1 MONTH OF
FREE
READING

at

www.ForgottenBooks.com

By purchasing this book you are eligible for one month membership to ForgottenBooks.com, giving you unlimited access to our entire collection of over 1,000,000 titles via our web site and mobile apps.

To claim your free month visit:

www.forgottenbooks.com/free833360

ISBN 978-0-483-16841-1
PIBN 10833360

CASES IN EQUITY

ARGUED AND DETERMINED IN

THE SUPREME COURT

NORTH CAROLINA

From December Term, 1845, to August Term, 1847.

BY JAMES IREDELL.

VOLUME IV.

RALEIGH:

PUBLISHED BY WESTON R. GALES.

1847.

Rec. Jan. 14, 1851

JUDGES

OF THE

SUPREME COURT OF NORTH CAROLINA,

DURING THE PERIOD COMPRISED IN THIS VOLUME.

Hon. THOMAS RUFFIN, Chief Justice.
Hon. JOSEPH J. DANIEL.
Hon. FREDERIC NASH.

JUDGES OF THE SUPERIOR COURTS.

Hon. THOMAS SETTLE.
Hon. JOHN M. DICK.
Hon. JOHN L. BAILEY.
Hon. RICHMOND M. PEARSON.
Hon. WILLIAM H. BATTLE.
Hon. MATTHIAS E. MANLY.
Hon. DAVID F. CALDWELL.

ATTORNEY GENERAL.

SPIER WHITAKER, Esquire.
EDWARD STANLY, Esquire.

CLERK OF THE SUPREME COURT AT RALEIGH.

EDMUND B. FREEMAN, Esquire.

CLERK OF THE SUPREME COURT AT MORGANTON FROM MAY 1847.

JAMES R. DODGE, Esquire.

REPORTER.

JAMES IREDELL.

INDEX

TO THE

NAMES OF CASES.

Adams, Moss v.	42	Clements v. Pearson,	257
Alexander, Williams v.	207	Closse, Denny v.	102
Allen v. Chambers,	125	Corpenning, Johnson v.	216
" McRae,	325	Councill v. Walton,	155
Alston, Hawkins v.	137	Cowles v. Carter,	105
Ashcraft v. Little,	236	Cox v. Williams,	15
Ballinger v. Edwards,	449	" Lewis v.	198
Bannar, Moore v.	293	Croom v. Wright,	248
Barnes v. Morris,	22	Darden, Beall v.	76
Barnet v. Spratt,	171	Deep River Gold Mining	
Beall v. Darden,	76	Co. v. Fox,	61
Bowden, Exum v.	281	Denny v. Closse,	102
Bowers v. Matthews,	258	Drake, Campbell v.	94
Bradley v. Parker,	430	Drumright v. Jones,	253
Bridges v. Pleasants,	26	Dunn v. Thorpe,	7
Britton, Exparte,	35	Edney v. King,	465
Brown, Gordon v.	399	Edwards, Ballinger v.	449
" Purvis v.	414	Ehringhaus, Pool v.	33
Bumpass, Rogers v.	385	Exum v. Bowden,	281
Campbell v. Drake,	94	Filhour v. Gibson,	455
Carter, Cowles v.	105	Fox, Deep River Gold	
" Liverman v.	59	Mining Co. v.	61
Chambers, Allen v.	125	Freeman, Newlin v.	312

Frost v. Reynolds,	494	Mills, Thompson v.	390
Gant, Rippy v.	443	Milton v. Hogue,	415
Gibson, Filhour v.	455	Moore, Hoyle v.	175
Gordon v. Brown,	399	" Murphy v.	118
Green, Logan v.	370	" v. Banner,	293
Greenlee v. McDowell,	481	Morris, Barnes v.	22
Guilford v. Guilford,	168	Morrison v. Meacham,	381
Harkins, Smith v.	486	Moss v. Adams,	42
Hawkins v. Alston,	137	Motz, Mauney v.	195
" Spencer v.	288	Murphy v. Moore,	118
Hill v. Spruill,	244	Nail v. Martin,	159
Hinton, Richardson v.	192	Nance v. Powell,	297
Hogue, Milton v.	415	Newlin v. Freeman,	312
Holden v. Peace,	223	Parker, Braddy v.	430
Horton v. Horton,	54	Peace, Holden v.	223
Howell v. Hooks,	188	Pearson, Clements v.	257
Hoyle v. Moore,	175	Pemberton v. Kirk,	178
Humphreys v. Tate,	220	Peterson v. Webb,	56
" Weir v.	264	Pleasants, Bridges v.	26
Hunt, Merritt v.	406	" Lindsay v.	320
Johnson v. Corpenning,	216	Pool v. Ehringhaus,	33
Johnston v. Shelton,	85	Powell, Nance v.	297
" v. Johnston,	9	Purvis v. Brown,	414
Jones, Drumright v.	253	Quinn v. Rippy,	181
Justice v. Scott,	108	Raper, Love v.	475
Kea v. Robeson,	427	Reynolds, Frost v.	494
King, Edney v.	465	Rich v. Marsh,	396
Kirk, Pemberton v.	178	Richardson v. Hinton,	192
Latham, Ex parte	231	Rippy, Quinn v.	181
Leigh, Wilson v.	97	" v. Gant,	443
Lewis v. Cox,	198	Robeson, Kea v.	427
Lindsay v. Pleasants,	320	Rogers v. Bumpass,	385
Little, Ashcraft v.	236	Scott, Justice v.	108
Livermore v. Carter,	59	Shannonhouse, Markham v.	411
Logan v. Green,	370	Shelton, Johnston v.	85
Love v. Raper,	475	Smith, Wagstaff v.	1
McDowell, Greenlee v.	481	" v. Turner,	433
McRae, Allen v.	325	" v. Harkins,	486
Marsh, Rich v.	396	Spencer v. Hawkins,	288
Markham v. Shannonhouse,	411	Spratt, Barnet v.	171
Martin, Nail v.	159	Spruill, Hill v.	244
Mask, Medley v.	339	Tate, Humphreys v.	220
Matthews, Bowers v.	258	Temple v. Williams,	39
Mauney v. Motz,	195	Tharpe, Dunn v.	7
Meacham, Morrison v.	381	Thompson v. Mills,	390
Mebane v. Mebane,	131	Turner, Smith v.	433
Medley v. Mask,	339	University, White v.	19
Merritt v. Hunt,	406	Wagstaff v. Smith,	1
Michael v. Michael,	349	Walton, Councill v.	155

Washburn v. Washburn,	306	Williams, Cox v.	15
Webb, Peterson v.	56	" Temple v.	39
Weir v. Humphries,	264	" v. Alexander,	207
Wheeler v. Wheeler,	210	Wilson v. Leigh,	97
White v. University,	19	Wright, Croom v.	248

EQUITY CASES

ARGUED AND DETERMINED

IN

THE SUPREME COURT

OF

NORTH CAROLINA.

DECEMBER TERM, 1845.

JOHN WAGSTAFF vs. CHARLES SMITH.*

A tenant in common in possession is protected by the Statute of Limitations from an account to his co-tenant, of the rents and profits received more than three years before the commencement of a suit.

Interest shall only be allowed from the time of an actual demand or from the commencement of the suit, if no previous demand has been made.

The case of *Wagstaff* v. *Smith*, 2 Dev. Eq. Rep. 264, overruled.

This was a petition to re-hear a decree made in this Court between the same parties, at December term, 1832, 2 Dev. Eq. 264. The Bill was for an account of the issues and profits of land, of which the plaintiff and defendant were tenants in common, the defendant having had the actual occupation. The defence was the Statute of Limitations. The Bill was filed in Granville Court of Equity, in February, 1829, and a partition had been made of the land held in common, in November, 1826.

---

*This opinion was delivered at December Term, 1833, but has not before been published. It is now reported at the request of the Court.

Nash and *Devereux*, for the plaintiff.
Badger, for the defendant.

GASTON, J. This case has been re-heard upon the petition of the defendant, and the Court is of opinion, that there is error in the decretal order in this, that it declared the plaintiff entitled to an account of rents and profits for more than three years before the filing of his bill. A legal demand, prosecuted in a Court of Equity, is barred by the same length of time, as constitutes a statutory bar at law. Upon legal titles and legal demands, a Court of Equity is *bound* by the statute of limitations. The claim in this case is one purely legal. The plaintiff demands an account from the defendant, with whom he had been tenant in common of a tract of land, of the plaintiff's share of rents and profits of the common property, the whole of which were retained by the defendant to his sole use. At common law, a tenant in common, unless where he had made his companion bailiff, could not have an action of account, but by the statute 4th Anne, ch. 16, it was enacted, that an action of account may be maintained by one tenant in common against the other, *as bailiff*, for receiving more than his share. It was doubted by the plaintiff's counsel, in the argument, whether this statute was in force here—but we see no foundation for that doubt. It is avowedly an " Act for *the amendment of the law* and the better advancement of justice," and one of those statutes for the amendment of the law repeatedly recognised as in force by our Colonial Legislature, and so declared in the Act of 1777, the Court law. It is by this statute, that at this day *payment* is a good plea to an action of debt on a single bill, or in debt, or a *scire facias* on a judgment ; and that payment of principal and interest due, *after* the day of payment, may be pleaded to debt on bond with a condition or defeazanee.

The bill being then a mere substitute for the action of

account, whatever time would be the bar at law, bars the account here. Our Act of limitations declares, that all actions of account rendered shall be brought within three years next after the cause of such action or suit, *and not after*, except such accounts as concern the trade of merchandise between merchant and merchant, and their factors or servants. This demand is not within the exception, but is within the enactment, and the enquiry is, when did the cause of action arise. It has been argued, that the cause of action did not arise until after the relation of tenants in common had ceased between the parties. or until after a demand and refusal to account; for that, during all that time, there was no withholding by one, of what the other was entitled to receive. We believe that this is a mistake. The receipt of the entire profits by one tenant in common, as such, is indeed no *ouster* of his companion—it affects not the possession of the *land*—but it imposes on him, who receives, an *immediate* accountability to the other, for the part of the profits to which he is entitled. The enactment of the statute, that " actions of account may be maintained by one joint tenant or tenant in common, his executors and administrators against the others, as bailiff, for receiving more than his share, and against the executors and administrators of such," is decisive, that the action lies while the relation of a common holding continues, and consequently that the cause of action may arise before the severance of that connection. It is sufficient in a declaration, after setting forth the holding as tenants in common, and the receipt of the whole rents, issues, and profits, by the defendant, and the obligation of the defendant to render an account to the plaintiff of his share thereof, to aver as a breach that such account had not been rendered, although the defendant " had been often required so to do." *See decl. in 3d Wilson*, 73, 74. Now it is a settled principle in pleading, that, where the cause of action does not arise until after a *demand* made, a spe-

cial *demand* must be stated, and the general allegation of
" *saepius requisitus*," or often required, will not answer.
The approved form of pleading the statute of limitations
in this action is, that the defendant did not receive the
profits " at any time within six years (with us *three*
years,) before the suing out of the original writ by the
plaintiff." which could not be good unless such receipt
did impose an immediate accountability.   The many decisions in equity, where, professing to act in analogy to
the statute, the Courts refuse to carry an account of rents
and profits further back than to six years before the filing
of the bill, are strong indications that the action of account rendered could not be sustained for rents antecedent-
ly received.   The *exception* in the statute, of accounts between merchant and merchant, would have been unnecessary, if, in *all* cases of confidential dealings, the statute
did not commence until the connection had ceased, or a
demand of account refused.   All the evils intended to be
remedied by the enactment—such as the loss of vouchers
or other proofs in discharge—would be left in full operation, if time had no effect to cure them.   Where one of
two tenants in common takes the whole of the annual
issues to himself, we hold that his companion has, thereupon, a right to an account for his share—and that the
statute of limitations will bar the assertion of this right,
unless it be made within the time declared by the statute.

  It is, however, further insisted on the part of the plaintiff, that he had a right to the entire account demanded,
because the defendant had, within three years before the
filing of this bill, *promised* and undertaken to render such
an account.   We have met with no authority to shew,
and on principle we are not disposed to believe, that a
promise will take any action out of the operation of the
Statute of limitations, but an action *founded on promises*
—the action of assumpsit.   See, *A'Court* v. *Cross*, 11 E.
C. L. Rep. 124. *Governor* v. *Hanrahan*, 4 Hawks 44.
Morrison v. *Morrison*, 3 Dev. 402.   If the assertion of the

present claim had been postponed in consequence of an agreement founded upon that promise, so as to make out a case of *fraud,* and thereby raise for the plaintiff an *equity* to the account, to which, but for the success of the fraud, he would have asserted his legal title, then the part of the decretal order complained of might be unobjectionable. But we deem it unnecessary to enquire very particularly into the effect of such a promise, because none such is *proved* in this case. To the allegations in the bill of a promise and of the facts from which it could be inferred, the defendant has returned an *explicit, full* and *positive* denial on his oath. The only witness, whose testimony may be said to conflict with this denial, is David J. Young. He states, that at the time of the division in December, 1826, he, as the agent of the plaintiff, *proposed* to the defendant to leave *all* matters in dispute between them to reference, and that, among other things, the balance of rents of the plaintiff's share in the land was expressly stated—that the defendant agreed to the proposal and "*mentioned something of the terms*"—that the witness, as agent of the plaintiff, *understood* such an agreement to be made, and *believes* that the defendant so understood it ; *soon* afterwards, the witness called on the defendant for the purpose of entering into bonds and choosing arbitrators, when the defendant said he would not leave it to arbitration ; that the improvements, which he had made, were more than equal to the rents, and that he would not give up the land to the plaintiff. Three other witnesses present on the same occasion have been examined, one of whom (Ellickson) represents that there was a long *debate,* which we understand as meaning an angry controversy, between the defendant and Young, and that he *thinks* the conclusion was to leave the matters in controversy (but does not state what *these* were) to arbitration. The other two, Jones and Amis, express their belief that *no* agreement took place, and say that they understood the *proposition* of Mr. Young not to extend to the rents, but only to the land claimed for the plaintiff. We do not hold ourselves justified upon this testimony, in opposition to the defendant's answer, to pronounce that *any* agreement to refer was made, much less that there was a well understood agreement to refer the question of rents—and still less an agreement to leave to the arbitrators the mere question of the *amount* due, thereby distinctly admitting an existing *liability*, and amounting to a *promise* to account for the excess received.

The exceptions filed by the defendant to the commissioner's report, have also been heard and argued. The two first exceptions are in substance a repetition of the objection taken to the decretal order upon the re-hearing, and for the reasons above stated are sustained and allowed. The last exception objects to interest upon the rents. This is sustained as to the interest accrued before the filing of the bill, and overruled as to that accrued since. We are governed in this by analogy to the rule, which prevails at law on a promise to pay money on demand. A previous request is not necessary to the bringing of the action—but interest will not be allowed for detention of the money, until after a demand or suit instituted.

The account which has been taken is to be reformed pursuantly to this opinion, and the complainant is to have a decree for the balance with costs.

PER CURIAM.   Decree accordingly.

ANNA DUNN *vs.* HARDY W. THARP, ADM'R., &c.*

The specific execution of marriage articles, and the reformation of settlements executed after marriage, because of their not conforming to articles
entered into before marriage, are among the ordinary subjects of Equity
jurisdiction.

Parol agreements, in consideration of marriage, entered into before our
statute of 1819, Rev. St. ch. 50, sec. 8, are valid, and will be enforced in Equity.

This case, after being set for hearing, was transmitted
from Franklin Court of Equity to this Court, at June
Term, 1837.

The plaintiff is the widow, and the defendant the administrator, of the late William Dunn, and the bill is
brought for the correction of an error in a marriage settlement, executed by the deceased, for the benefit of the
plaintiff. The case made in the bill is, that, previous to
the intermarriage of the plaintiff with the deceased, and
during the treaty for the said marriage, it was agreed
between them, that a settlement should be made of all
the slaves then belonging to the plaintiff, upon trust for
her, should she survive her husband, and for him, should
he survive the plaintiff; and it was expressly agreed and
contracted by the deceased, in consideration of such intended marriage, that a proper deed should be executed,
so as to convey the legal estate in the said slaves upon
the trusts aforesaid; that the marriage contemplated
took effect, (several years before the year 1819,) but that
from the confidence, which the plaintiff reposed in the
promises of the deceased, the hurry and bustle of the
wedding preparations, and the want of friends of the
plaintiff, skilled in business, to cause the proper deed to
be prepared, none such was executed, nor even any written articles drawn up previous to the marriage; that,
some years afterwards, the plaintiff's husband, intending
in good faith to carry out into execution the agreement

---

*The opinion in this case was delivered at June Term, 1837, but has not
heretofore been reported.

so made, caused an instrument to be draughted, whereby he was to convey unto certain trustees, the slaves aforesaid, upon the trusts aforesaid, and in the belief that the instrument, draughted in pursuance of these instructions, fully corresponded therewith, he duly executed the same ; that, recently, her husband had died, and the defendant had administered on his estate ; that, after her husband's death, it was discovered, that, through some inadvertence of the draughtsman, two of the negroes intended to be included in the deed, Polidore and Caroline, were omitted, and that in consequence of this omission, the defendant claimed to hold, and did hold, these two negroes, as a part of the estate of his intestate.

Badger, for the plaintiff.
E. Hall, for the defendant.

GASTON, J. The specific execution of marriage articles, and the reformation of settlements executed after marriage, because of their not conforming to articles entered into before marriage, are among the ordinary subjects of equity jurisdiction. Parol agreements in consideration of marriage are within the statute of 29th Charles 2nd, and, therefore, in the English Courts, they are not executed, nor do they constitute a ground for correcting settlements actually made. But for that statute, such agreements, clearly established, would have the same claims to be enforced, as if they had been manifested by writing. The reason of this provision in the statute was to prevent those unguarded expressions of gallantry and improvident promises thoughtlessly made, or artfully procured during courtship, being *perverted* into deliberate and solemn engagements, conferring a right to compel performance. When the alleged agreement in this case was made, we had no statute denying efficacy to it, unless reduced to writing. The only difference, therefore, which we can regard as existing between such an agreement by parol, and one in writing, is a difference in the degree of proof necessary to establish it. As an agreement, peculiarly liable to misapprehension and misrepresentation, it calls for the greatest caution in the consideration of the evidence, by which it is sought to be made out. In the present case, the extrinsic proofs are as full, clear, and satisfactory, as could have been desired, and the instrument itself furnishes no slight testimony of the alleged mistake, for, after conveying to the trustees seven negroes, by name, it proceeds to declare the trusts with respect to "the *nine* negroes aforesaid."

There is no contest here with creditors or purchasers, but it is one wholly between the widow and the administrator of the deceased.

The Court is of opinion, that she is entitled to have the mistake in the settlement corrected, as prayed for in her bill.

PER CURIAM.   Decree accordingly.

WADE H. JOHNSTON & AL. vs. ANTHONY M. JOHNSTON & AL.

Devises of real estate, by a parent to a child, are not to be brought into hotch-pot with land not disposed of by the will, but the land descended is to be divided, as if that were the whole real estate, of which the parent had ever been seized.

The case of *Norwood* v. *Branch*, 2 No. Ca. Law Rep. 598 overruled. The case of *Brown* v. *Brown*, 2 Ired. Eq. 309, approved.

This cause was transmitted from the Court of Equity of Warren County, at the Fall Term, 1845, to the Supreme Court.

The following case appeared from the pleadings. In the year 1843, Sterling Johnston died, leaving a will,

executed some time before, in which he devised to one of
his sons, John P. Johnston, a tract of land containing
800 acres.   He devised also to his six children, by his last
marriage, all the residue of his property, to be equally
divided between them and their heirs, share and share
alike.   The testator owned two tracts of land, one containing 2500 acres, and the other 700 acres, which formed a part of the residue.   One of the six children who
were the devisees of the residue, and who was named
Francis M. Johnston, died before the testator, without
issue.   The testator left also some other children by a
former marriage, and the issue of others, who had died
before him ; for whom he did not make any provision in
real estate. either during his life or by his will.   The bill
was filed by the five surviving children of the testator
by his last marriage, against his other children and the
grand-children, and prayed, in the first place, that partition of the two tracts of land, devised in the residuary
clause, might be made, so as to allot to each of the petitioners one equal sixth part in severalty ; and, in the
second place, that the remaining equal sixth part, which
had been devised to Francis M. Johnston and lapsed by
his death, should be sold and partition of the proceeds
thereof be made equally between the petitioners and all
the other children of the testator or their issue, as the
heirs at law of the testator.   The decree for partition
was accordingly made, and the share that would have
gone to Francis M. Johnston, had he lived, was sold, and
the master made his report, which was confirmed ; and
the cause was then removed to this Court, and was
brought on upon a motion for further directions as to the
division of the money arising from the sale of the one-
sixth part of the land, of which the testator died intestate.

Saunders, for the plaintiffs.
Whitaker, for the defendants.

Ruffin, C. J. The sole question is, whether, in the division of this fund, which is considered real estate, the son, John P. Johnston, and the children of the last marriage, who are the petitioners, are to be admitted to shares without accounting for the value of the lands, which those persons take by the devises in the will. The point, then, is precisely that decided in *Norwood* v. *Branch*, 2 No. Ca. Law Repos. 598. As was, mentioned by my brother Daniel, in *Brown* v. *Brown*, 2 Ired. Eq. 309, the profession has never been satisfied with that decision, and it is known that several, if not all of the Judges who made it, afterwards disapproved of it. The opinion given sets out with the observation, that the great object of the acts of descents, 1784 and 1795, is to make the estates of children, entitled to the inheritance, as nearly equal as possible. But surely that intention is not more clearly to be collected from those acts, which respect the division of real estate descended, than it is from the act of distributions of personal estate, 1766, and the English act of 22 and 23, Car. 2, from which ours is copied. Sir Joseph Jekyl said, that such equality of provision for children was the end and intent of the statute. Yet from the beginning, it was held, that land devised or legacies bequeathed, were not advancements, to be brought into hotch-pot in the distribution of a surplus undisposed of by the ancestor's will. Indeed, each of the acts particularly expresses that intent, and in the very same words : " as shall make the estate of all the children to be equal, as near as can be estimated." That, therefore, can afford no reason for a difference of construction. Chief Justice Taylor then mentions, that the use of the term " settle" in the act of 1784, and that of " life-time" in the act of Car. 2, and our act of 1766, authorises the different interpretations there adopted. And this is the whole ground of the opinion. Now, that is entirely a mistake, as it seems to us. For it will be seen that the acts of distribution use both the words " settle" and "life-time," applying the former to advancements in land, and the latter to portions. The words are, " one-third part of the surplus to the wife of the intestate, and all the rest by equal portions to and among the children of such person dying intestate, other than such child or children, (not being heirs at law) who shall have any *estate* by the *settlement* of the intestate, or shall be *advanced* by the intestate in his *life-time* by *portion* or *portions,* equal, &c." The construction plainly is, that if a child has a "settled estate," equal to a share of the other children in the distribution, *or* has " a portion advanced in the life-time" of the intestate, equal to a share, such child shall have no more. So that if the reasoning of *Norwood* v. *Branch* had been applied to the statute of distributions, it would have produced this result ; that gifts of real estate in the will would, as a settlement, exclude the devisee from any part of the surplus of personalty, not disposed of by the will, while a legacy in the same will would not exclude. But the true ground, on which, under the statutes of distribution, settlements or advancements were not to be brought into hotch-pot, when there was a will, is, that the language of the acts and their purpose, points only to an " intestate." *Walton* v. *Walton,* 14 Ves. 324. *Brown* v. *Brown,* 2 Ired. Eq. 309. The Legislature intended an inequality between children, when the parent did not himself produce an inequality. Therefore, when the parent dies intestate, the act operates. But, when he disposes of his own estate by will, the law does not interfere ; and, if he disposes of part only, the law does not interfere with his dispositions, as far as he has made them by his will, but suffers that inequality to stand and divides the residue equally. Suppose a father to have two sons, and to the elder he devises land worth £1000, and to the younger land worth £500 and personalty worth £500, and leaves personalty undisposed of to the value of £1000. It could not be possible the Legislature meant, that the second son should have all the land descended, making his share of the realty £1000, as well as his brother's, and then that they should divide the £1000 personalty equally, as it is admitted, notwithstanding his legacy of £500, they must do in respect of the personalty. So, the very giving to one son, by the will, more than to another, shews, that the parent, for reasons satisfactory to his own mind, intended a greater bounty to the one than the other; and that intention the law did not mean to counteract. It directs an equality, because it presumes the parent would naturally wish it. But here the parent creates the inequality by his own will, and the law never intended to thwart him. The rule, therefore, was not founded so much on "life-time" as "intestate;" the latter shewing, that the subject within the purview of the act was the estate of a man, who had not undertaken to divide his estate among his children, but had left the whole matter to the law to regulate. Now, the act of 1784, in like manner, in respect to descents to children, expressly uses the word "intestate"—saying, " when any person, having any right to any estate or inheritance of land in fee simple, *and such person shall die intestate*, his or her estate shall descend to all the sons, &c. other than such son as shall have lands settled on him in fee simple," &c. There seems, therefore, to have been no distinction between the statute of descents and the statute of distributions in this respect. We are not aware, that the question has ever come directly before the Court since. If it had come before the Judges, who adopted it, we are almost sure, from what we know, that they would have corrected the construction. But whether the present Court would have felt the same liberty of action is more doubtful, as it is better, perhaps, to leave it to the Legislature to enact a new law, as they may deem fit, rather than produce that uncertainty which arises from conflicting judicial decisions. And we believe that the Court would have adhered to *Norwood* v. *Branch*, if the Legislature had not, by recent enactments, plainly given us to understand, what is deemed by that body the proper principle applicable to such cases. By the Act of 1844, c. 51, the real and personal estates of parents are made one fund in respect to advancements, and it is expressly confined to cases where " any person shall die *intestate*, who in his or her *life-time advanced* to any child personal property," and " when any person shall die *intestate* seized and possessed of any real estate, who had in his or her *life-time settled* any real estate on any child." It is thus seen, that the Legislature thought it right to refer the settlement of land to the life-time of the intestate parent, as well as the advancement of a portion ; and, we think, it cannot be doubted that it was always so intended. This removes every difficulty ; because we cannot suppose the Legislature meant, that gifts of land by will, or in the life-time of a parent not dying intestate, should not exclude from the surplus of personalty, when there is a partial intestacy, but should exclude from the undevised realty, when at the same time it is not so *vice versa*—that is to say, that gifts of personalty by the will, or in the testator's life-time, would not exclude the donee from sharing in the land. We cannot thus suppose, because the act of 1844 puts the two kinds of estate, real and personal, on precisely the same footing in words, and must have meant that they should be so in fact. We think, therefore, that devises by a parent to a child are not to be brought into hotch-pot with land not disposed of by the will, but the land descended is to be divided, as if that were the whole real estate of which the parent had ever been seised. There must be a decree accordingly.

PER CURIAM.   Decreed accordingly.

JOHN COX, EXECUTOR OF MARY BISSELL *vs.* WILLIAM J. H. B. WILLIAMS & AL.

A bequest of Slaves to the American Colonization Society is a valid bequest under the laws of this State.

The cases of *Haywood* v. *Craven*, 2 No. Ca. Law Rep. 557, *Cameron* v. *Commissioners of Raleigh*, 1 Ired. Eq. 436, and *Thompson* v. *Newlin*, 3 Ired. Eq. 338, cited and approved.

Cause removed from the Court of Equity of Chowan County.

The case presented by the pleadings is this: Mary Bissell, by her will, made the following dispositions: " I direct that my servant women, Molly and Maria, Maria's two children, named Mary and John, and three other children, Nancy, Priscilla and Lucy, all of whom are my property, be made over to the American Colonization Society, or to any individual authorised by the American Colonization Society to receive them, on condition that said Society will engage to send them to either of its Colonies in Africa; and that the said Society may be at no expense in sending them as directed, I wish two vacant lots belonging to me in the town of Edenton, to be sold to defray their expenses, and certain other monies also to be appropriated to their use, as is hereafter directed." In a subsequent clause, there is the following provision: " If there should be any balance after the settlement of my estate, agreeably to the tenor of this will, I direct that it be all paid over to the American Colonization Society, for the exclusive use of the servants to be sent by them to Africa."

The bill is filed by the executor, against the next of kin of the testatrix and the American Colonization Society, and states the plaintiff's readiness to deliver the slaves, and pay over the residue of the estate to either the next of kin or the Society, whichever may be entitled to the same, and prays the Court to put a construction on the will, and declare who is entitled to the slaves and fund: The Colonization Society having offered to accept the slaves and transport them to one of their Colonies in Africa, there to be free persons, and also the pecuniary fund, in order to defray the expenses, and, as to any surplus thereof, in trust for the slaves themselves, when freed from the state of servitude; and insisting on their right thereto, for those purposes : And the next of kin, on the other hand, insisting that the provision for emancipation is against law, and the gift to the Society for that purpose is void.

The several defendants answered, and the cause was set for hearing on the bill and answers, and transferred to this Court for hearing. The answer of the American Colonization Society states that the Society has been duly incorporated by two acts of the General Assembly of Maryland, with power and capacity to receive gifts and bequests of slaves for the purpose of transporting them, with their own consent, to Africa, where several colonies of free persons of colour have been established, under the auspices of the Society ; and also with power and capacity to take gifts or bequests of money and other things needful to defray the expenses of transportation and to provide for the comfort of the colonists in Africa. And the answer further states, that the Society has been duly organized and has accepted the charter. The answer also engages, if the bequests to the Society should be held good, to remove the slaves, with their own consent, as soon as practicable, from this State to one of the said colonies in Africa, and thereby bestow on them emancipation.

No counsel for the plaintiff.
A. Moore, for the next of kin.
Iredell, for the American Colonization Society.

RUFFIN, C. J.   There can be no question, that a bequest of slaves for the purpose, or upon trust, to send them to another country, there to become and remain free, is

valid. There is no ground, upon which the validity of
such a bequest can be doubted. In the nature of things,
the owner of a slave may renounce his ownership, and
the slave will thereby be manumitted, and that natural
right continues, until restrained by positive statutes. It
was, indeed, early found in this State, as in most of the
others, in which there is slavery, that the third class of
free negroes was burdensome as a charge on the commu-
nity, and,.from its general characteristics of idleness and
dishonesty, a common nuisance. Hence the legislative
policy, with us, was opposed to emancipation, and restricted it to a particular mode and upon a special consideration—which was by license of the Court and for merito-
rious services. But that was purely a regulation of police,
and for the promotion of the security and quiet of the
people of this State. It sought only to guard against
evils arising from free negroes residing here. Except
for that purpose of policy, it was not intended to impose
any restriction on the natural right of an owner to free
his slaves. Emancipation was not prohibited for the
sake merely of keeping persons in servitude in this State,
and increasing the number of slaves, for the law never
restrained their exportation, either for the purpose of
servitude abroad, or for that of emancipation there. On
the contrary, all our legislative regulations had a reference exclusively to emancipation, within our limits, of
slaves, who were intended to remain here. That was
the ground of decision in the leading case of *Haywood* v.
Craven, 2 No. Ca. Law Repos. 557, and all the subsequent
cases ; in not one of which did the deed or will direct
that the emancipation should take effect abroad. It never
has been disputed, that the owner could send his slaves
away and emancipate them, where it was lawful for free
men to live. This State laid no claim at any time to hold
them here for the sake of their perpetual bondage. So
far from it, by a modern statute, 1830, c. 9, the policy is
avowed of encouraging emancipation, upon the sole con-

dition, that the people freed shall not disturb or be chargeable to us, but keep out of our borders.   And in *Cameron
v. Commissioners of Raleigh*, 1 Ired. Eq. 436, and in *Thompson v. Newlin*, 3 Ired. Eq. 338, the distinction is expressly
stated between a trust to remove slaves abroad, to be
emancipated, and one to have them emancipated here or
to hold them in a state of qualified servitude, nominally
as the property of the trustee, but really for the benefit of
the slaves themselves—holding the former trust lawful,
but the latter unlawful.   And the former case establishes,
that money given for the removal of the slaves to Africa,
and their preferment there, is a good charity, under the
common law and our statute.

The trust in this case must therefore be declared valid ;
and the Colonization Society authorised to receive the
slaves, and the surplus of the estate, (after paying the
costs of this suit,) for the purpose of removing them to
Africa, as directed in the will.   This direction, however,
is necessarily dependent on a fact, to be ascertained by
an enquiry ; which is, whether the negroes, who are
adults, are willing to go to Africa or not.   This fact
must be ascertained, that it may be seen whether the
Society has capacity to acquire the negroes, or remove
them, which, according to the terms of the charter, depends on the consent of the negroes themselves.   Indeed,
we are not sure that it would be proper to send them
abroad against their will, even if there were no such restriction in the charter of the Society—since, if a slave
has capacity to accept emancipation, it would seem that
he must have the power also of refusing it, when the offer of his owner is upon the condition of his leaving the
country, and when he is not compelled by law.   But,
however that may be, the gift being here to a corporation, with an express limitation on its capacities, it must
be considered that the testatrix knew that, and the disposition be construed, as if the provision of the will required their consent—at least, that of such of them as

are of years of discretion. For those who are under, say the age of fourteen—their parents may elect. If any adult should refuse to go, those refusing must, of necessity, be sold, and the proceeds will go into the residue for the benefit of those who will go—according to the last clause of the will, which excludes the next of kin altogether, unless all the slaves should refuse to go.

If any of the children have no parents, or their parents should elect for them not to go, liberty must be reserved to such children to make their election, when they shall arrive at the age of fourteen. It appears, indeed, that the money remaining in the hands of the executor is partly the proceeds of the sale of one of the negroes, which was rendered necessary for the payments of debts. Of course, all these charities must depend, for their validity, on the power of the party who creates them, without doing injustice to creditors.   Justice stands before generosity ; and the owner of a slave cannot defeat the rights of a creditor by manumitting the slave.   The Colonization Society can therefore claim only the slaves which remain unsold, and can have, immediately, only such as may be willing to go.

PER CURIAM.   Decree accordingly.

———

THOMAS WHITE, EX'R. &c. vs. THE ATTORNEY GENERAL, AND THE TRUSTEES OF THE UNIVERSITY.

A devise that land should be sold, and " the proceeds laid out in building convenient places of worship, free for the use of all Christians, who acknowledge the divinity of Christ and the necessity of a spiritual regeneration," is void for uncertainty.

A devise to a religious congregation is valid, if the Court can see, with certainty, what congregation is intended.

This cause was transmitted from the Court of Equity of Warren County, at the Fall Term, 1845, having been set for hearing upon the Bill and answer.

The case was this:

Richard Davidson by his will devised as follows: " I leave my real estate to be sold, and the proceeds to be laid out in building convenient places of worship, free for the use of all Christians who acknowledge the divinity of Christ, and the necessity of a spiritual regeneration ;" and he appointed the plaintiff his executor. The testator was a native of England and naturalized here ; and he died without kindred in this country.

The Bill is filed by the executor against the Attorney General and the Trustees of the University, and the object is to obtain a construction of the will, and the directions of the Court, in respect to the sale of the land and the investment of the proceeds. The Attorney General has not appeared in the cause. The Trustees of the University have answered and claimed the land, because the trust declared respecting it is not valid.

Badger, for the plaintiff.
Iredell, for the University.

RUFFIN, C. J. The doctrine of the Courts of this State is, that gifts to public and charitable uses will be sustained in equity, when not opposed to the express provisions or the plain policy of the law, provided the object is so specific that the Court can by decree effectuate it, by compelling the execution of the will, according to the intention of the donor, and keeping the subject within the control of the Court, so as always to have the will of the donor observed. This was carried as far as it could be, in the case arising under *Griffin's* will, 1 Hawks 96; which was a devise to trustees to establish a free school for orphan children or the children of indigent parents in the town of Newbern. And, as we have said in *Bridges* v. *Pleasants*, at this term, we suppose that a bequest to build Churches in this State for a particular religious denomination, where a congregation is already organized or with a view to the organization of one at such places, is suffi-

ciently definite to be established. We think so, because
the Legislature recognises the existence of religious congregations severally, and, recently, the whole Church of
each denomination in this State, (if it exist as one,) as capable of holding, either by themselves, or by trustees for them,
property of any kind, not exceeding in real estate a certain value and quantity. Those trustees, the statute
says, shall account with the congregation, and they may
be compelled, by suit in a method pointed out in the Act.
But the difficulty in this case arises from two circumstances; the one, that the will is silent as to the places
where the churches are to be erected; and the other, that
there is no ownership conferred on any religious congregation, nor any trustees for it; nor can there be, since,
from the nature of the charity, it appears to have been
the purpose of the testator, that no congregation of any
particular portion or sect of the Christian church should
be formed at his churches, as he makes them free for all
such as hold two doctrines of Christianity. Now, it
seems impossible for a Court to hold, that a charity for
religion is sufficiently specific, in which no part of the
Christian world has any property, legal or equitable;
which no one has a right to manage or preserve, and in
which the Court would, perhaps, be daily called on to
regulate the uses of the buildings, which the various
sects would endeavor to concentrate, each one in itself.
Every one is aware, that there are irreconcileable dif-
ferences of doctrine and discipline in the several sects
of even those Christians who are called orthodox; and
how bitter a spirit is engendered by the controversies
that must arise from the ministers of different sects
coming often into immediate contact. Hence, the Legislature, though Catholic to the utmost extent in allowing
all to be alike entitled to liberty of mind and conscience,
and to protection from the law for their property, has
plainly acted upon the assumption, that there can be no
common property between churches or sects of different

denominations. The act secures glebes, lands, and tenements for the support of "any particular ministers, or mode of worship," and all churches, chapels, and other houses, built for the purpose of public worship, to the use and occupancy of that religious society, church, sect, or denomination, to or for which they were purchased or given, or for which the churches, chapels, and other houses of public worship, were built. The Legislature had no hopes from a free church, in the sense of the word, that it was to belong to no church or sect ; and the testator lived in vain, if he thought that any importunity of his executor or authority from the Court could appease the conflicts among common possessors, the ministers of contending sects, without any property or authority in either. It seems to us, that it would be impossible for the Court to keep any control over such persons or property ; and, therefore, that this is a trust, which the Court cannot undertake to execute, since it cannot execute it effectually. It follows, that the land must be declared to belong to the University.

Per Curiam.   Decree accordingly.

JOHN C. BARNES & AL. vs. MORDECAI MORRIS & AL.

Where, on the petition of infants and *feme coverts*, for the sale of land, the land is sold, and the Court then passes this order: " Ordered, that the Clerk and Master collect the bonds as they become due, and make the purchasers title ;" *Held*, that under this order, the Clerk and Master had no authority to convey the title, until the purchase money was paid.

Held, further, that when, in such a case, the purchaser had conveyed the land to another person, who had notice that the purchase money was unpaid, the lien on the land in favor of the original owners still continued, and the surety of the purchaser at the Master's sale, who had been compelled to pay the bond, should be substituted to the rights of the original owners.

The cases of *Green* v. *Crocket*, 2 Dev. and Bat. Eq. 390, and *Polk* v. *Gallant*, 2 Dev. and Bat. Eq 395, cited and approved.

Transmitted by consent from the Court of Equity of Pasquotank County, at the Fall Term, 1845.

At the Fall term, 1839, of the Court of Equity for Pasquotank County, Alphia B. Harrell, his wife and others, tenants in common of several tracts of land, filed their petition under the Act of Assembly, to have them sold for the purpose of partition.

A decree of sale was made ; and the Master, by order of the Court, made sale of the lands—when the defendant Markham, became a purchaser of one of the tracts, and executed two bonds for the purchase money, with the plaintiff, Barnes, surety. The report of the Master of the sale was confirmed by the Court, and thereupon the following order was made : " Ordered, that the Clerk and Master collect the bonds as they become due, and make the purchasers title." The Master executed a deed of conveyance to Markham, before he paid the purchase money. And Markham has since paid one of the bonds and conveyed the lands to the other defendant, Morris, who had notice at the time, that the purchase money under the Master's sale was unpaid by his vendor. Markham is now insolvent. Barnes, as his surety, has been sued on the second bond and has been compelled to pay it.

Barnes, by his bill, prays to be substituted to all the rights and equities of Harrell, wife, and others, and to have the land now in possession of Morris, charged for his indemnity with the sum paid by him. The other plaintiffs are only formal parties. The defendants admit most of the facts set forth in the bill ; but they state that the first bond to the Master was paid, mainly by the money which Morris advanced to Markham on the sale to him ; and they insist, that if the plaintiff should obtain a decree, then the same should be credited to Morris, in the taking of the accounts. But they mainly insist, that the order made by the Court, and the deed executed to Markham by the Master in pursuance thereof, transferred to him all title, legal and equitable, in the bond. The case was then set for hearing.

Badger and *A. Moore*, for the plaintiffs.
Iredell, for the defendants.

DANIEL, J.   When the Clerk and Master shall sell any
real or personal estate, in obedience to a decree of a
Court of Equity, and shall be authorized by the decree
to make title to the purchaser, the deed of the Clerk and
Master shall be deemed as good and sufficient to convey
to the purchaser such title in the real and personal
property so sold, as the party of record owning the same
had therein. *Rev. Stat.* 183, *T.* 48. It is to be seen,
therefore, that a deed, executed by the Master, transfers
no title to the property sold by him, unless it is given in
obedience to the decree of the Court.   That brings us to
the consideration of the effect of the order to the Master
to make deed in this case.   The order was, "that the
Clerk and Master collect the bonds as they become due,
and make the purchasers title."   Had the Master any
authority, by this order, to make title to Markham, until
all the money was paid in ?   Where infants and *feme
coverts* are concerned, and can give no consent that a
conveyance of their lands should be made to the purchaser, before all the purchase money be paid in, the
Court is expected to be extremely cautious in making an
order, that shall have the effect of taking from them their
lien on the land for the purchase money.   And we see,
that there was a *feme covert* interested in the sale of these
lands, and also that other tracts of land were sold by the
Master for the petitioners, beside the one purchased by
Markham.   There was a strong inducement, therefore,
for the Court not to make an absolute order, that the
Master should immediately make title.   Taking these
things in our view, and then attending to the terms of
the orders, it seems to us that there was a condition precedent to the execution of the conveyance, to-wit, the
collection of the bonds as they became due : That was
not done, and therefore the deed to Markham was made

without authority, and did not transfer the legal title to the land. It is admitted, that the language is not as explicit as it ought to be, and therefore the decree is to be collected by construction, from the words and the circumstances. The Master is ordered " to make title." When, and upon what event? Why shall we answer, presently?

If the owners had taken out the bonds as cash, looking to the purchasers and intending to collect the money themselves, and to indulge the purchasers at their discretion, there might be a presumption, that, as the Court would not know when the purchase money was paid, it was intended the Master should make a deed at once, and be done with it. But as the collection was left in this case under the control of the Court, the presumption is the other way; and it cannot be intended, unless clearly expressed, that the Court meant to part with the security of the land, before the whole purchase money was paid. Therefore, the acts are to be taken to precede and follow each other, as they are stated in the order; that is, that the Master shall collect the bonds for the purchase money, and *then* make deeds to the purchasers respectively. That is the natural construction in Equity of even a contract of sale, where no time is specified for the conveyance; since Equity holds that the land was intended as a security for the purchase money, unless the contrary appeared; and much more of a decree, where the Court is dealing for others. Therefore, the deed of the Master, being unauthorized, did not pass the legal title, and Morris is but an assignee of Markham's equity. The surety of the purchaser has a right, upon the insolvency of the principal, who has not got in the legal title before the payment of the debt, as against one purchasing from him even *bona fide*, and without notice of the non-payment of the purchase money, to have the land sold for his re-imbursement, if he has paid the debt, or for his exoneration, if he has not yet paid it.

33

Green v. *Crocket*, 2 Dev. and Bat. Eq. 390. *Polk* v. *Gallant*, 2 Dev. and Bat. Eq. 395. We think, that the plaintiff's arc entitled to a decree, to have the land now held by Morris re-sold for their indemnity, unless Morris chooses to pay the plaintiff's demand, and take a new conveyance from the Master.

PER CURIAM.   ·   Decree accordingly.

WILLIAM H. BRIDGES & AL. *vs.* STEPHEN PLEASANTS.

A bequest of $1000, " to be applied to foreign missions and to the poor saints: this to be disposed of and applied as my executor may think the proper objects according to the scriptures, the greater part, however, to be applied to missionary purposes, say $900. Item—It is my will, that if there be any thing over and above," (after satisfying certain legacies and devises) " that it be applied to home missions," is too indefinite and therefore void.

To sustain a gift in trust by a testator, the trust itself must be valid ; and, to make it so, it must be in favor of such persons, natural or artificial, as can legally take.

In the case of devises to charitable purposes, the doctrine of *cy. pres.* does not obtain in this State.

A bequest for religious charity must, in this State, be to some definite purpose, and to some body or association of persons, having a legal existence and with capacity to take ; or, at the least, it must be to some such body, on which the Legislature shall, within a reasonable time, confer a capacity to take.

There is no provision in our laws for donations, to be employed in any general system of diffusing the knowledge of christianity throughout the earth.

The cases of *McAuley* v. *Wilson*, 1 Dev. Eq. 276. *Holland* v. *Peck*, 2 Ired. Eq. 255, and *State* v. *Gerard*, 2 Ired. Eq. 210, cited and approved.

This cause, having been set for hearing upon the Bill and answer, was transmitted, by consent of the parties, from the Court of Equity of Orange County, at the Fall Term, 1845, to this Court.

The following case was presented by the pleadings :

Stephen Justice made his will, and therein bequeathed sundry specific and pecuniary legacies; and then he directed as follows: "After my will is complied with, after the above directions, it is my will that $1000, if there be so much remaining, be applied to foreign missions, and to the poor saints: this to be disposed of and applied as my executor may think the proper objects according to the Scriptures; the greater part, however, to be applied to missionary purposes, say $900. Item: It is my will, that if there be any thing over and above, that it be applied to home missions."

There is no other residuary clause in the will; and the present bill was filed by the testator's next of kin, against the executor, for an account and distribution of the surplus, and claiming the above sums, as not being effectually given away.

Respecting the other parts of the estate, there seems to be no dispute, but the whole controversy turns on the validity of the charitable bequests. The answer states, that the defendant is, and has long been, an officiating minister in the Baptist denomination of Christians, and the testator was a pious and zealous member of the same denomination, and manifested a deep solicitude for the spread of the Gospel, as expounded by that denomination, and was charitable and liberal to its poor professing members; that by the terms, "poor saints," the testator meant his Christian brethren, who might be in needy circumstances; and that "foreign mission" and "home mission," apply to the efforts of the Baptist church to extend the knowledge of Christianity in foreign lands, and in our own country. The answer further states, that the defendant has accepted the trust conferred on him, and that he has formed a scheme for administering it, as follows: That he will pay the sum bequeathed for foreign missions, to the Treasurer of the North Carolina Baptist State Convention, (which is the highest assembly of that denomination in the State,) to be by them applied, with their other funds, in aid of the extension of Christianity in other countries, under the auspices of the General Baptist Convention of the United States. The bequest for home missions, he proposes to divide between the Beulah, Sandy Creek, and Flat River Associations; which, the answer states to be three inferior societies of the Baptist church, within the personal knowledge of the testator, in this State; to be applied by each association to the support of the Gospel ministry within its jurisdiction. The bequest to poor Christians, the defendant proposes to apply to the poor of Cane Creek congregation, in Orange County, (in which the testator habitually worshipped,) unless there should be objects of greater need elsewhere. The answer then refers to a pamphlet, published some years after the testator's death, as containing the proceedings and views of the Baptist State Convention, in relation to missions and charities to poor brethren. And the defendant states, that he is advised that he has, by the will, the right and trust to apply the funds according to his judgment, as the testator might himself have done; but he, nevertheless, submits to administer the charity as the Court may direct.

The answer further states, that two of the plaintiffs, William H. Bridges and William Duncan, executed to the defendant their releases by deed, of any further claim in the testator's estate; and it insists thereon as if the same matter were pleaded.

The two releases, referred to in the answer, are exhibited, and, in each of them, the receipt of the sum of $60 is acknowledged to be in full of the distributive share of the party in the estate of the late Stephen Justice, and the defendant is released from all further demands or claims on him, as executor of Justice, either at law or in equity.

The cause was set down for hearing without replying to the answer, and sent to this Court for hearing.

Badger, for the plaintiffs.

Norwood and *J. H. Bryan*, for the defendant.

RUFFIN, C. J. It is always painful to a Judge, to disappoint the intentions he believes to have been entertained by a testator, though he has not sufficiently expressed them; and it is so especially, when the testator's intentions were so praise-worthy as those which, as the defendant says, this testator entertained and which it is extremely probable he did entertain. But it is a perfectly well known principle of law, that a Court cannot go out of a will to construe it. The paper must tell us the testator's meaning, or we can never find it out; and if he hath not sufficiently disposed of his property, it falls, as a matter of course, to his next of kin.

An argument for the defendant is, that the next of kin are cut off by the gifts from them, which are to be applied in the discretion and judgment of the defendant; claiming for the defendant the largest authority of the testator himself. But with the exceptions of those bequests, which are technically called " charitable," the rule is quite the other way. When a gift is made, in trust, the donee cannot take it for his own benefit, in opposition to the intention of the donor. Then it follows, that, to sustain such a gift in trust, the trust itself must be valid; and, to make it so, it must be in favor of such persons, natural or artificial. as can legally take. Therefore, it was held, in *Morris* v. *Bishop of Durham*, 9 Ves. 390, 10 Ves. 522, that a gift to the Bishop, " to be disposed of to such objects of benevolence and liberality as he should most approve of," was void for its vagueness and generality; inasmuch as no person or persons in particular could claim the benefit of the gift or enforce the Bishop to bestow charity upon any person, while it was yet clear that the Bishop could not keep it to himself. Therefore, the subjects of such gifts result to the heir or next of kin of the donor. So far, then, as the attempt goes to support this bequest on the ground, that it is to be applied to the objects, which the executor might think proper, according to the scriptures, it must fail ; because, if the executor were dishonest enough to keep the money in his own pocket, there is no person that could institute an action to call for any part of the sum, unless it be the next of kin.

But it is further said, that these gifts are sufficiently precise to make them good as charities for religious purposes. And we have no doubt, that, in England, they would be so held, and that with the view of applying them to purposes quite opposite to those wished by this testator, upon the doctrine of *cy. pres.* But we have no authority in this country, which, like the King in England, or the Chancellor, can administer a fund upon that arbitrary principle. So it has been held in this State, more than once. *McAuley* v. *Wilson,* 1 Dev. Eq. 270. *Holland* v. *Peck,* 2 Ired. Eq. 255. In the former case, it was laid down, that, if there be a bequest to charity, which cannot take effect, the Court cannot conjecture that the testator would desire it to go in some other charity, and then take a step further, and say that the testator meant that the Court should select an object for the testator, which he omitted effectually to do for himself. Therefore, a bequest for religious charity must, like others, be to some definite purpose, and to some body or association of persons, having a legal existence, and with capacity to take. Or, at the least, it must be to some such body, on which the Legislature shall, within a reasonable time, confer a capacity to take. The Revised Statute, c. 99, authorises religious societies to choose trustees, and vests them with power to purchase and hold the churches, glebes and land, and to receive gifts of any kind, for the use of the society or congregation: provided, that no single congregation shall hold land to a greater annual value than $400, or in quantity more than 2000 acres. That has been extended, by an act of the last Assembly, 1844, c. 47, which allows the church or sect in the aggregate, as the Conference, Synod, or

Convention, representing a religious denomination in the State, to appoint trustees, who may receive donations, and take and hold property, real or personal. in trust for the church within this State.   So far, therefore, there is a capacity in religious congregations of particular denominations, and, now, in the aggregate church of the several denominations, to take property for the religious uses of the congregation or church.   And it is probable, that a gift to build a church at a particular place, for the purpose of forming or constituting a church of any one known denomination, might be sustained in favor of a congregation regularly though newly organized.   But it is clear, the statutes throughout have only those religious charities or purchases in their purview, which are made to or for the benefit in severalty of some church, sect or society, known as a denomination.   For the Legislature was fully aware of the existence of various sects or churches in the State, and of their general utility and harmonious action, when each moves in its own orbit, and is sustained by its own members; and, therefore, the requisite provision is made for securing the place of worship of each, and supplying such income from donations or purchases as the Legislature deemed adequate for keeping the congregation together, and enabling each church to fulfil its functions. of benevolence and instruction of its members, and of such persons as should resort thither for spiritual edification. But there is no provision for donations, to be employed in any general system of diffusing the knowledge of christianity throughout the earth.   That is left to those, who choose to administer their own means in such charities, or in their life-times to trust to others, in whose hands they place the funds: for in those cases the acts are personal or the confidence is so, and there is no call for the aid of the Court to compel the parties to their duty. Wherever the aid of the Court is invoked, there must appear some right in the person, who applies, or for whose benefit it is sought, to support a gift by will. In the present case, it is impossible, from any thing appearing in the will, to conjecture how, by whom, or in whose favour, these sums of money were to be administered. What kind of "foreign missions," whether diplomatic or religious, or, if the latter, of what sect, or to what countries, no man can say. So, likewise, of the "home mission." The gift to the "poor saints" is equally indefinite. If the testator had told us, who were meant by *him* by that description, the persons thus meant should have the benefit of the bequests, however much below the description of *saints* they might fall. But it is impossible at this day, and in this country, to say, judicially, that this or that man is a saint, or even a Christian ; much less can a bequest be supported for all poor saints indefinitely, that is, who are in the world. The poor of a County or City are proper objects of such a charity ; for the objects of bounty are readily known, and their number easily ascertained, and the gift is in fact to the public. *State* v. *Gerard*, 2 Ired. Eq. 210. But "poor saints," if it could be known who they are at all, are not mentioned in the will, as of any County, nor country ; but, if any can take, all such persons, throughout the world, are to share in it ; which is preposterous.

We think, therefore, that the several bequests must be declared to be too indefinite and void, and that the plaintiffs are entitled to an account, except Bridges and Duncan. They appear, upon the answer and exhibits, to have received their shares of the estate, and, at all events, for a consideration expressed, have given releases of any demand for a further share of the estate ; and therefore the bill must be dismissed as to them.

PER CURIAM. Decreed accordingly.

MARY JANE POOL vs. JOHN C. EHRINGHAUS.

When an infant and another person joined in a petition, in a Court of Equity, for a sale of land, held in common, the sale was made, and the Court ordered, that, when the money was collected, the infant's share should be paid to her guardian, upon his giving bond to the Clerk and Master with sufficient surety, that the same should be secured to the infant or her heirs, as real estate, and the Clerk and Master paid the money to the guardian without taking such bond and surety: *Held*, that he was liable to the infant by an action of law, or proceedings might be had against him in the Court of Equity, by a rule or attachment to pay the money; but that the infant had no remedy against him by an original bill in Equity.

This cause, having been set for hearing, was removed by consent, to this Court, at the Fall Term, 1845, of Pasquotank Court of Equity.

The present plaintiff and another person, who were tenants in common of a tract of land, filed their petition in a Court of Equity for a sale of the land for the purpose of partition; and a decree was made accordingly, a sale had, and the money paid into the office of the Clerk and Master. The plaintiff was, and still is, an infant; and when the money was collected, the Court ordered that her share of it should be paid to Jesse L. Pool, the guardian of the plaintiff, upon his giving bond to the Clerk and Master, with sufficient surety, that the same should be secured to the plaintiff and her heirs, as real estate. The present defendant afterwards became Clerk and Master, and received the fund into his hands, and paid it to Jesse L. Pool without taking any bond from him, as directed in the order, and Jesse L. Pool died insolvent. Upon this case the bill was filed in the name of the plaintiff, by her next friend, praying that the defendant may be decreed to pay the money to the plaintiff with interest from the time he paid the same to Jesse L. Pool.

The answer admits the facts, as above stated, and that the defendant is liable to make good the money to the infant. It states that the defendant paid the money to Pool, under the belief, that he had given the proper bond with sureties, when he was appointed guardian, and that such bond was a sufficient compliance with the decree. The defendant states, that his mistake on that point was an honest one, and that he has always been ready to pay the money again, when any person should be authorized to receive it; and he submits, therefore, whether he should be compelled to pay interest thereon, since the plaintiff treats the money, as being still in his hands. The answer then insists, that this is not a proper subject for a bill in the Court of Equity, as the remedy is plain by order of the Court upon the defendant as an officer of the Court, or by suit at law on his official bond.

A. Moore, for the plaintiff.
Badger, for the defendant.

Ruffin, C. J. The plaintiff lost the legal profit, which might have been made on her money, by the payment to a person unauthorized to receive it, who used and wasted it. The defendant is, therefore, clearly liable for both principal and interest, although he had the benefit of neither; for both stand on the same footing. The defendant says, indeed, that he has been always willing and ready to pay the principal; but we cannot understand that to mean that he has actually kept that sum by him, as the plaintiff's money, making no use of it—for. if so, he would have stated the facts with precision. On the contrary, the answer is taken only to admit the defendant's liability for the sum, and to say, that he at no time meant to resist the demand; and, consequently, the defendant cannot be supposed to have, in the mean while, lost the use of the money, which he is now called on to pay.

But, admitting the defendant's liability to the whole extent, the Court holds his objection to the remedy, here attempted, to be good. This is not the proper subject of equitable jurisdiction upon a bill. The plaintiff's right is not an equity, but it is in its nature legal—being merely the right to a sum of money paid into the office for her use. That the defendant is an officer of the Court does not change the jurisdiction, so as to make the matter cognizable by suit commenced by bill. The Court of Equity would have given the plaintiff summary and complete relief upon her petition in the original cause, or on her motion, and a rule on the Clerk and Master, to be enforced by attachment; or she might have instituted an action at law, against the defendant and his sureties on his official bond. But there is no ground, on which a bill can be sustained, without authorizing this remedy against every Clerk or Sheriff who misapplies or fails to pay money received in his office for another. Therefore, the bill must be dismissed at the costs of the next friend, without prejudice to any other remedy the plaintiff may have in the premises.

PER CURIAM.   Decree accordingly.

EX PARTE, R. O. BRITTON & AL.

Land was conveyed to a trustee in trust, " to receive and pay over the rents and profits of the land unto Mrs. A. B., to her sole and separate use, free and discharged from any contract or claim of her husband, C. D. during the natural life of the said A. B. ; and after her death, in trust to convey the said land unto all the children of the said A. B. that shall be living at her death, equally to be divided among them ; that is to say, only in default of any such appointment by the said A. B. in nature of a will, during her life-time, as is hereinafter mentioned. But if the said A. B. shall make any appointment in writing, witnessed by two witnesses, therein appointing or giving said land to any person or persons whatsoever, then in trust to convey said land to such person or persons as the said A. B. may appoint or name, by or in any such appointment in writing as aforesaid, or in any writing executed by the said A. B. as aforesaid." *Held*, that under this power, A. B. might appoint the land to any person she chose, by deed attested by two witnesses, and that her power was not restrained to an appointment by a writing in the nature of a will.

Appeal from a decree of the Court of Equity of Hali.

fax County, at the Fall Term, 1845, his Honor Judge SETTLE presiding.

The case was as follows: A petition was filed in the Court of Equity, under the statute, for the sale of a tract of land, for partition among tenants in common. The sale was decreed; and when it was reported, the purchaser opposed the confirmation of it, upon the ground that the petitioners' title was not good. It was thereupon referred to the Master to enquire and report upon the title; and he reported, that it was conceded by the purchaser that the title was good, if Martha M. R. Brownlow, wife of Tippo S. Brownlow, could limit and appoint the land, by deed attested by two witnesses, under a power vested in her by a deed for the premises, made by William W. Wilkins to Mark H. Pettway—of which he annexed a copy to his report. The Master also annexed to his report, a copy of the appointment made by Mrs. Brownlow, by deed attested by two witnesses, to one William B. Lockhart, from whom the petitioners derived their title. The deed from Wilkins to Pettway is, "upon trust to receive and pay over the rents and profits of the land unto Mrs. Martha M. R. Brownlow, to her sole and separate use, free and discharged from any contract or claim of her husband, Tippo S. Brownlow, during the natural life of the said Mrs. Martha M. R. Brownlow; and, after her death, in trust to convey the said land unto all the children of the said Mrs. M. M. R. B. that shall be living at her death, equally to be divided between them; that is to say, only in default of any such appointment by said Mrs. M. M. R. B., in nature of a will, during her life-time, as is hereinafter mentioned. But if the said Mrs. M. M. R. B. shall make any appointment in writing, witnessed by two witnesses, therein appointing or giving said land to any person or persons whatsoever, then in trust to convey said land to such person or persons as the said Mrs. M. M. R. B. may appoint or name, by or in any such appointment in writing as aforesaid, or in any writing executed by said Mrs. M. M. R. B. as aforesaid."

The only question was, whether, under that próvision in the deed made by Wilkins, Mrs. Brownlow was not restricted to an appointment by will, or an instrument in the nature of a will; or whether she might not also appoint by such deed as that to Lookhart. The Master submitted that question to the Court, and a declaration *pro forma* having been made that the title was not good, the petitioners were allowed to appeal.

Bragg, for the petitioners.

No counsel on the other side.

RUFFIN, C. J. As our brother DANIEL does not sit in this case, the other members of the Court have considered the question, and are of opinion that Mrs. Brownlow's appointment by the deed to Lockhart, which is attested by two witnesses, is effectual. The deed, containing the power, is obviously drawn by one who was but little versed in the form of such instruments, and who bungled in putting the different parts of this instrument together, probably, from some book of forms. For example, it says the land is to be equally divided between the children of Mrs. B., " only in default of any *such* appointment," though that is the first time that appointment is spoken of in the instrument. It is óbvious, that no effect will be allowed to the subsequent provision for an " appointment by writing, witnessed by two witnesses," if the execution of the power is to be by will alone. Yet the Court has no authority thus to strike out one provision for the sake of the other; but it is proper to give effect to the whole, if it can be done, by understanding the two clauses in such a way as to make them consistent. Perhaps that may be done in this case. Thus there is, first, a provision for Mrs. Brownlow's *children* to take *equally* at her death, in default of her making an appointment in nature of a will; and then, secondly, there is a provision for appointing or giving to *any person or persons*, in a writing witnessed by two witnesses. Now, children, or a particular child, may often exercise great influence over a mother, and might induce her, at an unguarded moment, voluntarily to appoint the land to some one or more of them, and thereby strip herself of her support from the profits of the land, and deprive her of the power of providing for another child, who, before her death, might turn out to be more needy; and it has occurred to us, that possibly the writer, being aware of these things, might have meant that, as to appointments among her children, which he took for granted would be voluntary, this lady should take her whole life for binding herself and concluding her other children, and therefore prescribed a will as the mode of appointing to those persons. But the same reasons did not apply to a disposition, by sale or otherwise, to any *other* persons besides the children; and, therefore, she was allowed to make such latter appointments by an act *inter vivos*, provided only it was in writing and attested as prescribed, as protections from fraud and perjury. We do not see how, otherwise, the different parts can stand together; unless it be, that the two sentences are to be treated as one, and read as if allowing an appointment to any person, whether a child or not, either by will or by any other writing, duly attested. Rather than render either provision wholly ineffectual, it would be the duty of the Court thus to blend them, as best effectuating the general intention. But it is sufficient for the present purpose, as Lockhart was not a child but a purchaser for value, to say, that the deed, by a fair construction, authorized such an appointment to be made by deed duly attested, as well as by will.

The decree was therefore erroneous, and ought to be reversed, and the title declared good, and the purchaser required to complete his purchase.

PER CURIAM.   Ordered to be certified accordingly.

NANCY TEMPLE *vs.* JOHN T. WILLIAMS & AL.

Where a wife and her husband turn her land into money, and she does not place her part of the money with some indifferent person for her, and as her separate property, but suffers the whole to be paid to the husband, the clearest proof is requisite to rebut the presumption that it was paid to, and accepted by the husband, for himself, and not in trust for his wife.

Cause removed from the Court of Equity of Pasquotank County, at the Fall Term, 1845.

The bill was filed in 1843, and states, that the plaintiff was the wife of Thomas Temple and was seised in fee of a tract of land; and that the husband made a proposition to her to sell her land, and with the proceeds purchase for her other land of equal value, that should have commodious buildings for a residence on it, and take the deed in the plaintiff's name; and that she assented thereto. The bill further states, that, in pursuance of the agreement, Thomas Temple made a contract to purchase a tract of land from one Carver, and that it was agreed between them and the plaintiff, that one hundred acres of the land so contracted for, including the buildings, should be conveyed by Carver to the plaintiff instead of her own land; and that in consideration thereof the plaintiff joined her husband in a sale and conveyance of her land for the sum of $1100, which was paid to the husband and by him paid to Carver in part of the price of the land purchased from Carver. The bill then states, that Temple, the husband, afterwards took a deed from Carver for the whole tract in his own name; and that subsequently he died and the land descended to the present defendants, who are his heirs at law. The prayer is for a conveyance of 100 acres, including the houses.

The defendants answer, that they have no knowledge upon the subject of the bill, and no information concerning it, except that derived from the statements of the plaintiff in her bill, and therefore they cannot admit the allegations to be true.

There are filed, as exhibits, a deed in fee from James Carver to Thomas Temple, bearing date the 2d of April, 1829, for a tract of land containing 161 acres, and the consideration stated is $1710, in hand paid; and also the copy of a deed, bearing date the 7th day of April, 1829, purporting to be made by Thomas Temple and his wife, Nancy, to Dempsey Richardson, for a tract of land containing 116 acres, in fee with general warranty, and the consideration is stated to be $1100.

A witness proves, that the land sold to Richardson was understood by him to belong to the plaintiff; that he was present when Temple and Carver made their contract in 1829, and that the plaintiff said, that she would not convey her land to any person, unless she should get as much of the land that was bought from Carver, as hers would pay for; and that Carver and Temple then said she should have it. Temple, at the time, said he thought he could sell the land he claimed in right of his wife, to Richardson.

Another witness proves, that he heard Temple once say, that he agreed to make his wife a separate deed for 100 acres, where the house stood; but he did not say that he was to do it, in consideration of his wife's having sold her land, and the proceeds having been applied in part payment of the land bought of Carver.

Badger and *A. Moore*, for the plaintiff.
Iredell, for the defendant.

RUFFIN, C. J. The bill is a mere skeleton, stating few particulars, and fixing no dates to any part of the transaction, nor to any event stated in it. In the most favorable view, the substance of the bill is, that there is a resulting trust to the plaintiff, upon a purchase by her husband with her land, or with the price of her land, which they sold for that purpose. Now, to sustain that case, the first step is, to shew her title to the land, which

she says belonged to her, and with which the purchase
was made ; and that is only done here by a single witness, and merely upon his understanding that it was hers.
It might. perhaps, be sufficient, *prima facie*, if the deed
from Temple and his wife stated the land to have descended to her, and to be hers or claimed as hers in fee.
But the extent of her title is in no manner to be gathered from that instrument. Besides, the bill does not shew
the state of the family of these parties, nor their ages,
nor any other matter from which the relative values of
the husband's interest in the land, and the wife's, can be
collected. But another and a decided objection is, that
the evidence contradicts the bill in its essential statement, that her land was sold and the proceeds invested
in this land for her ; for the two deeds shew that the land
was purchased from Carver, and conveyed by him, five
days before the plaintiff and her husband made their
conveyance ; and therefore, the most that can, *prima facie*, be made of the case for the plaintiff, is, that after
her husband had purchased and got his deed, she agreed
to sell her land to enable him to pay for his, provided
he would agree to sell to her 100 acres of his new purchase. But that is essentially a different case from that
charged by the bill, and, if that had been the case made
in the bill, the defendants would have met it at once
with a plea of the statute, to make void parol contracts
for the sale of land. 1819, c. 1016. It might have
probably appeared, if the plaintiff had taken the trouble
to take the testimony of witnesses, that the two contracts of sale were made some time before the conveyances, and that, in fact, the price of the plaintiff's
land was in hand, and laid out in purchasing the land
from Carver, and not merely in paying a debt contracted by the husband upon a previous purchase. But there
is no evidence to that point, and the only time to which
the witness refers, in speaking of the sale of the wife's
land, was prior to the sale of it. He says the husband

expected he could sell it to Richardson. Now, after
that, the plaintiff joined in a deed to Richardson, and
let the price go into the husband's hands, whereby it became his in law, at a time when the husband's own purchase was completed by a conveyance to himself; from
which, the conclusion is, that the wife then gave her
husband the money, whatever might have been her intention at a previous period. It is true, that a husband
and wife may, in Equity, deal with each other in respect
to her inheritance; but it is extremely difficult to do so,
with any security to her, without the intervention of a
third person as trustee, because it is hard to tell, in many
cases, whether she means to stand upon her separate
rights, or to surrender them to him; and, therefore, the
clearest proof is requisite to rebut the presumption,
when she and her husband turn her land into money,
and she does not place her part of the money with some
indifferent person for her, and as her separate property,
but suffers the whole to be paid to the husband, that it
was paid to and accepted by the husband for himself,
and not in trust for his wife. Here, there is no such
proof; and if the bill were properly framed, and sustained by evidence in other respects, it would be dismissed for this reason.

PER CURIAM.   Bill dismissed with costs.

JOHN B. MOSS & AL. *vs.* PETER ADAMS & AL.

If a debtor, who is indebted to the same creditor on different accounts, does
not make the application of a payment at the time such payment is made,
he cannot do so afterwards.

If the debtor fails to make the application, the creditor may do so at any
time afterwards before suit brought.

Where neither debtor nor creditor makes the application of the payment, the
law will apply it to that debt, for which the creditor's security was most
precarious.

This was an appeal from an interlocutory decree of the

Court of Equity of Guilford County, at the Fall Term, 1845, his Honor Judge Dick presiding, dissolving the injunction, which had been granted in the cause.

By the pleadings it appears, that the plaintiffs, Moss and M. W. Alexander, and the defendant, Bencine, as partners, took a contract from the government for carrying the Mail from Greensborough in this State, to Yorkville in South Carolina, to commence on the 1st day of January, 1839; and that they purchased from Peck, Wellford & Co. who had been the previous contractors on the line, horses, coaches, and other stock, to the value of $6,730. In liquidation thereof they gave four bonds—each for $1,682 50, and payable on the 1st of May, 1st of August, and 1st of November, 1839, and 1st of February, 1840; and the other plaintiffs, Long, D. Alexander, and Storkle, executed the bonds as sureties. A man by the name of Bowen took another Mail contract in South Carolina, to commence also on the 1st of January. 1839, and in like manner he became indebted to Peck, Wellford & Co. for which he gave them four notes—each for the sum of $1,675, payable on the same days with those before mentioned. In the spring of the year 1839, and after Bowen had paid his note which fell due on the 1st of May, 1839, the defendant, Bencine, purchased Bowen's contract and stock; and part of the agreement was, that Bencine should take up Bowen's notes to Peck, Wellford & Co. by substituting his own with satisfactory sureties. Accordingly, Bencine gave to Peck, Wellford & Co. his three notes for the sum of $1,675, each payable 1st August, 1st November, 1839, and 1st February, 1840, and the defendant, Adams, executed the notes as the surety of Bencine. A few months afterwards, the plaintiff, M. W. Alexander, and the defendant, Bencine, purchased from the plaintiff, Moss, his share of their joint contract and the stock; and part of the agreement was, that the purchasers should pay the debts to Peck, Wellford & Co. in exoneration of Moss. Sometime after that, Bencine purchased out the interest in the concern of the plaintiff, M. W. Alexander, and agreed with him, that he, Bencine, would pay to Peck, Wellford & Co. all the bonds of Moss, Alexander, and Bencine.

For some years previous to 1839, Bencine had been the agent of Peck, Wellford & Co. in conducting their line, and in the course of the business he became indebted to them in the sum of $2,720 59 1-4; and in liquidation thereof, he gave an acceptance, January 24th, 1840, for $120 27, in part, and on 5th of March, 1840, his note for $2,600 32 1-4, then payable.

In July, 1839, Bencine remitted the sum of $1682 50 to Peck, the acting partner of Peck, Wellford & Co. residing in Fredericksburg, Virginia, and he applied it in discharge of the bond of Moss, Alexander, and Bencine, which fell due 1st of May preceding, and charging no interest thereon. On the 23d of November, 1839, Bencine made a further remittance to Peck of $3,000, of which Peck applied at the time the sum of $1,713 90 in full of the principal and interest due on the bond of Moss, Alexander, and Bencine, which fell due 1st of August of that year, and the residue of $1,286 10 he applied as a credit to their bond, for $1,682 50, which fell due on the 1st of November: which left a balance due on that bond of $410 12, and the whole of their bond for $1682 50, to fall due 1st February, 1840.

Bencine made no further payment until August 3d, 1841, and he then remitted to Peck $2,024 07, with directions to apply it to his own note for $2,600 32 1-4, which he had given for the balance he owed upon his agency before 1839; and it was accordingly so applied.

Then at different times in 1842 and 1843, Bencine made eight remittances, amounting in the whole to the sum of $5,396 37, without any directions as to the application; and they were by Peck, Wellford & Co. entered generally to the credit of Bencine in account, without applying any one of them to a particular debt: though with an intention, as Peck states in his answer, and as Bencine says he expected, that it should be ultimately applied, in the first place, to the satisfaction of the balance due on the note of Bencine himself, and his acceptance for $120 27 to Peck, Wellford & Co. At those periods, Bencine was in possession of a large property and none of the parties suspected his credit, unless the plaintiff, Moss, might have done so. In the latter part of the year 1843, however, it was ascertained that he was not able to pay his debts, and he made an assignment.

In July, 1844, Peck came to Greensborough for the purpose of settling the business with Bencine. They did so by applying, by consent, the said sum of $5,896 37, first to the debts for which Peck, Wellford and Co. held no security but the note and acceptance of Bencine alone; and they applied the residue thereof to a part payment of each of the three notes for $1,675, given by Bencine and by Adams as his surety, which left a balance due on each of them, including interest to July 11th, 1844, which amounted in the whole to the sum of $1,951 83. The sum due for principal and interest up to the same day, on the two bonds aforesaid of Moss, Alexander and Bencine, which fell due the 1st of November, 1839, and 1st of February, 1840, was then ascertained to be $2,644 17. Peck at first expressed a reluctance to make any particular application of the money, except to the debts for which he had only the personal security of Bencine. But Bencine urged the application that was made, upon several grounds: first, that Adams was his surety, and never had any interest in the matter, while Moss and M. B. Alexander had been once principals, and had made a profit in selling out to him: secondly, that he had paid the sum of $4,651 10, which had been applied to the bonds given by Moss, Alexander and Bencine, in exoneration of the two former, and if the remaining sum, not before applied, should then be applied to the bonds to which Moss and Alexander were parties, those persons would get the benefit of all the payments that had been at any time made, and Adams have no benefit of them whatever, and sustain a total loss : and thirdly, that, although the notes given by the two sets of persons, were payable at the same days, the contract with Bowen had been made, and the notes, in which Adams was surety, had been given, before Bencine's contract of purchase from either Alexander or Moss. Finally, Peck declared that he would concur with Bencine in making the application, provided Adams would then pay the notes which had his name on them, and also pay the balance that would then remain on the bonds of Moss, Alexander and Bencine, namely, the sum of $2,644 17, and take an as·signment of those bonds without recourse to Peck, Wellford & Co. To that proposition, Adams assented, and the application of the payments was made accordingly ; and the two bonds of Moss, Alexander and Bencine, endorsed to Adams, who advanced for them the full sum thus appearing to be due on them, and instituted an action at law on them against the obligors.

The present bill was then filed by all the obligors, except Bencine, against that person, Peck, Wellford & Co. and Adams, praying for a perpetual injunction. The bill states, that Peck knew that Bencine had become the sole owner of the line, in which the plaintiffs had been concerned, and had engaged with them to pay the whole debt, and thereby made himself the sole principal debtor : that soon after the sale by Moss, he informed Peck by letter, that he feared Alexander was about to fail, and requested him to collect the bonds forthwith, and that Peck replied, that two of the bonds were paid in full, and on the third $1,286 10, and that he was not at all uneasy about the safety or payment of the balance : that Bencine soon afterwards informed Moss, that he had paid all those bonds except the sum of $1,200, and that he had promised Peck to pay that balance out of his next quarter's mail pay : that he, Moss, being induced by those representations of Peck and Bencine, to believe that he was in no danger, gave himself no concern about the bonds, and was prevented from keeping an eye, on the affairs of Alexander and Bencine, and saving himself before they were ruined, as he might and would have done, if he had not been thus lulled into security. The bill charges, that, in the belief of the plaintiffs, Bencine made payments to Peck, which were applied to those bonds and discharged them; but that they were not entered on the bonds, but only in a book, or that receipts were given for them, expressing the application, which were afterwards suppressed; and that the payments made on those bonds were in July, 1844, fraudulently transferred from them and applied to the notes on which Adams' name was.

The answer of Peck denies that he received from Moss or wrote to him a letter, of the purport stated in the bill; and there is attached to it a letter from Moss to Peck, dated February 2d, 1841, in which he mentions that he had sold his interest, and that the bonds were to have been changed: that he had learnt that they had not been changed, but that not long before, Bencine had stated to him that he had nearly paid them off; and he requested Peck to inform him what payments had been made. The answer then sets forth a copy of Peck's reply, which is dated the 10th of February, 1840, and states the four bonds of $1,682 50 each, and the credits of $4,651 10, which extinguished two of the bonds, and made a payment of $1,286 10 on the third, leaving a balance of principal on the two unpaid bonds of $2,078 90, as set forth in the letter. That is the whole of the letters, and the answer denies that any other ever passed between these parties, or that the defendant was ever requested to sue on the bonds, or represented that he was secure of the payment. The answers of Peck and Bencine deny that any part of the other payments were directed by Bencine to be applied, or were by him or by Peck applied to the bonds of Moss, Alexander and Bencine, or to any other debts, until they were applied on the 11th of July, 1844, as before stated; and that they were not transferred from one debt to the other.

The answer of Adams is to the same effect, as far as he has any knowledge or belief; and it states that this defendant was induced to advance the balance due on the plaintiffs' bonds to Peck, Wellford & Co. and to take an assignment of them, in order to prevent Peck from unjustly refusing to apply any of the money, remitted to him, to the notes on which, he, Adams, was—as the only means in his power to avoid a total loss. The injunction, which had been granted on the bill, was dissolved on the motion of the defendants, and an appeal allowed to the plaintiffs.

Morehead, for the plaintiffs.
Kerr, for the defendants.

RUFFIN, C. J. Those parts of the bill, which charge a misrepresentation to the plaintiff, Moss, as to his liabilities or concealment from him on that subject, or that payments were in truth made on the bonds with his name on them, which are the subjects of this controversy (except the sum of $4,651 10 which was applied to them) are, all, directly and satisfactorily denied. The cause therefore turns upon the rule of law, as to the application of indefinite payments. The defendant, Adams, stands in the shoes of his endorsers, Peck, Wellford & Co. as he took the bonds over-due; and he is, of course, no worse off than they would be. The payments were made in 1842 and 1843, and they were finally applied on the 11th day of July, 1844, by the debtor and the creditor concurring.

We do not find it any where said, that the debtor, if he fail to make the application at the time of the payment, can do so afterwards, although the creditor may not then have appropriated it. We suppose he cannot: for, by not exercising the power when he parted from the money, he allows it to devolve on the creditor, and submits to his exercise of it, if the latter will do it at all. The debtor, it would seem, could not therefore claim to resume the power. There could be no doubt, that the concurrence of both the parties in an application of payments *ex post facto*, would be effectual between them, although the rule was, that the creditor must exercise his power, that is, of his own motion, at the time of the payment, or within a reasonable time thereafter. For the law makes the application, on the failure of the parties to do it, on the presumption of the interest and intention of one or the other of the parties; and therefore it would give way to an actual application by both of the parties, as furnishing direct evidence and superseding the necessity for presumption. That would, probably, be the rule of law, even where sureties were concerned. But, if the law were, that the debtor, or creditor must, when each acts by himself and upon his single right, apply the payment when it is made, it would be an interesting question, whether in equity those two parties could subsequently, by concurring in the application, prevent the application by the law, so as to affect the rights of sureties. It would seem that on principle the insolvency of the debtor tied his hands and made it his duty to let the law operate between his sureties and his creditor, as things stood upon the happening of his insolvency. But we do not find it necessary to dispose of that question, as we believe the present case is to be decided against the plaintiff upon the rights of the creditor, independent of the assent of the debtor.

It has been sometimes thought, that the creditor lost his option as to the application, unless he acted on it at the time of the payment. The doctrine of our law upon this subject, is supposed to have been borrowed from the civil law; in which the rules certainly were, that if neither the debtor nor the creditor elected at the time of payment, the law applied it, and did so upon a presumed intention of the debtor, and, therefore, according to his interest, and to the most burdensome debt: as, to that carrying interest or secured by a penalty, before one that was not; and when the debtor could have no interest, as where the debts were alike, the application was made to the elder. It may be remarked, then, that if this were a case in which the creditor had not effectually applied the payments, because done out of due time, yet the applications made here were just such as the law would have made, according to the rule of the civil law. All the debts were secured alike, and drawing interest at the time of the payments; and the debt of Bencine, secured by his own name alone, though due upon securities more recent, was in fact contracted a considerable time before any of the others; and, though the other two classes of securities were payable at the same days, and the bonds of Moss, Alexander and Bencine were given to Peck, Wellford & Co. before those of Bencine and Adams, yet the former class became Bencine's own debt and payable by himself exclusively, after he had given the notes in substitution for Bowen's—he having purchased from Bowen before he did from Moss. But we are at liberty to pass by this point, also, for the same reason, that we did that respecting the concurrence of Bencine and Peck in the application in July, 1844. For, although the common law may be indebted to the civil law for the leading rule, which gives the option first to the debtor, and then, in succession, to the creditor, and to the law; yet it is certain, that the Roman law has not been followed throughout, but the English and American Courts have departed from it in several instances, and, indeed, reversed it, and allowed the creditor to make his election long posterior to the payment, and after material changes of the circumstances of the parties; and, in other instances, the law has applied payments according to the interest and presumed intention of the creditor, as, for example, to the debt not bearing interest, or the one more precariously secured, or one barred by the statute of limitations or the like. This doctrine was discussed, and first particularly explained by Sir William Grant, in *Devaynes* v. *Noble*, 1 Meriv. 528, *Clayton's case*, 570, 604. He did not conclusively decide any point on it; but he noticed the principal cases which had then been decided, and, although, as he remarked, they were not all reconcileable, it seems sufficiently plain, that, in his opinion, the weight of the authorities and principle authorized the creditor not only to apply a payment to what debt he pleased, but to make the application when he thought fit; and, further, that, in the absence of express appropriation by either party, the presumed intention of the creditor is to govern. The last case that had then been decided was that of *Peters* v. *Anderson*, in the Common Pleas, 5 Taun. 596, in which it was held, that, if not made specifically, the creditors may at any time elect that a payment shall retrospectively receive its application to the debt, for which his security was the worse. The old case of *Meggott* v. *Mills*, Ld. Ray. 287, and that of *Dawe* v. *Holdworth*, Peake N. P. 64, are there said by Chief Justice Gibbs to go on an exception founded on bankruptcy. Since that time, there have been a number of cases, which seem to settle the question definitely in England, and establish that the creditor may make the appropriation at any time before suit brought. *Bosanquet* v. *Wray*, 6 Taunt. 597. *Bodenham* v. *Purchas*, 2 B. and Ald. 39. *Simson* v. *Ingham*, 2 B. and C. 65. *Philpott* v. *Jones*, 2 Adol. and Ell. 41, and *Mills* v. *Fowkes*, 5 Bingh. N. C. 455. In *Philpott* v. *Jones*, the plaintiff could not have recovered on one of his debts, which was for spirits sold on credit, contrary to a statute; yet he was allowed to apply an indefinite payment to that debt; and Chief Justice Denman said he might so apply it at any time. The same language is used by all the Court in *Simson* v. *Ingham*, except that Judge Best said, the creditor must appropriate the pay-

ment in reasonable time, and except that it was agreed
by all the Judges that it must be before action. In the
case of *Mills* v. *Fowkes*, which is the latest that has
fallen under our notice, all the other cases are brought
forward; and it was there held, that where one of two
debts is barred by the statute of limitations, the creditor
may subsequently apply a payment to that debt, and then
recover the other. The old argument was revived again,
that, where the creditor failed to make the appropriation
at once, he could not do it, but the law did it afterwards.
But CHIEF JUSTICE TINDALL replied, that the decisions were
clearly the other way, and that the receiver had a clear
right to apply a payment " at any time before action."

Prior to those modern decisions, the questions arose in
the Courts of this Country, and the doctrines were distinctly laid down, which have since prevailed in England.
In *The Mayor, &c. of Alexandria* v. *Patton*, 4 Cranch 317,
Patton owed Ladd for goods sold to him, and also for the
proceeds of goods sold by Patton, as auctioneer. He
made a payment, which Ladd *ex post facto* applied to the
former debt, and then, as relator, instituted a suit against
Patton and his sureties on a bond given to secure his fidel-
ity as auctioneer. On the trial the jury was instructed,
that, although Ladd might apply the payment which Patton had omitted to apply, yet that " it must have been
recent and before any alteration had taken place in the
circumstances of Patton:" which denotes, that Patton
had then become insolvent. The judgment was reversed
in the Supreme Court, and CHIEF JUSTICE MARSHALL in
giving the opinion said, the error was in holding, that the
creditor's election was lost, if not immediately exercised.
It is not said in that case, that it may not be lost by any delay
to make it. But, if the creditor be not obliged to declare
his option immediately, to what other period can he be restricted? The only limitation must be that laid down in the
English cases; namely, suit brought. For when a person
brings suit, he must be taken to bring it on his demand

as it then stands, and he cannot subsequently change it. In accordance with which the Supreme Court also held in *The United States* v. *Kirkpatrick*, 9 Wheat. 720, that the creditor could not elect at the trial or after suit brought. And upon the question, concerning the application to be made by the law, where the parties omit, the same eminent Judge in 1810 laid it down in *Field* v. *Holland*, 6 Cranch 8, that it would be to the debt, for which the creditor's security was most precarious.

It follows from what has been said, that the payments were properly appropriated, in the first instance, to the debts for which the creditors hold only Bencine's own note and acceptance; and that the application by the creditors of the residue to the notes given by Bencine and Adams, is conclusive and cannot be controlled by the Court. It is important that the law should be settled on these points; and it is, perhaps, of more consequence that some certain rule should be established, than that it should be any one in particular—so that debtors may fully know the consequences of not availing themselves of the power of applying a payment when it is made, and allowing it to devolve on the creditor.

Perhaps it had been well to adhere to the original rule of the civil law, as more simple in itself, easily understood, and in its uniform operation doing as much justice, upon the whole, as any others however modified. But, with no previous predilection for them, we find the exceptions to it, on the points involved in this case, so firmly established in the tribunals of the common law, that we have no choice but to adopt them also; and possibly they were necessary to the advancement of credit in our more commercial ages, by affording to the creditor more facilities for securing himself upon the failure of his debtors.

The injunction was, therefore, properly dissolved, and it must be so certified to the Court of Equity; and the plaintiff must pay the costs in this Court.

PER CURIAM.   Ordered to be certified accordingly.

WILLIAM HORTON *vs.* EDWIN R. HORTON.

Whether or not a guardian is bound to go to another State to sue a former guardian, who has taken off his ward's property; yet when such former guardian has given a guardian bond in this State, the subsequent guardian is bound to sue on that bond to recover the value of the property so removed : and if he neglects to do so, he is answerable to the ward for the amount of the property removed.

This cause was transmitted to this Court from the Court of Equity of Chatham County, at the Fall Term, 1842.

The bill is filed by William Horton, against Edwin R. Horton, who was the guardian of the plaintiff, for an account. The facts are, that Joseph Horton was first appointed the plaintiff's guardian by the County Court, and entered into a guardian bond, in which the present defendant and another person were his sureties. This was in the year 1820, and the plaintiff was then seven or eight years old. Joseph Horton received, as legacies, from a deceased relative to his ward, the sum of $100, and a negro boy, worth $300. In January, 1823, Joseph Horton, being about to remove to Alabama, and to carry the slave with him, in order to induce the defendant and his co-surety to assent thereto, executed to them a conveyance for a tract of land in Chatham County to indemnify them from any loss in case he did not get from the plaintiff a release, when he came to full age ; and he then went with the defendant's approbation. In May, 1823, the defendant procured the removal of Joseph Horton, and himself to be appointed to the guardianship of the plaintiff. But he never afterwards took any steps to get in his ward's money and slave from Joseph Horton, who died in Alabama some years ago. The present bill charges that the defendant ought to have done so, and that he is liable to the plaintiff, among other things, for the value of the estate which ought to have been received from the first guardian.

The answer does not deny the facts, but insists that the defendant had not, under his appointment as guardian in this State, authority to receive or sue for the ward's property in Alabama.

There was the usual reference to the Master to take the accounts of the estate of the plaintiff in the hands, or that ought to have been in the hands, of the defendant. The Master has reported a balance of $1080 23 against the defendant, which includes the value of the negro and the pecuniary legacy to the plaintiff, which Joseph Horton received and wasted; and the defendant has excepted thereto.

W. H. Haywood, for the plaintiff.
Badger and *Manly*, for the defendant.

RUFFIN, C. J. The defendant is liable for the sums charged by the Master. Admitting that a guardian of a ward residing here is not bound to secure the estate of the ward in another government, a point we do not decide, that would be no excuse for this defendant. For he had it in his power to have justice done to his ward, without going out of this State, namely, by an action against the sureties of the first guardian. Indeed, he himself was one of them; and there can be little doubt, that the principal purpose, for which he procured himself to be appointed guardian, was to prevent those sureties from being immediately sued, as they would have been, if any other person had been appointed. The plaintiff, has therefore, a right to consider his estate to have been in the hands of the defendant, upon his receiving the office of guardian. He might have his remedy at law against the defendant, as the surety of Joseph Horton, or upon his own bond as guardian, or he may have it in this Court by bill for the breach of trust. The defendant's exception must therefore be over-ruled, and the report confirmed, and a decree according to it, with costs to the plaintiff.

PER CURIAM.   Decree accordingly.

ROBERT PETERSON *vs.* LORENZO S. WEBB & AL.

A. being about to be married, conveyed certain slaves to a trustee, in trust
for herself and future husband during their joint lives, and, if she survived
her husband, to her use only ; if he survived her, then to such person or
persons as she might bequeath them to by will, and, if she made no will,
then to the use of the husband for life, remainder " to the use of her next
of kin, under the statute of distributions." *Held*, that A. having died
without executing the power, the husband was only entitled to a life estate ;
that he was not one of her *next of kin* under the statute of distributions,
and the remainder of the slaves, after his death, belonged to her nearest
relatives of her blood, who were such next of kin under the statute.

Even if the conveyance had been to " her legal representatives, according
to the statute of distributions," the husband could not have taken, because
he is her legal representative, *jure mariti*, and not according to the
statute.

The case of *Jones* v. *Oliver*, 3 Ired. Eq. 369, cited and approved.

This cause was removed, by consent, from the Court
of Equity of Bertie County, at the Fall Term, 1845, to
the Supreme Court.

The Bill set forth that, in the year 1838, the plaintiff
intermarried with Mary Johnson ; that, previous to the
said marriage, a marriage settlement was entered into by
the said parties, in which the defendant was made a trus-
·tee. The material parts of the said settlement were,
" That the said Mary Johnson of the first part, the said
Robert Peterson, the plaintiff in this suit of the second
part, and Lorenzo S. Webb, the present defendant, of the
third part, entered into this indenture, and it witnessed,
" That whereas, the parties of the first and second part
were about to enter into the civil and religious contract
of marriage, and whereas it is intended between the said
parties, that such property as is hereinafter mentioned,
belonging to the said Mary Johnson, shall not vest absolutely in the said Robert Peterson, but shall be secured
for the joint use of the said parties of the first and second part, during the continuance of the marriage, and to
the survivor during his or her life, and afterwards to
such persons as the said Mary Johnson, by her last will
and testament, executed to pass personal property ac-

cording to the laws of North Carolina, shall appoint ; or, in default of such appointment by her, to her legal representatives according to the statute of distributions of this State. Now, therefore, &c." and the deed proceeded to convey certain slaves to the defendant, Lorenzo S. Webb, his executors, &c.; "In trust, nevertheless, for the purposes hereinafter declared; *first,* for the joint use, after the solemnization of the said intended marriage of the said first and second parties, during their marriage; *secondly,* if the said party of the first part shall survive the said party of the second part, then to the sole use of her, her heirs, executors or administrators; *thirdly,* in case of the death of the said party of the first part, before the party of the second part, to his use during his natural life, and, after his death. to the use of such person or persons as the said party of the first part shall, by will, duly executed according to the laws of this State, appoint; or, in default of such appointment, to the use of her next of kin under the statute of distributions." The Bill then alleged, that this marriage settlement having been duly executed, proved and registered, the said Mary died, without having made any appointment under the power therein contained; that the plaintiff, as her husband, took out letters of administration on her estate, and claims the whole interest in the said slaves, and prays that the defendant, Lorenzo S. Webb, may account, &c. The next of kin of the said Mary Peterson are also made parties defendant, and they insist on their right to the property, after the expiration of the life estate of the husband, the plaintiff in the cause. The trustee submits to any decree the Court may make in the premises, none of the facts being disputed on either side.

Bragg, for the plaintiff.

No counsel for the defendants in this Court.

DANIEL, J. The deed of marriage settlement, mentioned in the pleadings, was made in the year 1836, and by the

37

terms of it, the wife, if she survived her husband, was to have all the slaves mentioned in it; but if she died before him, she had a power to bequeath them by will to whom she pleased; and, in case she made no will, the slaves were to be held by the trustee, to the use of the husband for life, remainder to the use of her next of *kin*, "under the statute of distributions." Mrs. Peterson died without making any will. The husband, having taken administration on his wife's estate, has filed this bill, calling upon Webb, the trustee, to convey the said slaves to him absolutely. We do not think that he is entitled to any such decree. The next of *kin* of his wife, at her death, were her relations by *blood*, and the husband, in that sense of the term, was not of *kin* to his wife. *Watt* v. *Watt*, 2 Ves. 244. *Bailey* v. *Wright*, 18 Ves. 50. *Jones* v. *Oliver*, 3 Iredell's Eq. 369.

In the beginning of the deed, and before any conveying words are used, or trusts declared, the parties recite the inducement to the making of the same; and they state, that it is intended, if the wife should die before the husband, and in default of any appointment by her, then the slaves, after the death of the husband, should go "to her legal representatives, according to the statute of distributions." The husband is the administrator of the estate of his wife, and is her legal representative, *jure mariti*, and not according to the statute of distributions. It is therefore clear, according to the context, that he is not the person designated in the sentence, to take in the event which has happened. But, if it appear from the dispositions in the whole instrument, whether it be a deed or will, that those words (legal representatives,) were used in reference to other persons than executors and administrators, that interpretation will prevail and those other persons will take. 1 *Roper on Legacies*, 108, 110. We think, that it is here manifest, when the whole deed is read, that the trust for the husband is for his life only, in the event which has happened; and that the remainder

in the slaves, after the death of the husband, was to go
to the next of *kin in blood* of the wife, who were so, at
her death. The bill must be dismissed.

PER CURIAM.   Decree accordingly.

BENJAMIN S. H. LIVERMAN *vs.* STEPHEN D. CARTER.

A testator bequeathed all his property to his brother A., except $100, which
he " willed to B. to be appropriated to the use of schooling and educating
the said B., in that way and at that time that shall appear to be the most
advantage to the said boy. I also leave the said $100 in the hands of the
said A., to use the said money for the said purpose above written, if he
should have it in his power, and, if not, to remain in common with the
rest of the said property to A." The testator lived till B., the *boy*, had
become a man, married, and had a family. *Held*, that this was not an
absolute legacy of $100 to B., but only for his schooling and education,
and that, under the circumstances existing at the death of the testator, he
had no right to claim it, but it belonged to A.

If a bequest be to, or in trust for a legatee, to put him out apprentice, or to
advance him in any business or profession, it is an absolute bequest to such
legatee ; except in the case, where the legacy is given over to another, in
the event that the first object of the testator cannot be effected.

Appeal from the decree of the Court of Equity of Hyde
County, at the Fall Term, 1845, his Honor Judge BATTLE
presiding, dismissing the Bill.

The case appeared upon the pleadings, to be this :

Moses Carter, of the County of Hyde, in the year 1835,
made his will, and thereby gave to the defendant, his brother, all his real and personal estate, (amounting in value
to about $800, as the answer states,) " with the exception
of one hundred dollars, which I will to B. H. S. Liverman,
(the plaintiff) to be appropriated to the use of schooling and
educating the said Liverman, in that way and at that time,
that shall appear to be of the most advantage to the said

boy. I also leave the said hundred dollars in the hands of my brother, S. D. Carter, to use the said money for said purpose above written, if he should have it in his power, and, if not. to remain in common with the rest of the said property to the said S. D. Carter." The testator did not die until the month of March in the year 1842, nearly seven years after the writing of his will, when the plaintiff was more than twenty-one years old, married, and had two children.

No counsel for the plaintiff.
Stanly, for the defendant.

DANIEL, J. The hundred dollars, as it seems to us, was to be applied by the defendant to the use of the schooling and education of the plaintiff, in that way and at that time, that should appear to be of most advantage to the said *boy.* And if the defendant should not have it in his power to apply the fund to the schooling and education of the *boy*, then the same should sink in the general legacy. We do not think that the sum was to be raised for the general advancement in life of the plaintiff, and it does not appear that it ever was in the power of the defendant to apply it to the education of the plaintiff; nor is it now claimed by him for that purpose, but absolutely. The law is, if a bequest be to, or in trust for, a legatee, to put him out apprentice, or prepare him for Priests' orders, or to advance him in any business or profession, it is an absolute bequest to such legatee. This is, however, when the legacy is not given over to another, in the event the first object of the testator cannot be affected. *Nevile* v. *Nevile*, 2 Vern. 430. *Barton* v. *Grant*, 2 Vern. 254. *Barton* v. *Cocke*, 5 Ves. 451. *Cope* v. *Wilmot*, Amb. 704. *Sherwood* v. *Ryme*, 5 Ves. 667. In the case before us, the testator leaves the legacy in the hands of a trustee, to use it for schooling and educating the said *boy*, in that way and at that time, that shall appear to be of the most ad-

vantage to him, if the trustee should have it in his power;
and, if not, the fund is to remain with the rest of the property, before given to the trustee, for the benefit of the
trustee.   The plaintiff now insists, that he is absolute
owner of the $100; and he demands it on that ground only.
Suppose he was to get it and would never thereafter go
to school, what would become of the words in the will,
which give the said $100 to the defendant in that event?
Why, they would be nullified.   That, it seems to us,
would be contrary to all the known rules of construction
on wills.   We think, that the testator intended the $100
for his brother, unless it should be wanting for the schooling of the plaintiff.   We therefore think, that the decree,
dismissing the bill, was right, and that it must be affirmed;
but without costs in this Court.

Per Curiam.   Decree accordingly.

THE DEEP RIVER GOLD MINING CO. vs. RICHARD FOX.

It is a well established principle in Equity, that an agent cannot make himself an adverse party to his principal, while the agency continues; he can
neither make himself a purchaser, when employed to sell, nor, if employed to purchase, can he make himself the seller.   In both cases, he is but
a trustee for his principal.

But the rule applies only to agents, who are relied upon for counsel and direction, and whose employment is rather a trust than a service; and not
to those, who are merely employed as instruments, in the performance of
some appointed service.

Courts of Equity should be very cautious in granting injunctions to stop
mining operations, because such stoppage is alike opposed to public policy,
and to the private justice due to the party, who might ultimately be found
to be the owner.   The better course is not to prevent the working of the
mine, but to appoint a receiver.

The cases of *Bissell* v. *Bozman*, 2 Dev. Eq. 160, and *Falls* v. *McAffee*, 2
Ired. 239, cited and approved.

This was an appeal, both by the plaintiffs and the defendant, from certain interlocutory orders made by the

Court of Equity of Guilford County, at the Fall Term, 1845, his Honor Judge DICK presiding.

The bill charges, that the plaintiffs, by an Act of the General Assembly, passed in the year 1835, were incorporated by the name of the Deep River Gold Mining Company, and as such were organized and commenced business in the year 1835, and continued to carry it on until finally suspended. The officers of said company at the time the bill was filed, consisted of a President, Granville Sharp Patterson, and four Directors, to-wit: Roswell A. King, Lemuel Lamb, Joshua Phillips and Henry Ogden, all of whom were duly chosen, according to the act, and of whom, Roswell A. King alone lived in North Carolina. The others in New York and Philadelphia. That, by the provisions of the act of incorporation, all the property of the company is made liable to be sold for its debts, and that process, to subject it to such sale, may be served on the President or any Director or Stockholder. To carry on their operations, the bill charges that the company purchased, from Roswell A. King and others, several contiguous tracts of land, which were valued at the time at $200,000, and, at which price, they were taken as stock. When the company commenced operations, the defendant, Fox, was appointed the agent to manage and carry on the business at a salary of $1500 per year, and one F. Wilkerson was appointed their clerk at a salary of $400. The lands were found, upon examination, to abound in copper and gold ore, each very rich. Large quantities were sent to England and sold at a high price. The purpose of sending the ore to England was to ascertain its value, and to enable the company, by a sale of stock, to carry on their operations more extensively and profitably. Sales were effectuated upon certain terms, and in consequence of a misunderstanding between the company and the English purchasers, the business of the company was suspended. The agent, Fox, was, by letter dated the 1st of January. 1839, informed of this fact, and directed to discharge all the hands except two or three to take care of the property, and by letter, dated in the April following, and addressed to him, he was notified his services and Wilkerson's were no longer needed, and requiring him to forward a full statement of the situation of the firm, and the said Fox, subsequently, agreed with the plaintiffs to continue to act as their agent, at a salary of $100 per annum. This new arrangement was finally closed or made at a meeting of the board, held in May, 1841, at which the defendant was present. The bill charges that, while Fox was so acting as their agent, he caused process to issue against the company, returnable to the August Term, 1841, of the Court of Pleas and Quarter Sessions of Guilford County, and obtained a judgment at the November Term following, for the sum of $1166 36, which he claimed to be due for his said salaries as agent. Upon this judgment execution issued, returnable to February Term, 1842, and was levied on all the property of the plaintiffs in the County of Guilford, including the several tracts of land, so purchased and held by the company; that a sale took place at May Term, 1842, when the defendant purchased the whole of the lands at the price, in the whole, of $1,265—the several tracts having been sold separately, and being worth the amount at which they were taken as stock. The bill further states, that, at the meeting of the board in May, 1842, the defendant presented his account against the company, and made a representation of their affairs, at the same time stating the quantity of ore that was raised and on the surface of the mine, and which he agreed to take at the price of $500, deducting which from his account, would leave a balance in his favor of about $1000. He was fully informed of the causes which produced the suspension of the mining business, and of the embarrassed state of the plaintiffs' affairs, and in consequence thereof, promised not to press his claims, but that they might be paid at the convenience of the company. The bill charges, that the writ or process in the suit was not served on the President, but on Roswell A. King, one of the Directors, who lived in North Carolina, and while said Fox continued the agent of the company and was living on the land, and that no notice was given to the plaintiffs (except by the service) of the issuing of the writ or the obtaining of the judgment or the sale of the land, and that the judgment was taken by default, and without an appearance for them or defence. It charges, that it was the duty of the defendant to have taken care of the interest of the company, and to have notified the Board of Directors of the existence of the suit and its progress. The bill charges, that in the sale of the ore, lying on the ground as set forth, they were grossly deceived by the defendant, both as to the amount of the ore and its value, and that the defendant well knew both the amount and value, being an experienced miner, and that it was worth more than what the company owed him, and that, from it and from ore subsequently raised by him from the mines, preceding the sale to him by the Sheriff, he actually realized the sum of $6000, deducting all expenses ; and it calls for an account of the ore and its proceeds. The bill further charges, that, if all just accounts were taken between the plaintiffs and the said Fox, it would appear, that, at the time he took his judgment and sold the land, they owed him nothing, and that, at the sale, the defendant announced that nothing would be taken at the sale in payment by the purchaser but gold and silver. whereby purchasers were prevented from bidding, and the property of the plaintiffs was sacrificed, through the negligence and fraud of the defendant, who was their agent. The bill then charges, that as early as May, 1841, the defendant had formed the design of defrauding the plaintiffs out of their property, and, with that view, in his conversations depreciated the mines and the ore ; that the plaintiffs were ignorant of both, living at a great distance from North Carolina, and that they had implicit confidence in the mining skill and honesty of the defendant, but that, since his purchase, the mines have turned out to be extremely valuable, as proved by letters written by the said defendant in 1845 to John Rutter. It then charges that the defendant has little or no property, except that obtained from the mines, and that he is still working them, and prays an injunction; and, accordingly, an injunction was granted.

The answer admits the incorporation of the company, their regular organization, and the acquisition by them of the land, as stated in the bill. It admits the employment of the defendant as their agent at the salary of $1500, that the business of mining was suspended at the time specified and his dismissal from his agency in April 1839, and denies, that, after that time, he acted as their agent, but that he did agree, for the sum of $100 a year and the use of the land, to take care of the property of the plaintiffs. It admits that he did sue the company for money that was justly his due, and did obtain a judgment and caused the execution to be levied on the land and became himself the purchaser, and that the defendant now holds the Sheriff's deed for it and claims it as his own, and denies that his judgment was taken by default, but states that at the return term of the writ the plaintiffs were represented by counsel, who entered the pleas of the general issue, payment, and set off, release, and accord and satisfaction.

The answer alleges, that, in compliance with the directions contained in the letter of April 1839, he caused the clerk of the company, Mr. Wilkerson, to make out a full statement of the affairs of the company, from the commencement of operations to the time of suspension, which, together with an inventory of their effects in Guilford County, was by him laid before a board of the company, which was held in Philadelphia, in May, 1839, with which account and inventory they were well pleased. At this meeting he exhibited to the company his account and demanded what was due him for his services; it was admitted to be just, but he was informed by the board, that they had no funds. It was then proposed to him, that he should take care of the land and property for the company, for which service they would allow him $100 a year and let him have the use of the land, pay him then $100 of his account, his travelling expenses, and remit him, in the course of two or three weeks, $800 more on his account. He returned to North Carolina, but never received the money promised, except the $100. The defendant denies he then promised not to press his claims, or that he would wait the convenience of the company. The defendant was again present, at a meeting of the board in New York in May, 1841, when he again demanded payment of his account and received the same answer as before, when he distinctly informed them, if he was not paid before the next County Court of Guilford, he would put his claim in suit against the company. The Directors then promised in two weeks to send him $400, which they never did.

The answer admits that the company failing to remit the $400 as promised, a writ was taken out by him as returnable to August term, 1841, of Guilford County Court, and he had it served upon Roswell A. King, who was both a Stock-holder in, and Director of, the said company, and, at November term succeeding, recovered a judgment for what was justly due him and no more, and that he filed in the office a copy of his account. The defendant avers, that immediately upon commencing suit, he informed the company by letter, that he had done so, and, upon obtaining judgment, he notified John Rutter, one of the Directors, of the fact, and, that if funds were not forwarded to satisfy it, the lands would be sold at February term, 1842: That no sale took place at February term, in consequence of King's having prevailed on the Sheriff not to make it, promising to pay his forfeiture for him, to-wit, $100, which the defendant enforced. The answer further admits the purchase of the land by defendant, at May term, 1842, and that, at the preceding term, he had said he would take nothing but gold and silver, being vexed with King and the Sheriff, for the postponment of the sale at that term, but, when the land was offered, he informed the company he would take any current bank notes.

Defendant denies that in these transactions he was acting as the agent of the company. He avers that, after the sale, he had interviews and correspondence with some members of the company, when they were fully apprised of what had been done, and approved of the defendant's conduct, and that, in confirmation of this statement, he received from the President, Mr. Patterson, and Mr. Ogden, a letter bearing date the 30th of May, 1842, which is as follows:

New York, May 30th, 1842.

Sir: In answer to your enquiry, we can only say, that as the company *would* not pay you the money *due* by them to you, that, in purchasing the property when it was sold by the Sheriff, no blame can attach to you. As agent of the company, you certainly, both by your attention and competency, gave entire satisfaction, nor is any blame to be attached to you.

Signed, GRANVILLE S. PATTERSON,
HENRY OGDEN.

The answer denies the value set upon the lands in the bill, and if they were of that value, Roswell A. King, one of the Directors, lived within fifteen miles of them, and knew of the sale.

The defendant denies that he purchased the land and other property, with any view to a speculation, but simply to save his debt, as the whole that was sold fell short, by $900, of paying his claim, and, in confirmation of this allegation, states that, soon after making his purchase, he went on to New York, where Mr. Patterson, the President of the company, and Mr. Rutter, and Mr.

Ogden, two of the Directors, lived, and took with him the several Sheriffs' deeds, without having had them registered, and offered to surrender the deeds, both for the land and the personal property, if they would pay his debt and his travelling expenses. This they declined to do, saying the company had no funds; that the defendant must keep the property, and save himself out of it if he could. With respect to the ore, the answer states that he valued it at $400, but Mr. King insisted upon his giving $500, and placing implicit confidence in the judgment and integrity of Mr. King, he agreed to take it at t'iat price; and, in confirmation of this statement, refers to a letter from Mr. King to the company, under date of the 20th December. 1839, to that effect; and also to two other letters, one from Mr. Rutter, one of the Directors, and one from the President, Mr. Patterson, agreeing to let the ore go at the price of $500—the two last letters of a date subsequent to the one from Mr. King. The answer further states, that after purchasing the ore, he considered it his, and that he kept no account of the proceeds, and is now unable to state them, as he had ore from other mines, which he worked with it, but denies that, in his belief, he realized from it more than he had before been receiving by way of salary at $1500 a year.

The answer denies, that, upon a fair settlement, the defendant would be indebted to the plaintiffs: on the contrary, it avers that the sum. for which the defendant obtained judgment, was justly due to him, and as to the ore sold by the Sheriff, that a true account of it was contained in the inventory exhibited by the defendant to the President and Henry Ogden, at the time he offered to surrender his purchase. The answer further alleges, that by two deeds, the one bearing date the 30th day of May. 1842, and the other the 20th January, 1843, he appointed the said Patterson and Ogden his attorneys to sell said tracts of land, and that they accepted the agency, and made efforts to execute it, as was shown by their letters addressed to the defendant—copies of which letters and powers of attorney are appended to the answers, as parts thereof: And that, in June, 1845, John Rutter came on to the defendant's residence in North Carolina, and was, by defendant, and at his own request, appointed a co-agent with Henry Ogden, to make sale of the lands and mines, on account of, and for the defendant. Upon the coming in of the answer, on motion, the injunction was dissolved, so far as to allow the defendant to remove and use 10,000 bushels of the ore, then on the surface of the mines; and as to the residue, the injunction was retained until the hearing of the cause. From this interlocutory decree, both parties appealed—the plaintiffs from the first branch of it, and the defendant from the latter.

Badger, for the plaintiffs.
Morehead, for the defendant.

NASH, J. We think his Honor erred, and that the injunction ought to have been dissolved in full.

The plaintiffs, by their bill, rest their claim to relief upon three grounds: First, that the defendant, when he made his purchase, was their agent, and in this Court will be held to be a trustee for their benefit. 2d, that the judgment was fraudulently obtained, no process having been ever served upon the President of the company or any Stock-holder, and no defence having been made for them. And, 3dly, that the defendant was guilty of a fraud in purchasing from them the ore as set forth in the bill, in representing to them that it was not worth more than $600, when he knew that it was worth a great deal more, and when in fact he realized from it and other ore, six thousand dollars, whereby their debt to him was more than paid.

It is a well established principle in Equity, that an agent cannot make himself an adverse party to his principal, while the agency continues ; he can neither make himself a purchaser when employed to sell, nor, if employed to purchase, can he make himself the seller, and to this rule the exceptions are very limited. The justice and expediency of the rule are obvious and founded upon a plain reason. The principal does not get what he bargains for, in the employment, namely, the zeal and vigilance of the agent, for his own exclusive use. *Paley on Prin. and Agent*, p. 11, 33, 34. Equity therefore will consider an agent so acting as a trustee, in the case of a purchase, for his principal, and the purchase itself, but as a security for what may be found due him on a settlement of accounts between him and his principal. This case is not within the above principle. But the rule applies only to agents, who are relied upon for counsel and direction, and whose employment is rather a trust than a service, and not to those who are merely employed as instruments, in the performance of some appointed service. *Pal. on Prin. and Ag.* 12. If then the original employment of Fox, the defendant, was such an agency as forbad him to place himself, with respect to this property, in a position adverse to his principals, the plaintiffs, it is evident from the statement of the bill, that such agency had ceased before the commencement of his action against them. The bill charges, that the plaintiffs, through their President, on or about the sixth day of April, 1839, addressed a letter to the defendant, notifying him that his services were no longer required and directing him to forward his accounts. From the reception of that letter, the defendant ceased to be their agent, as an officer in conducting their mining operations.

The suit, which Fox instituted against the corporation, was commenced in the summer of 1841. It is true, that, after he was thus dismissed from their service, he entered into a new agreement to take care of the land and other property for the use of the land and $100 a year. But we do not think, that, by this new agreement or agency, he stood in such a relation to the plaintiffs, as to forbid his resort to the ordinary process of the law, to enforce the collection of a debt, which was justly due him.

The second ground upon which the defendant's purchase is assailed, is equally untenable. The bill charges, that the process was not served on the President or on any Director, and that judgment was taken against them by default, and without any defence. The act of incorporation, as set forth in the bill, subjects all the property of the company to the payment of their debts, and authorizes service to be made on the President, or in his absence, on a Director, or in the absence of both, on a Stock-holder—a provision usual in such acts, and, in this case, peculiarly proper, as all the officers and Stock-holders. but one, resided out of the State. In May, 1839, the defendant, in compliance with the directions contained in the letter from the President, and dated in the April preceding, met the board of Directors in Philadelphia: where, as he stated in his answer, he presented a general statement of the affairs of the company, and his own account, and demanded payment of the latter, and that no objection was made to his claim as not being correct, but he was told the company had no funds. At this meeting, the agreement was made as to taking care of the mines and other property. He received $100 and the promise of $800 more in two or three weeks, which was never sent. Again, in May, 1841, he met the board in the city of New York, and urged the payment of his account. No complaint was then made as to its correctness, and he informed them, that, if not paid by the next Court in Guilford county, he would sue them; and, no payment being made, the suit was commenced, returnable to August Court. The writ was served on Roswell King, who was both a Director and a Stock-holder, and, at the return term, the usual pleas were entered on the record by an attorney of the Court. And yet Mr. Patterson, the President, and one of the plaintiffs, swears that it was not served on any Director of the company. The suit, then, was regularly commenced, and, as stated in the answer, regularly conducted to a judgment. We see nothing unfair in all this. His claim against the company was admitted to be just; he had been informed by the President and some of the Directors at the North, that the company was without funds, and had been informed by Mr. King, himself a Director, and a Stock-holder and creditor of the company, that the individuals composing it were all bankrupt. There was no property to which he could look for his indemnity, but the lands and the property of a personal character connected with the mines. What was he to do? Did the law require him to stand by and see other creditors seize this very property, upon which his labor had been bestowed, and make no effort to save himself. We think not. But the defendant goes further. No sooner is his judgment obtained, than he informs the board of Directors of the fact—informs them when the sale will take place, and assures them, unless paid, the land will be sold. The lands were sold publicly, at the Court-house in Guilford County, on the sale day, as established by law, being the first day of the Court, and do not bring, by $200, what the executions called for. Mr. Fox again went on to New York—took with him the Sheriff's deeds, without having had them registered, and offered to surrender the deeds and give up all the property, if they would pay him what was justly due, and his travelling expenses. This proposition on the part of the defendant, is evidence that he had no wish to speculate on his late employers. It will be recollected the case is before us, not for hearing, but upon a motion to dissolve the injunction. In confirmation, however, of the statement made by the answer, is the letter of the 30th of May, 1842, written to the defendant by the President, G. S. Patterson, and Henry Ogden, one of the Directors of the company, in answer to one written to them by the defendant, informing them of the sale, in which they state that the company would not pay him his claims, and that, in purchasing the property at the Sheriff's sale, no blame could attach to him. With what propriety, then, can these plaintiffs allege, that the recovery by the defendant was a fraudulent one? As to the irregularity in the recovery, as alleged, but which is shown not to exist, this Court can take no notice of it, except so far as it may be evidence, with other things, of a fraud. Here, it is not alleged, upon this part of the case, that the plaintiff has recovered that by law, which in good conscience he ought not to retain; nor do the pleadings show, that although the judgment was recovered for a true debt, yet it was iniquitously used, in which case the Court would not hesitate to deprive the purchaser of the fruits of his iniquitous conduct, as was done in the case of *Lord Cranston* vs. *Johnston*, 3 Ves. Jr. 170, and cited for the plaintiff. Here the plaintiffs, or a part of them, not only admit, in their letter of the 30th May, that the defendant's claim was a just one, but that he had made a just and proper use of his judgment by purchasing at the sale. *Bissell v. Bozman*, 2 Dev. Eq. 160. In this case, the principles just stated are fully recognized and sustained. In addition to this, the plaintiffs, Patterson, Ogden, and Rutter, constituting a majority of the board of Directors, actually became the agents of the defendant to sell the mines thus purchased by him, and bargain for shares in the stock, and an interest in the mines. On this part of the case, it is urged by the plaintiffs' counsel, that these acts of the plaintiffs cannot be considered as confirming the title or acts of the defendant, because it is not shewn that they knew their rights; and the authorities cited by him sustain the position. These letters, and contracts of the plaintiffs with the defendant, are not offered as confirming his title. His title needs no confirmation; it is at law full and complete. but simply acknowledging that it is so. It has been further urged in the argument be-

39

fore us, that the defendant and Roswell King fraudulently combined together to injure and defraud the plaintiffs in the sale of the land. It is sufficient on this head to say, that it is not charged in the bill. Upon the third point made by the bill, the defendant's answer is full and satisfactory. It is charged, that, availing himself of the ignorance of the plaintiffs as to the quantity and value of the ore, which had been gotten out of the mine, he induced them to sell it to him at the price of $500, when he knew it was worth much more, and that, in truth and in fact, he had extracted from it a much larger sum—a sum much more than sufficient to pay his expenses and all that the company owed him, and that, therefore, at the time he obtained his judgment they owed him nothing. To this charge the defendant replies, that he is not skilled in gold ore, and that in giving $500 for it, he relied upon the judgment of Mr. King, both as to the quantity and value, and he produces the letter of Mr. King, directed to the plaintiffs, to sustain his answer. Mr. King was a Stock-holder and a Director, immediately 'interested in procuring from the defendant as high a price for the ore, as it was worth. It is not to be supposed, he would be willing to take less than what he believed its real value. But it is said the defendant's answer to this charge, when called on to state how much gold he got from that ore, is unsatisfactory and evasive. It may be so, but we consider it entirely unimportant; the sale was a fair one, and whether he realized much or little, has nothing to do with the question before us. But the answer states facts, that show the price given was a fair one upon the whole. We see nothing in the conduct of the defendant, of which the plaintiffs have a right to complain. So far as they were concerned as proprietors, his conduct has been fair, honest and honorable, and, if in any part of it he has lost sight of rectitude, it has been only, when listening to the suggestions and allurements of the plaintiffs themselves, in endeavoring to give to the mines a false and meretricious value, with a view to entice ignorant and unwary purchasers.

In closing this case, we would call the attention of our professional brethren to what fell from this Court, in the case of *Falls* v. *McAffee*, 2 Ire. 239. It was an action on a bond, given by the defendant on obtaining an injunction, restraining the plaintiff in working a mine. The Court after remarking upon the heavy loss the plaintiff had sustained by the operation of the process awarded against him, observe : " The case arose early after the business " of mining began, and the writ was improvidently " awarded, without recollecting at the time, that to stop " the working of the mine, was alike opposed by the " public policy and the private justice due to the party, " that might be found ultimately to be the owner, and ' that it would rather promote all interests to appoint " a receiver, or take some other method for having the " profits fully accounted for. · It is indeed remarkable that " the present plaintiff had not at the first opportunity, " moved to discharge the injunction, by submitting to have " a receiver appointed." We intend to express no opinion, nor even to intimate one that this is a proper case for the appointment of a receiver, at the present stage of it.

The interlocutory order of the Court below is erroneous and should be reversed, and the injunction dissolved absolutely, with costs, and the plaintiffs must pay the costs of this Court.

Per Curiam. Ordered to be certified accordingly.

WILLIAM BEALL, Adm's. &c. *vs.* RICHARD DARDEN, Adm'r. &c.

A husband is in Equity entitled to slaves, held in trust for his wife, (not for her separate use,) in the same manner as he would, at law, have been entitled to such as she legally owned and he had reduced to possession.

An executor, like other trustees, is not to be held liable, as insurers, or for any thing but *mala fides*, or want of reasonable diligence.

Where an administrator or executor delays an unreasonable time, as, for instance, three years, to sell slaves, and they are then lost, he is answerable for them as assets to the creditors.

And where an administrator or executor is guilty of gross neglect, in suffering slaves to remain with an improper person, as bailee, for a long period, and the slaves are sold by such bailee, so that they are lost to the estate, the executor or administrator will be answerable for their value to the next of kin.

The cases of *Murphey* v. *Grice*, 2 Dev. and Bat. Eq. 199, and *Miller* v. *Bingham*, 1 Ired. Eq. 423, cited and approved.

Cause removed from the Court of Equity of Hertford County, at the Fall Term, 1845.

The facts of the case appeared to be these :

On the 23d of August, 1821, Elisha Darden, of Hertford County, being entitled to a considerable estate, and aged and infirm, conveyed to Col. Carr Darden, of the same County, all his estate, real and personal, including therein twenty-two slaves. The deed is expressed to be made, "for, and in consideration of certain purposes hereinafter mentioned, to be done and performed by the said Carr Darden, and for divers other good causes and considerations me thereunto moving." After the *habendum* clause, the deed proceeds thus : "Provided the said Carr Darden shall well and truly pay all my debts, which I have contracted, and that I am at this time owing, out of the aforesaid property, but no unjust debts which may be presented against me ; and, furthermore, out of the remaining property, he, the said Carr, is to provide for me a decent support during life, both in health and sickness."

Carr Darden was a collateral relation of Elisha ; and, at the making of the deed, the latter had several children living, and grand-children, the issue of deceased children, among the latter of whom was Patsey, then the wife of Samuel Darden. Elisha Darden died intestate early in the year 1822, and Carr Darden took administration of his estate. About three years afterwards, Samuel Darden died, leaving his widow·and an only child of tender years surviving him ; and Carr Darden became his administrator also. Several years afterwards, Carr Darden died intestate, and the present defendant is his administrator. Subsequently, administration *de bonis non* was granted of the estate of Samuel Darden to the present plaintiff, who in 1837 brought this suit, for the purpose of obtaining an account of the estate of the intestate, Samuel Darden. By the original and an amended bill, it is particularly charged, that the deed made by Elisha to Carr Darden was not intended to convey the property to the grantee for his own use, either as a purchase or a gift, but merely as a mode of conveniently disposing of such parts of the property as should be needed to pay the grantor's debts, and provide for his support, and for the better management of what should remain ; and that, in fact, the conveyance was in trust for the grantor himself, who continued in the possession .and enjoyment of the property until his death. The bills further charge, that, after the death of Elisha Darden, the said Carr Darden, having administered on his estate, sold parts thereof, sufficient to discharge the debts, and then distributed the residue amongst the next of kin of the intestate, Elisha ; and that, in the division, a negro woman named Venus, and her children, were allotted as the distributive share of the said Patsey, then the wife of Samuel Darden, and were accordingly delivered to the said Samuel, who took them into possession and held them as his own until his death ; and that they afterwards came to the possession of Carr Darden, as his administrator, and have not been accounted for by him ; and the principal object of the suit is to make Carr Darden's estate chargeable with those negroes.

The answer states, that the defendant has no personal knowledge of the matters alleged in the bills; but it insists, that the deed from Elisha to Carr Darden vested an absolute property in the latter, not coupled with any trust. The answer admits, that the defendant had been informed, and believed, that the slave Venus and her children were, for a time before his death, in the possession of Samuel Darden, but that they were not claimed by him as his own property, but as bailed or lent to him by Carr Darden, who held them in trust for the wife of said Samuel. That so far from Samuel's claiming the *legal* title to the negroes, he disclaimed having any property, and was notoriously reputed to be insolvent, his creditors having, previously to his death, sold every thing that was known to belong to him. The answer further states, that one Samuel Carr intermarried with Patsey, the widow of Samuel Darden, and, by some means unknown to the defendant, got possession of the negroes, and sold them beyond the limits of this State.

Upon the evidence, it appeared, that, in the Spring of 1822, Carr Darden divided the negroes, that were left of those conveyed to him by Elisha Darden, amongst the next of kin of Elisha, as if they were the estate of the intestate; and that Venus and her children were allotted as the share of Patsey, the wife of Samuel Darden, and then delivered to him, and that he kept them until his death about three years afterwards. One witness says, that Col. Darden said, that he made the division at the request of his intestate Elisha, and that, when he delivered the negroes to Samuel Darden, he said he did so, "as his share of Elisha Darden's estate." Several other witnesses state, that Samuel Darden had the possession as described by the last witness, but that he was involved in debt, and was reputed to be insolvent, and it was further reputed that he did not claim the negroes as his own, but that they were his wife's, or that Carr Darden held the title in trust for his wife, and that, in consequence of those rumors, executions against him were not levied on the negroes. In one instance an execution was levied on the land on which he lived, and, although the sale was forbidden by Carr Darden, who also claimed the land, it was sold.

Upon the evidence it further appeared, that, after Samuel Darden's death, Carr Darden, as his administrator, sold some small crop, and other chattels of inconsiderable value; but he left the negroes above mentioned in the possession of the widow, who resided on the land where her husband died, which was in the same County and about eight or ten miles from the residence of Carr Darden. About eighteen months after the death of her first husband, she intermarried a second time with one Samuel Carr, who then took possession of the land and the negroes; and, about eighteen months afterwards, he sold them secretly to one Wright Allen, who immediately carried them away, and, as was supposed, sold them in parts unknown. They consisted of the woman and four children, the eldest of whom was ten years old. It is established that Samuel Carr was a man of bad character, and, "not considered trust-worthy," or "worthy to be trusted with such property." Two witnesses prove, that when Col. Darden heard that Allen had carried the negroes away, he left home in pursuit of them, and that, upon his return, he said, he had not been successful. They also state, that he sued Allen, when the latter came back; and that he afterwards said, he had recovered against Allen, but that he could not collect any thing, as Allen was insolvent. And one of the witnesses states, that Col. Darden then added, that he would be bound for a part of the negroes for letting them stay at Carr's.

It was also established by four witnesses, that Carr Darden purchased the land on which Samuel Darden lived, and that he took conveyance in his own name; but that he said, that the money, with which the purchase was made, belonged to Samuel Darden, except the sum of $80, which he, Carr, had lent to him; and that when that should be paid to him, he was to convey the land to Samuel's child.

A. *Moore* and *Iredell*, for the plaintiff.
Badger and *Bragg*, for the defendant.

RUFFIN, C. J. There can be no doubt entertained, that the deed to Carr Darden was purely upon trust for the grantor. The circumstances of the parties, and their relation and the contents of the deed, whereby every thing to be done by the grantee is to be " out of the property" conveyed, and the subsequent acts and acknowledgements of the grantee, taken together, establish the trust conclusively. Indeed, that was admitted in the argument by the counsel for the defendant; but he said that the trust was not for the next of kin of Elisha Darden, but for Elisha himself; and therefore, it was necessary, that Elisha should be represented by an administrator *de bonis non*. That would be true, if the bill was to have that trust declared and executed. But so far from that, it is a bill founded upon a title arising out of the execution of that trust many years ago. And it is proved, that, in 1822, when Carr Darden united in himself the characters both of trustee and administrator of the *cestui que trust*, he distributed the negroes as the personal estate of his intestate, Elisha Darden. It was, after that, an executed and not an executory trust; and the next of kin got in their several shares the same title, which is in other instances obtained from an administrator by distribution.

It would probably follow, as a consequence, that Samuel Darden became absolutely entitled to a legal estate in the negroes allotted as his wife's share, which he reduced to possession. It is true, that, owing to his embarrassments, it seems that, as an expedient to keep off creditors, it was held out by the parties, that the title of the negroes was in Col. Darden, for the benefit of Mrs. Darden, in some way, which prevented them from being liable on executions against her husband. In the same spirit, Col. Darden seems to have claimed also the land, although he held that, according to his own admission, upon trust for Samuel Darden. It argues but little, therefore, against the absolute legal title of the husband, that those persons held out to the world, that the title was in some sort in Col. Darden, so that the negroes could not be sold for Samuel's debts. But we do not consider it material to dwell on that; for supposing that, upon the division, Col. Darden still retained, by agreement, the legal title of the negroes allotted as Mrs. Darden's share. it does not appear that it was upon trust to the separate use of the wife. On the contrary, the answer states, that Samuel Darden did not claim the legal title. but admitted it to be in Col. Darden, " in trust for his wife," and in the same language do the witnesses speak ; which makes it plain that the idea of those persons was, that a trust for the wife, of slaves in possession, did not vest in the husband, and were not liable for his debts. But that is clearly a mistake, and the husband was in Equity entitled to the negroes, held in trust for his wife, in the same manner as he would, at law, have been entitled to such as she legally owned, and he had reduced to possession. *Murphy* v. *Grice*, 2 Dev. and Bat. Eq. 199. *Miller* v. *Bingham*, 1 Ired. Eq. 423. Therefore, in this Court, Carr Darden would be just as much liable to account for the loss, through his laches, of these slaves, which were the equitable property of his intestate, as he would be if they were his property, legally.

The question then remains, and it is the only serious one in the case, whether Carr Darden is chargeable for the value of the negroes, as for a *devastavit?* The opinion of the Court is, that he is. There is no evidence that the widow set up a title in herself, adverse to that of Col. Darden, as the administrator of her deceased hus-

40

band. If she had, it would clearly have been gross
negligence to have suffered her and her second husband,
however good their characters might have been, to have
held the possession upon an adverse claim, for three
years, without suit or any effort by the administrator and
trustee to regain the possession. But the Court understands, upon the evidence, that the widow kept the negroes by the assent of the administrator, and, in truth,
held under him, and therefore claiming only her distributive share, as widow. And we consider the case, therefore, as one in which the slaves came fully to the hands
of the administrator, and were wrongfully taken from him,
or were converted by his bailee; and the point is, whether
the circumstances are such as to put him in default and
make him chargeable for the value as assets. In the
first place, it is to be understood, that an executor, like
other trustees, is not to be held liable as insurers, or for
any thing but *mala fides* or want of reasonable diligence.
It is both plain justice and plain policy, to hold them
chargeable out of their own estates, only on that principle,
in order to get responsible and honest men to undertake
burdensome trusts. In England, both executors and trustees generally do not receive compensation, as an allowance by law, and therefore they may there claim all the
indulgence due to a person rendering gratuitous service.
And we are not prepared, or, rather, do not in this case, feel
called on to say, that the commission given to executors in
our law changes the rule of responsibility. It may be admitted, that there is a difference as to the administator's
liability to creditors and to next of kin, since he must, at
his peril, provide a sufficiency to pay debts, even by a sale
of slaves, if necessary, while distribution specifically between next of kin is contemplated, except when a sale
is rendered necessary for the purpose of an equal division. But there are several circumstances here, which
put the administrator in default, and in decidedly culpable default, in respect to the next of kin, and *a fortiori* in

Beall e. Darden.

respect of creditors, both of whom are represented by the present plaintiff. The lapse of three years before a sale or division, is, of itself, of considerable weight—sufficient to charge the administrator to creditors, at least; for Lord HOLT says, in *Jenkins* v. *Plombe*, 6 Mod. 181, that, if perishable goods, before any default in the executor to preserve them, or sell them at due value, be impaired, the executor shall not answer for the full value, but, upon evidence, shall be discharged—clearly implying, that if he has reasonable time to sell them at a fair price, he shall be charged with the full value. He also says, that if the executor omit to sell the goods at a good price, and afterwards they are taken from him, then the value of the goods shall be assets, and not what he recovers; for there was a default in him. We think it clear, therefore, that these negroes were assets in respect to creditors, though they had been stolen at the late period of three years, and had been wholly lost. And, under the circumstances, the default of the administrator, here, charges him to the next of kin also. It is true, if a trustee is robbed of money, it is laid down, that he is to be allowed it on account, the robbing being proved, although only proved by his own oath; and that so it is of an executor, as of trustees generally. 2 *Font. Eq.* 179. It may be the same as to a specific thing stolen from the executor. But very clearly, that is so, only when he was in no previous default. But this is not a case of theft. Here, the loss was occasioned by the administrator having, without reasonable precaution, selected an unfaithful person. with whom he entrusted the custody of the negroes, and one, of whose unfaithfulness he had sufficient means of judging, so as to be on his guard. It does not, indeed, appear upon what contract he allowed the negroes to remain with the widow. Perhaps, if the family was increasing and chargeable, it might have been prudent, and to the advantage of the estate, to have left them with Mrs. Darden, until the estate was so far

settled as to authorize a division, and have the child's
share allotted. But the defendant has offered no evidence on that point; and, as far as appears, the administrator left them without any stipulation, and as an act of
sheer neglect. It is true, the widow was entitled in distribution to one third of them; but that did not justify
the administrator to allow her to keep the whole, at the
risk of her disposing of them to the loss of the child. But
if that alone were not sufficient to charge him—and it is
not necessary to say that it is—the subsequent total neglect
to look after the negroes for one year and an half, after they
came into the possession of the second husband, being in
all three years, when the character of that person was so
bad, that he was generally considered not worthy to be
trusted with the possession of slaves, is almost an act of
abandonment of the property altogether. It was a duty
of the administrator to have taken the negroes into his
own possession upon that event, or to have hired them to
a responsible person, or to have distributed them. Instead
of doing so, he has, by neglect, allowed his own bailee
to convert them, and although he gives no reason why
they had not been divided, he asks not to be declared in
default, in having selected a person so improper, and in
having allowed him to keep the negroes so long. Besides,
it does not appear that the administrator made any well
directed or honest efforts to regain the slaves. It is true,
witnesses say he left home on that errand; but it does
not appear in any way, how long he pursued nor where
he went, nor even that he advertised the negroes, nor
made enquiries in the parts of the country to which slaves
are usually carried from this State. All he did was to
sue an insolvent man by whom they were carried away.
It seems to the Court, that both in the transaction anterior
to the carrying away the negroes, and in the subsequent
conduct of the administrator, as far as it has been made
to appear, there was an indifference to the interests of
those, for whom the administrator acted, which even the

most careless man would not have exhibited in his own affairs, and such negligence as would amount to gross laches. Col. Darden felt it, and acknowledged himself bound to make them good to the child. Therefore it must be declared, that his estate is chargeable for the value of the negroes and interest to the plaintiff.

It is very clear, however, if there are no debts of the intestate Samuel, which, at this late period, is not to be presumed, that the plaintiff ought not to raise out of Col. Darden's estate, the widow's share, inasmuch as her second husband has already received it. But as they are not parties to this suit, so that there is no means of enquiring into that matter in the present state of the case, liberty will be allowed the defendant, after the accounts shall have been taken, if necessary, to move to remand the cause, in order to enable the defendant to file a cross bill, and make those persons parties thereto.

PER CURIAM.　　　　　　　Decree accordingly.

JOHNSTON AND FRANCIS vs. SHELTON & AL.

A vague entry of lands is not absolutely void, but the defect may be supplied by a survey, which renders the party's claim more specific.

But if the entry be not so explicit, as to give reasonable notice to a second enterer of the first appropriation, and the same land is entered again, before a survey on the first entry, equity will not deprive the second enterer of his title.

An entry of " 640 acres of land, beginning on the line dividing the Counties of Haywood and Macon, at a point at or near Lowe's Bear-pen, on the Hogback Mountain, and running various courses for complement," is, in itself, too vague and indefinite.

The case of *Harris* v. *Ewing*, 1 Dev. and Bat. Eq. 369, cited and approved.

Cause removed from the Court of Equity of Haywood County, at the Fall Term, 1845.

The case, as far as concerns the questions determined in the Supreme Court, was as follows :

On the 30th day of August, 1842, the plaintiffs made their entries, in the office of the entry-taker of vacant land in the County of Haywood. The first was, " No. 1440, for 640 acres of land, beginning on the line dividing the Counties of Haywood and Macon, at a point at or near Lowe's Bear-pen on the Hogback Mountain, and running various courses for complement." The two others were, each, for 640 acres adjoining the first: the one lying east, and the other North of it. The Hogback mountain was in a wild tract of country, nearly all mountains, but little explored, and having very few inhabitants. The object of the plaintiffs, in making the entries, was to obtain lands that were then supposed to be rich in minerals, and particularly gold, at the heads of Tuckasegee river ; and about the same time, they entered a number of tracts on the opposite side of the line, in Macon. The plaintiffs were unacquainted with the part of the country in which the lands were situate, and received from other persons the information, on which they selected the locations and descriptions of their entries. The Hogback mountain consists of two distinct knobs, now known as " The Hogback" and " The Little Hogback," extending together about four or. five miles, and having between them a deep depression or gap, two miles wide or near it ; though, formerly, both knobs were known by hunters as " The Hogback" simply, and it so continued, as understood by some persons, to the beginning of this controversy. The Big Hogback and the Little Hogback are both in the line between Haywood and Macon, which there runs nearly East and West for six or seven miles. On the former was a Bear pen, which was known to some as " Lowe's Bear pen," and to others as the " Locust Bear pen" ; and West from the Little Hogback, near the County line, there were two Bear pens, that had been built by a hunter, named Lowe, which were within six or seven hundred yards of the Western foot of the Little Hogback mountain, in a valley or gap of the Blue Ridge.

In September, 1842, the defendants, Reeves, Shelton, and C. Hooper, made an entry of 640 acres, lying also on the County line West from the Little Hogback, somewhat more than a mile, and running North from the County line, and then West, South and East, to the beginning. At the time they made their entry, they saw the previous entries of the plaintiffs; but they say, that, from their knowledge of that part of the country, they believed their entry would not be within five miles of the plaintiffs' land, as described in their entries; and that, when the entry-taker saw the defendants' entries, he was of the same opinion. Thereupon, the defendants made their entry. At the same time, they took copies of the entries of the complainants, in order that they might submit them to the judgment of others, as to the lands they would cover, and with the intention of abandoning their own entry, in case it would interfere with the plaintiffs' entries. At that time, the defendants had discovered near the County line a deposit gold mine, and it was the object of their entry to obtain a grant for it; and their entry was so laid as just to include it in the South-east corner of the tract, being that part of it which lies nearest to the entries of the plaintiff. The defendants state that they made enquiry of several persons as to the location of the plaintiffs' beginning, and they were satisfied from the information obtained, that it was at the Bear pen on the Big Hogback, which was at least five miles from the gold mine. In December following, the defendants took out a warrant and delivered it to the County Surveyor, who made their survey and plat; on which they obtained a grant shortly after. At the time of making the survey, the defendants exhibited to the Surveyor, with their own entry, the copies of the plaintiffs' entries, and requested him to inform them, whether, from his knowledge of the country, he thought their entry would

cover any land of those embraced in the plaintiffs, saying,
that, if he thought so, they would go no further, as they
did not wish to lose their money or have a controversy;
and the surveyor also gave it as his opinion, that the entries were for different land. The survey was then proceeded in, and, when completed, the defendant sent to
Raleigh for the grant, in order to have the elder legal title, if there should be a dispute.

In the succeeding spring, the plaintiffs had their surveys
made, and the survey of entry No. 1440 was so made, as
to include the gold mine and other parts of the land granted
to the defendants aforesaid, and they paid the purchase
money to the State and obtained grants also.

The beginning was in the County line at the foot of the
West end of the Little Hogback Mountain, about six hundred yards from the Bear pen in the valley called
"Lowe's." The bill was then filed against the original
grantees of the gold mine and various lessees under them,
praying that those prior grantees might be declared to
be trustees for the plaintiffs, as they were the prior enterers and the others had notice of their entries, and that
they might be compelled to convey the legal title to the
plaintiffs, and in the mean time praying for a receiver.

A vast mass of depositions has been filed by the parties
for the purpose of establishing, which was "Lowe's
Bearpen" and what was known as the Hogback Mountain, and at which particular Bear pen and knob the plaintiffs meant to begin. For the purposes of the point on
which the decision of the Court rests, it is material only
to state a small portion of it. A witness states, that the
plaintiff, Johnston, mentioned, when he made his entries,
that he began on "the main Hogback Mountain" and
went out towards "the white oak flats"; which are on
the Tuckasegee, nearly North from the Big Hogback,
and seven or eight miles from the defendants' entry.
Another witness states, that, wishing to get a lease of a
part of the gold mine, he went to the entry-taker's books

and examined the plaintiffs' entries, and found that the beginning was at a *Locust* Bear pen on the Hogback mountain, and that he then applied to Johnston for a lease, and enquired of him, whether his entry began on the Big or the Little Hogback; and Johnston replied, "that he knew nothing of the Big Hogback or the Little Hogback—that he made his entry from information, and made it special, calling for a *Locust* Bear pen on the Hogback mountain in the County line." Another witness states, that Johnston employed a man to examine the land entered by him, for gold; and to enable the person to know the land, Johnston told him, that it commenced on a *Locust* Bear pen on the Big Hogback, and included the white oak flats. It also appears, upon the warrant of survey issued on the entry No. 1440, that, as first written, it called a for *Locust* Bear pen as the beginning, which was altered to "Lowe's." But the entry-taker states, that he altered it, and also the entry in the same way; because, in transcribing the entry on his books from the location furnished by the plaintiffs, he made an error in writing "Locust" for "Lowe's." On the other side, several witnesses state, that the persons, upon whose information the plaintiffs took their locations, gave him "Lowe's Bear pen" as the beginning, which was West from the Little Hogback, and is a different place from "The Locust Bear pen," which is on the top of the Big Hogback. And it appears very clearly from the Surveyor and others, that the plaintiffs did not intend to enter the particular land, where the gold mine is—for it was not then discovered—nor any other covered by the defendant's grant; for neither of the plaintiffs knew the place called for as their beginning, whether that be the one Bear pen or the other, nor any of the land subsequently included in their survey and grant. Indeed, when the plaintiffs went to survey, they could not designate to the Surveyor their beginning, and had to call on one Hooper to point it out. He designated

41

" Lowe's Bear pen in the gap," as that which he meant in giving the plaintiffs the description by which they made their entry ; though the same person, Hooper, has been examined as a witness in the cause, and in his examination says, that " the Locust Bear pen." on the top of the Big mountain, was the one he gave Johnston for a beginning, and that he purposely deceived the plaintiffs and the Surveyor, in pointing out a different one when the survey was made. After Hooper had designated Lowe's Bear pen in the gap as the beginning. the Surveyor commenced his survey at the point of the Little Hogback mountain nearest to " Lowe's Bear pen," and laid out the land very irregularly, and so as to include the gold mine and other parts of the land granted to the defendants. To that mode of making the survey, the defendants, who were present, objected, because in fact, the plaintiff's beginning, as described in the entry, was at a Bear pen on the Big Hogback, three or four miles off ; and because they, the defendants, had obtained a grant for some of the land, which would be included in the plaintiffs' survey, and had made their entry and survey, and obtained the grant, without the means of ascertaining from the plaintiffs' entries, whether they would interfere with the lands the defendants took up ; and further, because, in point of fact, there was still a sufficiency of vacant land to give the plaintiffs their quantity, without taking any of the defendants', if they would so run their lines. But the plaintiffs insisted, that as theirs was the oldest entry, no one else could enter and survey before the plaintiffs had surveyed, except at the risk of losing their land ; for that the prior entry gave the plaintiffs the right to be first satisfied, at all events, and to run in any direction they might choose, from their beginning, so that they got no more than their quantity. In obedience to the instructions of the plaintiffs, the Surveyor then completed the surveys, upon which the plaintiffs' grants were subsequently issued.

The cause, having been set for hearing, was transmitted to this Court.

Badger, for the plaintiffs.
W. H. Haywood. Avery and *Iredell*, for the defendants.

RUFFIN, C. J.   Without wading through the voluminous depositions, or discussing the various points of fact that arise on them, the Court may safely decide this cause upon the insufficiency of the plaintiffs' entry.   Its vagueness renders it void, as against a subsequent enterer, who surveys and pays his money before the plaintiffs had made their entry more specific, if the expression may be allowed, by a survey, identifying the land they meant to appropriate.   The construction of the entry laws, contended for by the plaintiffs, would change the meaning of them entirely, from what they have been understood; and would make an entry, not a mode of appropriating a particular piece of land as distinguished from all other land, but as creating a prior, and, in some degree, a floating right, to have a certain quantity of unappropriated land, any where the enterer might select within the two years, on a certain stream or mountain in the County.   It would consequently postpone all other persons in entering and surveying, until the prior enterers chose to make their selection, and in any form which their caprice or interest might from time to time dictate.   No construction of the acts could be more erroneous or mischievous—more directly opposed to the language or the policy of the Legislature.   In the case of *Harris* v. *Ewing*, 1 Dev. and Bat. Eq. 369, the Court held that a vague entry was not indeed absolutely void; because it was not material to the State, to whom she granted, and the defect might be supplied by a survey, which would render the party's claim more specific.   Therefore, there was a decree against another enterer, who made his entry after the prior vague enterer had actually surveyed, and with notice *of* it. That was, indeed, going beyond the words of the act, upon a very liberal construction, which was adopted with hesitation. It certainly can be carried no further in support of vague entries; which would be an encouragement to negligence or deception in enterers. And in that case, the Court used the language, that an entry ought to be so explicit as to give reasonable notice to a second enterer of the first appropriation; and that, if it do not, and the same land be entered again, the last purchaser has conscience on his side, while the fault is on the other. The present case falls precisely within that rule. The plaintiffs' entry is altogether indefinite, except in quantity, and except in the beginning—supposing that to be as now claimed by the plaintiffs. It is true, that from its lying on the County line it is seen, that it is to be on the North of the beginning. But it does not specify any thing else, and it cannot be told, whether the land is to laid out by running East or West on the County line from the beginning, nor how far in either direction, neither by calls for distance, or natural objects or other lines, or any other thing. It was therefore positively uncertain, what lands the plaintiffs would survey, for the description bound them to nothing but a beginning, and they might shift and change as they pleased, until the time when it would lapse unless ripened into a grant. No case could more strikingly illustrate the danger and error of the construction contended for by the plaintiffs, than this very one. The entry is vague in itself, and we find a multitude of witnesses disputing about the single object designated in it, and about the plaintiffs' declarations at different times, as to the point of beginning; and, moreover, it is absolutely certain, that they had, when they entered or for months afterwards, no view to the particular place which is the bone of this contention. Standing upon the entry alone then, the plaintiffs could not recover, according to the rule in *Harris* v. *Ewing*. But in that case the plaintiffs had made a survey and completely identified the land he wanted, and this the defendant knew before he made his entry; and upon that ground exclusively that decree proceeded. Now, that circumstance operates directly the other way between the present parties; for these plaintiffs let their claim rest in their vague entry, until the defendants had made an entry and survey, and got a grant. The reasoning therefore and principle of decision in *Harris* v. *Ewing* are directly against the plaintiffs in this suit. It is true, that the defendants had notice of the entry of the plaintiff; but, after they read it, they could learn nothing from it. Nobody could lay it down, unless he had the plaintiffs there to say, which land they chose. It is manifest, therefore, the very subject of the entry is not designated in the entry, but by the subsequent election of the enterers. Had the defendants gone to the plaintiffs themselves for information, as to the land they meant to take up, (if they had been under any obligation to do so in any case) the enquiry would have been unavailable in this case, for the plaintiffs did not then know how they would have their survey made. They could only have answered the defendants, that they must wait their pleasure to select the land, so as, in effect, to stop all entering after the first in a neighborhood, until the title on that is completed. But the defendants were not at all obliged to make any application to the plaintiffs on the subject. Where one is buying a legal title and has notice that a person claims an equity therein, he must take care in due time to ascertain the nature and extent of the claim. But that does not apply in a case of this sort; for an enterer has no equity or collateral claim independent of the entry itself, if the case still stands on the entry, and therefore the entry ought to give the requisite information, or, at all events, the enterer ought without delay to supply its defects by an actual survey, setting apart the land entered. Then an entry, made by one with knowledge of the survey as well as of the entry, would be *mala fide*, and convert the party into a trustee.

It is unquestionable, however, that these defendants did not and could not know or guess, that they were encroaching on the plaintiffs' entries. For, independent of the disputes as to the point intended and understood by different persons as the beginning, according to the present call for "Lowe's bear pen," it is certain, that the entry. as actually written in the entry book, when the defendants entered, called for "the *Locust* bear pen," which was five miles from the nearest point of the defendants' grant. Indeed, if the call therein had been "Lowe's" and not "Locust," it would still have been impossible for the defendants, by any experimental lines, to have first left the land for the plaintiffs, before they took that for themselves. The defendants, therefore, intended no wrong to the plaintiffs and did them no wrong. The whole wrong was with the plaintiffs themselves in not getting such knowledge of the land, as to be able to give a sufficient description of it in the entry, and then in delaying to identify it by a survey, so as by notice of it to affect the conscience of the defendants. Therefore the bill must be dismissed with costs.

PER CURIAM.   Decree accordingly.

JAMES A. CAMPBELL vs JOHN B. DRAKE & AL.

Where a clerk in a store pilfered money and goods from his employer, and laid out the proceeds in the purchase of a tract of land; *Held*, that the person thus robbed could hold neither the clerk, nor his representatives after his death, as trustees of the land for his benefit, so as to enable him to call for a conveyance of the legal title to himself.

Cause removed from the Court of Equity of Wake County, at the Fall Term, 1845.

The bill states that the plaintiff kept a retail shop in Raleigh, and that a lad, by the name of John Farrow.

Campbell v. Drake.

was his shop-keeper for several years; and that, while
in his employment, Farrow abstracted, to a considerable
amount, money and goods belonging to the plaintiff, and
that with the money of the plaintiff, taken without his
knowledge or consent, Farrow purchased a tract of land
at the price of $500. The bill states a great number of
facts, tending to shew that Farrow paid for the land with
the effects of the plaintiff, which he dishonestly converted
to that purpose. Farrow afterwards died under age, and
the land descended to his brothers and sisters; and the
plaintiff, having discovered his losses of money and merchandize, and that Farrow had purchased the land as
aforesaid, filed this bill against his heirs, and therein insists, that he has a right to consider the purchase as
made, and the land held, for the use of the plaintiff, and
that Farrow should be declared a trustee for him.

The bill was answered, so as to put in issue the various charges of dishonesty by Farrow, and the fact that
the land was paid for with money purloined from the
plaintiff: and much evidence was read to those points.

Badger, for the plaintiff.
Manly, for the defendants.

RUFFIN, C. J. The Court, though naturally inclined to
every presumption in favor of innocence, and especially
of a young person, who seems to have been so well thought
of while he lived, is satisfied from the proofs, that the
plaintiff was much plundered by this youth; and we have
no doubt, that every cent of the money with which he
paid for the land, he had pilfered from his employer.
Nevertheless, we believe the bill cannot be sustained.
The object of it is to have the land itself, claiming it as
if it had been purchased for the plaintiff by an agent
expressly constituted; and it seems to us, thus stated, to
be a bill of the first impression. We will not say, if the
plaintiff had obtained judgment against the administra-

tor for the money as a debt, that he might not come here to have the land declared liable, as a security, for the money laid out for it. But that is not the object of this suit. It is to get the land, which the plaintiff claims as his ; and, upon the same principle, would claim it, if it were worth twenty times his money, which was laid out for it. Now, we know not any precedent of such a bill. It is not at all like the cases of dealings with trust funds by trustees, executors, guardians, factors, and the like ; in which the owner of the fund may elect to take either the money or that in which it was invested. For, in all those cases, the legal title, if we may use the expression, of the fund, is in the party thus misapplying it. He has been entrusted with the whole possession of it, and that for the purpose of laying it out for the benefit of the equitable owner ; and therefore all the benefit and profit the trustee ought, in the nature of his office, and from his relation to the *cestui que trust*, to account for to that person. But the case of a servant or a shop-keeper is very different. He is not charged with the duty of investing his employer's stock, but merely to buy and sell at the counter. The possession of the goods or money is not in him, but in his master ; so entirely so, that he may be convicted of stealing them, in which both a *cepit* and *asportavit* are constituents. This person was in truth guilty of a felony in possessing himself of the plaintiff's effects, for the purpose of laying them out for his own lucre ; and that fully rebuts the idea of converting him into a trustee. If that could be done, there would be, at once, an end to punishing thefts by shop men. If, indeed, the plaintiff could actually trace the identical money taken from him, into the hands of a person who got it without paying value, no doubt he could recover it ; for his title was not destroyed by the theft. But we do not see how a felon is to be turned into a trustee of property, merely by showing that he bought it with stolen money. If it were so, there would have been many a bill of the kind. But we believe, there never was one before; and therefore, we cannot entertain this. But we think the facts so clearly established, and the demands of justice so strong on the defendants to surrender the land to the plaintiff, or to return him the money that was laid out in it, that we dismiss the bill without costs.

PER CURIAM.   Decree accordingly.

WILLIAM WILSON *vs.* JAMES LEIGH.

Where a creditor, on the trial of a suit at law against an administrator, relied upon his account of sales, as evidence of the assets in his hands, and afterwards discovered that the account was not correct, because the administrator, through an agent, who was returned as the purchaser of a large amount of property, had in fact bought the property himself at an under value: *Held,* that though the creditor might have called upon the administrator in equity, in the first instance, for an account of the assets, or might have filed a bill for a discovery, during the pendency of the suit at law, yet, having elected to pursue his remedy at law, he is bound by the verdict in such suit, unless he can shew that the administrator had fraudulently deceived him, by wilful misrepresentations of the state of the assets.

The cases of *Simmons* v. *Whitaker,* 2 Ired. Eq. 129, and *Martin* v. *Harding,* 3 Ired. Eq. 603, cited and approved.

Appeal from an interlocutory order of the Court of Equity of Perquimans County, at the Spring Term, 1845, his Honor Judge BATTLE presiding, by which a demurrer filed by the defendant to the plaintiff's bill, was overruled, and the defendant ordered to answer over.

The case made in the bill is, that the defendant is the executor of John H. Blount, and as such, sold his personal estate at public sale; and that he procured one Benjamin Skinner to bid for the crop of corn that was then growing, and to purchase the same for him, Leigh; and

42

that he returned an account of sales of the estate, to the
County Court, in which the said Skinner was set down
as the purchaser, although, in fact, Leigh was himself
the purchaser, through Skinner as his agent; that subsequently, Leigh cultivated the crop, gathered it, and sold
it for much more than it had brought at the sale, and
that he has applied the excess to his own use. The bill
further states, that the plaintiff was a creditor of Blount
by bond, and brought suit thereon against the executor,
who pleaded *plene administravit* and retainer; and that,
upon the trial of the issues joined thereon, the plaintiff
read, as his evidence to charge the executor with assets,
the accounts of sales which had been returned by him;
and the jury thereupon found, that the defendant had assets applicable to the plaintiff's demands, to the amount
of $653 99, and that he had no other assets; and that,
thereupon, the plaintiff took judgment for that sum of
$653 99, and for the residue of his debt, namely, $2,130 16,
he took judgment *quando.* The bill states, that the plaintiff read the account of sales in evidence, under the belief that it set forth the assets truly, and that the persons
were really the purchasers of the property, who were
there stated to have been so, and at the prices therein set
forth; and that the plaintiff did not know to the contrary, until recently before the filing of this bill; and that,
upon the discovery that the defendant was, himself, the
real purchaser of the corn, and that, by reason thereof,
the first sale was void, and that he had re-sold it for a
great advance in price, he applied to the defendant to
account with him in respect of such additional sum as
was realized from the corn, by applying the same to the
discharge of the balance due the plaintiff on his judgment; which the defendant refused. The plaintiff then
filed this bill, and the prayer is for a decree to the same
effect.

A. *Moore*, for the plaintiff.
Badger, for the defendant.

RUFFIN, C. J.   If the crop was still growing, when the trial at law took place, it is probable it might be reached at law by a *scire facias* on the judgment *quando*, and there would be no necessity for resorting to this Court. *Mara* v. *Quin*, 6 T. R. 10.   It does not appear in the bill how the fact was, as it ought, properly speaking.   But we take it for granted, that the crop had been gathered and sold the second time, for the advanced price mentioned in the bill.   Still, we think the bill cannot be sustained.

There is no doubt that creditors may come into a Court of Equity against executors, or against them and the heirs or devisees, for accounts and for payment out of the proper fund.   It seems to be the common mode in England, at the present day, for administering estates, and is certainly much the most convenient, as it saves vast expense and trouble in trying issues at law, as to the assets, where every voucher is to be proved, over and over again, against every creditor, and as considerable portions of the assets in that country, in almost every case, are equitable. We hold the same thing here.   *Simmons* v. *Whitaker*, 2 Ired. Eq. 129.   The subject was much discussed and fully explained by Chancellor KENT, in *Thompson* v. *Brown*, 4 John. C. C. 619.   But, in those cases, the creditor comes into the Court of Equity *ab origine* for himself, or for himself and the other creditors ; and the accounts are ordered there, and relief granted, for the greater convenience, and to prevent multiplicity of suits at law, although the question, as to the amount and administration of legal assets, is properly cognizable at law.   That, however, is essentially different from the present case. This plaintiff did not file his bill, but elected, in the first instance, to sue at law, and to try the issue on *plene administravit*, without a bill of discovery, and upon such evidence as he thought proper to risk his case on before the jury. The question being legal, the tribunal legal, and the trial regular, the result must be conclusive on the one party as well as the other, unless there was fraud practised by one of them on the trial, so as to prevent it from being a fair trial. In *Martin* v. *Harding*, 3 Ired. Eq. 603, the plaintiff had by mistake admitted the executor's plea of *fully administered*, and proceeded against the land, and then filed a bill for satisfaction out of the personal estate. On demurrer, the Court dismissed the bill, and said, if a creditor chooses to go on at law, and has the plea of fully administered found against him or confesses it, there is no possible ground for relief in equity, where the executor has been guilty of no fraud in misrepresenting the state of the assets. And what would be a fraud, in such a case, is explained by the subsequent observation, that it is not sufficient, for example, that the creditor has discovered, that the executor had assets at the time of the trial, which the executor did not disclose, nor the creditor know of or prove; for an executor is not bound to give evidence against himself at law, and there are methods of obtaining discoveries, in which the executor would have a right to discharge himself, as well as be bound to charge himself, by his answer. Now, there is no communication between these parties stated in the bill. The executor does not appear to have been present at the trial, much less to have misled the plaintiff in the mode of proving his case. or to have made any representation to him whatever. The whole stress of the bill is, that the defendant returned an account of sales, in which Skinner was mentioned as the purchaser of a crop of corn, of which the defendant himself was the purchaser. Now, that, in itself, amounted to no fraud, nor any thing like a fraud, upon any body, or at any time. The Court holds, that an executor cannot purchase at his own sale, as a rule of policy to prevent fraud, which might be practised. But that is only at the election of creditors and legatees, and the executor runs the risk of their making the election within any reasonable time. For if he agrees to give a great deal more than the value of the thing, the other parties may hold him to it. Besides, the defendant may not even have known, that he could not purchase through an agent at his own sale; and, therefore, although his ignorance of the law will not help his purchase, yet it would repel the allegation of fraud. But giving to the return the full effect the plaintiff attributes to it, that it did not truly state all the facts respecting the sale, yet it it was his own folly to rely upon that, as evidence of the assets. It bound the defendant as his declaration, and as such the plaintiff used it; but surely a plaintiff, who chooses to prove a fact, not by direct evidence to it, but by the defendant's declarations respecting it, is not entitled to be loosed from the verdict upon the ground, that he afterwards discovered that the defendant did not admit in the declaration all he might or ought to have done. The account of sales concludes no person—not even the executor, for he may undoubtedly prove a mistake in it. The law requires him to return it, for the ease of creditors and legatees; and, if they think proper to use it, they may do so as part of their evidence, giving other evidence to surcharge and falsify it, or they may rely simply upon the account by itself. Either is the creditor's own act exclusively, unless, upon a communication with the executor, the latter take means to prevent the creditor from obtaining or using other proof, by inducing in him the belief, that the creditor could not establish any thing in opposition to the statements in the account. In truth, however, this bill seeks to avoid the obligation of the judgment at law, upon the mere ground, that the plaintiff might have offered cumulative proof as to the assets, which would have charged the defendant with more, if he had taken the trouble to search for it. He says, indeed, that the reason he did not search for other evidence was, that he believed the account of sales stated the truth, though he has since discovered, that it did not.

But if it be admitted, that it did not, that would be a fraud in making the account, and not in the trial between the plaintiff and the defendant. It is impossible that every creditor of Blount can come into this Court, after a trial at law, for a fresh account of the assets, upon the ground, that the executor's account of sales contained some inaccuracy, either through a mistake, or, if you please, through design. If so, every verdict on *plene administravit* will be overhauled in equity, upon separate bills by each creditor, if the creditor should, after the trial, discover, that he could have given better evidence as to the assets: For in every case it is the duty of the executor, by his inventory and account of sales, to charge himself with the whole. The Court cannot assume any such jurisdiction. Therefore it will be certified to the Court of Equity, that the decree was erroneous and should be reversed, and the demurrer sustained and the bill dismissed.

The plaintiff must pay the costs in this Court.

PER CURIAM.   Decree and order accordingly.

JAMES M. DENNY & AL. *vs.* JAMES CLOSSE & AL.

A testator bequeathed to his wife a certain slave for her life, and, after her death, the slave to be sold, and the issue of the slave together with the money arising from such sale, to be equally divided among all his children "that are then living." *Held*, that the issue of such of the children, as died during the life-time of the legatee for life, took no interest under this bequest.

The word "children" in a will sometimes, but only under peculiar circumstances, is construed to mean "grand-children:" as where the meaning of the testator is uncertain, and the bequest must fail unless such construction be given.

Cause removed by consent from the Court of Equity of Guilford County, at the Fall Term, 1845.

The Bill was filed to obtain a construction of the Will of James McMurray. By his Will, the testator, after giving to his wife some perishable property, bequeathes as follows: "I also give and bequeath to her my negro girl Mary, to be enjoyed by her during her natural life, and at her death, I allow the said negro to be sold, and her issue, if she should have any, and the money arising from the said sale, to be equally divided among all my children that are then living." At the time of his death, James McMurray left seven children surviving him, two of whom, to-wit, Jane, who intermarried with William Denny, and Polly, who intermarried with William Doak, died before the widow, the tenant for life. The plaintiffs are the children of Jane. The widow is dead, and the Bill claims, that the plaintiffs, the children of Jane Denny, are entitled to one-seventh part of the proceeds of the negro Mary and her increase, as standing in the place of their mother, and representing her in the division of the property.

Morehead, for the plaintiffs.
Kerr, for the defendants.

NASH, J. The claim of the plaintiffs rests upon the ground, that the bequest to the children, after the death of the widow, was a vested remainder, and vested in all the children of James McMurray, who were alive at his death; and that, consequently, it made no difference at what time any of the children might die, whether before or after the falling in of the life estate. The testator seems to have been aware, that questions of that kind had before then arisen upon the construction of wills, and entangled and perplexed the settlement of estates, and has clothed *his* intentions in language that cannot be mistaken. The intention of the testator is the governing rule in the construction of wills, upon the principle, that the law accords to every man the right to dispose of his property after his death, as he shall please. If, therefore, his intention can be ascertained from the will, and it contravenes no rule of law, that intention shall be carried into effect. It sometimes becomes very difficult to ascertain, what is the true meaning of a will; and the Courts have been compelled to adopt various rules, as indicating the will of the testator, which in such cases will be observed. Here there appears to be no difficulty in ascertaining the wishes and design of the testator. The remainder men are such of his children as shall be alive, at the time the life estate falls in. The words are precise—" to be enjoyed by her (his widow,) during her natural life, and at her death, &c. to be divided among *all* my children, that are *then alive*." The testator does not choose to leave any thing to speculation. He not only fixes the time at which the property shall be enjoyed, but by whom. It is impossible, by authority or argument, to make his meaning more apparent, than he has himself done; and the will furnishes abundant evidence, that the phraseology used was not lightly nor ignorantly adopted. In the clause of his will next succeeding, he gives to his wife the remainder of his lands, not previously disposed of, during her life, &c., remainder to his son, John McMurray, *if he is then living*, " but if he shall die before *that* time, the land previously given to his wife for life, &c. is to be sold, and the proceeds to be equally divided among all my children *then living*." In a subsequent clause he directs, that certain property shall be put into the possession of his wife, upon her giving bond, &c. and, if she declines taking it upon the conditions specified, then it is to be sold, and, after payment of his debts, " to be equally divided between my wife Elizabeth McMurray, my son John, my daughter Uphia, and my daughter Hannah." And again, in the succeeding clause, he leaves a negro man to his wife for ten years, to assist in raising his youngest children, and, at the expiration of that time, to be sold, and the money " to be equally divided between my wife, and my children that are *then* living." It is manifest the testator well. understood the meaning of the words he used, and that he varied them, as occasion required, to meet his wishes in the disposition of his property. The objects of his bounty were his *own* children; and he had a legal right to dispose of his property as he chose.

We have examined the authorities to which our attention has been directed. There is nothing in them, to change the view we have taken of the case. They only prove that the word "children" may, under peculiar circumstances, mean "grand-children;" as where the meaning of the testator is uncertain, and the bequest must fail, unless such construction be given. That is not the case here. The Bill must be dismissed with costs.

PER CURIAM.   Decree accordingly.

COWLES AND WILCOX *vs.* THOMAS W. CARTER.

A preliminary injunction, granted *ex parte* upon the bill alone, should be dissolved, upon an answer fully denying the facts, upon which the bill raises the plaintiff's equity.

A general allegation in a bill, specifying no facts upon which it is founded, requires no answer; or, at most, a general denial in the answer is sufficient to meet it.

Appeal from an interlocutory order of the Court of Equity of Surry County, at the Spring Term, 1845, his Honor Judge BAILEY presiding, by which order, the injunction, which had been granted in the case, was directed to lie over until the final hearing.

The Bill charged that the defendant had been employed by them, as their clerk and agent in a certain store owned by them, in Surry County; that he had mismanaged

43

their concerns wilfully and corruptly; that he had been guilty, in the course of his employment, of divers frauds upon them, which were specified; and, among other things, that he was in the habit, during such term of employment, of using his private funds in "iniquitous, usurious" operations with their customers, whereby they sustained great damages; and calling upon him to account, &c., and praying for an injunction against a judgment at law he had obtained against them for his wages.

The defendant, in his answer, denied specifically all the charges of fraud, corruption and mismanagement, alleged against him, and denied, also, generally, the charge of usurious operations to the prejudice of the plaintiffs.

An injunction having been granted upon the filing of the plaintiffs' bill, on a motion to dissolve the same, the Court below directed the injunction to be continued to the hearing, from which order the defendant, by leave of the Court, appealed.

Badger, for the plaintiffs.
Boyden, for the defendant.

Ruffin, C. J. The decree, continuing the injunction to the hearing, was erroneous, we think. The established rule of the Court is, that a preliminary injunction, granted *ex parte* upon the bill alone, is to be dissolved upon an answer, fully denying the facts upon which the bill raises the plaintiffs' equity. In the present case, the answer could not be more direct, unequivocal, full, and, apparently, founded on probable truth, than it is. It is nearly incredible, that the defendant could have been carrying on dealings on his own account, of the character imputed to him, for so long a period, without the knowledge and, therefore, the presumed concurrence of the plaintiffs, who were residing in the immediate neighborhood, and who had a personal agency in some of the cases, in which joint securities were taken for debts due to the plaintiffs and those due also to the defendant. At all events, the answer is positive, that the plaintiffs well knew of those transactions, and not only acquiesced, but they approved of them. The charge in the bill, that the plaintiffs lost a number of debts, which are mentioned, because their debtors became insolvent by reason of " the outrageous usury," which the defendant had practised on them, is of such a character, that it cannot be answered with any precision, nor be acted on by the Court. Pleaders ought to be aware that in judicial proceedings epithets avail nothing; and that the Court requires *facts* to be alleged and proved as the grounds of relief. The bill sets forth nothing, whereby it can be seen that the defendant perpetrated usury in a single instance; and, therefore, even if the matter itself would entitle the plaintiffs to relief, if properly stated, we do not require an answer to that part of the bill. It is to be remarked, however, that the defendant does answer it as far as he can; that is, by a denial in general terms, similar to those in which the allegation was made. When the allegations are precise, in respect to particular acts of negligence or unfaithfulness in respect to deeds of trust and the like, the answer meets the bill fully. And it states, that the debts, lost by the plaintiffs through the insolvency of customers, were not greater than must be expected in such extensive dealings; on which, upon a capital of about $8000, the defendant in four years made for the plaintiffs and paid over to them, upwards of $8,000 clear profit, after returning the stock. And it further states, with respect to losses from persons, who were debtors to both the plaintiffs and the defendant, that the losses of the latter were fully equal to those of the plaintiffs, in proportion to their debts. The justice of the debt recovered at law by the defendant cannot be contested, and there is nothing in the transactions embraced in these pleadings, (according to the answer, at all events,) on which the plaintiffs ought to be relieved from any part of it. Therefore, the injunction ought to have been dissolved with costs in the Court of Equity. That will be accordingly certified; and the plaintiffs must pay the costs in this Court.

PER CURIAM.   Decree accordingly.

JOHN R. JUSTICE vs. JOSHUA SCOTT & AL.

The probate of a deed of settlement upon a man's family, before the Clerk of the County Court, as if it were an ordinary deed of trust, and its subsequent registration upon that probate, are void as against creditors and subsequent purchasers.

Where an action is brought at law for the recovery of negroes, conveyed by a deed in trust, which it is alleged was fraudulent in its inception, the defendant at law may avail himself of that objection in the suit at law, and cannot transfer the jurisdiction to a Court of Equity. He can only apply to the Court of Equity for a discovery of the facts, to be used in the suit at law.

But where a trustee, in a deed made nine years before, institutes an action at law, against a purchaser under execution against the maker of the deed, and the purchaser alleges that all the debts were paid and the whole trust resulted to the debtor; while the debtor, who united in himself the character of creditor, by administering upon the estate of one of the creditors secured in the deed, says, that a certain debt is not paid, and the trustee says he does not know whether it is or is not paid, a Court of Equity will entertain a bill by the purchaser, as the most convenient and comprehensive mode of determining the rights of all the parties.

Where a bill is for relief upon the footing, that, as a trust, the subject is one of equitable cognizance, the injunction ought not to stay the trial at law, but only the suing out of an execution, should the plaintiff at law get a judgment.

The cases of *Smith* v. *Castrix*, 5 Ired. 518, and *Henderson* v. *Hoke*, 1 Dev. and Bat. 119, cited and approved.

Appeal from an interlocutory order of the Court of Equity of Craven County, at the Fall Term, 1845, his Honor Judge BATTLE presiding, which order directed the dissolution of the injunction, theretofore obtained in the cause.

The case, as presented by the pleadings, was this:

On the 8th of April, 1834, the defendant, Bryan Jones, conveyed to the other defendant, Scott, sundry pieces of land, a stock of merchandize, and several slaves, including two, named Henry and John; in trust to sell, and out of the proceeds of sale, pay a debt for $910, due from the grantor to his mother, Sarah Jones, and then to pay all the other debts of the grantor. It is admitted by all the parties, that every debt secured in the deed, except that to Sarah Jones, was paid soon after the execution of the deed. Sarah Jones died intestate in 1838; and Bryan Jones, her son, administered on her estate. In 1843, the two slaves, Henry and John, were sold by the Sheriff upon writs of *fieri facias* on judgments then recently obtained against Bryan Jones, and the present plaintiff became the purchaser, having, as he says, no notice of the deed to Scott, and believing the title, as well as the possession, to be in Bryan Jones. Soon afterwards, an action at law was brought by Scott and Jones, in the name of the former, against Justice, for the negroes, which the latter defended, and the same is now pending. Afterwards, Justice filed the present bill. It charges, *first*, that the deed of trust was in its inception fraudulent, having been made to secure debts that were not owing; and *secondly*, that, if the debts really existed at that time, they had been paid many years ago, and that Jones had used and enjoyed the property as his own—had sold some of it, and particularly, that, in 1838, he settled that part of it, which he had not before sold, on his wife and children, by conveying the same to a trustee for their use, including the two negroes before mentioned; and that the settlement was void, because it was voluntary, and made when the settler was insolvent. The bill further charges, that, on the 9th of January, 1843, being the day of the sale at which the plaintiff purchased, Jones, at the instance of Scott, executed to the latter a declaration and release, under his hand and seal, in which he, in his own right, and as administrator of Sarah Jones, acknowledged that the debt to Sarah Jones, and all the others mentioned in the deed, were satisfied. and released and discharged Scott from all claims and actions in respect of the said trust and trust property. The prayer of the bill is, that the deed of trust may be declared to have been fraudulent and void, as against the execution creditors, and for an injunction against prosecuting the suit at law, and for general relief.

The defendants answered separately. They both state, that the debt to Sarah Jones was justly due at the date of the deed. and that the other debts had been paid by sales of parts of the property conveyed; and they aver, that the deed was not intended to defraud creditors, but was executed to secure debts truly owing. The defendant, Scott, says, that he does not know whether the debt to Sarah Jones was ever paid or not, and he admits that Bryan Jones, after the death of his mother and of his wife, told him, Scott, that the debt was not due. He also admits, that Jones executed the release to him, as stated in the bill, and says that he took it, "because he thought he was entitled to it, and for his own protection." He states that he, afterwards, allowed the action at law to be brought in his name, for the benefit of the children of Bryan Jones, who claim the beneficial property in the slaves, under the settlement made by their father in 1838, and that at that time. Bryan Jones, he believes, was clear of debt; and he denies that the suit is prosecuted for the benefit of Bryan Jones himself. The defendant, Jones, further answers, that the debt to his mother was for money borrowed from her, and that it was raised by the sale of a tract of land by her, as executrix of her husband, John Jones, deceased; and that, by the will, the same belonged to the mother for her life, and then to such child or children as this defendant should leave. With the answer is exhibited a copy of the will of John Jones, and it appears thereby, that the testator appointed his wife executrix, and gave her all his estate during her life ; and, at her death, he gave certain parts of his real and personal estates to John S. Morris, including therein a certain plantation in Craven County, in trust to permit the defendant, Bryan Jones, to enjoy and use the property, real and personal, and receive the rents and profits thereof during his life, and then in trust for such child or children of the said Bryan, as might be living at his death. By a subsequent clause, the testator authorized his wife, if she deemed it expedient, to sell the plantation mentioned, and, with the proceeds, purchase other real or personal property, and, after the death of his wife, he gave the property so purchased to the said Morris, to be held upon the same trusts as the plantation was held on.

He further states, that after the death of his mother, to-wit, on the 29th of August, 1838, this defendant, at a time when he owed nothing, conveyed to John S. Morris the negroes Henry and John, and six others, in trust for the separate use of the defendant's wife during the coverture, and if she should survive, to be conveyed to the wife, upon the death of the defendant, with a power of appointment by deed or will to the wife, and in default of appointment to the child or children she might leave. The answer then states that the wife did appoint by will to her children, and died, and that her will was duly proved. With the answer is exhibited a copy of the settlement, made by the defendant to Morris ; and it appears thereon to have been proved before the Clerk of the Craven County Court, September 3d, 1838, and to have been proved before a Judge of the Superior Court, June 26th, 1843.

This defendant further says, that the debt to his Mother was never in fact paid ; but, considering that he had conveyed to a trustee all his estate for the benefit of his wife and children, and that to the latter belonged the money secured by his bond to his Mother, he destroyed his bond, without paying any part of the principal or interest due thereon. The answer thereupon insists, that the negroes and other property conveyed in the deed to Scott are properly applicable to the payment of that debt. The defendant says that his reason, for giving to Scott the release of January 9th, 1843, was merely to quiet his apprehensions of liability in consequence of the sale of the slaves that day to the present plaintiff; and that it was not meant as an abandonment of Scott's right to the slaves, as trustee; and that, so far from it, both Scott and Jones gave notice of the title of the former openly, and forbad the sale by the Sheriff. The defendant denies that he has any interest in the property, and says that he has been discharged as a bankrupt.

Upon the filing of the bill, an injunction was granted as prayed for; and upon the coming in of the answers, the defendant moved for its dissolution, and it was ordered *pro forma* accordingly, and the plaintiff appealed.

J. W. Bryan and *J. H. Bryan*, for the plaintiff.
Badger, for the defendants.

RUFFIN, C. J. The Court is of opinion, that the injunction ought not to have been dissolved, that is, not absolutely. The claim set up for the children of Jones under his settlement may be put out of the way at once. To say nothing of the *prima facie* fraud in it, as being a voluntary settlement upon his family by one, who, as he now says, was then indebted to his Mother's estate, and so soon became indebted to others, and insolvent; and, as he says, bankrupt; yet the deed is void for want of due proof and registration. *Smith* v. *Castrix*, 5 Ired. 519. We collect from the answer of Scott, that it was in reference to this claim of the children he regarded himself as trustee for them; considering that their father had assigned to them, or to Morris for them, his resulting trust, which was for the whole property after the debts were paid. If, then, the settlement by Jones be not effectual, the resulting

trust is still in him, and that amounted to the whole beneficial property, as this defendant supposed, from the representations of Jones, and from his formal release, that
the debt to the mother was paid as well as all the others.
It was consequently wrong for Scott to set up his legal
title, in opposition to the right of the plaintiff, derived by
his purchase, under execution against the sole *cestui que
trust* of the property; for the plaintiff, by his purchase,
stood, in this Court, in the place of Jones in his relation
to Scott, and the latter is therefore endeavoring to recover the possession or the value of the negroes, from his
own *cestui que trust*.

But it is said by the other defendant, that his children
have another interest in this property. He states that
the money which his mother lent him, was, under their
grand-father's will, theirs after the grand-mother's death;
that in truth it has never been paid by him; and therefore he insists, that it ought now to be raised for their
benefit. There are several answers to this claim. This
is new matter, brought forward in the answer, in avoid-
ance of the plaintiff's equity, and not responsively to the
bill, and in denial of the equity. Therefore, the injunction should have been kept up to the hearing. In the
next place, the children have not the right to the money
at present, but only the capital after the death of their
father, who is entitled to the profits during life. But in
the last place, and chiefly, the children have no equity as
against these negroes, unless it were to appear, that
their father has not satisfied them, and is not able to satisfy them. He borrowed the money, and he settled on
them six other negroes besides these two; and it is no
where stated, that, unless they should receive that sum
out of these negroes, they will lose it, inasmuch as they
cannot get it in some other way from their father or their
grand-mother's estate. *Prima facie*, the declaration under seal of the defendant, Jones, who is administrator of
his mother, the creditor, that the debt had been paid, dis-

charges therefrom the trustee of the trust property. If the children have a right in the money, and an equitable lien on this debt therefor, let them file their bill, and put the questions, upon which their title depends, directly in issue. They cannot be brought forward in a way, which will not enable the Court to investigate the whole case, upon which the merit of the claim depends.

Those supposed rights of the children being thus disposed of, there remains nothing to shew, that the whole equitable ownership of the property was not in Bryan Jones, and liable to execution under the act of 1812; unless it be, that his right passed to his assignees in bankruptcy. As to that, the answer states nothing but the fact, that, before it was put in, the defendant had been discharged as a bankrupt; but when that was, or whether these negroes were included in the assignment, is not stated. So that no right appears in the assignees, even if it were competent for this party to set up such a right for the assignees, instead of leaving it to them to do it. It is very clear, that the suit at law was not instituted for the benefit of the general creditors; but only to get the negroes for the debtor's children.

It was, however, objected at the bar, that all the questions, arising upon the facts stated in the bill, were legal questions, properly triable in the suit at law; and that the plaintiff could not transfer the jurisdiction to this Court, after a suit properly constituted for the trial of them at law. With respect to this point, it is to be observed, that the bill is framed with two sets of allegations, having a view to relief upon different, and, indeed, opposing grounds. There is not, it must be admitted, a clear discrimination made between them in the bill, but much confusion in mingling together the facts, upon which the two grounds of relief, taken separately, depend. But we collect, that the bill was framed with the intention of trying here the question, whether the deed was or was not originally covinous, as a security for feigned debts, and deceptive to creditors; and also the further question, whether the debts secured by the deed—admitting it to be *bona fide*—had not been paid, so as to vest the whole equitable right, as a resulting trust, in Bryan Jones. As to the first point, we think the objection sound. The bill alleges no defect of proof of any fact, on which the question of fraud depends. If it had, it would only be matter for discovery, to be used on the trial at law, and not for relief. In its nature, the controversy, whether a deed by a debtor is fraudulent, as to his creditors, under the statute of Elizabeth, is a legal one; though, in particular cases, it may be made the subject of a suit in equity. But here it was in a course of litigation at law : and it is plain that it ought not to go on there, and one be carried on here at the same time, upon the very same subject. Then, upon what principle has the defendant at law a right to change the forum, and say that *he* will have the matter tried by the Judge in the Court of Equity, and not by a Judge and Jury in a Court of Law? If, therefore, that were all the bill, the Court would not sustain it.

But, in the second aspect, the case, we think, is properly a subject of equitable jurisdiction. The case, that a trustee in a deed, made to secure creditors nine years before, instituted an action at law against a purchaser, under an execution against the maker of the deed, and the purchaser alleges, that all the debts were paid and the whole trust resulted to the debtor, while the debtor, who also unites in himself the character of creditor, by administering upon the estate of one of the creditors secured in the deed, says, that a certain debt is not paid, and the trustee says he does not know whether it is or is not paid. It is true, if all the debts were paid, that, under the Act of 1812, the sale by the Sheriff transferred to the purchaser both the trust and the estate of the trustee; and that he might set up that title and defend himself at law. But that does not oust the jurisdiction of the Court of Equity over the trust, which it originally had, according to a well established principle. Besides, the relief in equity is more effectual, because the investigation is more complete, and the decree will conclude more persons than the judgment at law. Trusts often lie in confidence, and the party may not be able to shew them at law, whereas, in equity, the parties may be made witnesses against themselves. It is plain, too, that a decree in this Court in a suit against the trustee, the debtor and the creditor, declaring the trusts, and such and such debts to have been paid, and the whole equitable ownership to be in the debtor, and compelling the creditor to execute a release or acknowledge satisfaction, and the trustee and the debtor to execute conveyances of their several interests and for perpetual injunctions, will obtain for the purchaser muniments of title, more plain and permanent, than a judgment in his favor, in a suit brought at law by the trustee for a detention or conversion of the slaves. After such a judgment at law, the purchaser might, perhaps, still be harassed by suits in Equity brought by some of the creditors. But, by making proper parties to his bill, he can, by one suit, settle all controversies touching the equitable claims, as well as the legal title, to the property. Hence, in *Henderson* v. *Hoke*, 1 Dev. and Bat. Eq. 119, the Court sustained the bill, where the plaintiff claimed under execution sale against a *cestui que trust*. And it is remarkable, that there was an ejectment by Hoke against Henderson, 3 Dev. 12, for the same premises. It is true, that Henderson did not, upon the filing of his bill, pray an injunction against the trial at law; for there was, after the first judgment was reversed in this Court, a second trial at law, and an appeal to this Court, which was pending when the decree was made in the suit in Equity brought by Henderson. But the bill was entertained, notwithstanding the action at law; and when the decree was made, it followed, of course, that the defendant in Equity was restrained from further proceeding in the ejectment, and the appeal therein was never brought on. The case, therefore, is, in our opinion, a proper one for relief in this point of view.

But as the bill is for relief upon the footing, that, as a trust, the subject is one of equitable cognizance, the injunction ought not to have staid the trial at law, but only the suing out execution, should the plaintiff at law get a judgment. The plaintiff has no right to delay the trial at law, until his cause shall have been heard here, and, perhaps, his bill dismissed, by which time the other party may not be able to prove his case at law, by the death or removal of witnesses, or the loss of documents. All the plaintiff can justly ask is, that, as he has an undetermined equity, the plaintiff at law shall not proceed to execution. If the plaintiff means to rely altogether on his relief in equity, then he ought to let judgment go, inasmuch as his defence is on an equitable, and not on a legal title. But, as in this case, he, no doubt, insists that he has a good defence at law, as well as a good ground for his bill in equity, we do not see that he may not resist the recovery at law, if he can, or that the Court should require him to submit to a judgment. While, however, that is so, it would be an injury to the other side to stay the trial. It ought not to have been done before the answers, because the object of this suit was not to get answers to be used in the defence at law; and, much more, the injunction to stay the trial ought not to be continued after the answers. If the plaintiff chooses to try at law, he ought to be at liberty to do so, as he will run the double risk of paying the costs; first, by having the judgment against him, and, secondly, by having a perpetual injunction against the judgment, if in his favor, should there finally be a decree against him here.

Therefore, the decree should be reversed, and the injunction modified so as to stay execution upon the judgment, if the plaintiff at law should obtain one. The

Court cannot give costs to either party. The defendants are not entitled to costs, because they took a decree, which has been reversed. And the plaintiff ought not to have them, because his injunction was too extensive at first, and, chiefly, because the bill, instead of presenting simply the case on which the plaintiff's equity arises, complicates a good and a bad case together. It will be sufficient to let the costs abide the result at the hearing.

PER CURIAM.　　　Ordered to be certified accordingly.

PATRICK MURPHY rs. DANIEL C. MOORE & AL.

A bill cannot be brought by one, who indemnifies another, upon an equity of the principal, without making the principal himself a party.

Though, in an action of detinue for slaves, juries generally and properly, when their verdict is for the plaintiff, find the value of the property higher than it really is, in order to enforce the delivery of the slaves; yet, that is not the case, where it is known that the defendant cannot discharge himself by a delivery, as if the slaves be dead or owned by another person.

Appeal from an interlocutory order of the Court of Equity of Sampson County, at the Fall Term, 1845, his Honor Judge CALDWELL presiding, which order directed the injunction heretofore granted in this case, to be dissolved.

The following case was presented by the Bill and answers.

The plaintiff, as the equitable assignee of a judgment for about $800, interest and costs, which had been recovered by Samuel Houston against William McGee in his life-time, issued an execution on the same, and indemnified the Deputy Sheriff of Duplin, (one Hussy,) to levy on and sell five certain slaves, as the property of William

McGee, to satisfy said execution. Thomas McGee, one of the present defendants, brought an action of detinue for the said slaves against the Deputy Sheriff, and obtained a judgment for them. And their value, in *toto*, was assessed by the jury at $1,600, and damages for their detention, at $30. Thomas McGee issued a *distringas*, with a *fieri facias* clause, against Hussy, for the production of the said five slaves, damages and costs. Murphy then filed this bill in his own name, and as the administrator of William McGee, who had recently died, praying the Court to enjoin Thomas McGee's execution against Hussy. The bill alleges, that Thomas McGee, Sen., was the father of Thomas McGee, Jun., Elizabeth McGee, (now the wife of Daniel C. Moore,) and William McGee, (the plaintiff's intestate) ; that he, in the year 1842, conveyed a number of slaves to his daughter, Elizabeth McGee, by an absolute deed of gift, but upon a secret trust and promise on her part, that she would convey a certain portion of the said slaves to his son, William McGee, (who was then insolvent and a fugitive from justice,) whenever it was safe for her to do so. Afterwards, the bill alleges, the father procured Elizabeth to deliver up the said deed to him, and place it in the hands of one Gillaspie, in order that two other deeds might be drawn, to be executed by the father, one conveying absolutely a portion of the said slaves to her, Elizabeth, and the other conveying the balance of the said slaves to her upon trust for William McGee. But that, before Gillaspie could prepare the said two draughts of deed for execution, the father died. The bill further states, that afterwards Elizabeth applied to Gillaspie for the original deed, which had been deposited with him for the purpose aforesaid, and that she received it, and that she has since set it up, and is now claiming under it; that, afterwards, in the year 1843, the said Elizabeth conveyed by deed to Thomas McGee, (the plaintiff in the action of detinue) in trust for

William McGee, the slaves now in controversy; that either through mistake or fraud, no words of perpetuity were inserted in the trust for the representatives of William McGee: whereby the plaintiff is advised, that an interest for life only was created in William, leaving a resulting trust for the benefit of Elizabeth, the maker of the deed. The bill further charges that, at the Sheriff's sale, the negroes were purchased at the price of $1,025 by one Bowden, as the agent of the defendant Moore, and that Moore has them in possession, and therefore ought not to enforce or require the trustee to enforce the judgment at law, at all events, for more than he paid for them. The bill furthermore seeks of the trustee an account at least of the rents and hires of the said slaves during the life of William McGee. The injunction was granted.

The defendants answered the bill; and they deny any knowledge of any trust, secret or otherwise, created by the father, Thomas McGee, Sen. in favor of William McGee. Elizabeth, now the wife of Daniel C. Moore, another defendant, answers and says, that her father shortly before his death, did convey to her, by a deed of gift, certain slaves; but she denies, that the said deed was made and executed upon any condition, that she should convey any of the said slaves to William McGee her brother, or a trustee for him, or that any promise or agreement was ever made by her to her father, that she would hold any portion of the said slaves, in trust for William. She states, that the said slaves were conveyed absolutely to her by her father, by his own free will for her own benefit. She admits, that some time after the execution of the deed, her father, in a conversation with her, remarked—"My daughter, you must provide, or I know you will provide, for my son William"; when she desired her father to make some provision for William, by conveying a portion of the slaves given to her, for his benefit. And to this end, she delivered the deed to Gillaspie, with instructions to prepare other deeds. But she denies that she surrendered the deed to Gillaspie, upon any request made by her father, to carry out any previous agreement made with him at the time of its execution. She states that her father lived several weeks after she placed the deed in the hands of Gillaspie. This defendant states, that she has reason to believe, that her father had advanced to William several slaves, and had paid debts for him, equal to the share of his estate given to her. This defendant admits, that she did, in the year 1843, convey to Thomas McGee, (another defendant) certain slaves in trust, for the support and maintenance of her brother William for his life; but she denies, that the same was done with any fraudulent intention to evade any engagement she had made with her father. She knew that her brother William was in very indigent circumstances, and she desired to make some provision for him for his lifetime, and to this end, just before her marriage with Mr. Moore, she applied to Dr. Gillaspie, a man of integrity, to write a deed conveying certain of her slaves to Thomas McGee, in trust for the support of her brother William for his life-time; which was accordingly done. She admits that William lately died, and that the plaintiff is his administrator, and that she and her husband claim a resulting trust in the said slaves. The answer of Moore denies, that he purchased the negroes at the Sheriff's sale, or that Bowden purchased them for him, or sold them to him afterwards. He says that Bowden bought for himself; that for a short time after the sale, he, Moore, had the negroes in his possession for Bowden, but that he did not claim them, and that Bowden now owns them and has them in his possession.

Thomas McGee, the trustee, after denying any knowledge of any trust made by his father for William his brother, as stated in the bill, says that he has paid $460 since the date of the deed to him, for his brother William's maintenance and support, and that he has promised to pay $80 more, for his medicine bill in his last illness.

45

That he has never received but $50, as rents and hires for the said slaves; and that he has nothing now in his hands to account to the administrator of William McGee.

On the answers coming in. the Court dissolved the injunction; from which the complainant appealed.

W. H. Haywood, Strange, and *Warren Winslow,* for the plaintiff.

D. Reid, for the defendants.

DANIEL, J. The defendants have denied, in their answers, any knowledge of any trust in the slaves for William McGee, created by Thomas McGee, Sen. either by any secret or public agreement with his daughter Elizabeth, or any one else. They furthermore deny any belief that such a trust was ever created or intended. Elizabeth Moore, (formerly McGee,) denies positively, that her father ever requested her, before or after he executed the deed of gift of the said slaves, that she should hold any portion of them in trust for her brother, William McGee. Thomas McGee, the trustee under the deed executed by Elizabeth, denies that he has one cent for rents and hires, to account to the administrator of William McGee. He avers that he had advanced about $400 for his, William's, support, after the date of the deed from his sister to him, in trust; and that he had promised to pay $80 more, the medicine bill in his last illness; and that he had never received, or was entitled to receive, more than about $50 for rents and hires of the slaves he had charge of for the use of William McGee. Hussy, the defendant in the judgment at law, should regularly have been a party plaintiff in that bill. A bill cannot be brought by one, who indemnifies another, upon an equity of the principal, without making the principal himself a party. But in looking into the case, we thought the merits so plain in favor of the defendants to the bill, that we concluded to decide the cause, upon the strength of the answers themselves.   As for the equity, which the bill sets up by reason of the purchase of the negroes by or for Moore at the Sheriff's sale ; there are two answers to it.   *First,* the fact is positively denied in the answer.   *Secondly,* if it were true, the plaintiff could not be relieved on it.   If he had thought proper to have gone into the Court of Equity, in the first instance, to obtain satisfaction out of the negroes as the equitable property of William McGee for life, the life estate been sold, and then, the plaintiff, as the creditor, would have got whatever that would have brought in the market—the purchaser running the risk of W. McGee's life.   That sale would not have disturbed Moore's interest in remainder, nor been wrongful to the trustee ; and there would have been no cause of action to any one.   But the plaintiff and the Sheriff did not adopt that course, but sold the negroes out and out, as the absolute property of William, liable to execution under the Act of 1812. That made it the duty of the trustee to bring the action at law, in which, as the case turns out, the recovery is in money. Now, pending that action, William McGee died, and the plaintiff insists, that he ought to have a deduction from the judgment proportional at least to the value of his life estate, at the time of the sale, compared with the value of the remainder.   But we think clearly, that he cannot. For, by the plaintiff's own act, the negroes have been turned into money in the hands of the trustee ; and the only right the plaintiff could claim therein would be the interest of the fund during William's life.   That, in truth, he has ; for the value of property recovered in detinue does not bear interest, and, therefore, there is not and will not be, when the judgment at law is collected, one cent, as regards the sums recovered for the value of the negroes, in the hands of the trustee, which ought to belong to William McGee, or to the plaintiff as his administrator. Thomas McGee is the trustee as well for Moore as for his brother William ; and it is not against conscience that

Moore should claim, upon the falling in of William's life estate, the capital or full value of the negroes—for he ought to have had them specifically, and may therefore rightfully claim the whole value of them. It is not intimated in the bill, that the verdict, found the value higher than it truly was. It cannot be presumed that it did; for although juries often and properly so find in order to enforce the delivery of the slaves, yet that is not the course, where it is known that the defendant cannot discharge himself by a delivery, as if the negro be dead or is owned by another person. From that circumstance, and the sum found compared with the number of slaves, and the silence of the bill on the point, we must take it, that only the true value was given. Now, it is manifest that there is no reason why Moore should not have that. If he bought at the Sheriff's sale for less, it was his good fortune and the plaintiff's fault; and, as he would have lost the whole of his purchase money, if William McGee's title proved defective, he may justly claim any advantage from a purchase at less than the real value. It is true, the verdict includes also the hires of the negroes while the suit was pending, and that they do belong to William McGee, as the profits in his time. But that cannot avail the plaintiff upon these pleadings, because the trustee swears, that he was in advance for William a much larger sum, besides his expenses in this litigation. There is, therefore, nothing in this part of the case on which the plaintiff can have relief.

We are unable to see any ground, for the reversal of the decree ; and it must be affirmed with costs.

PER CURIAM.   Ordered to be certified accordingly.

DRURY ALLEN *vs.* MOSES CHAMBERS.

A Bill, praying for the specific performance of a contract for the conveyance of land, is defective, if it does not contain so particular a description that the Court may know with certainty the land, of which they are asked to decree a conveyance.

If a Bill be brought for the specific performance of a parol contract for the conveyance of land, although the defendant does not rely upon the plea of the statute, rendering such contracts void, yet if he denies the contract as stated in the Bill, and insists that the real contract was a different one, this Court will not permit parol evidence to be heard in support of the plaintiff's claim.

Part performance, such as the payment of the whole of the purchase money and the delivery of the possession to the vendee, will not, in this State, dispense with a writing, if the statute be insisted on, nor admit a parol proof of a contract, different from that stated in the answer.

The case of *Ellis* v. *Ellis*, 1 Dev. Eq 180, 341, cited and approved.

Cause removed from the Court of Equity of Person County, at the Fall Term, 1845, by consent of the parties.

The bill was filed in 1844, and states, that, in 1840, the defendant made a parol contract to sell to the plaintiff " a certain parcel of land in the County of Person, to contain by contract 200 acres, at $2 per acre"; that, some time in the same year, the plaintiff and defendant partly performed the said parol agreement, by the payment to the defendant by the plaintiff of the sum of $240, for which the defendant gave receipt in the following words: " Received of Mr. Drury Allen, two hundred and forty dollars, in part for a certain tract of land lying on Flat river, including Taylor Hicks' Spring-house and lot &c., and adjoining the land of Lewis Daniel, Womack, and others."

The bill further states, that, upon such payment, the defendant let the plaintiff into possession " of the said land," in pursuance of the agreement, and that the plaintiff has offered to pay the residue of the purchase money, and requested the defendant to convey to him the land in fee ; but that the defendant refused to do so, for the reason, that the defendant denies the contract as herein

stated, and sets up another agreement in relation thereto, and threatens to turn the plaintiff and his tenants out.

The prayer is for a decree for the specific performance
of the said agreement, and that the defendant be compelled " to convey to the plaintiff the said land as agreed
between them."

The answer admits, that, in 1840, the parties entered
into a parol contract for a tract of land, and that the
defendant received a sum of money, either $220, or $240,
thereon, as a part of the purchase money. But the defendant denies positively, that the contract was as set
forth in the bill, and says that it was essentially different.
The answer then states, that the defendant is the owner
of a tract of land containing between six and eight hundred acres, and that the plaintiff applied to him to purchase a part of the said land, to be laid off at the west
end of the tract; that the plaintiff at first spoke of buying 200 acres, and the defendant agreed to sell him that,
or any other quantity he might want, at the price of $2 50
per acre and not at $2, as stated in the bill; and the
plaintiff concluded to take a parcel of land on those
terms; and that it was further agreed, that the parties
should employ a surveyor to lay off the quantity the
plaintiff might choose, at the West end of the tract, and
to run, so as, at the least, to include therein a house and
small farm occupied by one Taylor Hicks, who then
lived on a part of the land, as a tenant of the defendant.
The answer states, that, not long afterwards, the parties
employed a surveyor, who made a survey precisely as he
was directed by the plaintiff, who was present, and marked the lines and corners himself: that when the surveyor
had run East far enough to make 200 acres by running
across the tract to the opposite North line, he informed
the plaintiff and the defendant of the fact, and the former said he wished to include the Spring and Hicks' improvements, and ordered the surveyor to proceed on the
former course, until the plaintiff should tell him to stop;

and so it was accordingly done : that the land thus laid off was plotted by the surveyor and the quantity ascertained to be 366 acres ; for which, in a few days, the surveyor prepared a deed, which the defendant executed, and had attested and tendered to the plaintiff, requesting him to accept it and pay the residue of the purchase money ; but that the plaintiff refused. The answer states, that, nevertheless, the plaintiff entered into the land and settled his son thereon, and that neither the farm nor the houses are within a tract of 200 acres, laid off at the West end of the tract. The answer further states, that the defendant would have been willing the plaintiff should have taken only 200 acres, or any other quantity, if he would have designated the particular quantity and part ; but that, having selected the tract of 366 acres, and entered into possession of it, and then refused to accept a deed for it, and also denying the price agreed on, the plaintiff seemed, as the defendant believed, determined to baffle him, by keeping possession without paying for the land, and, therefore, the defendant tendered back the money he had received from the plaintiff, and gave him notice that he would annul the contract ; but the plaintiff still refused to receive the money and rescind the bargain, and, at the same time, refused to accept the deed and pay the residue of the purchase money. And the answer insists, that the defendant is not now bound to convey any part of the land.

Replication was taken to the answer, and the parties took proofs. The plaintiff proved the execution of the receipt for $240, of the tenor set out in the bill. Several witnesses for the plaintiff prove, that the price agreed on was $2 per acre ; while others, more numerous and, apparently, unconnected with the parties, state that the plaintiff offered $2, but finally agreed to give $2 50, and frequently afterwards, acknowledged the latter to be the price. Two or three witnesses state, that when the land was surveyed, the plaintiff said that, although he wanted

Hicks' improvements, he was not able to pay for more than 200 acres and would not take more; while others, preponderating in numbers and opportunities of information and including the surveyor selected by the plaintiff, depose positively, that the plaintiff, when informed that the survey had proceeded far enough for 200 acres, directed the surveyor to go on, and include Hicks' improvements and a particular parcel of good wood-land, and, indeed, that the tract, as surveyed and containing 366 acres, was selected by the plaintiff himself, who fixed on the corners and marked them and the lines with his own hands and that the plaintiff entered into the house and fields before occupied by Hicks, which would not be included in a tract of only 200 acres.

Venable, for the plaintiff.
E. G. Reade, for the defendant.

RUFFIN, C. J. The plaintiff could get no decree on his bill, as at present framed, if it were admitted by a demurrer or in an answer; for it contains no description of the land, of which he seeks the conveyance, from which the Court could decree an immediate conveyance of any land in particular, or could ascertain the land by ordering a survey. In the beginning of the bill it states the land to be "a certain parcel of land lying in Person, to contain 200 acres." It then sets out the defendant's receipt for $240, as paid in part "for a certain tract of land lying on Flat river, including Taylor Hicks' Spring-house and lot adjoining the land of Lewis Daniel, Womack, and others." The receipt is but little more specific than the "200 acres in Person County;" for it mentions no quantity, nor how any land is to be laid off around the improvements of Hicks. Of course, there can be no decree, when the parties leave it altogether uncertain, what was the subject of their contract. It seems highly probable, that there never was, in truth, any final and precise contract between the parties, for any particular piece or quantity of land. At all events, the plaintiff states none in the bill, in such terms as to obtain an effectual conveyance for any land, even if the deed were made in the very terms in which he asks it.

But, besides the difficulty mentioned, there is that of the nature of the alleged contract: it being by parol and denied by the answer. If the receipt had sufficiently described the land and price, it would have authorized the relief. But of itself it amounts to nothing, and no contract can be made out from it, unless by the help of parol evidence; and the reception of that is forbidden by the statute of frauds, *Rev. St.* c. 50, s. 8. The defendant, if he had chosen that mode of defence, might have brought the cause to an end at once by a plea of the statute. But the defendant has thought it due to himself, to state his willingness and endeavor to deal fairly, and this he does by denying the contract, as set out in the bill, in the two most essential particulars: the one is in the price, being a difference of one-fifth between them; and the other is in the quantity of the land agreed for. The parties are, therefore, directly at issue as to the substance of their contract; and, as it is admitted to be in parol, there is no mode of ascertaining which is right, but by hearing the oral testimony of witnesses. That, the Legislature must have meant in such a case to exclude. If, indeed, a defendant submits to perform a parol contract charged in the bill, there is no difficulty in decreeing it; for the danger within the purview of the Act is excluded. Perhaps, it may be the same, if the defendant admits the alleged contract in his answer, and neither by a plea nor the answer insists on the statute. But, if the defendant deny the agreement charged in the bill altogether, or deny it as charged, and set up a distinct and inconsistent agreement, it is impossible to move one step further without doing so in the teeth of the Act; which, as a rule of evidence, upon a point of fact disputed between the parties, must be as binding in this Court as in a Court of Law. It was so laid down in *Whitaker* v. *Revis*, 2 Bro : C. C. 567, and seems so evident from the nature of the thing, that there can scarcely be need for authority on it. The propriety of that construction and the value of the statute, thus understood, could not be rendered more evident, than by the case before us; in which, although the proof preponderates very directly in favor of the defendant, there is the most direct conflict between numerous witnesses, both as to the land contracted for and its price. We have read the proofs, as they are filed; but merely as a matter of curiosity; and the danger of hearing such evidence upon a question of this kind and of inducing persons, thereby, to rely on it, could not be better exemplified than in this case.

The alleged past performance could avail nothing, were the contract established in respect to the identical land and the price; as in this State it was finally settled, in *Ellis* v. *Ellis*, 1 Dev. Eq. 180, 341, that doctrine did not prevail, and that even the payment of the whole purchase money and the delivery of possession to the vendee would not dispense with a writing, if the statute be insisted on, nor admit a parol proof of a contract, different from that stated in the answer. A vendor may in some cases practice a fraud under this rule; but the opposite one would open a door to numberless perjuries, alike, if not more, productive of frauds on the other side.

PER CURIAM.   The bill dismissed with costs.

JAMES MEBANE *vs.* ALEXANDER MEBANE & AL.

A. devised certain property to a trustee, in trust to apply the proceeds to the maintenance of his son, and with a proviso that no part of the property should be subject to the debts of his said son. *Held*, that this proviso was inoperative, and the creditors of the son had a right to have their claims paid out of the property.

By the use of no terms or art can property be given to a man, or to another for him, so that he may continue to enjoy it, or derive any benefit from it, as the interest, or his maintenance thereout or the like, and at the same time defy his creditors and deny them satisfaction thereout.

The only manner, in which creditors can be excluded, is to exclude the debtor also from all benefit from, or interest in, the property, by such a limitation, upon the contingency of his bankruptcy or insolvency, as will determine his interest and make it go to some other person.

The cases of *Dick* v. *Pitchford*, 1 Dev. and Bat. Eq. 480, and *Bank of the State* v. *Forney*, 2 Ired. Eq. 184, cited and approved.

Cause removed from the Court of Equity of Orange County, at the Fall Term, 1845.

The following were the facts of the case:

David Mebane, by his will, dated April 7th, 1842, gave to Alexander Mebane in fee, a tract of land, called the Hodge Place, and four slaves, "in trust for my son Anderson; and the said Alexander, as trustee, may at any time take possession of said land and negroes, and lease the land and hire the negroes, and apply the proceeds to the maintenance of my son Anderson—it being my will and intention, that the aforesaid property shall not in any wise be subject to the debts of my said son Anderson." In a subsequent clause, the testator added: "I give unto my son Alexander, all the horses, cattle, hogs, and the farming utensils on the Hodge Place, and also one bed and furniture, in trust, nevertheless, for my said son, Anderson; it being my will and intention, that the said property shall not in any wise be subject to the debts of said Anderson. It is also my will, if the said Anderson should die without issue. that then the Hodge Place shall belong to my grand-son, Thomas R. Mebane."

By other clauses of the will, the testator gave to his son Anderson a share, with his other children, of the debts that might be owing to him at his death, but directed that his son Alexander, as the money might be collected, should, "as trustee, take possession of it, and pay it over in the manner directed in the former clauses of this will."

The plaintiff is a judgment-creditor of Anderson Mebane; and, after a return of *nulla bona* on a *fieri facias*, he filed this bill against Anderson Mebane and Alexander Mebane, for satisfaction out of the trust property. The answers raise the question, whether the property is liable to the debts. The trustee further states, that in the maintenance of his brother Anderson, who is blind, and in necessary expenditures in conducting the farm, he has anticipated the income about $200; and he submits that at all events he has a right to be reimbursed what he shall be found to be in advance.

Badger. for the plaintiff.
Norwood and *Iredell,* for the defendants.

Ruffin, C. J. In the case of *Dick* v. *Pitchford*, 1 Dev. and Bat. Eq. 480, the question arose upon a conveyance of negroes to one, in trust, annually to apply the profits to the use of the donor's son, H. P., so that they should not be subject to be sold or disposed of by H. P., or the rents and profits anticipated by him, or in any manner subject to his debts; and it was held, that the son's conveyance was, nevertheless, effectual to pass his interest, as *cestui que trust*, for the term of his life. The doctrine rests upon these considerations: that a gift of the legal property in a thing includes the *jus disponendi*, and that a restriction on that right, as a condition, is repugnant to the grant, and therefore void: And that, in a Court of Equity, a *cestui que trust* is looked on as the real owner, and the trust governed in this respect by the same rules which govern legal interests; and, consequently, that it is equally repugnant to equitable ownership that the owner should not have the power of alienating his property. There is, indeed, an exception to that general rule, which is founded on the peculiar incapacities of married women, and their subjection to their husbands. A gift in trust for the separate use of a married woman, or in contemplation of her marriage, may be coupled with a provision against alienation or anticipation; for, in truth, the restriction is imposed for her protection, and, as she is *sub potestate viri*, it will more frequently operate as a beneficial protection, than in prejudice to her. But restraints, as conditions merely, upon alienation by a person *sui juris* have been held in a great number of cases to be null, as regards property given through the medium of a trust; and several of them are cited in *Dick* v. *Pitchford*. In the case of *Brandon* v. *Robinson*, 18 Ves. 429, for example, LORD ELDON, after speaking of the exception in respect to *feme coverts*, says, "but the case of a disposition to a man, who, if he has the property, has the power of aliening, is quite different." It is true, that property may be given in trust upon a condition, so expressed as to amount to a limitation, whereby the interest of the first taker ceases upon a particular event, and the property goes over to some other person in particular, or falls into the residue. But there is nothing like that here. By this will, the entire equitable ownership of the slaves and other personal effects, is given to the son Anderson, and of the land also, subject however, as to the last, to a contingent limitation over upon the event of Anderson's dying without leaving issue living at his death, as the will must be read since the Act of 1827. Then, there is no doubt that the donee, Anderson, has, upon the principles and precedents mentioned, the absolute right to assign his interest in these gifts, and that his assignee would have the right to take the estates under his own control.

That being so, it follows, that the interest of the *cestui que trust*, whatever it may be, is liable in this Court for his debts. For it would be a shame upon any system of law, if, through the medium of a trust of any kind of contrivance, property, from which a person is absolutely entitled to a comfortable, perhaps an affluent support, and over which he can exercise the highest right of property, namely, alienation, and which, upon his death, would undoubtedly be assets, should be shielded from the creditors of that person during his life. There is no such reproach upon nor absurdity in our law; for we hold, that whatevery interest a debtor has in property of any sort may be reached by his creditors, either at law or in equity, according to the nature of the property. Terms of exclusion of the donee's creditors, not amounting to a limitation of the estate, can no more repel the creditors, than a restraint upon alienation can tie the hands of the donee himself. Liability for debts ought to be, and is, just as much an incident of property, as the *jus disponendi* is; for, indeed, it is one mode of exercising the power of disposition. This is the first occasion on which the point has come directly into judgment; but in the case of *Bank of the State* v. *Forney*, 2 Ired. Eq. 184, the Court said, however anxiously the benefit of the donee personally may be looked to by the donor, the policy of the law will not permit property or a trust to be so given, that the donee may continue to enjoy it after his bankruptcy, or, in other words, against his creditors. In *Brandon* v. *Robinson*, there was a trust to pay dividends, from time to time, into the proper hands of a man or on his receipt, and that they should not be grantable or assignable by way of anticipation; and it was held, that this interest passed to assignees in bankruptcy: Lord ELDON remarking, that an attempt to give property, and to prevent creditors from obtaining any interest in it, though it be his, the debtor's, could not be sustained; and that the gift must be subject to the incidents of property, and it could not be preserved from creditors, unless given to some one else, that is, limited over. Following that case, was that of *Graves* v. *Dolphin*, 1 Sim. 66, in which estates were devised in trust to pay an annuity to a son for his personal support for life, not liable to his debts, and to be paid from time to time into his own proper hands, and not to any other person, and his receipt only to be a discharge; and Sir John Leach declared, although the testator might have made the annuity determinable by the bankruptcy of his son, yet, as he had not done that, the policy of the law did not permit property to be so limited, that it should continue in the enjoyment of the donee, notwithstanding his bankruptcy; and therefore that the annuity passed under the commission. In the case of *Piercy* v. *Roberts*, 1 *Mylne and Keen* 4, there was a discretion given to the trustee, but it was held not to make a difference. It was a bequest of £400 to executors, upon trust to pay the same to a son, in such smaller or larger portions, at such time or times, and in such way or manner, as they should in their judgment and discretion think best, and, upon the insolvency of the son, Sir John Leach, then Master of the Rolls, said, that the legacy could not remain in the hands of the executors, to be applied at their discretion, for the benefit of the legatee. He held that the discretion of the executors determined by the insolvency of the son, and the legacy passed by the assignment; for the insolvent being substantially entitled to the legacy, the attempt to continue in him the enjoyment of it, notwithstanding his insolvency, was in fraud of the law. In *Snowden* v. *Dales*, 6 Sim. 524, the language of the will is still stronger against any absolute right in the donee. It was an assignment of a sum of money, in trust during the life of J. D. H., or during such part thereof as the trustees should think proper, and at their will and pleasure and not otherwise, and, at such times and in such sums as they should think proper, to pay the interest to him, or, if they should think fit, to pay it in procuring for him diet, apparel and other necessaries, but so that he should not have any right or title in or to such interest, other than the trustees should, in their absolute and uncontrolled power, discretion, and inclination, think proper and expedient, and so as no creditor of his should have any lien or claim thereon, in any case; or the same be in any way liable to his debts, and disposition, or engagements—with a limitation over upon his death. The Vice Chancellor, Sir Lancelot Shadwell, admitted it to be plain, the grantor did intend to exclude assignees in bankruptcy. and that it might have been effected, if there had been a clear gift over; but he said as there was no direction to the trustees, upon the bankruptcy of J. D. H., to withhold and accumulate the interest during his life, so as to go over with the capital upon his death, that the life interest of the bankrupt went to the assignees.

The foregoing cases sufficiently establish, that by the use of no terms or art can property be given to a man, or to another for him, so that he may continue to enjoy it, or derive any benefit from it, as the interest, or his maintenance thereout or the like, and at the same time defy his creditors and deny them satisfaction thereout. The thing is impossible. As long as the property is his, it must, as an incident, be subject to his debts, provided, only, that it be tangible. The only manner in which creditors can be excluded, is to exclude the debtor also from all benefit from, or interest in, the property, by such a limitation, upon the contingency of his bankruptcy or insolvency, as will determine his interest, and make it go to some other person. It follows, that the interests of Anderson Mebane are liable to the plaintiff's satisfaction, and that they must be sold for that purpose, unless, within a reasonable time, the plaintiff's debt should be otherwise paid. But, of course, the trustee is entitled, first, to be re-imbursed out of the fund any expenditures made by him *bona fide*, and his costs in this cause; and, in order to ascertain what may be thus due, and also what may remain due on the plaintiff's judgment for principal, interest, and costs, and his costs in this Court, there must be an enquiry by the Master.

PER CURIAM.   Decree accordingly.

––––––––

JAMES B. HAWKINS vs. MICAJAH T. J. ALSTON & AL.

When property is conveyed by a deed of trust to satisfy certain alleged debts, and the parties stand in a near relation to each other, as father and son, or brothers, and the deed is impeached for fraud, it is incumbent on the parties to offer something more than the naked bond of the one to the other, as evidence of the alleged indebtedness, especially when the bond is followed, immediately after its execution, by the deed of trust.

And more especially will the Court, when a bill is filed by a creditor to set aside such conveyance, refuse to admit the validity of the bond so attempted to be secured, when the parties, being particularly interrogated, decline or refuse to set forth, fully and sufficiently, what was the consideration of the bond.

A bond may be voluntary, and such an one, though binding between the parties, cannot stand before other debts arising out of contracts for value.

Sales by execution must be made before the return of the writ, without respect to price, because the mandate of the writ is peremptory; but the obligations of a trustee are not precisely like those of a Sheriff. A trustee, under a deed of trust conveying property for the purpose of a sale to pay debts, is charged with the interests of both parties, and ought not, except under very special circumstances, to sell at an enormous sacrifice.

Cause removed from the Court of Equity of Warren County, at the Fall Term, 1845.

The case as exhibited by the pleadings and process, was as follows:

On the 31st day of January, 1843, the defendant, Micajah T. J. Alston, by a deed, to which he and the defendants, Spencer H. Alston and Christopher B. Allen were parties, conveyed to the said Allen all his property, real and personal, consisting of eleven slaves, which he owned absolutely and in severalty, of a negro woman named Caroline, of whom the said Micajah owned three undivided fourths, and the said Allen owned the other fourth, and of three other slaves, being a woman and her two children, which the said Micajah owned for the term of his life: The said effects conveyed, consisted further of all the said Micajah's household and kitchen furniture, namely, 4 beds, bedsteads and furniture, a cradle and cradle bed, 2 tables, 1 press, 1 dozen chairs, looking glass, dishes, plates, knives and forks, cups and saucers, pots, pans, and ovens, and six old trunks; also, 3 head of horses, 8 head of cattle, 1 waggon, corn and fodder, 4 cows, and 21 pigs, and also the plantation on which Micajah lived, which he had leased for the year 1843, and a negro boy whom he had hired for the same period, and about 1,200 or 1,500 lbs. of bacon: upon trust to secure and pay certain debts therein recited to be owing from the said Micajah to the said Spencer, that is to say, one debt of $284 47, due by bond dated the 20th of July, 1841; one other of $54 34, due by bond bearing date the 15th of December, 1842; one other debt of $1,475 60, by bond bearing date the 30th day of January, 1843, and payable one day after date; and one other of $408, or thereabouts, besides interest, due on a bond, given by the said Micajah as principal and Spencer as surety, to John H. Alston, which had then been due about a year; with power and directions to the trustee, in case Micajah should fail to pay all those debts on or before the 1st day of March, 1843, at the request of Spencer, to sell the property to the highest bidder for ready money, having first advertised the time and place of sale fourteen days, and out of the proceeds of sale discharge the expenses and debts, and then pay the surplus to Micajah or his order. Spencer H. Alston is the brother of Micajah and Allen his brother-in-law.

At the time of making the deed, the defendant, Micajah, was indebted to the plaintiff, Hawkins, on his bond, then due, for $500, the price of land sold him ; on which the plaintiff instituted suit, in which he recovered judgment in October, 1843, for the principal sum, and $36 for interest, besides costs.   The plaintiff then issued a *fieri facias*, on which the Sheriff returned *nulla bona* to April, 1844 ; and thereupon, the plaintiff filed this bill against the said Micajah and Spencer, and the said Allen, and therein states that he cannot obtain satisfaction of any part of his debt, unless it be out of the effects so owned by Micajah and conveyed to Allen, and charges that the said conveyance was intended to delay and hinder him of the recovery of his debt, and prays that the same may be declared fraudulent and void against him, and that satisfaction may be decreed to him out of the property, or out of the proceeds or value thereof in the hands of Allen and Spencer H. Alston.   The bill charges, that the value of the property conveyed was more than sufficient to pay all the just debts of the said Micajah, if fairly disposed of; but that Micajah declared, that he would never pay the debt to the plaintiff, and he executed the deed in question with the express intention to defeat the plaintiff, and upon a contrivance between the three parties to it to encumber and cover all Micajah's property with that view : And, as evidence thereof, the bill further charges, that the debts mentioned in the deed of trust were not due from Micajah to his brother Spencer, or, if any part of them was due, it did not exceed one half the amount therein mentioned : And, furthermore, that in a short time after the deed was made, namely, on the 10th of April, 1843, while the plaintiff was prosecuting his suit, the defendants proceeded to make a pretended sale of the property conveyed, at the residence of Micajah, in the country, without due notice, and when but few persons were present ; and that, at the sale, the defendant, Spencer, purchased all the negroes and the other property without competition, and for very low prices, much below the true value, and not amounting to the debts recited in the deed.

The bill charges, that the few persons, who were present at
the sale, were induced not to bid by the belief, that the sale
was a matter of family arrangement, and that such belief
was produced by the contrivance and conduct of the defendants or some of them; and that in fact the defendant,
Spencer, having no bid against him, purchased at his own
prices, not exceeding one third of the value of the property, and that, notwithstanding such ruinous sacrifices,
the said Allen did not suspend the sale, nor did the said
Micajah request him to do so, but the sale proceeded upon
a previous design of those parties, until the said Spencer
bought every thing in, upon the terms mentioned. The
bill further charges, that the purchases of the defendant,
Spencer, were intended for the benefit of his brother Micajah and upon a secret trust for him, while the property
should, at the same time, be covered from the claims of
the plaintiff and his other creditors; and that, in fact, all
the property or nearly all of it continued in the possession
and enjoyment of the said Micajah after the sale as before, during the year 1843, and that then the defendants
Spencer and Micajah removed the slaves out of this State
to parts unknown, and the said Micajah was preparing
to remove himself and his family, and settling where the
slaves had been carried. The bill further charges, that,
if the said Spencer did not purchase wholly in trust for
Micajah, yet that he did so, as to all the property that
might remain after Spencer should, by re-sales of part of
it, or otherwise, be satisfied for the debt really due to him,
if any; and that he has been thus satisfied and yet holds
slaves, money and other things in trust for Micajah, to a
greater value than the principal money, interest, and costs
due to the plaintiffs. The bill then specially interro-
gates the defendants as to the several matters charged,
and, particularly, what debts Micajah owed Spencer,
when and how contracted, and upon what considerations
respectively: why Micajah conveyed so much property,
being all he had, to secure the debt, if any, to his brother,

when much less than half of it was of value sufficient, if fairly sold, to pay the debts mentioned in the deed, even if the said debts were all just: what was the value of the several slaves and other property, what the said Spencer gave for them, whether the prices were not less than half the values, and how it happened that he was able to purchase at such a great under value all the slaves and other effects: why Allen, the trustee, continued the sale, when he discovered the property was selling so greatly below its value: whether the sale was thus continued with the acquiescence of Micajah, or whether he made request to his brother or the trustee to defer the sale until better prices could be had: And whether, in fine, it was not intended, that Micajah should still have the enjoyment of the property purchased by his brother, or some part of it, and whether the purchase was not for the benefit of Micajah, either in whole or in part.

The defendants answered together. Allen, the trustee, states that he had no interest in the subject matter of the controversy, and that he was merely trustee; that he supposed the debts mentioned in the deed to be true debts, and that, after due advertisement at several public places, he made the sale, for the purpose of satisfying those debts, upon the terms prescribed in the deed. All the defendants state that it was conducted in the usual manner of sales to the highest bidder for ready money, and fairly, and without any attempt by any or either of them to prevent competition or induce other persons not to bid. They annex to their answer an account of the sales of the property, from which it appears that the defendant Spencer purchased every thing that was sold, at prices, which amounted in the whole, to the sum of $1,740 50. The price of a woman Hester and her child was, for example, $250; that of a boy Trim, $22; that of three-fourths of Caroline, $150; that of a boy George, $50; those of woman Grace and her two sons, for the life of Micajah, $125; and those of other negroes in proportion. The prices of four beds, bed-steads and furniture, amounted to $17 50 ; of a wagon and harness, $10 ; of three horses, $15 ; and 8 head of cattle, $10 ; and of 500 lb. of bacon $20. The answers admits, that the prices, might be something below the value of the property, but not so much below it as is charged in the bill.

The defendants. Mieajah and Spencer, state, that the debts from the former to the latter were due upon bonds, as described in the deed ; and that said bonds were exe-cuted in part for moneys advanced by said Spencer, at different times, either as loans to said Micajah, or to pay debts for him, or for debts for which the said Spencer was bound as surety for Micajah ; all of which they aver were justly due and remained unpaid at the time of exe-cuting the said deed of trust. They further answer, that the conveyance was made with the view of certainly se-curing the payment of those debts. and not to cover Mi-cajah's property or to defeat the plaintiff or any other creditor : And they deny that Spencer purchased any part of the property. upon any secret trust. or otherwise, for the use or benefit of Micajah, or that there was any agreement or understanding to that effect, either when the deed was executed, or at the sale, or at any other time ; and they say, that Spencer purchased *bona fide* for his own use and benefit alone, and that the defendant, Spencer, is under no promise, nor in any way bound, in consequence of his purchases, to render any aid or as-sistance to his brother Micajah, but that such aid and as-sistance as he may render him, will be voluntary on his part.

Replication was taken to the answer, and the parties proceeded to proofs. It was sufficiently established, that notice was given of the time and place of sale as re-quired in the deed ; and that the whole sale took place at the residence of Micajah Alston, in Halifax, and was at-tended by about five and twenty persons. among whom were three persons, Mr. Bachelor, and Mr. Marcus A.

Allen, and Mr. J. N. Faulcon, who were creditors of Micajah Alston—of whom the former has not, and the two latter have been, examined in the cause. One or two low bids were made during the sale by other persons, but there was no serious competition against Spencer Alston for any thing, and he purchased all at the prices specified in the account of sales set forth in the answer. Four or five witnesses, who were at the sale, say that they saw nothing unfair in conducting it, and that the articles were exposed and cried openly and sufficiently. and that there were some persons present, who pursued the business of buying and selling slaves, and that no persuasion or other means were used by either of the defendants, as known to or discovered by the witnesses, to induce any person not to bid. Two witnesses for the plaintiff state, however, that an impression prevailed in the company, that the property was to be purchased, in part at least, for the benefit of Micajah Alston, and one of those witnesses, Marcus A. Allen, says that was his own impression, produced from the manner of the sale, and from the declaration of Micajah to him, " that he might rest satisfied ; for that, notwithstanding the sale, his debt should be paid"—which prevented him from bidding. All the witnesses state, that the property sold very low, and several of them say, for not more than half price. W. Skinner, a witness for the defendants, deposes that he was present at the sale, and that, as far as he is a judge of sales, this was fairly conducted. But he says the negroes sold very low ; that, before he left the place, he gave Spencer Alston $337 50 for 3-4ths of Caroline, for whom the latter had given that day $150 ; that the negroes, to which Micajah was entitled in severalty and absolutely, were worth $2,050, and that the woman and two boys (of whom one was 13 years old,) to which he was entitled for life, were worth $800, if he had owned the absolute property ; that Micajah continued in possession of all the negroes and other property, except

Caroline, until the latter part of the year 1843, when Spencer Alston sold to the witness, Hester and her child, at the price of $500, and the boy Trim at the price of $400, and sold another woman and child to some other person, but at what price he did not know ; and that he sent the remaining negroes, except one, to the South, by John Alston, a brother of the parties, and that one was taken by Micajah. who also removed from this State, but to what parts the witness does not know.

The defendants also offered evidence of the debts mentioned in the deed of trust. That, to John H. Alston is admitted by the plaintiff, and appears to have been due on a bond for $404 86 dated 19th October, 1841, given by Micajah and by Spencer as his surety, and to have been paid by Spencer, June 13th, 1844. The defendants further proved three bonds given by Micajah to Spencer, of the dates and for the sums mentioned in the deed. Neither of them has a subscribing witness. and the proof is by the hand writing of the obligor. It is established that the defendant, Spencer, on the 9th of March, 1841, gave his bond to Yarborough and Perry for a store account or bond of $239 83, which Micajah Alston owed them, and that he paid it in August following. It is stated by several witnesses, that Micajah was a younger brother of the defendant Spencer, and that he made Spencer's house his home for about four years, from 1834 to 1839, except about one year, during which he was absent in Mississippi in 1837 or 1838, and that, just before he set out on that trip, he purchased a horse from Spencer at the price of $150 ; and that in 1841 or 1842, after Micajah's marriage, he purchased a horse from another person at the price of $175, to discharge which his brother Spencer advanced $75, and gave his note for the residue, as Micajah told a witness. It is also stated by two or three witnesses, that Micajah Alston said, that, when he wanted money, he was in the habit of applying to his brother Spencer and that he supplied him, and that sometimes Micajah said, he owed his brother a large debt and then would deny that he owed him much.

W. H. Haywood, for the plaintiff.
Saunders, for the defendants.

RUFFIN, C. J. If the grounds, upon which the bill impeaches the transactions between the defendants, be founded in facts, there can be no hesitation in holding, that they amount to a fraud in law against the plaintiff, as a creditor. For no device can be more deceptive and more likely to baffle, delay, or defeat creditors, than the creating incumbrances upon their property by embarrassed men, for debts that are fictitious or mainly so. The false pretence of a debt, or the designed exaggeration of one, is an act of direct fraud. That is one of the allegations of the bill against this deed.

Another is, that property. to a much greater value than the alleged debt from the one brother. to the other, was conveyed, and that this was done with the design, that, before the plaintiff could get a judgment, the property should be brought to a sale, so conducted as to enable the defendant, Spencer, to buy it at prices far below its value, as a mode by which, under the form of a public sale, *prima facie* fair, the one brother's property could become vested in the other, without an adequate valuable consideration, or by which the one should get the title, apparently for himself, but in reality upon some confidence for the maker of the deed. And there can be no doubt, allowing even the whole debt mentioned in the deed to have been owing, that the conveyance of property to secure it, and with the further intentions supposed, would be fraudulent, for the want of *bona fides*. It would be an attempt by a debtor, so far as the value of the property exceeded the debt, indirectly to convey it to a friend, voluntarily and without valuable considera-

48

tion; or, in the other point of view, it would be a conveyance to enable the creditor, under cover of obtaining payment of his debt, to make purchases either wholly, or in part, upon a secret trust for the debtor. Such a contrivance, if directly proved, amounts to express fraud; and, if to be fairly collected from the conduct of the parties, and the attendant and subsequent circumstances, the same consequences must follow. It is calculated to deceive the world by putting the title out of the debtor, and vesting it in the purchaser, pretendedly for the sole use of the latter, so as to exempt the property from execution, while the debtor is to enjoy, in some way, a benefit from the profits, or, perhaps, the possession of at least part of the property. It is, then, to be considered, whether the allegations of the bill are sustained by proofs or rational presumptions.

Upon the point of the indebtedness of Micajah Alston to his brother Spencer, the Court is obliged to say, the defendants have not given satisfactory evidence; and that there are very strong grounds of suspicion against it, and, especially, as to its amount, or any thing near it. The debt to John H. Alston, for which Spencer was surety, appears to have been nearly as stated in the deed. That is the only debt, the origin and amount of which are established with any certainty. The others are stated to be due to Spencer himself, on three bonds, as follows: One, of July 20th, 1841, for $284 47; a second, of December 15th, 1842, for $54 34; and the third, of January 30th, 1843, for $1,475 60—making, in all, the sum of $1,814 41. The bonds have no subscribing witness, and are proved merely by the hand-writing of the obligor. The deed was executed on the day after the last bond was given.

Transactions of this kind, between near relations, are naturally so much more the objects of suspicion, than those between strangers, that it is to be expected that parties, when father and son, or brothers, should offer something more than the naked bond of the one to the other, as evidence of the alleged indebtedness. especially when the bond is executed recently, and followed immediately by a deed of trust for all the debtor's property. A bond may be voluntary, and such an one, though binding between the parties, cannot stand before other debts arising out of contracts for value. Rev. St. c. 50, s. 1. *Lachnere* v. *Earl of Carlisle*, 3 Pr. Wms. 211. *Jones* v, *Powell*, 1 Eq. Cas. Abr. 84. Indeed, it may be fabricated for the occasion of creating the encumbrance, as an obstacle to *bona fide* creditors. Therefore, all persons may be called on to offer some probable proof of dealings, out of which a debt might have arisen to the amount of the bonds produced or approaching it; and, especially, persons very nearly connected ought to be provided with stronger evidence on those points. It is an act of but common precaution, which every man owes to his own character, when a bond is executed between brothers for such a sum as $1,475 60, under such circumstances, and upon a settlement, as alleged, for previous dealings running through several years, that the parties should come to their settlement in the presence of disinterested third persons, capable of understanding and proving what, in fact, were the subject matters of the settlement, so as to afford other creditors the opportunity of investigating the correctness both of the charges and the credits in it. Indeed, in the ordinary course of business, no one lets accounts run up to such sums without some entry in a book or some statement of the items on paper. It can hardly be possible, that all the items in dealings for so long a period as nine years, from 1834 to 1843, should have all been on one side. Therefore, some account must have been stated between these parties, as the basis for the bond of $1475 60; which the defendants ought to have been able to identify by an indifferent witness, or, at least, to have produced and verified by their own oath. But there is no witness to that point, nor document of that kind; which certainly could not fail to excite surprise, as very extraordinary, if the settlement was a real settlement between debtor and creditor, in which each stood up for his rights. Instead of that, there is nothing but the three bonds; neither of which was ever seen, or heard of by any one else, as far as appears, until the execution of the deed. There is an attempt, however, to prove by witnesses, that there have been, in former times, some dealings between the brothers, on which Micajah became the debtor of Spencer. It appears, that in March, 1841, the latter did assume for the former, a debt to Yarborough and Perry for $239 83. We are not informed why that was done. It does not appear that the creditors suspected Micajah's credit, but merely that Spencer took the debt on himself. The legal inference would be, perhaps, that he was thereby paying a debt of his own to his brother. But admit it to be otherwise; and that may account for the first bond of $284 47, of July 20th, 1841. If that bond included the payment to Y. and P. the debt may be assumed to be that far just. But there the case hangs, we believe. There is no probable proof to uphold the other bonds. It is, indeed, stated that, in 1841 or 1842, Micajah purchased a horse in the neighborhood for $175, and that he said his brother lent him $75 at the time for a payment in part, and gave his bond to the seller for the residue. But no reason has been given, why the seller of the horse has not been examined to prove these facts, instead of relying on Micajah's declarations alone. Again it is stated, that, between 1834 and 1839, Micajah lived in his brother's family about four years, for which $500 would be a moderate charge, and that, in 1836 or 1837, he purchased a horse from Spencer at $150. Upon that, several observations may be made. It does not appear that Spencer intended to charge board. Nothing was ever said by either of the brothers to that effect. If Spencer intended to make the other pay for board, as he, no doubt, did for the horse, it is hardly possible that he should have waited until January, 1843, without receiving any payment on account, or taking a bond for those demands, as he had, in the meanwhile, done for the other of $284 47. It must strike one, therefore, as highly probable, that there were mutual dealings, and those demands—if that for board ever existed—were satisfied in account. But there is another objection to all these last items, which is insuperable under the circumstances. It is, that the defendants, who knew the fact perfectly, and were called on to state it on this point particularly, would, not venture to swear in their answers, that any part of the sums for which the bonds are given, was for the horse sold, or for board. The bill charges, that the debts or the greater part of them, were not really owing, and therefore, that the principal bond of $1,475 60 was devised of express covin; and it proceeds further to interrogate the defendant specially, what debts Micajah owed Spencer, when and how contracted, and upon what considerations. Now, although the defendants had been incautious enough to act without a witness to their dealings, yet, when the opportunity was thus afforded them for offering full explanation, and making their answers, responsive to the charges and interrogatories of the bill, evidence for them, one could not have expected less than that they would have gone into the matter, in detail, stated the account on both sides particularly, and accounted for the delay in taking the bonds. But instead of such a narrative, not equivocal nor evasive, but full and direct, as they could have given, and. if the bonds were fair, would probably have given, the answer only states, that the debts were due upon bonds, as described in the deed; that they were justly due, and remained unpaid when the deed was executed; and that " the said bonds were executed in part for money advanced by said Spencer at different times. either as loans to Micajah, or to pay debts for him, or for debts for which the said Spen-

cer was bound as surety for him." It is obvious, that this
is no answer to the points on which the discovery was
sought. The defendants say the bonds were unpaid; and
no doubt that is true. They say also, that they were
justly due; which may likewise be true, in a certain
sense—that is, as between themselves, although they
were in the main voluntary bonds. The true enquiry is,
whether the debts were justly due as opposed to other
debts, that were *bona fide;* that is, whether they were
true debts, that arose entirely upon real contracts. And
upon that essential point, the answer is, " that the bonds
were *in part* for money lent or advanced." But what
part, to whom it was paid, or when, is not disclosed; and
for the other parts of the debts, besides the money, the
answer assigns no cause but the bonds themselves. Five
shillings lent or paid by Spencer, would satisfy the answer
and save the defendants from the penalties of a false
statement, touching the considerations of these bonds.
There is no suggestion that the price of board or of a
horse was included in them. The defendants would not
make that statement, and therefore they cannot ask the
Court to give them the benefit of remote probabilities,
founded on the testimony of witnesses with imperfect information on the subject, when they, themselves, in whose
knowledge the whole matter is, refuse, though demanded,
to give any answer whatever. They do not even attempt
to explain, why the bond for the small small sum of $54 84
was taken so recently as December 15th, 1842, if, at that
time, the pretended debtor owed the other large debt of
$1,475 60, for which he gave a bond January 30th, 1843;
nor is it intimated, that this large debt arose upon any
intermediate transaction.

The truth is, then, that there is not evidence, upon which
a rational reliance can be placed, to sustain the debts of
$54 84, and $1,475 60. The bonds themselves, being executed to a brother by an embarrassed man on the eve of insolvency, as alleged by the parties, and with a view to found

on them an immediate conveyance of all his property, are entirely insufficient to establish the *bona fides* of the debt, and require the aid of extrinsic proof of the probable justice of it, which does not exist in this case.

The opinion of the Court on the foregoing point is sufficient to dispose of the cause. But we think it our duty to the cause of fair dealing and the justice due to creditors to say, that our opinion is equally strong against the defendants upon the other parts of the case. There are seldom collected more circumstances, than are here presented, of grave suspicion, that the deed and sale under it were not *bona fide*, with the intent to pay a debt, but, under color thereof, to provide for the grantor through favor of the preferred creditor; or, at all events, to defeat another creditor, as one of the primary motives for making the deed. The debtor and creditor are brothers; the trustee is a brother in law; the deed conveys every thing the grantor had on earth, down to his wife's bed and his child's cradle, and the most trifling articles, as old trunks; with a provision for an early sale, before the present plaintiff could recover his judgment; an actual sale in little more than two months, at which every thing was, without complaint on the part of the debtor, bought by the secured creditor at grossly inadequate prices; and, with the exception of one negro woman, the former owner retained possession of all the property for about eight months after the sale, when the plaintiff was getting into a situation to seize it; and then some of it was sold to third persons and the residue partly spent by Spencer Alston and partly carried by Micajah out of the State. These facts, which are unquestionable, raise a conclusive presumption in a mind, at all familiar with real fair dealings among mankind, that the conveyance was made for the purpose of turning over the debtor's property without an adequate consideration to his brother, thereby to defeat other creditors, and, probably upon a secret confidence for himself, to some extent at least. The subsequent possession and enjoyment of the property by the debtor serves strongly to establish those intents. It is not now held to be conclusive of the fraud, as a matter of law it is true. Nevertheless, it is a very cogent sign of bad faith in every case, and in the present case is in the highest degree evidence of it. A person may naturally enough convey property to secure a particular creditor, from whom he wishes forbearance, in the hope of paying the debt without a sale. So a person, who is insolvent, may probably assign his property with a view to an immediate sale, where a number of creditors are provided for, whose interest it will be to compete in bidding, so that the effects shall bring their value and exonerate the debtor as far as possible. But here is a case, which shews views of the parties of quite a contrary nature from either of the foregoing. There was but a single person provided for, and that by means of a deed authorizing a sale at a very short day. Why was that? If the object was really to pay the debt, and nothing more, why did not the parties at once agree upon a sale, at a fair price, of enough for that purpose? The reason for an assignment of the whole property, instead of a sale of part, upon those terms, is but too easily given. If there had been a sale at fair prices, there would have been a residue of the property left in the debtor, and exposed to execution. If it had been at grossly inadequate prices between brothers, it would have been easily questioned, and could not stand the trial, especially where the pretended debtor retained the enjoyment after the alleged sale. But sales to the highest bidder have an appearance of fairness as to price, which renders it more difficult to ferret out a fraud in them; although it is obvious that a preferred creditor has a great advantage over other bidders, by not being obliged to advance money at the time, and if he can collude with the trustee, by fixing the time and place of sale; and the retaining of possession for a period is not so conclusive of a secret trust. The sale under a deed of trust may thus really be devised, as a better

cover and mode of effecting a conveyance to the creditor
at an under value, or in secret trust for the debtor. Such
a motive for this deed, as it appears to the Court, must
be inferred from the circumstances under which it was
executed, its provisions in favor of a single person, and
for so speedy a sale, the mode of conducting the sale, and
the continued enjoyment by the debtor afterwards. Spencer Alston bought every thing; and, according to the evidence, at about half price, or less. That is beyond contradiction; for, within that year, he sold four negroes for
$1,237 50, for which he gave $620; and one of them he
sold on the spot for $337 50, for which he gave $150.
Now, this is said, in the answer, to have been a fair sale;
and it is called so, because it was a public sale, and neither of the parties persuaded persons not to bid. The
witnesses, for the same reasons, say, that as far as they
are judges of such matters, it was fair. But they must
estimate the morals involved in such cases, very loosely,
if they hold this transaction fair. It is true, that sales
by execution must be made before the return of the writ,
without regard to price, because the mandate of the writ
is peremptory. But the obligations of a trustee are not
precisely like those of a Sheriff. He is selected by the
parties, and is charged with the interests of both, and
ought not to sell at an enormous sacrifice, as in this
case—at all events, he ought not, unless under very special circumstances. Now, suppose the present plaintiff
and the other creditors of Micajah Alston had been secured in this deed, instead of Spencer Alston; would
Micajah have stood by, a silent and heedless spectator of
a sale, at which the creditor was buying, without competition, at his own half prices, all the property he meant
to take and keep? Would he not certainly have urged
the trustee to adjourn the sale to some time and place
where bidders might be had? And would not the trustee—
an impartial and fair man, not to speak of his being a
brother-in-law—as certainly have done so? Then, why

49

was not this sale stopped? The answer is plain: the sale was going on precisely as the debtor, the creditor, and the trustee—all three near relations—wished, and from the beginning intended it should. So far from complaining of the ruin brought on him, Micajah Alston said to one of his other creditors, who is the only one examined to the point, that, notwithstanding the sale then proceeding, he would pay his debt. and accordingly he still kept the property, and thus had the means of paying him, if he would. Micajah Alston was unquestionably willing that his brother should purchase at the prices he did, and that, the spectators felt and acquiesced in, rather than offend neighbors. It is impossible that Micajah Alston could have been willing to such a sale, if it had not been to his brother, and if he had not expected a benefit from it, and to defeat the present plaintiff. The witnesses may, perhaps, have meant, when they called it a fair sale, that it was so in respect of Micajah Alston, as he assented to it. But as respects that person's creditors, it was not a fair sale, but a most unfair one—devised and conducted with the view of disposing of his property, not at a fair price in satisfaction of a just debt, but, under cover of a sale for that purpose, to get the property, or much of it, into the hands of his brother for his own use. It is true, these defendants deny, that there was any agreement or understanding between them, that Spencer should purchase in trust for Micajah, or that he is bound or under promise to render him assistance ; and they say that such assistance is altogether voluntary. No doubt that is in form, at least, true ; for there never is, upon such occasions, a plain and express declaration of trust, which, indeed, would defeat the objects in view by placing in the debtor an admitted interest, that would plainly be subject to his debts. Therefore, the purpose always is, that the purchaser shall appear to be the exclusive owner, and that the rights of the grantor shall rest in mere personal confidence between the parties, and dependent upon the pleasure of the grantor. It is that very circumstance that constitutes the fraud, where it is collected that the deed was made, because the grantor thereby expected a profit or benefit to himself from such pleasure and favor of the grantee ; while his creditors cannot reach that interest in any way. And the facts attending the sale, and the subsequent enjoyment of the property by the grantor, naturally reflect back on the previous parts of the transaction, and open to view the motives for making the deed.

The deed must, for these reasons, be declared fraudulent and void, as against the plaintiff. As parts of the property have been sold by the defendant, Spencer, for more than sufficient to pay the plaintiff's debt, and the residue removed beyond the process of the law, and Micajah Alston is insolvent, except in respect of this property, and has removed from the State, the plaintiff is entitled to a decree against the defendant, Spencer, directly, for payment of the principal, interest and costs of his judgment at law ; which may be ascertained by an enquiry. We suppose this will be sufficient, as there is no suggestion to the contrary. But, if the money should not be raised from him, liberty is reserved to the plaintiff to move for further directions in respect to the liability of the defendant, Allen. The defendants must pay the costs.

PER CURIAM.   Decree accordingly.

JORDAN COUNCILL *vs.* A. Y. WALTON & AL.

Where there are two defendants in a bill of injunction, and one of them answers that he is ignorant of the facts charged, the Court will not hear a motion to dissolve the injunction, until the answer of the other defendant is put in.

Appeal from an interlocutory order of the Court of Equity of Ashe County, at the Fall Term, 1845, his Honor

Judge BAILEY presiding, which order directed the injunction to be continued, refusing a motion to dissolve it.

The following case was presented by the pleadings:

The plaintiff charges, that, in February 1839, he and one David E. Bowers, his partner, became indebted to the mercantile firm of A. Y. Walton and J. W. Y. Walton, of Charleston, South Carolina, which was conducted in the name of J. W. Y. Walton, and gave the note of the firm for the amount, to-wit, $344 65. At the time of giving this note, the plaintiff transferred, by endorsement, to the two Waltons, a note which he held on one John Clark for two hundred dollars, to be applied, when collected, in part discharge of his note: the said Clark being a citizen of Charleston. In the year 1842, he was again in Charleston, and the firm of Walton and Walton having been dissolved, he was called on by their clerk to give a new note, which he at first declined doing, unless he received a credit for the Clark note, which the agent of the Waltons declined giving, as he knew nothing about it; and the plaintiff at his earnest solicitation and repeated assurance, that he would see his principals and enter the credit, gave his note for the full amount, having full and entire confidence in the integrity of J. W. Y. Walton, with whom he had been doing business many years. The principals were both absent from the city at that time, and John Clark assured the agent, that he had paid his note to the principals at maturity. In 1843, being in Charleston, he endeavored to have the matter arranged, but J. W. Y. Walton being dead, and A. Y. Walton too unwell to do business, he failed in doing so. Thomas Walton, the defendant, is the administrator of J. W. Y. Walton, and, having obtained possession of the note, brought suit against him and obtained judgment for the full amount, principal and interest. In March, 1844, previous to the said judgment being obtained, A. Y. Walton, at his instance, wrote to the defendant, Thomas Walton, to suspend the collection of the $200, as there was an entry, on the books of the firm, of the transfer of Clark's note to them. At the time the judgment was obtained, as he was informed by his counsel, the letter of A. Y. Walton was mislaid, and not being able to ascertain the exact amount of the credit, it was agreed by his counsel, that the judgment should be taken for the full amount, upon the promise of Thomas Walton, that, when the letter was found, the credit should be entered; afterwards, when the letter was found, the defendant, Thomas Walton, refused to permit the credit to be entered, unless the plaintiff would produce a receipt from A. Y. Walton. The judgment has all been paid but the amount of the Clark note. The plaintiff prayed and obtained an injunction for that amount.

The defendant, A. Y. Walton, did not answer. The defendant, Thomas Walton, while he does not admit that A. Y. Walton was a partner with J. W. Y. Walton, does not deny it, but does admit that most of the capital was advanced by A. Y. Walton, and, that when the establishment was dissolved, it was agreed between the partners, that A. Y. Walton should take all the debts due the firm, &c., and pay to J. W. Y. Walton a certain amount of money for his interest in, and services in conducting, the business. He admits the death of J. W. Y. Walton, and that he is his administrator; the bringing of the action and the obtaining of the judgment. He admits, that, while the suit was pending, the letter of A. Y. Walton was shown to him by the defendant's counsel, who required that a credit should be entered for the Clark note, which he refused, upon the ground that he was not so instructed by the letter of A. Y. Walton. He denies all knowledge of the Clark note, or that he agreed, when judgment was obtained, to allow the credit when the letter was found, but that he did agree, if an absolute receipt could be procured or produced from the said A. Y. Walton, that it should be allowed. Denies any such receipt has been produced, and admits the payment by the plaintiff of all the judgment, except the amount of the Clark note.

Upon the coming in of the answer, a motion to dissolve the injunction was refused; from which decree the defendant appealed.

Dodge, for the plaintiff.
Avery and *Boyden,* for the defendant.

NASH. J. This case is now before this Court on the motion to dissolve the injunction. The equity of the plaintiff is so manifest from the defendant's answer, that we do not hesitate to refuse the motion. The bill charges, that A. Y. Walton and J. W. Y. Walton were partners. This averment is not denied by the defendant, but he answers it by saying, that " A. Y. Walton was not known or recognized as a partner." We consider the answer in this particular, as evasive and disingenuous. Again, he admits, that most of the capital was advanced by A. Y. Walton, upon some arrangements between them, the *exact* nature and terms whereof, he does not know ; and, further, when the *establishment* was broken up, that the amount of the sale of stock, &c., the debts due the said *concern,* and all the effects appertaining thereto, should be taken and belong to A. Y. Walton. It is impossible not to see from the answer, that the two Waltons were partners. By the law, A. Y. Walton, as surviving partner, was entitled to the note of the plaintiff, and he was entitled to it also, by the agreement, as set forth in the answer. As, however, it was made payable to J. W. Y. Walton singly, the action was well brought in the name of his administrator ; but in collecting it, the defendant, Thomas Walton. was the agent of A. Y. Walton, who had a right to control and direct him in so doing. He is informed by A. Y. Walton, by letter, before the judgment is obtained, that upon looking over *our* ledger, there is a memorandum of the payment of the Clark note, and directing him to stay collecting the amount of the two hundred dollars. This direction from his principal, if not at law, at least so considered in this Court, he refuses to obey, upon the flimsy pretext that it is not an absolute receipt. We consider the answer as confirming the plaintiff's equity. And the defendant, T. Walton, had no right to ask the Court to dissolve the injunction upon his answer alone, as he professes to know nothing about the matter. The other defendant does not answer, and the matters upon which the plaintiff's equity rests, are within his knowledge, and, before the dissolution of the injunction, the plaintiff has a right to his answer, and the production of the books, in which the entry of the receipt of the Clark note was made.

The interlocutory decree of the Court below is affirmed, and the defendant, Thomas Walton, must pay the costs of this Court.

Per Curiam.   Decree accordingly.

RICHMOND NAIL vs. THOMAS S. MARTIN.

Though it is the usual course, in a suit brought by a *cestui que trust* against his trustee, for an account of the trust fund, to order a reference, yet such reference will not be ordered, when objected to by the trustee, where it appears satisfactorily on the hearing, that there is nothing due from the trustee.

Pleadings ought to be plainly written, and the words spelt in full and without contractions, especially papers that are sworn to. If papers of a different description are sent to this Court, the Court will put the parties to the expense of making fair copies, and perhaps order the originals to be taken off the file, or dismiss the suit.

Cause removed from the Court of Equity of Davie County, at the Fall Term, 1845.

The plaintiff was indebted to Christian Sheek in the sum of $2000, for which Thomas Foster was surety;

likewise to several other persons in considerable sums,
for which Foster and James F. Martin were his sureties,
or one of them was; and to Foster himself in the sum
of $500, and to Martin in the sum of $250, and to other
persons. Being so indebted, he executed on the 4th day
of May, 1840, to the defendant, Thomas S. Martin, an
assignment of all his property, in trust to secure, and, by
a sale, to pay, the debts above mentioned. Among the
estates conveyed was Nail's "interest in a lot and steam
saw-mill in Mocksville," which was subject to an encumbrance for the debt to Christian Sheek. Thomas Foster
was at that time Sheriff of Davie County, in which the
parties lived.

The bill was filed in April, 1842, by Nail alone, against
Martin, the trustee; and, as far as it is legible and intelligible, it purports to state, that, at the time of executing the deed, there were a considerable number of
judgments and executions against Nail, in the hands of
certain constables, and also of Foster, the Sheriff, which
had a lien on the property, preferable to the deed; that
some of those executions were for some of the debts
mentioned in the deed; and that, by sales thereon by the
constables and the Sheriff, the whole of the property conveyed was disposed of, (except the lot and steam saw-
mill,) and thereout the whole of the executions satisfied,
and that a surplus of the proceeds of those sales remained in the hands of Foster, as Sheriff, amounting to $218.
The bill further states, that on the 24th of August, 1840,
the plaintiff, with the consent of the defendant, sold to
John Sheek his interest in the lot and saw-mill, for the
sum of $384 33, over and above the encumbrance of C.
Sheek; and that, for that sum, John Sheek then made
his note to the plaintiff, and he delivered it to the defendant, who accepted it as a part of the trust fund, instead of the lot and saw-mill; that the defendant allowed Foster to use the note, in a settlement between
him and John Sheek, of their own accounts, upon an

agreement by Foster with the defendant, who was then a clerk in a store of Foster, and his agent, that he, Martin, might take that amount and the other sum of $218, held by Foster, out of the store or any funds of Foster's in his hands; and that he accordingly did reimburse himself, or that, if he did not, he was guilty of gross negligence in not doing so. The bill further states, that, although the debts, that were in judgment and execution, were all satisfied, yet several others remain unsatisfied; and that, after applying thereto the effects in the defendant's hands as aforesaid, or that ought to be in his hands, there will be a surplus resulting to the plaintiff. The prayer is, that the defendant may come to an account of the sums due upon the debts mentioned in the deed, of the funds in his hands or that ought to be, and that they may be applied, in the first instance, to the balance due on the debts, and the residue be decreed to the plaintiff.

The answer states, that the deed of trust was arranged between the plaintiff and Thomas Foster, who was chiefly interested in it, as the principal creditor and surety of the plaintiff; and that the defendant was not privy to it, until it had been prepared and he requested to execute it, as a formal trustee, upon the promise of Foster and the plaintiff, that it should give him no trouble. It states that, in point of fact, no part of the property was ever in the defendant's possession or power; for that, when the deed was executed, all the property was subject to executions, under which it was sold and exhausted, except the sawmill and lot, and that the defendant knew of no surplus, of the proceeds of those sales, being in Foster's hands after satisfying the executions.

With respect to the sale of the lot and saw-mill, the answer states, that the plaintiff and Foster informed the defendant, that they could make an advantageous private sale of it to John Sheek, which would extinguish C. Sheek's large debt, for which Foster was bound, and they requested the defendant to come into the arragement;

50

and that he replied that he had no objection, if all the parties, who were interested, desired it; that thereupon the plaintiff and Foster made the sale, as they informed him, to their satisfaction, and the defendant had nothing to do with it, and supposed the price paid and applied properly by those parties, and never suspected to the contrary, or heard of the note of John Sheek for $384 33, until after November 1840; that in November 1840, Foster executed to the defendant an assignment of his stores and other property, in trust to pay specified debts, far beyond the value of the effects; and that, sometime afterwards, the plaintiff and Foster brought to him Sheek's note for $384 33, cancelled, and informed him, that it had been given for the saw-mill, and that the money on it, had been, by the consent of the plaintiff, paid to Foster, and that Foster (who had become insolvent) wished, if he could, to secure it, or as much of it as exceeded the debts to Foster, for the benefit of the plaintiff's trust fund; and to that end Foster then agreed to place in the defendant's hands, notes and accounts, not included in his previous assignments, to cover the amount that might be due from him in respect of Sheek's note. The answer states, that the defendant was desirous of securing in that way, debts which Foster owed to him, and also this trust fund, which the plaintiff had improperly allowed Foster to misapply; and that he endeavored to obtain from Foster an assignment of debts for those purposes, according to his promises; that Foster did deliver to him some notes and accounts for his own debts, which nearly all proved worthless; and also other notes and accounts on account of the debt he might be found to owe by reason of Sheek's note; that the defendant immediately brought suits thereupon, and that upon the trials, judgments were rendered in nearly every case, against the plaintiff, upon proof or Foster's acknowledgement of payment; so that not enough was recovered on them to pay the aggregate of the costs on them. The answer finally insists, that the defendant is not answerable to the plaintiff in respect to Sheek's note, as the transaction was that of the plaintiff himself and not of the defendant; and that if he would be liable under any circumstances, he is not under those existing, because he has never received any effects under the deed, and, also, because there are balances due to the creditors provided for in the deed, besides Foster, to a larger amount than the bill claims as the surplus due from Foster on both parts of the case.

The answer then offers, that, if the plaintiff thinks it worth his while and will indemnify the defendant against the costs, he may prosecute a suit against Foster or any other persons he may elect, in respect of any of these claims, and submits, that, as he has no funds and Foster and the plaintiff are both insolvent, he is not bound to bring any such suits without an indemnity.

The plaintiff examined several witnesses. One is John Sheek, who says, that when he purchased the saw-mill, he gave his note to the present plaintiff, who delivered it to Foster, upon an agreement between them, that Foster should account for it upon the settlement of Nail's trust. The witness says he afterwards paid Foster the note, and heard Foster tell Martin, that he, Foster, was to account for the note upon the trust.

James S. Martin states, that he heard the plaintiff several times state to Foster, that he had more money in his hands, than he had claims to cover, and request a settlement; that Foster became utterly insolvent in the summer of 1840, and executed an assignment before November Court in that year, which, however, will not yield the creditors a dividend of more than fifteen cents in the dollar, and that the defendant could not have recovered any thing from him, by a suit brought after May, 1840; that, after Foster made his assignment, the plaintiff and Foster came to a settlement, on which, with the assistance of the witness, they found the balance due from Foster to the trust fund to be $216; and that there is still due upon the debt to the witness, and on those for which he is surety, provided for in the deed, about the sum of $800.

A witness proves, that the defendant held a bond given by the witness to Foster for $170, which the defendant told him Foster had transferred to him, in part of a debt which Foster owed the defendant for wages on his own account.

Another witness, who is a constable, proves that the defendant placed in his hands a number of notes, payable to Foster, with directions to warrant on them, in the name of Foster, to the use of Martin, as trustee for Nail; that he did so, but failed in nearly every one by proof of settlements, and that he did not collect on all enough to pay the costs of the warrants dismissed at the plaintiff's costs.

Craig, for the plaintiff.
Boyden, for the defendant.

Ruffin, C. J.   The trust between the parties, created by the deed, being admitted, it would, generally, be a matter of course to refer the accounts to the Master. But the defendant objects to the unnecessary expense and trouble of their reference in this case, because it appears clearly upon the pleadings, and the plaintiff's own proofs on file, that the account cannot result in favor of the plaintiff; for the defendant has not, and never had, any trust fund, and, if he had the amount charged by the bill, he would not be accountable to the plaintiff upon this bill.   And the Court is of opinion, on those points, with the defendant.

The creditors secured by the deed are not parties to the cause, but the bill is brought by the debtor alone, and prays for the payment to himself of an alleged surplus, remaining after the payment of all the debts.   Now, he has himself proved that there is no such surplus; for his witness states, that, to that witness alone, $800 remains due, and both of the sums claimed in the bill amount only to $602 33.   It may be admitted, that, even in those sums the plaintiff has an interest, as, by the application of them to the debts, he would be personally exonerated to that amount ; and he has a right to call on the trustee and the creditors to make the application : and, there-fore, that the bill ought not to be dismissed, but allowed to stand over in order to make the creditors parties. But even that would not sustain the bill, for the plaintiff can only insist on being exonerated from the debts, as be-tween him and the defendant, as far as the defendant is liable by his own default, and not by that of the plain-tiff, to answer to the creditors; for the plaintiff, in this suit, is endeavoring to take care only of his own interest, and not that of the creditors.   Now, it is very certain, that the whole sum with which the defendant can be charged to any one, is that which may be found to be in Foster's hands, on account of the surplus of the sales on execution, and of Sheek's note, the latter of which is ad-mitted to be $384 33, and the former the bill states to be $218.   But those two sums, amounting together to $602 33, are not in fact due. as appears upon the evi-dence of the plaintiff's witness, James Martin, but only the one sum of $216.   For, Foster, as a creditor, was se-cured in the deed to the amount of $500, besides indem-nified as a surety ; and in August, 1840, the plaintiff let him have Sheek's note, to be applied to Foster's own use, and to be accounted for by him in the settlement of the deed of trust.   There is no evidence of any balance due from Foster, except that the answer states, that he ad-mitted to the defendant, that there was one on account of Sheek's note, but to what amount he did not state ; and except what appears upon the deposition of James S. Martin—which is, that after Foster made his assignment, that is, after November, 1840, the plaintiff and he settled their respective demands, under the deed and execution sales, and that Foster was found to be in debt $216. That was the whole balance, and must have included Sheek's note, for no one states that there was any surplus of the sales on execution, except the plaintiff in the bill. The witness, Martin, does not intimate it, and the answer denies it, as far as the defendant knows. No doubt, in the settlement, Foster included the debt to himself, which it is not pretended was in judgment and satisfied out of the execution sales ; and so, it must be understood, it was intended he should do, when the note was delivered to him by the plaintiff, because he was to account for it upon the deed. The whole debt of Foster, therefore, arose upon the transaction respecting Sheek's note ; and, whatever fault the other creditors may have a right to find with the present defendant, for allowing the mill to be thus sold and the proceeds applied, the present plaintiff surely cannot complain, inasmuch as it was his own act. Therefore, he has no right to ask. that the defendant should exonerate him from that amount of the secured debts.

But the bill brings forward a claim, founded upon the opportunity the defendant had, and his consequent obligation, to secure this balance out of the effects of Foster. In respect to the plaintiff, the defendant was not under any obligation to secure the sum in question : for the loss had been occasioned by the plaintiff, and it was his look-out to repair it. But in truth, the witnesses prove, that the defendant did all he could. It was in vain to sue Foster, for the sale to Sheek was in August, and, before November, Foster had conveyed all his tangible estate. Then nothing remained but to get whatever Foster would voluntarily offer of the debts due to him. Those the defendant took, as far as he was able to get them, for aught that can be seen ; and a witness for the plaintiff again proves, that the defendant was not able to realize one cent from them.

It is therefore a case, in which the defendant has nothing, and never had any thing to account for, as between

Nail v. Martin.

him and the plaintiff, and in which he is endeavoring to make the defendant liable for the consequences of his own blind confidence in Foster and the latter's insolvency. As this appears clearly upon the plaintiff's own proofs, read at the hearing, the Court allows the objection of the defendant to a reference, and dismisses the bill with costs.

There is an inconvenience, to which the Court is often subjected, and which has been so particularly felt in this case, as to make it proper to draw the attention of the profession to it. Pleadings ought to be plainly written and the words spelt in full, and without contractions—especially papers that are sworn to. As the profession is not remarkable for good hand-writing, and, from much use to a variety of hands, can read almost any paper that has the words with all their letters, the Court is not disposed to be very particular. But, really, bills and answers are often submitted to us, in which there are so many contractions, words half spelt, and carelessness in hand-writing, that, with all our experience, we find it difficult to decipher them. In many instances words are to be guessed at from the context; for it is impossible to read them by themselves, as, indeed, they are not words, but only some of their component letters. A conviction for perjury could not be had on them. If such papers be sent to us again, we shall be compelled to put the parties to the expense of making fair copies, and, perhaps, order the originals to be taken off the file, or dismiss the suit.

PER CURIAM.   Bill dismissed with costs.

NOAH W. GUILFORD *vs.* GEORGE W. GUILFORD & AL.

A. bequeathed as follows: " I leave my negroes (except Dan) to be sold by my executor, and divided into three shares," &c. *Held*, that this was a specific legacy of the negroes, of which the testator was possessed at the time of his death ; and that one of the legatees, to whom, after the date of the will, the testator had given two negroes, was not bound to account for their value in the division of the legacy.

By another clause, the testator bequeathed the negro Dan to his daughter A. M. and directed as follows: " I wish my executor to hire him out, and apply the proceeds, or so much thereof as may be necessary, to raise, clothe and educate the said child : And if the said A. M. should die before she arrives at the age of twenty-one years, then the negro boy Dan to go back and be sold by my executor, and the proceeds to be divided between E. L." and others. *Held*, that A. M. was entitled absolutely to all the hires of Dan, that accrued during her life-time, and was not restricted to so much only as was necessary " to raise, clothe and educate her."

Cause removed from the Court of Equity of Beaufort County, at the Spring Term, 1845.

The following case was presented by the pleadings :.

Joseph W. Guilford made his will in the year 1837, and thereby appointed the plaintiff his executor, and died in the year 1840. The widow of the testator dissented from his will and has since married Lewis.

The testator left a son (G. W. Guilford) who is unprovided for, and was born after the making of his father's will. Lewis and wife, and the infant son, (G. W. Guilford) have filed petitions in the County Court of Beaufort, to recover of the executor their distributive shares of the testator's estate, according to the several Acts of Assembly in such cases made and provided. The testator bequeathed as follows : " At the expiration of two years, *I leave my negroes*, (except Dan) to be sold by my executor, and divided into three shares ; one third to George Guilford and Gulana Guilford, his sister ; and the other two thirds between Noah W. Guilford and Elizabeth Langly, equally." The testator further bequeathed the negro boy Dan to Alvana Morris, an infant, and says, " I wish my executor to hire him out, and apply the proceeds, or so much thereof as may be necessary to raise, clothe and educate said child.   And if the said Alvana Morris should die before she arrives at the age of twenty-one years, then the negro boy Dan to go back and be sold by my executor ; and the proceeds to be divided between Elizabeth Langly," and others.   The testator gave his executor a power to hire out the negroes for the two years, and to divide the proceeds of hire among the very same persons, and in the same proportions, as the slaves were directed to be divided at the expiration of the two years.   The executor has sold the slaves as directed by the will; and the proceeds of sale are now in his hands ready for distribution. After making his will, the testator gave, by deed of gift, two of his slaves to his daughter Elizabeth Langly.   The other legatees, under this clause of the will, insist, that she should bring the value of the said two slaves into the fund for division ; as they say, she has been already advanced to that amount.   Elizabeth Langly insists that the two slaves, given to her by her father, compose no part of the legacy of negroes, bequeathed to be sold by the executor, and the money divided among the four legatees as above described.   *Secondly*, the guardian of Alvana Morris insists, that all the hires of the slave Dan belong to her : And that no part of his hire, during her life, is limited over to others, on the event of her dying before she arrives to the age of twenty-one years.   The plaintiff, the executor, has brought all the parties interested in the above controversies before the Court.   And he prays, that the trust fund in his hands, may be administered by the Court, according to the just rights of the said parties to the same.

J. H. Bryan, for the plaintiff.
Badger, for the defendants.

Daniel, J. *First.* As to the legacy, " I leave *my negroes* (except Dan) to be sold by my executor, and divided into three shares."   This is not a general legacy ; it is

51

not by law chargeable upon the whole personal estate undisposed of. It is a specific legacy of all the negroes (except Dan) the testator owned at the time of his death; for, at that time, the will legally speaks. If a testator bequeath all the horses, which he may have in his stables at the time of his death, it is a specific legacy; or, " such part of my stock of horses which A. shall select, to be fairly appraised to the value of £800," is a specific legacy. *Fontain* v. *Tyler*, 9 Price, 98. *Richards* v. *Richards*, 9 Price, 236. *Wil. on Ex.* 739. At the time of his death, the testator, Joseph W. Guilford, did not own the two negroes, Asa and Sally; he had given them before to Elizabeth Langly. And, although she is one of the legatees of " *all my negroes*," she is entitled to a share, as directed by the will, as if those two negroes had never belonged to the testator, and she is not compelled to bring their value into the fund to be divided, before she shall share.

Secondly. The testator gave the slave Dan to Alvana Morris, with the executory devise over to others, on the event of her dying before she arrived at twenty-one years of age. But all the hires of the said slave during her life, go to her absolutely. These hires are not confined to so much as may be necessary to her raising, clothing and education. Those words in the will are only directory to the executor, how the testator wished the hires of Dan to be applied. He could not expect, that there would be a surplus of hires after these objects had been accomplished. But he has declared in his will, that if Alvana Morris should die before her age of twenty-one, then the said negro boy Dan to go back and be sold by my executor, and the proceeds to be divided equally among G. W. Guilford, and others. No part of the hires, to arise during the life of Alvana Morris, are directed by the testator to accumulate upon any event whatever, and go over to the contingent legatees. The guardian of A. Morris is therefore entitled to all the hires of the slave Dan.

Thirdly. Some of the defendants have offered evidence *de hors* the will, tending to prove, that the testator intended, when he made the deed of gift of the two slaves to Elizabeth Langly, to alter his will, and charge her with the value of the same, in the division of the legacy of his negroes after his death. But that, if established, cannot affect the construction of the will ; for, if the gift of the negroes would not be a satisfaction or ademption of the legacy to her of a share of the negroes, an intention to *make* a new will, and therein make her legacy so much less, cannot diminish the legacy left to her in the present will.

Per Curiam.   Decree accordingly.

JAMES BARNETT *vs.* JAMES SPRATT'S ADM'R. & AL.

Where a contract is shown to be grossly against conscience, or grossly unreasonable, as that the price given bore no proportion to the real value of the property conveyed, this may, with other circumstances, authorize the interference of a Court of Equity.

But where these circumstances are not proved, and no complaint is made by the party, now alleging that he was circumvented, for more than twenty years after the contract was entered into, the Court will not interfere, to set aside the contract.

Cause transmitted, by consent, from the Court of Equity of Mecklenburg County, at the Fall Term, 1845.

From the pleadings and proofs, the following appeared to be the case :

The plaintiff charges, in his bill, which was filed in 1838, that, in the year 1817, being in the possession of considerable property, both real and personal, the latter consisting of negroes, stock of all kinds, and farming utensils and household furniture, the intestate, James Spratt, proposed that he should convey to him, the said

Spratt, all his property of every kind, and that he would pay all the debts he owed, and support him during the remainder of his days. This proposition he rejected, but, being a man of weak mind, he yielded to the persuasions and threats of the said Spratt, and did, by deed, in November 1818, convey to him seven negroes, worth at that time $3000. He further states, that, being about to go to Georgia, Spratt proposed he should lease to him his land, at an annual rent of $400; and accordingly a paper writing was prepared, which he signed, without reading, and that Alexander Grier and James Dinkins were present; that he did not know it was a deed for his land; that this took place also in 1818, and, though he often saw James Spratt from that time up to 1831, he never heard of the deed for the land until that year. He charges, that the bill of sale was procured from him by the false pretences and the threats of James Spratt, and the deed for the land by fraud; and that James Spratt, during his life, was a trustee for him, and that his administrator and the heirs of James Spratt, all of whom are defendants, and who are in the possession of the said land, and of the personal property so conveyed, or of such portions of the latter as the said James did not sell and waste, are now trustees for him; and prays they may be decreed to re-convey the land to him and account for the rents thereof, and also account for the value and hires of the negroes and other property.

The answers deny all personal knowledge of the manner in which the two deeds were obtained from the plaintiff by James Spratt, the intestate; but aver, that, according to their belief, the charges of fraud and threats, as stated in the bill, are false and unfounded. They further aver, that the consideration set forth in the deeds, copies of which are filed as exhibits, is $3000, and that is a full value, as they believe; and that the full amount has been paid by James Spratt, either to the plaintiff or to his use in the discharge of his debts. They further aver, that the parties had three different settlements, the last in February, 1822, all of which were made by respectable men of the neighborhood, in the presence of the parties; and these settlements are filed at the call of the plaintiff, as exhibits in the cause; that from them it appeared, that James Spratt had paid on account of the plaintiff, $2,592 24, and that the balance was paid afterwards.

Replication was taken to the answers, and the case removed to this Court for hearing.

No more of the pleadings are set out, than is necessary to shew the ground upon which the opinion of the Court is founded.

Boyden, for the plaintiff.
Alexander, for the defendants.

Nash, J. The plaintiff does not allege, that, from imbecility of mind, he was legally incapacitated from making a contract, but that it was so weak, as to render him an easy dupe to the artful designs of those who might be desirous to take advantage of it. He charges that James Spratt, who was his brother-in-law, availing himself of his knowledge of his weakness, procured from him a bill of sale for seven negroes, and that it was procured by persuasion and by working on his fears by threats, and that the deed for the land was obtained by fraud, as he was induced to sign it, under the belief that it was a lease for the land. To support these charges, the plaintiff does not produce any direct testimony whatever, and the bill making them is preferred in 1838, after the death of James Spratt, and after the lapse of twenty years from the execution of the deeds. But the case is equally destitute of any *circumstances*, to sustain the charge. The declarations of James Spratt, as proved by the witnesses, with the exception of those testified to by Mrs. Pettis, amount to nothing more than evidence, that the purchase money was not paid at the time the contract was made, and the mode in which it was done. Mrs. Pettis is so discredited, that she would need very strong corroborating circumstances to entitle her to belief. If the witnesses to the transaction were dead, or if there were no persons present at the time, still the plaintiff *might* have entitled himself to relief, by proof of circumstances showing fraud and oppression on the part of Spratt. If he had shown that the contract was grossly against conscience or grossly unreasonable, as that the price given bore no proportion to the real value of the property conveyed, it might, with other circumstances, have authorized the interference of a Court of Equity. 1 *Sto. Eq.* 324, s. 331. But we see nothing in the case to justify us in declaring that such is the fact. The bill charges that the negroes were worth $3,000, the other personal property $1,000, and the land $10,000, amounting in the whole to $14,000. There is no evidence as to the value of the personal property, and, as to the value of the land, it is contradictory. One witness for the plaintiff says it is worth $5,000, and a witness for the defendant, that, on a liberal credit, it might be worth $2,500; but, at the time of the sale, it could have been purchased at less than $2,000, and other witnesses vary from $2,000 to $3,000. If then, there was any difference between the real value of the land, and that stated in the deed, it certainly is not of such a gross character, as to evidence any thing like fraud and imposition. And as to the true character of the deed, we think that the fact, that the plaintiff never claimed any rent, and that, in the different settlements, which took place, it was not brought into account, is evidence, that, at that time, at least, the plaintiff did not consider himself entitled to any, and this is proof beyond all doubt, taken in connection with the delay in bringing this suit, that the deed is what it was intended to be.

PER CURIAM.   Bill dismissed.

ANDREW HOYLE, EX'R. &c. vs. ALEXANDER MOORE'S DEVI-
SEES AND LEGATEES.

All the persons, however, numerous, who are interested in the subject of a
suit in Equity, must be made parties, and, as in a declaration at common
law, the circumstances constituting the case must be set forth in the Bill
at large.

The parties intended to be made defendants in a suit in Equity, must be specially named in the Bill, and process prayed against them. None are parties to a Bill, against whom process is not prayed.

Therefore, where the prayer of the Bill was, " that the clerk be ordered to
issue subpœnas to the proper defendants," &c. without naming them:
Held, that the Bill should be dismissed, though certain persons came in and
filed answers.

Cause removed from the Court of Equity of Lincoln
County, at the Spring Term, 1845.

The Bill is filed for the purpose of obtaining from the
Court directions to the plaintiff, how to distribute property
in his hands, which he holds as representing Alexander
Moore, deceased. Alexander Moore, by his will, gave to
his wife, Elizabeth Moore, considerable property, both
real and personal, during her life, and, at her death, to be
disposed of as she might think proper, among her children. Elizabeth Moore, by her will, gave a certain portion of the property, so devised to her, to the children of
her deceased son, James Moore, naming them. The
plaintiff is the administrator with the will annexed of
Alexander Moore, and he may be the executor of Elizabeth Moore, though it is not stated in the Bill, nor is her
will exhibited. The Bill then states, that, after selling a
large portion of the personal property, preparatory to dividing it among those who were entitled, he was " by
some of the legatees ordered to pay over none of the legacies or bequests, &c."; " that some of the negroes are
claimed by Margaret Moore, relict and widow of James
Moore, dec'd. who is the guardian of the children of A.
Moore, dec'd. The other children claim that the negroes
shall be sold and divided among the other children of Alexander Moore;" " that James Moore and William Moore,

sons of A. Moore, died after the making of the will and before the testator. William left five children ; and John Moore died many years before, leaving" — with a space, to insert, as we presume, the names of his children, but setting out none. The Bill then proceeds: "Robinson Moore is still living, Alexander is still living, John Rhinehardt married Ann, Michael married Polly, since dead; William Scott married Rosanna, both dead; they left issue William Scott, who died without issue, Alexander Rankin married Elizabeth, still living"—not stating the period when any of the foregoing died. The Bill then prays, that "the proper parties may be made defendants, and if there are others than those set forth, they may be made parties, &c."—"that the clerk may be ordered to issue his State's writ of subpœna to the proper defendants, &c." Answers were filed by several persons, and replication taken, and the cause set for hearing.

No counsel for the plaintiff.
Alexander, for the defendants.

NASH, J. We much regret it is not in our power to grant to the plaintiff the relief he seeks. The Bill, no doubt from haste, is so inartificially drawn, that we cannot give him the instructions required. It is a general rule in Equity, that all the persons, however numerous they may be, who are interested in the subject of a suit, must be made parties, either plaintiffs or defendants, if known ; and like a declaration at common law, the circumstances constituting the case must be set forth in the Bill at large. Mr. Cooper, in his Equity Pleading, page 9, states, that the second part of the Bill sets forth the *names* of the parties. In order to obtain the answer upon oath, the Bill must pray, that the writ of subpœna issue to the defendant ; and, although persons may be named in the Bill, none are parties to it, against whom process is not prayed. Coop. Eq. Plead. 16. 1 P. Wil. 593. 2

Dick. 707. A defendant is as necessary to the just and proper construction of a Bill in Equity as a plaintiff. In the case we are now considering, there is no defendant whatever—process is prayed against no one. The prayer is, " that the clerk be ordered to issue subpœnas to the proper defendants, &c." But who are they? No name or names are given. How is he to find them out? Is it to be left to his discretion to say, who ought to be made defendants? This, in fact, is what the plaintiff does ask. It is not, as before remarked, sufficient that the names of individuals are contained in the Bill. Process is not asked against them, nor against any one in particular. There is, then, *no party defendant* to the Bill. But the Bill is liable to other objections, equally fatal. It is, among other things, stated, that John Moore died before the testator, leaving children, and a blank is left in the Bill, after the word " leaving," apparently for inserting the names of his children, and perhaps of his representatives, if he had any. It is not stated whether there is a representative or not. The Bill does not state who are the children of Alexander Moore. The names of certain persons are mentioned, but whether they are such children, we are left to conjecture. Some of those, so mentioned, are said to be dead, but when they died we are not informed. It would be impossible for the Court, upon this executor's bill, to know to whom to decree the money.

The Court has gone very far, in sustaining Bills defectively drawn—but we think this so essentially wanting in one of the points, necessary to the institution of a suit in any Court, that we cannot sustain it.

PER CURIAM.   Bill dismissed.

THOMAS PEMBERTON vs. PARHAM KIRK.

A Bill of discovery does not ask relief, but, generally, only seeks the discovery of facts, resting in the knowledge of the defendant, or of deeds or
writings in his possession or power, in order to maintain the right or title
of the party asking it, in some suit or proceeding in another Court.

Where a verdict has been recovered at law, the defendant in that action
cannot have relief in Equity, upon the ground that he can now produce
cumulative proof as to the facts on which his defence rested at law.

The case of *Peagram v. King*, 2 Hawks, 605, cited and approved.

Cause removed from the Court of Equity of Montgomery County, at the Fall Term, 1845.

The following was the case :

The plaintiff, in his bill, charges, that in the year 1826,
the defendant was Sheriff of Montgomery County, and
Samuel Pemberton, brother of the plaintiff, was appointed his deputy, and gave bond with the plaintiff as his
surety, for the faithful performance of his duties. The
defendant put into the hands of his said deputy the tax
lists in districts No. 2 and No. 11, for collection, and for
which Samuel Pemberton gave his receipt. He further
charges, that, in the year 1827, Samuel Pemberton was
Sheriff of Montgomery County, and Parham Kirk, the
defendant, acted as his deputy, and collected the taxes
in the districts No. 6 and No. 12, and that afterwards
they, the said Pemberton and Kirk, came to a settlement,
when it was ascertained that the defendant owed the
plaintiff $10. Samuel Pemberton died, and Abraham
Cochran qualified as his executor, and an action was
brought by the defendant against the plaintiff and the
said executor, upon the bond of the said Samuel as
deputy Sheriff ; upon the trial of which suit, the defendant recovered judgment for the sum of $397 45, be-
ing the amount of the tax list put into the hands of his
deputy including the interest. The Bill charges that the
plea of fully administered was found in favor of the executor, and that there is no real estate descended to the
heirs of the said Samuel, his estate being entirely insolvent. The plaintiff avers, that nothing was due to the

Pemberton v. Kirk.

defendant from the estate of his brother Samuel, as he could have proved by Abraham Cochran, to whom the defendant admitted that a settlement had taken place as before stated, but that he could not avail himself of his testimony, as he was a defendant with the plaintiff, and that he had no other witness by whom it could be proved. He further states, that he is ignorant himself of the situation of the business between his brother Samuel and the defendant, but that he had obtained from the executor, Cochran, a receipt of the defendant to his brother for $70, for which he is entitled to a credit on the judgment as so much money paid, and that there are other receipts of a similar kind. The prayer of the bill is for an account of the dealings between the parties in the collection of taxes, that the receipts of Samuel Pemberton from the defendant may be allowed, and the defendant decreed to pay such balance as might be found due to Samuel Pemberton.

The answer admits the appointment of Samuel Pemberton, as the deputy of the defendant, and of the defendant, as the deputy of Pemberton; admits his recovery of a judgment against the complainant, as the surety of his brother Samuel, and that the plea of fully administered was found in favor of Abraham Cochran, executor of Samuel Pemberton, and that the estate is entirely insolvent. But the defendant denies, that he recovered judgment for more than was justly due to him, except a receipt for $70, the amount of which he did not, at the time, distinctly know; as to which he alleges, that at the time of the trial, Cochran had it in his pocket, and declined introducing it. After the trial was over, in a conversation with the present plaintiff, he agreed to allow the $70 receipt, and instructed his counsel to credit the judgment with its amount, whenever it was brought forward, and that he is now willing to allow it as a payment. The answer further avers, that, as to the pretended settlement, which he denies ever did take place, on the trial at law, Allen was examined on behalf of the then defendants, as being present, and that the jury found that there was no settlement of the taxes between the parties, at the time he spoke of.

The plaintiff took replication to the answer, and the cause being set for hearing, was transferred to this Court.

Strange and *Winston*, for the plaintiff.
No counsel for the defendant.

NASH, J. This is not properly a bill of discovery. Such a bill asks no relief, but seeks the discovery of facts resting in the knowledge of the defendant, or of deeds or writings in his possession or power, in order to maintain the right or title of the party asking it, in some suit or proceedings in another Court. Coop. Eq. Pl. ch. 1, sec. 4, p. 58, 60. Mitford 8, 53, &c. And in general, to maintain such a bill, an action should be depending in another Court, to the maintaining of which the discovery sought, is material, and therefore the power of the Court of Equity is ancillary in such a case. *1st vol. Sto. Eq.* 701. Neither is it a bill, to procure a new trial of the case at law, but it is an original bill, seeking relief against a judgment at law upon the ground, that the defendant in this action did not give the present plaintiff credit for the $70 received, and because he could not prove the settlement set forth, in consequence of his witness, Cochran, being a party to that suit. A Court of Equity will not sustain a bill of review, upon the ground of newly discovered testimony of a cumulative character. *Livingston v. Herbbs*, 3 John. Ch. Ca. 123, particularly when it relates to a matter, which was principally controverted on a former trial. *Peagram v. King*, 2 Haw. 612. In the case at law of *Kirby v. Pemberton and Cochran*, the settlement between the parties of their tax accounts was the matter, principally controverted, and a witness, Allen, was present at the settlement as the parties were closing it, and was examined as to the matters contained in the settlement produced.   To permit the present plaintiff now to produce Cochran, in this controversy, would be granting him a new trial here, simply for the purpose of introducing cumulative testimony upon that point.   But Cochran is here an interested witness, and can no more be introduced than could Samuel Pemberton, if alive; he is a party defendant to the judgment, against which relief is sought.

As to the $70, it is shown, that the plaintiff had it in his power and knew of its existence, at the time of the trial at law; it was then in the possession of Cochran, one of the defendants, and not produced.   The presiding Judge, very properly, refused the defendants a new trial on that ground.   Nor would we now give the plaintiff any relief, but for the fact, that the defendant admits it was paid, and was willing it should now be credited on the judgment.   He cannot, therefore, in conscience, retain it, nor does he ask so to do, as the judgment has been collected by the plaintiff at law.   The plaintiff, here, is entitled to a decree for that sum, and interest from the 10th of July 1828, the date of the receipt, but out of it the master will pay the costs of this suit, and, if not sufficient for that purpose, the plaintiff must pay what will be necessary to cover all the costs.

PER CURIAM.   Decree accordingly.

OLIVER QUINN vs. EDWARD RIPPEY & AL.

One, the title of whose land, as alleged by a creditor, has been sold by this creditor at execution sale, is an incompetent witness in a suit between other parties, to prove that the title was really in him.

The case of *Waller v. Mills*, 3 Dev. 515, cited and approved.

Case removed from the Court of Equity of Cleaveland County, at the Fall Term, 1845.

Quinn v. Rippey.

In 1832, Peter Mauney was seised of the land in fee, which is the subject of this controversy, and contracted to sell it to the defendant, Leguire, who went into possession. Leguire did not pay any part of the purchase money, and Mauney brought an action of ejectment against him in Rutherford Superior Court. When the case was about being tried, at October term. 1836, the parties came to a new agreement, by which Mauney was to dismiss the suit, if Leguire would give a new bond for the purchase money, with the defendant, Edward Rippey, and one Epps, as his sureties; which was then done. At the same time, Leguire executed a deed to one Michael Borders, dated November 5th, 1836, for the same land, upon trust to sell, and, out of the proceeds of sale, to pay the debt to Mauney, if it should not be paid by Leguire, when it became due. The deed is very informally drawn, and contains no words of inheritance, so that the trustee got but a life estate, at any rate. At the Superior Court of Lincoln, which was the week afterwards, one Collins obtained judgment against Leguire, on which he issued a *fieri facias*, and delivered it to the Sheriff of Rutherford, on the 9th of January, 1837, and he levied it on this land, on the 14th of February following; and, upon a *venditioni exponas*, it was subsequently sold, and purchased by the plaintiff, Quinn, who took the Sheriff's deed and got into possession, Leguire having abandoned it. Afterwards, Mauney brought an action of ejectment against the present plaintiff, and judgment was obtained therein by the plaintiff, as the defendant at law, Quinn, being unable to shew that Mauney ever conveyed to Leguire. Mauney having died, Quinn filed this bill against his heirs, Rippey and Leguire, and therein charges, that, in fact, Mauney did execute a deed for the premises to Leguire, when the new bond, with sureties for the purchase money, was given; and that, after the plaintiff's purchase, and with the view of favoring Rippey, and defeating the plaintiff of his purchase, of which they were well informed, those three persons, Leguire, Rippey and Mauney, agreed to cancel the contract of sale to Leguire, and the latter, thereupon, surrendered the deed, which Mauney had made to him, and which had not been registered; and they then destroyed it. The prayer is for a conveyance from Mauney's heirs to the plaintiff, as the purchaser of the land at the Sheriff's sale, and, in the mean while, for an injunction against suing out execution on the judgment at law.

The answer of Mauney's heirs states, that they have no knowledge or information, that their ancestor ever made a deed to Leguire for the land; that those persons made the contract in 1832, and that, at Fall term, 1836, of Rutherford Superior Court, a new arrangement was made between them on the subject, as these defendants have understood, but what it was they do not know. And they state, that afterwards Mauney claimed the land as his own, and instituted the suit at law, against the present plaintiff.

The answer of Rippey states, that it was known, when he and Epps became Leguire's sureties, that he, Leguire, was much embarrassed, if not insolvent; and that, for that reason, it was agreed that Mauney should not convey the land, but retain the title, as a security for the purchase money; and that it was further agreed, that, if Leguire did not pay the money, and Epps or Rippey should pay it, the land should be conveyed by Mauney to the party making the payment for it. This defendant also states, that, fearing that they might be afterwards embarrassed by the creditors of Leguire proceeding in some way against his interest in the land, it was further agreed that Leguire should, at that time, secure to his sureties whatever interest he had therein, by a conveyance to a trustee for that purpose; and that, in execution of that agreement, Leguire made the deed to Borders, when the bond was given to Mauney for the purchase money.

He denies positively, that Mauney made a conveyance to Leguire, at that time, or at any time to his knowledge, or that he ever had it, or that it was surrendered by Leguire to him. He states, that, after the land had been sold by the Sheriff, Leguire abandoned it, and became insolvent; and that then Mauney, in February, 1838, applied to him, Rippey, for payment of the bond, and that he, thereupon, went for Leguire that he might consent, according to the original agreement, that Mauney should make the deed to him. Rippey, upon his payment of the purchase money, as he was obliged and intended to do; and that Leguire came to his house and was present when he, Rippey, paid to Mauney the whole principal and interest due on the bond, and saw Mauney make a deed for the premises to Rippey, and fully approved thereof, and did not then intimate that Mauney had ever conveyed to him, Leguire. The answer states, that, in the next month, Mauney applied to him, Rippey, to re-purchase the land, and proposed to pay him back the same price he had received; and that this defendant, not wanting to keep the land, acceded thereto, and received from Mauney what he had before paid to him, and at the same time surrendered the deed which had been made by Mauney to him, Rippey, and it was destroyed—that, being deemed by the parties sufficient, as that deed had never been proved or registered. And the defendant says, that he never afterwards had any claim against Leguire, for having paid the bond as his surety, nor any claim to the land, after Mauney returned to him the money he had before paid.

The answer of Leguire was also filed, but was not read at the hearing, as the plaintiff took his deposition under an order.

The plaintiff examined the wife of Leguire, as well as Leguire himself, and their depositions were read without objection. She states, that, about 1838, Rippey came to Leguire's residence in his absence, and asked her for the deed from Mauney to her husband; and that she handed

him all her husband's papers, and, after looking over
them, he took out one, and said that was the deed he
wanted. She did not see that it was a deed, nor does she
know that her husband had such a deed, except as stated
by Rippey on that occasion.

Leguire says, that Mauney did make a deed to him for
the land and he then made the deed of trust to Borders
for the counter security of his sureties ; that he saw Rippey the same day ; that Rippey had been at his house
and was told by him, that he had got the deed from his
wife, and that he then went with Rippey to his house and
there saw Mauney, who asked him, if the deed had been
registered, and when the witness told him that it had
not, Mauney remarked, that was all he wished to know.
He denies that he ever said that Mauney had not made
him a deed, or that he was present when Mauney conveyed to Rippey, or consented that he should do it. And
he says, that he is not on good terms with Rippey, but has
sued him for slander.

Another witness for the plaintiff states, that he saw
Mauney as he was going to Rippey's in February 1838,
and asked him whether he had made a deed to Leguire ;
and Mauney replied that he had, but that Rippey and
Epps took a deed of trust for the land, and that would
hold it ; and he mentioned further, that the deeds were
written and witnessed by a man named Perry Roberts.

On the other hand, a witness for the defendant states,
that Leguire told him, that Mauney gave him a bond for
a title, and that he was to get a deed, when he should pay
for the land.

Three other witnesses state, that, at the time Leguire
came to Rippey's with him and saw Mauney there, he
declared that Mauney never had conveyed the land to
him: that at that time, by his consent, and in his presence,
Mauney conveyed it to Rippey, who then paid the purchase money ; and that the person, who was writing the
deed from Mauney to Rippey, asked for the deed from

53

Mauney to Leguire, (which he supposed to have been made) in order to get the boundaries of the land from it, and thereupon, both Mauney and Leguire said, that no such deed had ever been executed.

The deed of trust is exhibited, and it bears date the 5th of November, 1836, and is attested by Perry Roberts, and was registered February 6th, 1837.

Alexander, for the plaintiff.
Guion, for the defendants.

RUFFIN, C. J.   If the statement of this transaction, which Leguire gives, be true, a legal question would arise, which, perhaps, is not clear of doubt. For, as the conveyance to Leguire and the deed of trust by him were executed together, upon one treaty and as different parts of the same transaction, and as the deed to him was never registered so as to complete his legal title, it is quite debateable, whether a Court of Equity would set up the deed, as though it were registered, or would supply its place, upon any other condition than that the plaintiff should first pay the purchase money and interest. But as that question was not discussed, and its decision is not necessary for the purpose of this cause, in the view the Court takes of it, we shall not further consider it.

The bill is not framed upon the idea, that Leguire had an equitable interest, merely, in the land, in the nature of the right of a mortgagor, and it does not offer to pay Mauney's purchase money. But the whole equity is founded on the fact, that a deed was made to Leguire, which was an incipient legal title, and only lacked registration to constitute a competent title, and that, after his purchase, it was suppressed in fraud of the plaintiff. It therefore behooves the plaintiff to establish the execution of such a deed. The only direct evidence to the point, is that contained in Rippey's answer and Leguire's deposition : and they are irreconcilably contradictory to each

other. The answer, however, is entitled, upon a rule of
the Court, to preponderate, unless the credit of the witness
be propped by other witnesses, or collateral circumstances. But, as they seem to the Court, the circumstances
here operate against, rather than for, the witness. In the
first place, he is a biassed and an interested witness. The
land was sold under execution for his debt, and he comes
to support his title and the sale, and thereby to be discharged from the judgment debt. *Waller* v. *Mills*, 3
Dev. 515. The debt to Mauney or Rippey is gone, upon
the admissions in the answer of Rippey; and consequently
Leguire's interest is all on one side. The same remarks
are equally applicable to the testimony of his wife. But
the truth is, that she proves nothing of any consequence,
as she really does not pretend to know, that there was
such a deed as the plaintiff sets up, and it would be un-
safe, against the *positive* answer of the defendant, to decree upon a loose declaration, proved under the circumstances in which she was. In the next place, three witnesses expressly and directly contradict Leguire in essential parts of his testimony, and prove, that he explicitly
stated that there had not been a deed to him; and that
he made the settlement under circumstances, which would
naturally have induced him to state the contrary, if the
contrary had been true. Besides, a fourth witness deposes, that at a different time he told him, that it was not
a conveyance for the land which he had, but a bond for
title, as he called it, when he should pay for the land.
Then, it is a consideration entitled to much weight, that
the plaintiff upon whom the affirmative lies, has not examined either Roberts or Epps, who appear to have been
present, when the deed of trust was made, and therefore
must have known of the deed of conveyance, if, as Leguire says, one was made to him at the same time. But
neither of them has been examined, nor any account given
of them, nor any reason for not taking their testimony,
but the plaintiff has preferred relying on Leguire alone.

The circumstance, that Leguire made a deed of trust, would, indeed, afford some presumption, if unexplained, that he had the title. But it may be otherwise; and the answer states it to have been otherwise, and that the reason for taking the deed of trust was, that the parties feared that even the equitable title might be sold, to the exclusion of the sureties for the purchase money. That point was not so entirely plain, that these persons, who appear to be illiterate, might not have entertained that opinion. At all events, we cannot decree for the plaintiff upon a fact, thus denied and thus defectively proved, when it was in the plaintiff's power, if the fact had been, as he alleges, to have proved it clearly by two other unsuspected witnesses.

Upon the whole, then, it must be declared, that the plaintiff has failed to establish that Mauney made a conveyance of the premises to Leguire; and therefore, the bill must be dismissed with costs.

PER CURIAM.　　　　　　　　　Decree accordingly.

HAMILTON HOWELL & AL. vs. CURTIS HOOKS' ADM'R.

A bequest of a particular bond is a specific bequest, and the executor is not bound to collect the money due on the bond, but must deliver the bond itself to the legatees.

Cause removed from the Court of Equity of Wayne County, at the Fall Term, 1845.

The following is the case presented by the pleadings and proofs:

In the year 1817, Edward Sasser, who had married a daughter of Benjamin Howell, gave to the latter his bond for $415 77, payable two days after date. In November, 1828, Benjamin Howell made his will, and died in 1829. The 11th clause of the will is as follows: "I give and bequeath unto the daughters of Edward Sasser, one note which I hold on said Sasser, to be equally divided between them, the amount probably $500." The will was duly proven, and the executor, therein named, Benjamin Howell, Jun. qualified as such, and took into his hands the property of his testator, including this bond. Benjamin Howell, Jun. died in the year   , and the defendant was, by the proper authority, appointed his administrator; and the bond in question came into his hands, together with property to a large amount, belonging to his intestate. The bill charges that it was the duty of the executor. Benjamin Howell, to have collected the bond, which is still due and unpaid, and to have distributed the proceeds among those entitled, who are the complainants in this case; that, in consequence of his negligence, the bond cannot now be recovered, as from the length of time which has elapsed, the law will presume it has been paid; and prays that the defendant may be decreed to pay to them the amount of principal and interest due thereon.

The answer states that more than twelve years elapsed, from the time the bond became due and payable, to the death of Benjamin Howell, Sen.; and that letters testamentary did not issue to him, until more than sixteen years after its so falling due. It further states, that, soon after the issuing to him his letters testamentary, he did call on the obligee, Edward Sasser, and requested him to become guardian to his children, and receive the bond. This he declined, saying he never meant to pay it. That he then offered to transfer it to Hamilton Howell, one of the plaintiffs, that he might recover it to the use of himself and wife, and the other parties interested; but Howell refused to receive it. It then alleges that the bequest is a specific one, and that it was not the duty of the executor, Benjamin Howell, to collect it, but to deliver it over to the plaintiffs, or some one of them, whensoever required to do so; which obligation was discharged by his offer to Hamilton Howell.

The evidence taken in the cause proves, that Benjamin Howell, the executor, did offer to deliver the bond to Hamilton Howell or Ransom Rose, two of the plaintiffs, that they might, if they chose, take the necessary steps to collect it; and they refused to receive it.

The cause has been regularly transferred to this Court for hearing.

Mordecai, for the plaintiffs.
J. H. Bryan, for the defendant.

Nash, J. The only question presented by this case, and which the Court is called on to decide, is, whether or not it was the duty of the executor, Benjamin Howell, to collect the money due on the bond of Edward Sasser, and divide it among his children. We think it was not; it results from the very nature of the legacy, that such was not his duty. It is a bequest of a specific article, of a particular bond, and not of the money due upon it. The testator gives the *bond*, due to him from Edward Sasser, to his-daughters. Such a legacy can only be satisfied by the delivery of the identical article or subject. 2 Wil. on Ex'rs. 740. Fonb. Treat. on Eq. B. 4, Part 1, ch. 11, sec. 5, n. a. Thus, if a particular horse or negro is bequeathed, the executor cannot sell the horse or negro and tender the money in his discharge; nor can he, with the money, purchase another horse or negro and tender that. He must keep the particular article, and have that ready to deliver, whenever a demand is made. It is true, the money due on this bond is its essence, and, if when the legacy was demanded, the executor had it ready to pay over, it is not to be supposed but what the legatees would take it. But what, if in the collection of the bond, he had received counterfeit money in payment, or the notes of a Bank, which had subsequently failed—

would the legatee be bound to receive them? Clearly not. He would say, my legacy was of a bond, not money; and I demand the bond. We think, then, that the executor was not bound to bring an action on the bond against Edward Sasser, the obligor. On the contrary, it was his duty to retain it, subject to the demand of the legatees. This view of the case is an answer to the cases cited in behalf of the plaintiff, from the 2d and 3d Brown's C. R. In *Lawson* and *Copeland*, Lord THUR-LOW decided, that an executor was liable, when he neglected to *sue* for money due the estate, so long as to enable the debtor to protect himself under the statute of limitations, because it was his duty to collect it. But it is said, the words, " to be equally divided," in the bequest, show that it was the intention of the testator, that the executor should collect the bond and distribute the money. The answer is, if such was his intention, he would have bequeathed the money and not the bond. We consider those words as indicating on the part of the testator, how the legatees should hold the bond. The executor offered the bond to Hamilton Howell and to Ransom Rose, two of the plaintiffs, to collect for their use and the use of those who were jointly interested with them, thereby authorizing them, if necessary, to use his name in its collection ; and he would, no doubt, at their request, have endorsed it without recourse, as it would have been his duty to do. In making this offer, we consider the executor as having discharged himself of all responsibility to them, and his administrator having the bond ready to deliver to any one legally authorized to receive it, the plaintiffs have no equity against his estate. We consider this an ungracious claim on the part of the plaintiffs. Edward Sasser, the obligor, was the father and father-in-law of the complainants—a man of wealth. Moreover, he is entitled, as the next of kin of those of his daughters who have died intestate, to their shares in the bond.

Richardson v. Hinton.

The plaintiffs are entitled to a decree for the delivery of the bond; but they must pay all costs.

PER CURIAM.   Decree accordingly.

BARBARA RICHARDSON *vs.* PETER W. HINTON & AL.

A testator devised to his wife a large real and personal estate, and then directed as follows: "It is my wish that my widow and cousin Barbara Richardson should continue to keep house together; but should they not, I wish my executor to pay over to cousin Barbara Richardson $1,000, or that amount out of the property left my wife." The parties continued to live together until the death of the widow. *Held,* that, on the happening of that event, B. R. was entitled to receive the legacy of $1000.

Cause removed from the Court of Equity of Pasquotank County, at the Fall Term, 1845.

The case was as follows:

Samuel Halstead died in the year 1832, having made his last will and testament. In it he devises to his wife, Eliza E. Halstead, a large real estate and much valuable personal property, and by the 6th clause, he bequeaths as follows: "It is my wish that my widow and cousin Bar- "bara Richardson, should continue to keep house together, "but should they not, I wish my executors to pay over to "cousin Barbara Richardson $1,000, or that amount out "of the property left my wife." William S. Hinton, one of these defendants, and Edwin H. Hinton, were appointed executors; of whom the former alone qualified as such, and assented to the legacy to the widow, who took possession of the property devised to her. After the death of the testator, the complainant and the widow continued to keep house together, up to the time of the marriage of the latter with Peter W. Hinton, the other defendant. After that event, the plaintiff continued to live with Peter W. Hinton, until the death of his wife in 1846, soon after which she left his house and family.   The property, which was devised to the widow Halstead, and which she possessed at the time of her intermarriage with the defendant, Peter W. Hinton, came into his hands.   When the plaintiff expressed her intention of leaving his family, the defendant. Peter, told her she was at liberty to remain still with him, as she had before done.

The bill is filed to compel the defendants to pay to the complainant the $1000, so bequeathed to her.

The answer of Peter W. Hinton resists the plaintiff's recovery, upon the ground, that the only fair construction, which can be put upon the clause of the will in question, is, that the plaintiff should have her election, either to live with the widow or to take the legacy of $1000, and that her election should be made either at the death of the testator, or in some reasonable time thereafter; and that she had elected to live with Mrs. Halstead, and cannot now claim the money.

Badger, for the plaintiff.
A. Moore, for the defendants.

Nash, J.   We cannot yield our assent to this construction.   We believe the testator intended a substantial benefit to the plaintiff.   The construction claimed by the defendant would make it entirely illusory, and dependent upon the will or caprice of the widow.   The clause is not very explicit, and is somewhat peculiar.   The language is, "I wish that my widow and cousin Barbara Richardson should continue to *keep house* together, but should they not," &c.—not simply live together.   His wish was, that they should continue together, and, while they did so, that Barbara was to be, equally with his widow, mistress of the family, and enjoy equal privileges with her.   While so keeping house together, Barbara is not to receive the money, because she, in that case, is already provided for; nor does he make her contingent right to receive her pecuniary legacy dependent wholly on her own will or on that of Mrs. Halstead ; the words are—" but should *they* not," &c. If, then, after the death of the testator, they continued to keep house together, it would not have been in the power of the plaintiff, at any time thereafter, capriciously to put an end to their joint house-keeping, and then demand her legacy ; neither would it have been in the power of the widow to put an end to it, and thereby deprive her, not only of a home, but of the bounty of the testator. If the widow had refused to permit the plaintiff to live with her, or, after they had so begun to live, she had ordered her to leave the house, or by her conduct rendered her further residence with her intolerable, or they had mutually agreed to separate ; in either of these cases, the right of the plaintiff to receive her legacy could not be questioned. It is not, therefore, a case of election, for her rights depend not alone on her own will, but in part upon that of another ; nor is her *right* to enjoy both the interests bequeathed to her, though at different periods, inconsistent with the intention of the testator ; nor does it defeat any portion of the will. We consider the subsequent marriage of Mrs. Halstead as an event, which, in itself, put an end to their jointly keeping house. She had ceased to have the right to permit the plaintiff to live with her ; she had, by her own voluntary act, transferred it to another, and, if the plaintiff had then left her, she would have been entitled to her pecuniary legacy. The subsequent death of Mrs. Halstead, then Mrs. Hinton, produced the same effect. The power to keep house together had ceased. That the death of the widow would restore to the plaintiff her right to the legacy, is obvious. What, if the widow had died a month or a year after their joint house-keeping had commenced, it could not be pretended, that, in such event, from no fault of hers, the plaintiff would have lost the benefit intended her by the kindness of the testator.

We are of opinion, then, that, upon the death of the testator, the plaintiff was at liberty either to separate from the widow, and claim the money, or, with the consent of the latter, to continue with her, in which case she could not claim the legacy during the continuance of their joint residence: but as soon as that ceased, without any fault of hers, her right was restored. The plaintiff is, therefore, entitled to her legacy, and interest on it from the time she demanded it, upon her leaving the defendant's house.

The defendant, Peter W. Hinton, states that he is entitled, if a decree is made in favor of the plaintiff, to an allowance for the maintenance of a negro woman and child belonging to her. This would much depend upon the fact, whether these negroes were attendants upon the person of the plaintiff, which does not appear. The defendants may have an enquiry upon this subject if they require it.

PER CURIAM.   Decree accordingly.

EPHRAIM MAUNEY vs. HIGH SHOALS MANUFACTURING COMPANY.

A corporation can only sue or be sued in its corporate name, unless the act of incorporation enables it to come into Court in the name of any other person, as its President, Cashier, &c.

Cause removed from the Court of Equity of Lincoln County, at the Fall Term, 1845.

The following is the case:

The bill is filed against Andrew Motz, President and Stock-holder of the High Shoals Manufacturing Company, against Samuel R. Simpson, Eli Hoyle, and John Motz, Directors and Stock-holders, against Michael Hoke and

Henry W. Burton, Executors of Robert H. Burton, dec'd. and against Henry Fullenwider. It charges that Robert H. Burton, dec'd. had been President of the Company, and, while so, by virtue of the authority of his office, and various resolutions, passed by the said Company, for and on behalf of the Company, made a contract with the defendant Henry Fullenwider, to furnish them with a certain quantity of ore, for the use of their furnace. It alleges, that although the contract was made with Henry Fullenwider, yet, in fact and truth, it was made between the company and Fullenwider and the plaintiff, he being a partner with Fullenwider, equally interested with him in the contract, and entitled equally with him to all its benefits; and this was well known to Robert H. Burton, and to the Company, who recognized him as such.

The bill then sets forth that a great quantity of ore was raised and delivered by him and Fullenwider, and upon the death of Robert H. Burton and the appointment of A. Motz as President of the Company, he demanded a settlement of accounts arising under the contract set forth, and the payment to him of his share of what was due to him, but that his demand has been refused, on the ground that the contract was made by the Company with Henry Fullenwider, and that they had claims against him, to an amount equal, or more than equal, to what was due on the contract for the ore. Fullenwider is entirely insolvent. The bill further alleges, that he obtained from Fullenwider orders upon the Company for the sum of $600, which were presented to A. Motz, the President, who said he could not accept them without consulting M. Hoke, and that they were returned to him, and he claims them as equitable assignments, which the Company are bound to pay.

The answers admit the contract with Fullenwider, but deny that the plaintiff was any party to it; admit the plaintiff did assist in raising and delivering the ore, but not under any contract with the Company; and if he was interested, it was in consequence of some subsequent agreement with Fullenwider; and allege that Fullenwider is indebted to the Company to the amount of what they owe under the contract; but, if, upon a final settlement between the Company and Fullenwider, it should be found any thing is due to him on the contract, they are willing to pay it over to the plaintiff.

Alexander, for the plaintiff.
Guion, for the defendant.

NASH, J. This Company was incorporated in the year 1838, by the name of the " High Shoals Manufacturing Company," and it is enacted. " by that name and style, shall sue and be sued." In that name alone. can they declare when plaintiffs, and in that name do they answer when sued, unless the act of incorporation enables them to come into Court in the name of any other person, as their President, Cashier, &c. *Brown on Actions*, 155. In the case of this corporation, no power is given to sue or be sued in any other but their corporate name. The bill, though filed against the individuals named, is for the settlement of an account growing out of a contract made with the Company, and to enforce it. The corporation is the debtor, and the corporation ought to have been a party to the suit, which it is not.

The bill is subject to another and equally fatal objection. The contract set forth is one, as stated in the bill, made between the Company and Henry Fullenwider. It is true, it alleges that he, the plaintiff, was interested in the contract, and insinuates, but does not aver, that he was a party to it. The answers deny that the plaintiff was a party to the contract, and aver it was made with Fullenwider alone. They admit, that the plaintiff may, after the contract was made, have been admitted by him to a participation in it. From the evidence, we are satisfied this was the fact, and that the plaintiff was not a party to the original contract, and that any interest he may have in it is derived from Fullenwider. To him he must look. As against the plaintiff, the Company had a right to have their claims against Fullenwider fully settled, before they would hold any thing subject to his claim. They are therefore justified in obeying the orders of Fullenwider, in disposing of the money, arising under the contract.

We could not refer the case to the Master, to ascertain whether the Company have paid Fullenwider all that they owe him, on account of the ore delivered under the contract, because the bill is not framed with that view. The plaintiff claims not as assignee of Fullenwider, but as an original contractor.

PER CURIAM.   Bill dismissed with costs.

JAMES O. LEWIS & AL. vs. FRANCIS S. COXE & AL.

A Court of Equity will not interfere to enforce the performance of a contract, after the lapse of forty years from the time when it should have been executed.

The case of *Tate* v. *Conner*, 2 Dev. Eq. 224, cited and approved.

Cause removed from the Court of Equity of Rutherford County, at the Fall Term, 1845.

The following case was presented by the pleadings and process:

Prior to the year 1802, Tench Coxe, of Philadelphia, obtained patents for very large tracts of land in Buncombe, Rutherford, and other Counties in the Western part of this State. Among them was a tract, situate in Rutherford, containing 14,720 acres granted by patent, No. 1023; and Coxe had conveyed that and others of his lands in this State to Peter Stephen Duponceau and others, as trustees for certain purposes. On the 14th of May, 1802, Tench Coxe and his trustees united in a letter of attorney to Peter Fisher, whom they sent out from Pennsylvania, authorizing him to make sale of the lands or any parts of them. On the 17th of July, 1802, Fisher entered into a written agreement with James Miller, who resided at Rutherfordton, for the sale of 600 acres. part of patent No. 1023, and described as " lying on the waters of Glaghorn's creek ; the same to be run in a long square, and include the shoal on the stone-cutter fork of the said creek ;" for which Fisher bound himself to make title in ten days, in consideration of a certain roan gelding then delivered to Fisher. A considerable number of sales and conveyances were made by Fisher to other persons, and he reported them, from time to time, to his employers in Philadelphia, until the revocation of his power in 1807 ; but this sale to Miller does not appear to have been reported. In 1807, Tench Coxe and his trustees conveyed to Coxe's son, Tench Coxe the younger, 7360 acres ; being the northern part of the tract No. 1023, excluding such lands as had been previously sold to other persons. Tench Coxe the younger, then came to Rutherfordton and resided there until his death in 1814 ; and during the same period James Miller also continued to reside there. He, T. Coxe, Jun., continued to make sales of parts of the land, and, upon his death, his lands descended to his brothers and sisters, who are the defendants in this suit ; and all of them, except Francis S. Coxe, united in a conveyance to Francis S. Coxe.

In 1823, Francis S. Coxe employed two surveyors to survey and make a map of the large tract, with a view to ascertain what parts of it belonged to or were claimed by other persons, and to have the residue laid off into parcels, best fitted for sale. He instructed the surveyors to ascertain, if they could, the validity of the interior claims ; and that, wherever they could not arive at a cer-

tainty, that a claim was bad, they were to act, in surveying
and making the map, as if it was good. The instructions
then proceed thus : " The two following claims must in
this manner (for the purpose of surveying) be treated as
if they were good. although I am ignorant, whether they
are valid or not : First : For a sale said to have been
made to General James Miller by Peter Fisher, agent, for
640 acres of land on the Stone-cutter creek, claimed by
Col. Richard Lewis. Secondly, for a sale," &c. The
survey and map were accordingly made in June, 1823 ;
and from the map it appears, that 66 tracts or different
parcels were claimed under various titles by different
persons within the large patent, No. 1023, of 14,720 acres,
and were so situated within it, as to leave the unsold or
unclaimed residue to consist of 44 separate parcels, containing in the whole 7,121 acres. Of the 66 tracts thus
claimed by others, that said to have been sold to James
Miller is one. It is laid down on the map in his name,
as containing 600 acres on Stone-cutter's Fork, not in a
square or parallelogram, but in a very irregular figure,
having thirteen lines, and they, except two, the lines of
tracts laid down as having been sold to other persons or
to be claimed by them. The report of the surveyor states
the titles of the several claimants to the different parcels,
all of which they deemed valid except 12 ; and of those
12, the claim of Miller is one. Of it, the report speaks
thus :

" No. 15 : 600 acres claimed by Richard Lewis, &c. un-
" der a bond given by Peter Fisher to James Miller in
" 1802, to make him a title—see copy of bond—not lo-
" cated or surveyed, no place of beginning, or courses
" or distances stated in the bond ; unimproved—we can-
" not judge whether it be valid or not—it is put down
" in draft by suppositions."

Francis S. Coxe soon afterwards removed to Tennessee, and appointed Francis Alexander, of Rutherford, his

attorney, with power to take care of his lands, and sell and convey them. F. Alexander was the public surveyor for Rutherford, and in February, 1835, he made, at the instance of the heirs of Miller, a survey and plan of 600 acres of land on Stone-cutter's creek, including the shoal, but in a different form from that in the map of 1823, that is to say. having only nine lines, and conveying different land in a great degree.

The present bill was filed in July, 1843, and charges, that, although the contract was made in the name of Fisher himself. yet that it bound his principals, and that, in fact, the horse, that was given for the land, was received by Tench Coxe the elder, and that he recognized the sale made by Fisher, as did also Tench Coxe the younger. The bill charges, that, from the time of the contract, Miller and those claiming under him were in possession of the land, and claimed it as theirs; that none of it was cultivated or cleared, but that they cut timber on it, and their claim was notorious; that Miller paid the taxes on it, and that neither of the Coxe's did so after the sale; and it charges, that the several surveys and maps before mentioned were intended, and were, in fact, acknowledgments by Francis S. Coxe, or his agents, of Miller's purchase and title. The bill also states, that Miller was prevented by age and infirmity from having the land laid off in his life-time, and getting a conveyance executed in Philadelphia; that he " died in the year   , leaving Sarah, the wife of Richard Lewis, and another daughter, the wife of James Erwin, his only children and heirs at law; and that the said Richard and James are both dead, and the said land hath descended to your orators and oratrixes as heirs at law." The prayer is for a specific performance, by a decree that the defendants convey to the plaintiff in fee simple " the said lands."

The answers deny all knowledge or information of the sale made by Fisher to Miller, except as the same ap-

pears on the face of the instrument executed by Fisher,
which the defendant, Francis S. Coxe, first saw and
heard of in the year 1823. They deny that either Tench
Coxe, the elder or the younger, was, as the defendants believe, informed thereof, or recognized the sale, or received
the horse or any other consideration for the land; and
they state that Fisher did not include this in any of his
reports of sales to his employers; and that, from that circumstance, and the laches of Miller in not getting from
Fisher a conveyance, and not making known his claim
to either Tench Coxe, the elder or the younger, or to the
defendant, Francis S., during Miller's life, the defendants
believe that the contract, if made, was abandoned in a
very short time afterwards. The defendants also deny,
and particularly, the defendant Francis S., that Miller,
or any other person under him, ever was in possession of
any land under the contract, or cut timber thereon, or
paid taxes therefor, to their knowledge or belief; for
they say, that the Coxes' respectively paid taxes on that
part, with the other unconveyed portions, of the large
grant No. 1023, and that, in fact, the Miller claim was
never laid off by Miller or any one claiming under him,
or in any manner identified, until the survey made in
1835 by Francis Alexander—which, they say, was made
for Richard Lewis by Alexander, as the County surveyor,
and not for Francis S. Coxe, or as the agent of Coxe.
The defendant, Francis S. Coxe, denies that he intended
to recognize and confirm the sale to Miller, by his instructions to his surveyors in June, 1823, or that they did
by the survey and map made for him; and he says, on
the contrary, that the sole purpose of the survey was for
his private use, to enable him to settle correctly with
his father's trustees for the lands sold by them to his
brother Tench Coxe the younger, for which the title was
unquestionable, and to enable him to discover what land
he might subsequently sell to others, without danger of
any controversy respecting the title: and, consequently,

that his instructions and the report both expressly declare, in respect to this claim under Miller, that it was uncertain, whether it was good or not, and, particularly, the report specifies objections to it, which prove it to be invalid, though the surveyors would not undertake to judge thereof.

The answers then insist on the great length of time that has elapsed, the death of all the immediate parties to the alleged contract long ago, the staleness of the claim, and the difficulty of establishing the actual facts affecting the merits of the claim. An account of the sales of lands within this patent was made up by Tench Coxe, the elder, in Philadelphia, in August 1819, and signed by him with a view to a settlement with his trustees, and it does not include any sale to Miller. This document is proved by several witnesses to be in his hand-writing, who say also that he died at an advanced age in 1824. It further appears, that Fisher has been dead many years, and also Miller. At what particular time Miller died, is not stated, though it appears that he was alive in 1814.

The land appears to be situated in the mountainous part of Rutherford, and it is stated by the witnesses, that the average price of such land in 1802 was twenty-five cents an acre. It is proved by one witness, that Fisher got from Miller a fine roan gelding in 1802, and that it was generally understood that it was for land on Stone-cutter's fork; and by several witnesses, that it was further understood then, and continually since, that 600 acres of land, around the Shoal of Stone-cutter's fork, had been bought by Miller from Fisher, as the agent of Coxe, and was claimed by Miller and his heirs. Two persons, who purchased land from Tench Coxe, the younger, situate, as appears in the map of 1823, on the North of the land laid down therein as Miller's, state that they always understood, that Miller's purchase adjoined them to the South, and that the land there was always reported to be Miller's; and, further, that Tench Coxe, the younger, though often on their land, did not in their hearing set up title to the particular tract called Miller's.

The surveyors state, that Francis S. Coxe never recognized to them the claim of Miller; and that it was laid down in the map merely for his information, as to its situation, whether it was good or bad, and not as acknowledged by him to be good. And Francis Alexander states, that the survey of 1835 was not made by him for Coxe or with a view that he. as Coxe's agent, should convey the land; for that Coxe did not instruct him to convey it, nor ever admit that it ought to be conveyed.

No counsel for the plaintiffs.
Alexander, for the defendants.

RUFFIN, C. J. It will be at once perceived, that the plaintiffs cannot have a decree, for the want of an allegation or proof of the death of their mothers, Mrs. Lewis, and Mrs. Erwin. The bill states that they were the surviving daughters of James Miller, and were his heirs; and that they were then married, and that the husbands subsequently died, and thereupon that the land descended to the plaintiffs as heirs at law. But it does not state, to whom the plaintiffs are heirs; and, from the structure of the sentence, the grammatical construction is, that the land descended from the plaintiff's father. This is the unavoidable construction, when it is perceived that in no part of the bill does it appear. that the mothers are dead.. Consequently the land belongs to Miller's daughters and not to their husbands' children. We have no doubt, however. that this was a mere slip of the draftsman, and therefore would allow the cause to stand over for an amendment, if the claim itself had merits, or it were at all probable that the plaintiffs could ever entitle themselves to relief. But we are satisfied, they could not get a decree, and consequently that the bill might as well be dismissed at once.

The great lapse of time, and, especially, taken in conjunction with the vagueness of the contract in respect to the particular land sold, and with the further circumstance, that nothing was ever done under it, furnishes strong grounds for believing that the contract was abandoned, and, at all events, repels all claim to the interference of the Court of Equity. It was forty-one years after the bargain, before the bill was filed, or any distinct claim set up, as far as is seen. There was, indeed, a sort of reputation, that Miller or Miller's heirs owned land around the Shoal of Stone-cutter's fork; but it is not pretended, that even the reputation fixed upon any land in particular, except that two witnesses, who owned land in one direction, say, they understood that it came up to their lines—though how they came by that understanding, they do not state. It is certain, that the land they reputed to be Miller's, is altogether different in form from that contracted for; and that Miller never, either in conjunction with Fisher or Coxe, or even by himself, proceeded to survey, or in any way set apart, any particular parcel as his under the contract. And to this day there has been no such appropriation, that can be respected. Indeed, the bill does not and could not claim any land in particular, for none has been identified, at least as at all corresponding to the description in the contract; and the plaintiffs are unable to describe any land in their bill, for which they are willing to take a deed. Such being the state of the case, the inference seems a fair one, that Miller and Fisher rescinded the contract; for, otherwise, it would be very extraordinary, that Miller did not take a deed from Fisher, who had authority to execute it for five years after the contract, nor claim one from either of the Coxe's, nor even take any step to identify the land he was to have.

The probability is, therefore, that Fisher paid for the horse in some other way, and that in fact the sale was expressly rescinded—especially, as Fisher, though he re-

ported other sales to his principals, never reported this.
But if it was not expressly rescinded, the Court must treat
it as abandoned. Not one act has been done under it, as
a subsisting contract for about forty years. The bill, indeed, endeavors to excuse this *laches* by a statement of
Miller's age and infirmities. But there is no evidence on
those points, and the persons, from whom he could get the
title, were resident in the same village with him. The
bill also states acts of ownership, such as paying taxes
and cutting timber; but even those equivocal acts are
not proved, nor any thing approaching towards a prepa-
ration to get a title, until Miller's son-in-law, Lewis, in
1835, employed F. Alexander to see if he could not lay
off 600 acres of land around the Shoal in some form. It
is very clear, that not one of the Coxe family ever acknowledged the contract as obligatory or subsistent, and
that Francis S. Coxe did not mean to do so. or in the
least to confirm it by his instructions to his surveyors,
and any thing done under them—for they were acts *di-
verso intuitu.* There is, then, nothing whatever to account for the want of diligence on the part of the alleged vendee, or to shed that light upon the transactions between Miller and Fisher, which will enable the
Court to see them clearly, so as to be reasonably sure
that we see the whole of them, through the dim obscurity of so long an interval as forty years. The case is not
more favorable to the plaintiffs than that of *Tate* v.
Conner, 2 Dev. Eq. 224, in which relief was refused after
thirty-four years.

For these reasons, the bill must be dismissed with
costs.

Per Curiam.   Decree accordingly.

CATHARINE WILLIAMS *vs.* BENJAMIN W. ALEXANDER.

The compromise of a doubtful right, fairly entered into, with due deliberation, will be sustained in a Court of Equity.

Cause removed from the Court of Equity of Mecklenburg County, at the Fall Term, 1845.

. The following was the case :

The plaintiff charges, that her mother, Catharine Simmons, in 1822, conveyed to her, by deed of gift, a negro
girl by the name of Jenny—" to have, hold, and enjoy
" to the sole and separate use of her, the said plaintiff,
" during her natural life, free and separate from the con-
" trol of her husband, Thomas B. Williams, and, after
" her death, to be conveyed to her children"; that her
husband never claimed the negro Jenny, or any of her
children as his property, but, upon leaving his family
and removing to the State of Tennessee, he was induced to sell and convey his right in them to the defendant, Alexander, who, when he purchased, had full
knowledge of the plaintiff's right. She further states,
that the defendant sued her for Jenny and her children,
and, being deranged in her mind, and not knowing what
she was doing, she was led, by the false suggestions
and threats of the defendant, to enter into a compromise, and to sign a paper conveying to him her right
to all the negroes but Jenny and her child John, which
were secured to her. The prayer of the bill is, to have
the compromise set aside, as being obtained by fraud
and oppression, and a re-conveyance of the negroes.

The defendant alleges, that, by the terms of the deed
set forth in the plaintiff's bill, the title of the negroes
was in Thomas B. Williams, the husband of the plaintiff, from whom he purchased them for a full and valuable consideration, with full knowledge of the above
deed; that, having made this purchase, he brought suit
for them against Elizabeth Buchanan, the sister of the
plaintiff, with whom she lived, and James Miller her

nephew, and who was in possession of the negroes, having purchased the right of the plaintiff's children in them. At the instance of the plaintiff, he was induced to enter into a compromise, and agreed to let her have Jenny and her child John, she agreeing that he should have the remaining three, and that writings under seal were executed for the purpose of settling their respective rights. He denies, that at the time this compromise took place, the plaintiff was deranged or out of her mind, and avers that, on the contrary, she was in full possession of her faculties, and understood what she was doing, as the deed was deliberately read over to her. He further states, that the former name of the plaintiff was Catharine Simmons, the same as her mother's, and that, in the year 1813, she purchased the negro girl Jenny, then an infant, from her brother James Simmons, for the sum of $100, and took from him a bill of sale, and that after her intermarriage with Thomas B. Williams, in order to protect the negroes from his debts, he having become much involved, the deed set forth in plaintiff's bill was executed by her mother, Catharine Simmons, to her.

Replication being taken to the answer, the case was removed to this Court for hearing.

Boyden, for the plaintiff.
Alexander, for the defendant.

NASH, J. We do not deem it necessary to give any construction of the deed of 1822, as to the rights of the husband, Thomas B. Williams, or of the plaintiff under it, whether property can or cannot be conveyed to a *feme covert* to hold to her separate use, without the intervention of a trustee. It is sufficient for the present · purpose to say, it was, with the parties concerned. a doubtful question. The defendant purchased the negroes from the husband. and instituted a suit to recover them. While the title is thus in contestation, or while he is claiming them as his property, and the plaintiff holding them as hers, they agree, in order to put an end to the dispute, to divide the property. The compromise of a doubtful right, fairly entered into, with due deliberation, will be sustained in a Court of Equity. It is reasonable and proper it should be so ; parties must be at liberty to settle their own controversies, by dividing the property in controversy, and public policy upholds the right. 1*st* vol. *Story's Eq.* 134, *sec.* 121. The plaintiff in her bill sets out the compromise and endeavors to get rid of it, as obtained from her, while not possessed of mind sufficient to make a binding contract. If such be the case, unquestionably it is not binding on her. It is sufficiently proved, we think, that the plaintiff's mind was naturally a weak one, and that, at some period of time, before the compromise took place, it was unsettled ; but there is no sufficient evidence that such was its condition at the time of the settlement. On the contrary, the evidence is satisfactory, that she was in the full possession of her understanding at the time. She exhibited anxiety that it should be executed by her sister, Elizabeth Buchanan, and James Miller, and it was done. The terms of the compromise were agreed on at one meeting, and executed at a subsequent one. So that the plaintiff was not hurried in the matter, but had time to deliberate and consult her friends. David Galloway, a subscribing witness to the deeds, and who lives a half mile from the plaintiff, states he knew her well, and that she knew, at the time, very well what she was doing, and he heard nothing of her derangement until after the compromise. She requested him to testify, that, at the time it took place, she was deranged, which he refused. The counsel, who managed the suit at law in behalf of Mrs. Buchanan and Miller, states that the plaintiff was examined as a witness in that suit, and he saw no cause to doubt the sanity of her mind. He advised the compromise, because he thought the title of his clients not good. We repeat, then, that we are satisfied from the evidence, that whatever may have been the state of her mind previous to the compromise, at that time she was not deranged, but knew and understood what she was doing; and it is fortunate for her that such is the fact. By the compromise, she has secured to herself two of the negroes, when in fact she was entitled to none of them. The defendant alleges in his answer, and proves it by his witnesses, from the declarations of the plaintiff herself, made before her marriage, that *she* had purchased the negro girl Jenny from her brother, James Simmons, and had given him for her $100, which she had made by selling spirits. No evidence in the case shows that the title of the girl ever was in Catharine Simmons, the mother. This purchase, according to the allegation of the answer, was made in the year 1813, and the conveyance by the mother in 1822. If the fact was as she admitted—and we see no reason to doubt it—the title of all the negroes was in the defendant, Alexander, by his purchase from Thomas B. Williams, the husband. The compromise, however, secures to the plaintiff the two conveyed by him to her.

PER CURIAM. The Bill dismissed with costs.

ELIZABETH A. WHEELER & AL. vs. CLAUDIUS B. WHEELER & AL.

If there be two clauses in a deed, repugnant or contradictory to each other, the first shall stand and the other be rejected.

Cause removed from the Court of Equity, of Davie County, at the Fall Term, 1845.

The following case was presented by the pleadings.

The plaintiffs are the infant children of Claudius B. Wheeler and Anne his wife. They sue by their next friend, and state in their bill, that their maternal grandfather, Nathan Chaffin, made a deed of settlement, for their benefit, in the following words, to-wit:

STATE OF NORTH CAROLINA, }
     Davie County.   } December 27th, 1838.

Know all men by these presents, that I, Nathan Chaffin, of the County and State aforesaid, have this day given to the children of my daughter, Anne J. Wheeler, which she now has or may hereafter have, the following slaves, viz: Sam," &c. (naming them) "which slaves are to remain in possession of my son-in-law, C. B. Wheeler, and his wife Anne J. Wheeler, to their own proper use, until the eldest child gets married, or arrives at the age of twenty-one years, for boarding, clothing and tuition of the said children, which is to be agreeable to the property which they may have. And then the above slaves and increase to be equally divided between said C. B. Wheeler, his wife Anne J. and said children, so as for the said C. B. Wheeler and his wife Anne J. to have a child's part of said property, which they are to have, hold and possess, as long as they shall live; and then to descend to the children of the said Anne J. Wheeler; and the said C. B. Wheeler and his wife Anne J. are to deliver each child's part of the property to each child, when they get married or arrive to the age of twenty-one; and if all the children should die without having a child or children, then, after the death of the said C. B. Wheeler and his wife Anne, the property to revert to my estate and be equally divided between my children, N. S. Chaffin, Elizabeth Chaffin and Mary W. Taylor, or their children after their death, which slaves I warrant and defend the title unto the above persons above expressed. If the said Anne J. Wheeler should have a child or children, after the division of the slaves, as above expressed, then the children, that have received their property allotted them, in the division as above, shall pay over to those born after the division, as above expressed, so as to make all the children of the said Anne J. equal in property."

Which instrument was properly executed by the grantor, attested, proved and registered.

The Bill goes on to state, that their father, C. B. Wheeler, became much indebted; and under judgments and executions against him, certain of the slaves, covered by the above deed of settlement, were sold by the Sheriff as the property of their father, when their maternal uncle, N. C. Chaffin, became the purchaser; that he has since made a conveyance of the said slaves to Giles Pearson, in trust for certain of his creditors. The plaintiffs further state, that Pearson is about to sell the said slaves to satisfy the trust; and that they are apprehensive that some person may purchase them, and remove them beyond the jurisdiction of this Court. And the plaintiffs further state, that their father has conveyed five others of the said slaves to William Locke, in trust for the benefit of certain other of his creditors; and that Locke is about to sell the said five slaves; and that they are apprehensive the purchasers will take them beyond the limits of the State. The plaintiffs, in their bill, insist that their father was only a trustee under the above deed of settlement, for their use and the use of any subsequent born children of their mother, and that he had no interest in the said slaves to convey to Locke, or that was subject to be sold by the Sheriff for his debts. The plaintiffs, in their bill, pray that the trust fund may be secured for their benefit; and that the defendants may be enjoined from making absolute sales of the entire interest in the said slaves; and also for general relief.

Writs of injunction were granted, and, on the answers coming in, the injunctions were ordered to be continued to the hearing. The defendants have answered, and they admit that the complainants are the infant children of Claudius B. Wheeler and Anne his wife. They admit that Nathan Chaffin executed the deed of settlement mentioned in the bill; and they insist, that, by the said deed, C. B. Wheeler had an estate for life in the slaves therein mentioned. They admit all the other material facts and charges, as set forth in the bill. But Locke and Pearson say, that they only intend to sell such interest in the said slaves conveyed to them in trust, as C. B. Wheeler had under the said deed of settlement; which, they are advised, is for his life-time. They, however, submit to any decree the Court may deem right. The case was set for hearing on the bill and answers.

Boyden, for the plaintiffs.
Osborne, for the defendants.

DANIEL, J. The Court is called upon to put a construction upon the deed mentioned in the bill, and to declare the respective rights of the several persons claiming interests under it. We have examined this very curiously framed deed, and have come to the following opinion, as to the rights of the several parties claiming under it:

First. That all the slaves mentioned in the deed, and their increase, are to remain in the possession of Claudius B. Wheeler, " *to his own proper use,* until the eldest child gets married or arrives to twenty-one years of age." This clause in the deed, we think, gives the legal interest to C. B. Wheeler in all the slaves, until the happening of either one or the other of the events mentioned in it. The words contained in the next following parenthesis in the deed, are not to be taken as declaring an immediate trust for the benefit of Wheeler's children, for such a construction would make void the antecedent declaration in the deed, that the slaves were to be to C. B. Wheeler, " *to his own proper use, until,*" &c. For if there be two clauses in a deed repugnant or contradictory to each other, the first shall stand and the other be rejected. 1 *Touch.* 88, *sec.* 7. We have said nothing of the gift in the deed to Mrs. Wheeler, because all the interest she had was immediately vested in her husband, there being no separate estate, declared in the deed, for her benefit.

Secondly. On the eldest of the children of C. B. Wheeler and his wife Anne, coming of age or marrying, all the slaves mentioned in the deed are to be equally divided between C. B. Wheeler and all his children then born. And the share in the slaves allotted to C. B. Wheeler in this division, " he is to have, hold, and possess," to himself, his executors or assigns, during his own life and the life of his wife, then remainder as to this share, to the children of Anne Wheeler, his wife.

Thirdly. The settlor, expecting that the children would remain as members of their father's and mother's family, until they either married or arrived at the age of twenty-one years, and that the slaves would all be divided among them, when the eldest child married or came of age (which event would probably take place before any of the younger children married) therefore attempts to appoint the father and mother guardians or trustees of their childrens property or shares in the said slaves, until they (the children) respectively marry or come of age. For the deed says, " and the said C. B. Wheeler, and his wife " Anne, are to deliver each child's part of the property " to each child, when they get married or arrive at twen- " ty-one years of age. And if *all* the children should die " without having a child or children, then (after the death " of C. B. Wheeler and his wife) the property is to revert " and belong to the other children of the settlor, to-wit: " N. S. Chaffin, Elizabeth Chaffin, and Mary Taylor," &c.

It is very probable that the settlor intended, when he penned the aforesaid clause in the deed, that if it should happen that all the children of his daughter, Mrs. Whee-

ler should die without children, then the said slaves should
be to the use of Wheeler and wife for their lives, remainder to his (the settlor's) other three children for life, then
remainder to their children. But it is unnecessary for us
now to decide, what would, in law, be the effect of these
ulterior limitations ; for in no possible contingency could
C. B. Wheeler (under the deed) get a larger interest in
the slaves, than we have before mentioned. For, if *all*
his (Wheeler's) children should die without issue, and in
his life-time, he could not, under the deed, take a life estate in all or any of the slaves by implication ; for the
expression in the deed, (" after the death of C. B. Wheeler
and wife, the property is to revert") would not give him
a life estate, by implication, or in any other manner, unless it should be in right of his wife, as one of Nathan
Chaffin's next of kin.

Fourthly. The interest of C. B. Wheeler in *all* the slaves,
until the period of division, was liable, at law, to be sold
in execution, or assigned by him for the benefit of his
creditors, or for his own benefit. And so, likewise, is the
share of Wheeler in the slaves, to be ascertained by division at the proper time, liable to execution, or assignment by him, for the lives of himself and wife.

Fifthly. The complainants are the *cestuis que trusts* of
the slaves, subject to the particular interest of their father in the same, as aforementioned. And we think, that
they have a right, under the circumstances of the case,
to have their interest in the same secured, so that it shall
certainly be forthcoming to them, when their father's interest in the said slaves, or any of them, shall have expired.

Sixthly. It is unnecessary, now, for this Court to remark
upon the last clause in the deed of settlement ; which directs, that those children, who may receive shares, on the
division of the slaves as aforesaid, shall contribute to make
up shares to any after born children of Mrs. Wheeler.
For the bill is framed with a view only, *first*, to ascertain

the exact interest of Wheeler in the fund; and, *secondly,* with a view, that the residue of the fund, after his interest is ascertained and taken out, may be secured for the benefit of the present and all after born children of Mrs. Wheeler. We think, that the injunction should be held up, and continued, until such security shall be given to the satisfaction of the Court.

Seventhly. It is also improper, upon these pleadings, to say, which of the two, Nathan L. Chaffin or Locke, will be entitled, upon the division of the negroes between Wheeler and his children, to the share that may fall to Wheeler and wife. At present, each of those persons is entitled to the profits of the negroes, purchased by him, and will be so entitled as long as Wheeler would have been to the whole profits. But when the division shall take place, which of them is to be preferred or how they are to divide between themselves, must be determined at that time, or when they shall raise the question as between themselves.

PER CURIAM.   Decreed accordingly.

WILLIAM T. JOHNSON vs. JOSEPH CORPENNING.

Where the deceased had a residence in this State, a grant of administration on his estate, by the Court of any other County than that in which he resided, is absolutely void.

The cases of *Smith* v. *Barham*, 2 Dev. Eq. 420, *Etheridge* v. *Bell*, 5 Ired. 87, *Collins* v. *Turner*, No. Ca. T. R. 105, and *Smith* v. *Munroe*, 1 Ired. 345, cited and approved.

Cause removed from the Court of Equity of Henderson County, at the Fall Term, 1845.

Upon the pleadings and proofs, the case appears to be this: Abraham A. Strange made his will on the 13th of

October, 1814, and therein, after some small specific legacies, gave all the residue of his estate, real and per-. sonal, to his wife Mary A. Strange, during her natural life, and then to his twelve children, who are mentioned by their several names, equally to be divided between them ; and appointed his wife, and his son, Nelson A. Strange, and his son-in-law, James Coffee, the executors. The testator died soon afterwards in Wilkes County, where he resided at the time of his death, and for several years before. In July, 1815, the will was proved in the County Court of Wilkes, and probate was granted to the widow and Nelson A. Strange, who alone qualified. The estate consisted of land, several slaves, and other articles of personal chattels ; and after disposing of enough to pay the debts, the whole residue was taken and held by Mrs. Strange, as devisee and legatee, until her death in November, 1842, except as hereinafter mentioned.

The bill was filed in September, 1843, and states that, while Mrs. Strange was seised of the land and possessed of the slaves, under the gift to her for life, Nelson A. Strange pulled down and removed a barn and other houses, situate on the land, and also sold one of the slaves for the price of $400, which he converted to his own use ; and that in like manner he disposed of other parts of the personal property, and that he never accounted for any part thereof.

The bill then states the subsequent death of Nelson A. Strange, intestate, and that administration of his estate was granted to his widow, Ann Strange, and Joseph Corpenning, who are defendants in this suit; and that afterwards, namely, in February, 1843, James Coffee, who was appointed one of the executors of the will of Abraham A. Strange, renounced the said office, that is to say, in the County Court of Henderson County, and thereupon, that Court granted letters of administration *cum testamento annexo de bonis non* to the plaintiff, William T. Johnson. The prayer is for an account in the premises and payment.

The defendant, Mrs. Ann Strange, did not administer on the estate of her deceased husband, and she insists thereon in her answer.

The defendant, Corpenning, after admitting that he is the sole administrator of Nelson A. Strange, insists in his answer on several matters of defence; of which it is not material to mention more than the following, as they have been deemed by the Court fatal to the plaintiff's case. The first is, that in respect to the injury to the real estate, the plaintiff had no right, but that the right was exclusively in the devisees in remainder. Another is, that the testator charged his executors with no duty touching the personal estate after the death of his widow, and that the executor's assent to the legacies to the tenant for life, vested the slaves absolutely in her, and in the remainder men according to their respective interests. Thirdly, that none of the other personal chattels were used by Nelson A. Strange, but all were kept and enjoyed by Mrs. Mary A. Strange alone, and were consumed or worn out in the necessary use of them by her as tenant for life; and also, that if any person were chargeable therefor, the said Mary A. was, and that she left personal assets more than sufficient to cover the value thereof, and that the plaintiff is the administrator of her estate, and the assets as aforesaid came to her hands. Lastly, that the Court of Henderson County had no jurisdiction to receive the renunciation of Coffee, the surviving executor of Abraham A. Strange, or to grant the administration to the plaintiff.

Francis, for the plaintiff.
Avery, for the defendants.

RUFFIN, C. J. With the land, the personal representative has no concern. The will creates no trust respect-

ing it; and upon the death of the widow, it went directly to the remainder-men. As to that, therefore, the bill
would have to be dismissed.

Upon the second point, the rule is clear, that, like specific legacies, the slaves, given in the residue, vested by
the assent of the executors in the tenant for life and the
remainder-men. There are several decided cases in this
Court on the question; but it is only necessary to refer
to *Smith* v. *Barham*, 2 Dev. Eq. 420, and the late case of
Etheridge v. *Bell*, 5 Ired. 87, as they are directly in point.
Therefore, the plaintiff, as administrator, could have no
redress, even supposing Nelson A. Strange sold the negro and converted the price to his own use.

It may be that Nelson A. Strange might be liable, because as an executor he did not attempt to sell the other
articles constituting the residue, so that the tenant for
life should have the interest of the fund, instead of allowing her to consume the articles. Without considering the effect on his liability, of the fact that the widow
was also executrix, and was as much entitled as he was
to the possession of the assets, and to assent to the legacy to herself, but supposing that he might be chargeable
therefor, yet it is clear, that he ought not to be chargeable to the plaintiff in the first instance, if it be true that
the executrix and tenant for life had the sole benefit of
those articles, and left assets to more than their value,
which have come to the plaintiff's hands, as her administrator. That would be a proper subject for an enquiry,
which would be directed, if a result thereof favorable to
the plaintiff could possibly enable him to maintain this
suit. But, as the Court thinks that could not be, on the
ground that will be next mentioned, it is useless to direct
the enquiry.

The fourth objection is to the validity of the grant of
administration to the plaintiff; which goes to the whole
bill. Upon that, the Acts of Assembly of 1777 and 1789,
Rev. St. c. 46, *s.* 1, and c. 122, *s.* 6, are decisive. They

require wills to be proved, and letters testamentary and letters of administration to be granted in the Court of the County where the testator or intestate resided at the time of his death. If done in any other Court, in case the party deceased had a residence in this State, it is void. *Collins* v. *Turner*, No. Ca. T. R. 105; *Smith* v. *Munroe*, 1 Ired. 345. Besides, it is a contradiction and absurdity, after the probate of a will in one Court, that another Court should pretend to grant a probate thereof to another person named therein an executor, or receive the renunciation of such person, and grant, to yet another, administration *cum testamento annexo*. For such grants consist of a copy of the will, as proved, and the acts thereon of the Court taking the proof, officially certified. 1 *Wms. Ex'or.* 158; and that cannot come from any Court but that which has the custody of the original. When, therefore, the bill states that the Court of Henderson granted to the plaintiff letters of administration " with the will annexed," it states that which cannot possibly be true; and, unless it were true, the plaintiff could not institute this suit.

The bill must therefore be dismissed, and costs to each defendant.

Per Curiam.   Decree accordingly.

SUSAN J. HUMPHREYS *vs.* THOMAS R. TATE & AL.

A Bill should contain a statement of the title of the plaintiff and defendant, so that the pleadings may shew the titles claimed by the parties, without looking for it in the evidence alone.

Cause removed from the Court of Equity of Guilford County, at the Fall Term, 1845.

Badger and *Kerr*, for the plaintiff.
Morehead, for the defendants.

RUFFIN, C. J.   In this case, two of the defendants, Sarah
L. Humphreys, and Absalom H. Tate, are infants, and no
answers have been put in for them.   The defendant,
Thomas R. Tate has put in an answer; which is stated
in the beginning of it to be put in by him for himself, and
for the two infant defendants—of the former of whom,
he says, he is guardian, and of the latter the father.   But
there does not appear to have been any order appointing
him guardian *pendente lite* to make defence for either of
those persons.   For that reason alone, the Court would
be unable to make a decree. that would be binding on
the infants; and therefore, the cause would be remanded, that the infants might be properly brought before the
Court.   We observe from the copies of the wills of Henry
Humphreys, deceased, and of that of the plaintiff's late
husband, which are filed with the bill as exhibits, that
those infants are interested and essential parties to the
suit.   Absalom H. Tate is the devisee, in the latter will,
of a house and lot in Greensborough, which is one of the
parts of the real estate in which the plaintiff, as we suppose, claims dower.   But the truth is, that the bill is so
drawn as not to show on its face, how any of the persons
named therein as defendants have any interest in the
subject.   It calls " Thomas R. Tate and his wife Nancy,
Sarah L. Humphreys, and Absalom H. Tate, defendants,"
and states that they " are the only persons interested in
the estates in which your oratrix is entitled to dower."
But it does not charge that either of them is the heir at
law of Absalom Humphreys, the plaintiff's late husband,
nor a devisee from him.   It undertakes to state how that
person became seised, namely, under a will of his late
father, Henry Humphreys; but it does not state that the
will has ever been proved, nor set out any devise therein
to Absalom Humphreys, nor to any of the other persons

who are made defendants. There are annexed to the
bill copies of the papers it calls wills ; but that does not
dispense with a statement of the title of the plaintiff and
defendants in the bill, so that the pleadings may show
the titles claimed by the parties, without looking for it
in the evidence alone—for it is not even alleged that the
persons sued are the persons mentioned in the respective
devises. As the cause has to go back, the attention of
the counsel is drawn to the defects in the bill, as well
as that respecting the answers, in order that they may
avail themselves of the opportunity of amending, or,
rather, remodelling the pleadings. The cause was removed by consent to this Court for hearing, and must be
remanded at the costs of the parties equally.

PER CURIAM.   Ordered accordingly.

EQUITY CASES

ARGUED AND DETERMINED

IN

THE SUPREME COURT

OF

NORTH CAROLINA.

JUNE TERM, 1846.

WILLIAM W. HOLDEN, ADM'R. OF JOSEPH PEACE *vs.* WILLIAM PEACE.

Where a co-partnership owned a dwelling house, which was exclusively occupied by one of the partners and his family, *Held*, that this partner was liable for rent, though there was no special agreement to that effect, and though no charge against him for rent was made on the books of the firm during his life-time.

The general rule for interest on accounts in ordinary dealings, is, that it is chargeable only after an account has been rendered, so that the parties can see which is the debtor and what he has to pay, unless it be agreed otherwise, or the course of business shews it to have been otherwise understood.

In the case of a co-partnership, without some agreement or understanding to the contrary, interest is chargeable by one partner against another only on the balance found due from the latter at the time of the dissolution of the partnership, whether that dissolution be by death or otherwise, and only from and after that period.

This cause, having been set for hearing, was transmitted to this Court from the Court of Equity of Wake County, at the Spring Term, 1846.

The pleadings presented the following case :

In November 1798, Joseph Peace and the defendant, William Peace, entered into co-partnership as retail dealers in dry goods and other merchandise, in Raleigh, and carried on their business actively and prosperously until the year 1832, when their stock of goods and shop were burned. They began to trade with very little capital, but from diligence and skill they made considerable profits, and, during the period mentioned, they invested the surplus profits, which were not needed in their regular business, in loans, stocks, lands, houses, slaves, and other things. After 1832, they made no more purchases of merchandise for sale again, but never dissolved the partnership, and continued to invest their funds, as they were collected, in real and personal property and stocks, as before mentioned, until December 1842, when Joseph Peace died suddenly and intestate.

These two gentlemen were brothers and were both unmarried, and jointly conducted their trade personally, and resided together, generally in lodgings in the building in which their business was carried on. Joseph Peace, however, had a family of children, whom he recognized, and for whom and their mother he provided a house and servants and other necessaries, and defrayed the expenses of their education, as a parent. In consequence of this difference in their situation, the demands of Joseph for money were much greater than those of William; and as neither of them had any other resources than his share in the partnership, Joseph's account became much the larger of the two, as appearing on the books at the death of Joseph.

Among the real estate purchased for profit by the firm, were two lots, with a house on one of them, in Raleigh, at the price of $1,612 50. Soon afterwards, Joseph Peace expressed a wish to give up the house he had before leased, and to take this for the use of his family aforesaid; and he did so. In consequence thereof, expenditures were made in repairs and erecting other buildings, and various outlays on it to render it comfortable, which, together with the first cost, made the property stand the firm in the sum of $4,405, as stated in the books. After the fire in 1832, Joseph Peace removed, himself, to the same house, and lived there with his family for the ten years preceding his death; and during that period, William Peace paid for his lodging and board at other places, and charged himself with the sums he took from the joint funds for that purpose, as well as for all other personal uses; and, for several years before the death of Joseph, William resided with his brother, but during that time, he, William, regularly charged himself to Joseph, on the books of the firm, with his board. But, at no time during the life of Joseph, was he charged with rent for the premises so occupied by his family for one period, and by himself and his family for another period. After the death of his brother, however, Mr. William Peace, in bringing up the books with a view, as a surviving partner, to stating a final account between the two partners, in order to settling with his brother's administrator, entered, as a charge in Joseph's account, the rent of the house and lots during the period they had been thus occupied, amounting to about $4000.

There never was a settlement between the two brothers. Having the greatest confidence in each other, and living in the greatest intimacy, each was suffered to take what he wished and to charge himself with it; and the items were merely posted into the ledger, and the accounts carried on from year to year and from book to book, without ever having been added up, much less closed. But, after the death of Joseph, the surviving partner ascertained the amount of the annual dealings of each partner, and computed interest upon the several balances from the end of each year, including interest on the sums before mentioned, and charged the same in the several accounts of the brother and himself, whereby a very large balance of interest appears against Joseph Peace. When his administrator and the surviving part-ner came together to settle, the former objected to the charges of rent and the interest thereon, and all the other interest, and he then filed this bill for an account. In order to render it the easier to take between the parties themselves, or by the master, the pleadings were framed so as to obtain the opinion of the Court on those questions, which seem to form the chief obstacles to the adjustment of the business. As to the point respecting the interest besides the facts already mentioned, the answer admits, that there was no agreement between the parties, that the interest should be charged, and that the subject was never mentioned between them. But the defendant insists on the propriety of charging it, upon the ground, that the moneys withdrawn from the joint funds by the respective partners would have been actively employed, either in trade or by investments yielding interest, or in property increasing in value, and that there is no danger of doing injustice to either side, as the items of account all appear in the books, and making up the interest account is mere matter of computation. The defendant states that he was advised, in the life-time of his brother, of his right to charge interest upon a final settlement ; and, though he is not called on to decide whether he would have insisted on his right, if they had, themselves, made a settlement, yet under existing circumstances, he is unwilling to sur-render any thing, to which he is entitled, since his brother's sudden death prevented him from bestowing his property on his own family, as he would no doubt have done, and the law casts it on persons who have not as strong claims on him.

The case was heard upon the bill, answer and exhibits.

W. H. Haywood, for the plaintiff.
Badger, for the defendant.

RUFFIN, C. J. Joseph Peace is justly charged with a reasonable rent of the premises, occupied by himself or his family. There is no ground on which he could have the use of the property gratuitously, more than he could take merchandize from the store without being charged for it. He did·not purchase the property as his own, but the firm bought it, took the conveyances, and made all the outlays on it. If it was decayed or was burned, the loss would have been that of the partnership; and, as he exclusively enjoyed it, he ought to pay to the partnership a fair rent. Of course the Court cannot undertake to enquire into the period of his occupation, nor the proper rent to be charged, nor is it supposed the parties expect it, or that the Court should do more than determine the principle. If they cannot agree upon those points, they must be referred to the master.

With respect to the heavier item of interest, the law, we think, is against the defendant. The general rule for interest, on accounts in ordinary dealings si, that it is chargeable only after an account has been rendered, so that the parties can see which is the debtor and what he has to pay, unless it be agreed otherwise, or the course of business shews it to have been otherwise understood. This applies still more forcibly, as between partners, because their accounts cannot be fully made up between them without, in truth, taking all the accounts of the firm; in other words, without a dissolution: and it is impossible to tell before, what either would be bound to pay or entitled to receive. Therefore, if the parties mean, that interest should be charged on the accounts of the partners, for dealings in the shop and money withdrawn for personal expenses or other things, from year to year, the course is to come to an agreement to that effect, and then for balances appearing upon those individual accounts annually or oftener, according to the agreement, charges of interest are made from time to time, or, if omitted, will be allowed in making the final settlement. If there be no agreement upon the subject, it must be understood, that the parties, especially when they have no separate property, were aware that each must draw from the firm the means of supporting himself and his family, and that an exact equality could not be expected in those matters ; and therefore, that it was not intended that interest should be charged during the partnership. In *Dexter* v. *Arnold*, 3 Mas. Rep. 284. Mr. Justice STORY lays it down, that interest is not allowed upon partnership accounts generally, until a balance is struck on a settlement between the partners, unless the parties have otherwise agreed or acted in their partnership concerns. And Chancellor KENT, in *Stoughton* v. *Lynch*, 2 John C. C. 209, says, that the time of dissolution is the period to adjust the balance between the partners, and the party, then found the debtor, becomes so with obligation to pay, and is, therefore, charged with interest on that debt. In that case, the partners had made no settlement, but the master in taking the accounts in a suit to settle the partnership, found the balance at the period of dissolution, and thenceforward allowed the interest thereon ; and the Chancellor approved of it, saying that it was the general practice, as well as the good sense of the thing, that a rest should be made on the liquidation and adjustment of accounts, at the period of the dissolution of the concern. These positions render it clear, that there can be no charge of interest before the death of Joseph Peace, and that interest ought to be charged after that event, on the amount found to have been then due from him. It cannot be allowed before, because it is admitted that there was no agreement for it, nor even a suggestion of it in conversation ; and the accounts had just been kept on in the books, without being examined or even added up, upon the entire confidence of the brothers, in the good faith of each other, that all proper charges were respectively made by each against himself. It is absolutely certain, we think, that Joseph Peace had no idea that he was to pay interest, else he would have charged it, or mentioned it at least ; and it is nearly certain, that the defendant had had as little thought of charging him with it, though he is now from peculiar circumstances, induced to prefer the claim against his administrator. But the benevolence of his view, as to the disposition of what he might gain by the charge, cannot change the law. If he had been dissatisfied with the amount of his brother's expenditures, he might either have stopped the business, or made an agreement as to interest. Having done neither, and knowing that no interest had been charged at any time during forty-four years, it is presumed that it was not intended to be charged The omission of this charge has a very different effect from the omission merely of the charge of rent, since the latter required an adjustment, as to the proper amount between the parties, while the other would have required but computation. We have said, that interest cannot be allowed before the death of Joseph Peace—which is, because there had been no dissolution before. It is true the buying and selling of goods had been stopped ten years, but nearly all their property remained joint, and all their accounts went through the books of the firm, regularly kept up to his death, which event alone dissolved the concern. But upon the principle held in *Stoughton* v. *Lynch*, the balance then due must be ascertained, and interest computed thereon from that time until the settlement be made.

The pleadings also raise another question, upon the following facts stated in the answer. One John W. Young married a daughter of Joseph Peace, who took charge of their advancement and also of the support of their children, and from time to time supplied them with necessaries or money to purchase them. For some of those advances he took memorandums or notes from Young; and upon one occasion the defendant, finding a number of them in the store, computed the amount due thereon

and took the bond of Young to the firm therefor. Other
memorandums of the same kind were found, upon the
death of Joseph Peace, among his private papers. There
were also on the books other small debts charged to some
"other members of said Joseph's family." The defendant
states his belief, that Joseph Peace did not expect or intend that Young and "the other members of his family"
should pay any part of those debts, and considered himself accountable for them, as he recorded them as advancements or supplies to his family, and would not have
thought of the defendant's contributing to them. In consequence of these views, the defendant, after the death of
Joseph, transferred to his debit the debts before charged
to Young and "the other members of his family," and
also charged him with the amount of the due bills of
Young, that were found in Joseph Peace's desk, and the
interest thereon. It is submitted to the Court whether
that charge or any part of it is proper. The statement
is so deficient, as to the period and amounts of the several
advances, which form the subject of this part of the controversy, and also as to what other sums Joseph Peace
laid out for advancements to Mrs. Young, or for the benefit of the "other members of the family," that the Court
is not able to speak conclusively on the subject. It would
seem from the circumstances, that Joseph Peace generally
charged to his own account immediately the sums expended
for the maintenance or advancement of the dependent
members of his family, that he did not intend to take on
himself the debts contracted for those persons by Young
himself or the others, and for which he took notes or made
charges in account against them. Why charge them instead of himself, if he meant the debts to be his own?
This reason is particularly strong in respect of the bond
of Young, which was taken by the defendant for a number of those demands, whereby all parties made Young,
and not Joseph Peace, debtor to the firm therefor. It is
possible that Joseph Peace purposed to take the debt on

himself in the final settlement, especially, if Young was unable to pay, and was known to be at the time his debts were contracted. But it does not sufficiently appear, that it was so intended between the parties, or that even he had a distinct intention upon the subject. Nothing seems to have been said upon it at any time; and the presumption is, that the debts were exclusively those of the persons against whom a note was held or a charge made in the books. For the sums, for which Young's notes were found in Joseph Peace's private papers, it is natural to suppose he had already charged himself on the books of the firm; otherwise, he would have placed those notes among the papers of the concern, as he had done the others. Upon the whole, therefore, the Court holds that it was improper to charge Joseph Peace with the bond of Young, which the defendant took as before mentioned; and we incline to the opinion, that no part of Young's debt was chargeable to Joseph Peace—the same is probably true, for the same reasons, in respect to the debts of the "other members of the family," but as the facts in relation to those debts, do not sufficiently appear, we are unable to come to any definite decision of the point.

Per Curiam.   Declared accordingly.

IN THE MATTER OF THOMAS LATHAM, GUARDIAN, &c.

Before the Court will direct any of the property of a lunatic to be applied to the payment of his debts, it will set apart a sufficient fund for the maintenance of the lunatic, and his wife and infant children, if he has any. Nothing that has been advanced for the prior maintenance of the lunatic shall be chargeable on this fund.

This was an appeal from certain interlocutory orders made in the course of the proceedings on this petition in the Court of Equity of Beaufort County, at the Fall Term, 1843, his Honor Judge PEARSON presiding.

The following are the facts of the case presented to this Court.

Daniel Latham was duly found to be a lunatic. He had a wife and some children, and was deeply involved in debt. The Court appointed the petitioner, Thomas Latham, to be his committee. The said committee filed this petition, to have the real and personal estate of the lunatic sold, for the purpose of paying his debts, and for the purpose of maintaining him and his family. At spring term, 1841, of Beaufort Court of Equity, there was an order made, that the committee should sell the real and personal estate of the lunatic. The property was sold, and a report made by the committee to the next Court, when the report was set aside, and the clerk and master was ordered to make the said sales. At spring term, 1842, the case was continued. At spring term, 1843, an order was made by the Court, at the instance of H. Wiswall, a creditor, that the committee should himself report in full, as to all the property, which had, or might come to his hands, before the next term of the Court; and also to report as to all his expenditures and his disbursements for the lunatic: and that the creditors of the lunatic, prove their debts before the master. And it was then further ordered, that the house and land belonging to it be sold by the master. At fall term, 1843, the master reported a sale, made by him, of the home house and plantation; and this report was confirmed. And the master also reported on the accounts of the committee, from the date of the appointment, up to that term; including the sale of the personal property, under an order of the County Court, made at December term, 1840; and also, the amount of property sold under a former interlocutory decree, made in this cause. The master also reported the amount of debts due to the several creditors of the lunatic, and the balance of debts still due to the committee; and the master allowed the said balance to the committee, and also allowed him commissions, 2 1-2 per cent. on the receipts, and 5 per cent. on the disbursements. To this report of the master, two of the creditors of the lunatic, Wiswall and Winfield, excepted; *first*, because the committee paid other creditors their debts in full, after he knew or had reason to believe that the lunatic was insolvent. They insist that he should pay all the creditors *pro rata.* And the Court sustained this exception, and ordered, that the account and report be re-committed to the master, so as to distribute the whole fund. *pro rata*, among the several creditors. This order was resisted by the committee, because he said, that his payments in full to the several creditors had been rightfully made before the filing of this petition. And, secondly, he insisted, that, if the creditors were to be paid, as directed in the said order, then he should be deemed a creditor. Also a motion was made for a proper allowance, out of the fund in Court, for the maintenance of the lunatic and his wife and infant children; and also for an allowance to the committee, for the previous maintenance of the lunatic and his wife and family. The Court was of the opinion, that any previous necessary maintenance of the lunatic, his wife and children, should be allowed to the committee. But, as against the claims of the creditors, the Court thought, that no prospective allowance for maintenance could be hereafter made. The Court overruled the exception as to commissions allowed to the committee. From the decision of the Court upon the exceptions, and also from the judgment of the Court, upon the motion for an order for maintenance prospectively for the lunatic and his family, the committee prayed an appeal, which was allowed by the Court. Wiswall and Winfield, two of the creditors of the lunatic, prayed an appeal from so much of this decree, as allows the committee of the lunatic, for sums expended for maintenance of the lunatic and his family heretofore, which appeal was allowed by the Court. The master reported the receipts by the committee of the lunatic $3,730 51, and that his disbursements were $4,360 07. The committee was allowed for commissions $259 32, leaving a balance due the committee from the estate of the lunatic, $886 86. The master further reported, that there was now in his office the sum of $942 14 unexpended, belonging to the lunatic, being the proceeds of the real estate sold in this cause by the master. And he further reported $3,160 40, unsatisfied claims, now outstanding against the lunatic.

No counsel in this Court for the petitioner.
J. H. Bryan, for the creditors.

DANIEL, J. Before we give any opinion upon the exceptions taken by the creditors to the master's report, we must first see that there is a balance of estate on hand, sufficient to maintain the lunatic during his lunacy, and his wife and infant children. *Shelford on Lunatics,* 356. In England, the grant, under the great seal, of the custody of the person and estate of the lunatic, contains, among other things, an authority to the bailiff or committee, to take the property and effects of the lunatic, for his profit and advantage; "and for the maintenance, sustenance and support of the said A. B. and his family, (if he has any, or in time to come may have)." *Shelford,* 635. In England, it has been questioned, whether the seizure of the estate of a lunatic by the King; *first,* for the maintenance of him and his family, and *secondly,* for the benefit of his creditors, as the Court of Chancery might from time to time make orders for the same, was not solely by force of the statute, *De prerogativa regis,* 17 *Ed. 2d. ch.* 10. (See the translation into English of that statute, *Shelford,* 498.) But the better opinion is, that the said statute was not introductive of any new right, but was only declaratory of the common law.

In the matter of Latham.

Beverly's Case, 4 *Steph.* 126, 127, 2 *Ves. Jr.* 71, *Bac. Abr. title Idiots and Lunatics*, C., *Shelford*, 12. And we take it, that the King, as *parens patriæ,* by the common law, had the protection of all his subjects, and that, in a more particular manner, he is to take care of all those whc, by reason of their imbecility and want of understanding, are incapable to taking care of themselves. *Bac. Abr. Idiots and Lun. C.* All the lunatic's estate has been converted into money, and only the sum of $942 14 is now within the reach of this Court. We think that this fund must be retained by the committee, not to pay his balance or the debts of any of the creditors, but for the purpose of maintaining the lunatic and his wife and infant children. That the Court must reserve a sufficient maintenance for the lunatic, before making an order for payment of debts, or allowing to the committee sums already applied by him to that purpose, is clear from the nature of the jurisdiction in lunacy, as well as from the decisions. In *Ex parte Hastings,* 14 Ves. 182, Lord El- bon said, he could not pay a lunatic's debts and leave him destitute, but must reserve a sufficient maintenance for him; and in *Tally* v. *Tally,* 2 D. & B. Eq. 385, that is cited with approbation by this Court. With respect to the maintenance of the wife, and such of the children as, from tenderness of age or other causes, are dependent upon the parent, this Court, in *Brooks* v. *Brooks,* 2 D. & B. Eq. 389, gave the opinion, that, though it was not mentioned in our statute, it was a proper charge upon the lunatic's estate—it not preventing the maintenance of the lunatic himself—upon the ground, that the lunatic himself was chargeable with it; and, among the demands on his estate, to be provided for by order of the Court, none can be more meritorious, certainly, and no disposition of the lunatic's estate is so likely to promote the comfort and due care of the lunatic himself.

These being appeals from interlocutory orders on the petition, this Court can do no more than decide the par-

59

ticular points sent here; and therefore, we refrain from saying more than this: that, for the present, the whole of the sum in the Court of Equity should be declared a fund necessary for the maintenance of the lunatic and his wife and infant children, and be ordered to be put out at interest by the committee, to answer such orders as may be made by the Court, from time to time, for those purposes; referring it to the master to inquire of the proper allowance for those purposes, according to the fund and the state of the family. We leave it to the Judge below or the County Court, whichever be the proper tribunal, now or in future, as they shall be moved, to deal with the committee in respect to the estate already disbursed by him.

The Court being of this opinion, it is unnecessary now to decide the other points raised in the cause.

The costs in this Court must be paid equally by the parties.

PER CURIAM.   Decreed accordingly.

EUNICE ASHCRAFT vs. ALEXANDER LITTLE AND OTHERS.

A husband cannot be deprived of his right to property given to his wife, except by clear and unequivocal expressions in the deed of gift or devise, leaving no reasonable doubt that the property was given to the separate use of the wife.

Where a deed of gift of a negro was made to a married woman and her children, (two sons,) and these words were added, "but the said gift to extend to no other person"—Held, DANIEL, J. dissentiente, that these words did not create a separate estate in the wife, especially as they extended equally to the gift to the sons, and that therefore the husband was entitled to the share of the negro so given to his wife.

The case of Rudisell v. Watson, 2 Dev. Eq. 430, cited and approved.

This was an appeal from a decree of the Court of Equity of Anson County, at the spring term, 1846, his Honor

Judge DICK presiding, by which decree a demurrer, which had been filed by the defendants to the plaintiff's bill, was sustained and the bill dismissed with costs.

The bill states that Solomon Marsh. the father of the complainant, gave by deed certain negroes to the plaintiff and her children, which is in the following words: "Know all men by these presents, that I, Solomon Marsh, for and in consideration of the natural love and good will which I have and bear towards my daughter. Eunice Ashcraft, have given and granted, and by these presents do freely give and grant unto the said Eunice Ashcraft and her children, a negro girl ten years old, by the name of Clarissa, and her increase; but the said gift to extend to no other person." At the time this gift was made, Eunice was the wife of James Ashcraft and had two children who were boys, both of whom are since dead. James Ashcraft, the husband, being largely indebted, judgments were had against him, and under the executions issuing thereon, the negro Clarissa and her children were by the sheriff levied on and sold as the property of the defendant Ashcraft, and the defendant Little became the purchaser. The bill claims, that under the deed of Solomon Marsh, the plaintiff, who is the Eunice Ashcraft mentioned in the deed, was entitled to the sole use and benefit of one-third of the negro Clarissa and her children, or to one-third of their value, and prays that they either may be divided and one-third allotted to her or to some person for her sole use, or sold, and one-third of the value so allotted; and that the defendant Little may be decreed to account with her for one-third of the hires of said negroes since they have been in his possession.

The defendants have filed a demurrer, and assigned for reason, that it appears, by the plaintiff's own showing, that she has not any separate estate in the negroes mentioned in the bill. Upon argument, the demurrer was sustained and the bill dismissed with costs.

Winston, for the plaintiff.
Strange, for the defendants.

NASH, J. We concur with his Honor, in his opinion. The plaintiff contends, that, under the expression used in the deed, "but the said gift to extend to no other person," she has in one-third part of the negroes a sole property, separate and distinct from her husband, and over which he has no control, and which is not subject to his debts or incumbrances. Do these words, taken in connexion with those which immediately precede them, give her such property? It is admitted, that no technical words or particular form of expression is required, to convey to a married woman property to the exclusion of her husband, but that any words are sufficient, which leave no doubt that such was the intention of the devisor or settlor. It is the intention of the donor, which is to govern, but this intention of excluding the husband must not be left to inference, but must be clearly and unequivocally declared. If the intention be clear, the Court will execute it, though it may not be expressed in technical language. *Lew. on Trusts*, p. 150, and the authorities there referred to. The governing principle is, that the husband is not to be deprived of what the law gives him, by the *jus mariti*, by inference. In the case of *Heathman* v. *Hall*, 3 Ired. Eq. 420, this doctrine is fully recognized. The words, " for the *entire* use and benefit, profit and advantage of Mrs. Eleanor Kincaid," being equivalent to *for the sole use*, &c. Words which were held to be sufficiently explicit, in the case of *Adamson* v. *Armitage*, 19 Ves. Jr. 416, also reported in *Cooper*. 283, and also in the case, *Ex parte Ray*, 1st Mod. 199, and *Lynes'* case, 1st Younge, 562. So also the case of *Rudisell* v. *Watson*. 2 Dev. Eq. 430, expressly and strongly enforces the same doctrine. " It will not do (the Court say,) to guess. The husband cannot be excluded without plain recorded words or a necessary implication." These cases abundantly show, that, to exclude the husband, the intention of the settlor must be clear, certain, and unequivocally declared. This certainty, it is said, exists in this case by force of the clause, "but the said gift to extend to no other person." Taken by themselves, they might have that effect; but coupled, as they are with others preceding them, we do not think so. Our attention has been drawn to the case, *Margetts* v. *Barringer*, 10th Cond. Ch. Rep. 158, 7th Simons 482. The condensed report is very concise. The case is as follows: John Eustace devised to Louisa Margetts and Ann Margetts, all the residue of his property to be equally divided between them, for their own use and benefit, independent of any other person. The Vice Chancellor Sir Launcelot Shadwell decided, that the words "independent of any other person," meant "independent of all mankind," and of course included the husband. In the previous case of *Wagstaff* v. *Smith*, 9th Ves. Jr. 520, it had been declared by the Master of the Rolls, Sir William Grant, that a devise to a trustee to suffer a married woman to take to her own use, &c. "independent of her husband," the interest of certain stock, was a devise to her separate use. For such expressions are clearly inconsistent with the idea of any interference on the part of the husband. The only question, which appears to have been brought to the attention of the Court in *Margett's case* was, whether the husband was included in the words "independent of any other person," by force of the words themselves, and the Vice Chancellor so declared. The words "for their own use and benefit" are not noticed, because, if the husband was included in the words of exclusion, then it was admitted, she had the property to her sole and separate use. There was nothing in the devise, in that case, inconsistent with such an intention on the part of the settlor, and indeed his obscure purpose could not be carried out under any other construction. The husband therefore was excluded by a necessary implication. Is there any such necessary implication in this case? The words are, "but the said gift is not to extend to any other person." These words extend to the whole gift, as well to the children as to the mother. These children being sons, the words, as to them, could not have been used, to create an estate to their separate use, but for some other purpose; as to show the intention, that, upon the death of one of them, the other should take and not some other person. But whether this last was the intention or not, it is clear they could not create a separate estate in them, and therefore we cannot say that the same words, connected as they are with others, create a separate estate in the mother. But in the case of *Margetts*, the gift was to a mother and her daughter; the purpose, therefore, was consistent and applied to both. Here the children of Eunice Ashcraft were boys, and to put upon the words, as to them, the construction that is urged on the part of the mother, would be absurd. This view of the case is sustained by the case of *Wardel* v. *Claxton*, 16th E. Cond. Ch. Rep. 324. The testator bequeathed his residuary estate to trustees, to invest, &c. and to pay the interest and dividends thereof to his wife, for her life, to be by her applied for the maintenance of herself and children, &c. The question was, whether the widow, who had married again, was entitled to the income of the property to her separate use. The Vice Chancellor observed, "I do not think that this is a gift to the separate use of this lady. In all the cases that have been cited the sole object of the bounty was the woman, &c. But in this case, the words to be by her applied, have reference not only to the testator's widow, but to all the children." The Chancellor admits, if the words applied only to the widow, she would have had a separate estate. Such might have been, in the case before us, the intention of the donor. "It is possible," as the Court say in *Rudisell* v. *Watson*, "nay, very probable, that the donor did intend, that his daughter should have the sole, separate use of her share of the negroes." We are inclined to.think he did so intend; but we cannot say he did, for we are not sure of it. But it will not do to guess. The donor might further have supposed, that, without the use of those words, the gift to the children of Eunice might embrace all the children she might thereafter have. The question is not, whether he was expert in the law, whether he was right or wrong in that supposition, if he did entertain it, but what was his intention in using the expressions. As before stated, it is probable it was to give the property to the sole use of the wife; but a probable, a possible intention, will not sustain the wife's claims. Hence, although the words might have the construction contended for, yet if they will have the other also, as being in the mind or intention of the donor, though he was wrong in his conclusion, the claim of the wife is repelled: not because the donor did not intend the sole and separate use to her, but because he has not used such language as to enable us to say he did so intend. See the case of *Rudisell* v. *Watson.* The opinion pronounced by the Court in that case, it appears to me, governs and control this. The husband cannot be deprived of his marital rights by conjecture, however strong. There must be a certainty, to that degree which shows that the donor must have so meant, and could not have meant otherwise. If such was the intention here of the donor, from the words he has used, we cannot declare it so to have been. By the gift of Solomon Marsh, one-third of the negro Clarissa and her future increase vested absolutely in James Ashcraft, the husband, by virtue of " the *jus mariti*," and the other two-thirds in his children then born of his wife Eunice. Upon their death, their interest passed to him, and the whole title vested in him, and was liable to the payment of his debts.

The decree of the Court below must be affirmed, the demurrer sustained, and the bill dismissed with costs.

DANIEL, J. On the 15th day of December 1822, Solomon Marsh made the deed in question, and delivered it to James Marsh, to be kept for the benefit of the plaintiff and her two sons, as the bill alleges. The deed recites, that for the natural love and good will that the donor had for his married daughter, (the plaintiff,) he, " by these presents, do freely give and grant to the said Eunice Ashcraft and her children, a negro girl ten years old, by the name of Clarissa, and her increase ; *but the said gift to extend to no other person.*" Clarissa has now several children. The bill is filed by the plaintiff. against her husband and Alexander Little and others, who claim the slaves under a judgment and execution against her husband, to have one-third of them secured to her sole and separate use. The defendants have demurred. The demurrer was sustained in the Court of equity for Anson county, and the bill was decreed to be dismissed. The plaintiff then appealed.

Any person may make a gift to the wife of another man, and shut out the husband's interference, by clearly expressing such an intention in the instrument creating the gift, *Lewin on Trusts*, 148. But whether a trustee is appointed or not, the intention of the testator or settlor, of excluding the husband, must not be left to inference, but must be clearly and unequivocally declared. For, as the husband is bound to maintain his wife, and bears the burthen of her incumbrances, he has, *prima facie*, a right to her property. But provided the meaning be certain, the Court of equity will execute the intention though the settlor may not have expressed himself in technical language, *Lewin*, 148, 150 (*marg. page*,) and 2 *Story's Eq.* 909, 610, where all the authorities are collected and remarked on. If Marsh had said thus in his deed of gift, " but the said gift is not to extend to my daughter's husband," or " she is to have it independent of her husband," it would then have been clear, that the husband was intended to be excluded, and the property would go to the separate use of the wife. *Wagstaff* v. *Smith*, 9

Ves. 520. *Simons* v. *Howard*, 1 Keen 7. So if the gift had been to Eunice Ashcraft and her children, "*independent of any other person*," it would have been a separate estate to the wife of her share, *Margetts* v. *Margetts*, 10 Cond. Eng. C. Rep. 158. This case is, in my opinion, very much in point. It was as follows: John Eustice, by his will, gave all the rest and residue of his estate and effects unto Louisa Margetts (a married woman) and Ann Margetts, her daughter, to be equally divided between them, share and share alike, for their own use and benefit, "*independent of another person*" The Vice Chancellor said, that the words, "independent of any other person" meant, "independent of all mankind," and therefore included the husband, and the wife had a separate estate. This case was well considered, I presume, as the reporter informs us, that Mr. Barber and Mr. Parker were counsel in the cause. It seems to me that the words, "independent of any other person," are in meaning, the same as the words, "and to extend to no other person." If, therefore, the first set of words, when applied to Mrs. Margetts (a married woman) and her daughter, gave the *feme covert* a separate estate in the legacy, (as we see they did,) it is plain and clear, that the latter set of words, ("and to extend to no other person") must also exclude the husband; and give the negroes to Mrs. Ashcraft and her two sons then born. The case reported is a gift to Mrs. Margetts and her daughter Ann Margetts; the case before us is a gift to Mrs. Ashcraft and her two sons. I ask, where is the difference? The case of *Rudisell* v. *Watson*, 2 Dev. Eq. 430, was a decision that has no bearing on the case now before the Court. It was a devise and bequest, by a father to his married daughter, "to her and her heirs proper use;" and this Court said, that the words "to her proper use" did not clearly mean to convey the estate "*to her separate use.*" As to the two children of Mrs. Ashcraft, the deed would have conveyed to each of them, his one-third part of the slaves, without supple-

60

mentary words used by the donor. But as Mrs. Ashcraft was a *feme covert*, the donor used the words, " independent of any other person," to exclude her husband: he being the only person in the world, that the said words could have any effect or bearing on. If the donor did not mean to exclude him, I would ask whom did he mean to exclude? The words have no meaning at all, if they do not exclude the husband. To say that the husband is not clearly meant to be excluded by the words used, is to say that no words in the English language, which may be used in deeds or will, can exclude the husband, unless he is expressly or particularly named ; and such a decision has not yet been made in any Court. I think the demurrer ought to be over-ruled.

PER CURIAM. Decree below affirmed, the demurrer sustained and the bill dismissed with costs.

WHITMELL J. HILL, ADM'R. &c. *vs.* MARY L. SPRUILL & AL.

A testatrix bequeathed, as follows, all her estate consisting of personal property: " It is my wish that all my property be equally divided among my grand-children, that are living at the time of my death; and that their parents have the use of it as long as they live." *Held,* that the grand-children took the property *per capita.*

Held, further, that all the parents, whether the children of the testatrix or their husbands or wives, took a life estate in the shares of their respective children.

The cases of *Freeman* v. *Knight,* 2 Ired. Eq. 72, *Bryant* v. *Scott,* 1 Dev. and Bat. Eq. 155, and *Ward* v. *Stowe,* 2 Dev. Eq. 509, cited and approved.

Cause transmitted by consent from the Court of Equity of Halifax County at the Spring Term, 1846.

This is a bill filed by the plaintiff, as administrator with the will annexed of Rebecca Hill, to obtain a construction by the Court of certain clauses in the will. The points presented are stated by the Chief Justice in delivering the opinion of this Court.

B. F. Moore, for the plaintiff.
Badger, for the defendants.

Ruffin, C. J. Mrs. Rebecca Hill made her will and therein bequeathed as follows: " It is my wish, that all my property be equally divided among my grand-children, that are living at the time of my death; and that their parents have the use of it as long as they live." The testatrix had had six children. A daughter had married James B. Urquhart and died, leaving her husband and children, who survived the testatrix. Another daughter married George E. Spruill, and he died just before the testatrix. The other four, two sons and two daughters, were married and had respectively unequal numbers of children at the death of Mrs. Hill.

The property consisted entirely of personalty, and chiefly of forty-one negroes.

The bill was filed by an administrator with the will annexed, and brings before the Court James B. Urquhart and his children, Mrs. Spruill and her children, and the two surviving sons and their wives and children, and the other two daughters and their husbands and children; and the object of it is to obtain a declaration of the rights of the several legatees under the will, and the duties of the administrator and directions to him upon certain points stated.

The first is, whether the estate is to be divided *per capita* among the grand-children, and then the shares allotted to each family of grand-children be enjoyed by their parents for life ; or, whether the division is to be among the parents equally, with remainders in their respective shares, after their deaths, to their respective families of children that were living at the death of the testatrix, so as to make the grand-children take *per stirpes*. The Court is of opinion, that the division is to be equally among the grand-children according to their whole number, allotting to each an aliquot part. The authorities are decisive, that they take *per capita*, as the gift is to them under the common denomination of "my grand-children," with a direction for "an equal division" among them. It is not necessary to refer to other cases than those, which have been before the Court at recent periods, as in them the point was sufficiently discussed and most of the previous cases cited. *Freeman* v. *Knight*, 2 Ired. Eq. 72. *Bryant* v. *Scott*, 1 Dev. & Bat. Eq. 155. *Ward* v. *Stowe*, 2 Dev. Eq. 509. It was, indeed, said at the bar, that this case might be taken out of the rule, because there is a gift to the respective parents of the several families of grand-children, which, though not coming first in the will, is really and necessarily prior to that to the grand-children themselves, as it is to be first enjoyed; and it was insisted, that this would enable the Court to make the division among the grand-children *per stirpes*. But the argument goes too far, so as to show it to be clearly wrong. For if the division be between the parents of the grand-children, then each person within that description takes, and, consequently, where both of the parents are alive, the grand-children of that family would have double as much as those who had but a single parent living: which would produce the very inequality between the families, against which the argument is directed. The donation to the children of the testatrix and their husbands and wives is not, in truth, made to them as such, but as being "the parents of the grand-children, then living," whose shares their respective parents are to enjoy during their lives. The division is therefore to be made immediately among the grand-children *per capita;* but the enjoyment, during the lives of their respective parents or the survivor of them, is to belong to the respective parents, and then go into possession of the grand-children themselves. But, although the share of each grand-child is measured, in point of value, by dividing the property by the whole number of grand-children, yet, as the grand-children do not come to the enjoyment, as long as their respective parents or the survivor of them be alive, it is not necessary that, as between the grand-children themselves of a particular family, such a division should be made, as would allot to each of them particular slaves *in presenti.* On the contrary, in order to equalize the loss and gain from the death or birth of slaves, it would be most prudent, that those allotted to all the grand-children of the same family should be thrown together or remain as one stock, until their period of enjoyment shall arrive by the death of both their parents—when they can divide among themselves.

The next question raised in the bill, is, whether both of the parents of the several sets of grand-children take, or whether only such parent as was a child of the testatrix. From what has been already said, it will have been seen, that the Court is of opinion, that all the parents, whether a son or daughter of the testatrix, or his or her wife or husband, take the slaves of their respective children. The gift is to them as " their parents," and that includes all and each of their parents. The testatrix did not mean, that, while a parent of one of her grand-children was living, the grand-child should possess the means of living and acting independent of the parent.

The plaintiff likewise presents a point, as to the interests of the parents as between themselves. But, although there does not seem to be much difficulty in it, the Court deems it improper to make any declaration on it in this cause, because it is a question between the husbands and wives exclusively, and does not concern the administrator, who therefore has no right to raise it. No controversy can arise on the point, unless one of the married ladies should survive her husband; and it will be time enough, when asked by her and the husband's executor, to determine whether the life estate in the shares of their children survived to her or went to the executor.

PER CURIAM. Declared accordingly.

CHARLES CROOM & AL. vs. JOHN WRIGHT.

A testator bequeathed as follows: " I give and bequeath to my five sons and daughters, to wit, C. C., J. C., N. C., S. C. and J. H. fifteen negroes, &c. Those fifteen negroes I give to be theirs at my death, and my wife's, &c.; these I give them with all the future increase. I hereby appoint my son C. C. guardian to my daughter N. C. The legacy I leave her is to be free and clear, and independent of her present husband, T. C., or in any wise to be subject to his debts, engagements or control, but to be wholly under the management of the guardian C. C. to act with it as he thinks best for her profit ; and after her death, all the negroes, &c. to go to his six children, &c." *Held*, that the wife was entitled to a sole and separate estate in this property ; that the legal title did not pass by the words of the will to C. C. who is called guardian, but vested in the husband. But that the husband, there being no trustee interposed, is considered in Equity as the trustee for the wife, holding the property to the sole and separate use of the wife, in the same manner as another trustee would have done.

Held, therefore, that one who purchased these negroes from the husband with notice of the trust, held them subject to the trusts in the will in favor of the wife and her children.

The case of *Freeman v. Hill*, 1 Dev. and Bat. Eq. 389, cited and approved.

This was an appeal from a decree of the Court of Equity of Wayne County, at the Spring Term, 1846, his Honor Judge MANLY presiding, by which decree a demurrer filed by the defendants was sustained and the plaintiff's bill dismissed.

Charles Croom. the elder, died in Wayne county, having first made his will, and therein, amongst other things, bequeathed as follows: "I give and bequeath to my five sons and daughters now in the Western countries, viz: Charles Croom, Isaac Croom, Nancy Coor, Sarah Cook, and Jemima Hollowel, to them 1 leave fifteen negroes, by name, Will, &c. Those fifteen negroes, I give to be theirs at my death and my wife's, either to divide the negroes or sell them and divide the money equally—these I give to them with all the further increase. I hereby appoint my son Charles as guardian to daughter Nancy Coor. The legacy I leave her is to be free and clear and independent of her present husband, Thomas Coor, or in any wise not to be subject to his debts, engagements, or control but to be wholly under the management of the guardian, Charles Croom, to act with it as he thinks best for her profit; and, at her death, all the negroes or other property arising from them to go to her six children Charles, Thomas, &c." Mrs. Croom, the testator's widow, died in February, 1844, and thereupon a division of the negroes was made and a share allotted for Mrs. Coor and her children, and delivered to an agent for Mrs. Coor and her brother, Charles Croom, who were residents of Tennessee. After that had been done, John Wright had the negroes, that had been allotted as Mrs. Coor's share, seised under original attachment against the husband, Thomas Coor, and they were afterwards sold on the execution and purchased by Wright, who had notice of the provisions of the will of Charles Croom the elder, and of Mrs. Coor's claiming under it, but yet took the negroes into his, Wright's, possession, claims them as his own and refuses to deliver them either to Mrs. Coor or to Charles Croom for her.

The bill is filed by Charles Croom and by Nancy Coor by the said Charles, as her next friend, and by Mrs. Coor's six children against Wright and Thomas Coor, the husband, and, after setting forth the foregoing facts, states that it was the intention of the testator, in that clause of his will, to vest the legal title of one-fifth of the negroes in the plaintiff Charles Croom, for the separate use of Mrs. Coor during her life, clear of her husband's control, and after her death in trust for her said children; but that the plaintiffs are advised, that the terms used by the testator are so vague and inapt as not to pass the title to him, or, at the least, that it is doubtful whether he, C. Croom, can maintain an action at law for the slaves, and that it is thereby rendered necessary for the plaintiff to apply to this Court, to have the rights of the parties under the will declared and secured by proper conveyances.

The defendant, Wright, put in a demurrer for want of equity, which, upon argument, was sustained, and the plaintiff appealed.

No counsel for the plaintiffs.
Husted and *Mordecai*, for the defendants.

RUFFIN, C. J. The negroes are given to Mrs. Coor for life, and then to her children; and it admits of no doubt, that the intention was that her interest should be her separate property. The words are perfectly clear: " the legacy I leave her is to be free, clear and independent of her husband, and not subject to his debts or control." His exclusion could not be more expressly declared. He therefore can take no beneficial interest in this property under the will, whether the legal title be vested in his wife's brother as trustee, or be vested in the husband himself, for want of the interposition of another trustee, since it has been long held, that, when there is a clear intention to give a separate estate to a married woman, it shall not fail for want of a trustee, but be effectuated by converting the husband, in respect of the legal title, which comes to him *jure mariti*, into a trustee for her. *Rich* v. *Cockell*, 9 Ves, 375. *Porker* v. *Brooke*, Id. 583. It follows, if Coor was trustee for his wife, that Wright, as a purchaser with notice, or as purchaser under execution against the trustee, *Freeman* v. *Hill*, 1 Dev. & Bat. Eq. 389, takes the negroes subject to the same trust. The only question, then, which exists in the case, and the only one, indeed, which was argued, is, whether Charles Croom, the son, takes this share as trustee. It is said for the defendant, that C. Croom did take the legal title, and therefore, that he might have brought detinue or trover, and that, as he had remedy at law, there is no reason why this Court should take the jurisdiction. This reduces the dispute to a single point, as to the mode of redress; it being admitted that Mrs. Coor must be entitled to it here, or at law by an action by her trustee. Upon that point, the opinion of the Court is against the defendant. Without determining whether a bill would or would not lie, under the circumstances of this case, by Mrs. Coor and her children, to have their respective interests declared and secured, although the construction of the will had vested the legal title in Charles Croom, the son, the Court holds, that such is not the proper construction of the will, and that an action at law could not be sustained by him. We have little doubt that the statement in the bill is correct, that the intention of the testator was to vest the title in his son as trustee for his daughter; or, rather, if he had been fully advised of the advantages of a trustee, properly speaking, in more effectually and cheaply protecting the interest of his daughter, he would have given the legal title to the son. But we think, as the will is expressed, that intention is not sufficiently declared. The testator seems not only to have been *inops consilii*, but it is apparent that the instrument is very loosely drawn, and is the production of an uninformed and confused mind, so that, as is often the case, after a disposition in terms sufficiently precise to leave no doubt of the primary intention or as to its legal effect, if that disposition stood by itself, other language is used, conveying a glimmering of an intention somewhat inconsistent with that previously declared. But in such cases, the plain legal import of what is explicitly set down ought not to be defeated, upon the other

61

dubious and imperfect expression of intention. Now
this will in the beginning contains words of direct gift
to Mrs. Coor : " I give and bequeath to my five children,"
" to them I leave fifteen negroes," "those fifteen I give *to*
be theirs at my death and my wife's," "these I give *to*
them with their future increase." The gift of Mrs. Coor's
share *to her* is just as clearly and by exactly the same
terms, as the gifts of the shares of the other children are
to them. But as the testator meant that the gift to Mrs.
Coor should be to her separate use, he not only declares
that intention in the next sentence, but expresses himself
so as to shew very plainly that there was at least some
vague notion floating in his mind, that it was necessary
or might be useful to substitute, for the husband, some
other person to take care of the daughter's interest, as
regards the productiveness of the property, and, perhaps,
its protection from the husband or his creditors. To that
end he appoints his son Charles "the guardian" of his
daughter, and adds, "the legacy *I leave her* is to be wholly
under the *management* of the guardian, to act as he thinks
best for her profit." The natural sense of this passage
is to constitute the son the manager merely of the negroes. If it stood alone, it might be taken as an implied
gift to the son in trust for the daughter. But there is
no necessity of such implication to raise an interest in
the daughter ; for there has been a previous express gift
to her, which dispenses with any implication on the subject. And we think that the operation of that express
gift, anxiously repeated several times, as we have seen,
cannot be overcome by inferences from the terms in which
an interest or an authority is conferred on the son, but it
is uncertain which was intended, or which the testator
conceived would be best. The testator, as a parent,
charged his son with the duty of affording a brother's
care and protection to his sister, but he does not take
from her the title, which he had just vested in her, and
bestow it on the son. The consequence is, that the title

of the wife under the will, devolved by law on the husband, but in trust for her to her separate use; and therefore his legal title, though subject at law to be sold for his debts, was acquired by this purchaser upon the same trusts. The decree must therefore be reversed with costs, and the demurrer over-ruled, and the cause remanded for an answer or further proceedings thereon.

PER CURIAM.　　　　　Decreed accordingly.

JONES DRUMRIGHT & AL. vs. ROBERT JONES & AL.

Where an executor is in possession of a sum of money, to which his testator was entitled for the life of another, who is still living, a Court of Equity will not compel the executor to give security for the payment of the amount at the expiration of the life-interest, unless he be insolvent or in failing circumstances, or, from some other good cause, there is reason to fear the money will be lost.

Cause removed from the Court of Equity of Person County, at the Spring term, 1846.

The following facts appear from the pleadings.

Henry Baily died in the year —— having made and published in writing his last will and testament, which, after his death. was by the surviving executor, James Drumright, one of the plaintiffs, duly proved before the proper tribunal. In the said will is the following legacy: "I give and bequeath to my wife Mary. one thousand dollars, either in cash or property belonging to my estate, to that amount, to be taken by valuation; also one negro girl named Mary and a good feather-bed and furniture; to hold the above named property, money, &c. during her life-time, and, at her death, to return to my estate and be distributed as hereinafter directed." At the sale of the property of the testator, made by the executor, Mary

Baily, the widow, purchased a couple of negroes, Billy and Joe, and it was agreed between her and the executor, that she should hold them, as a part of the $1,000 legacy, at the price at which she should bid them off, as a convenient mode of valuing them. The two negroes were bid of for the sum of $446 06. The widow subsequently married Robert Deshazo, to whom the executor of Baily paid the balance of the pecuniary legacy in money, and took his receipt for the whole $1.000. Robert Deshazo is dead, having made his will and therein appointed Robert Jones, one of the defendants, his executor, who has caused it to be duly proved. By his will Robert Deshazo made provision for his wife, Mary, who is one of the plaintiffs, and from which she duly dissented, and gave the rest of his estate to the other defendants. The bill charges, that the legacy received by the plaintiff, Mary Deshazo, from the estate of her first husband, Henry Baily, passed into the possession of her second husband, Robert Deshazo, and is now in that of his executor, the defendant, Robert Jones, who holds it for the life only of the said Mary; that Mary Deshazo, having dissented from her husband's will, is entitled to a third part of his personal property, the said husband having left no child—the other legatees in his will not being such; that they live beyond the limits of the State, and threaten to carry the property to their place of residence. The bill prays that the executor, Jones, may be compelled either to deliver over to the plaintiff, Drumright, as the executor of Henry Baily, the whole of the property constituting the legacy of the plaintiff, Mary, taking a bond to pay over to him the interest of the money and the hire of the negroes annually, or that he give bond and security, that the said property shall not be carried beyond the limits of the State, and that it shall be forthcoming on the death of the said Mary, and it further prays that he may come to an account with and pay over to her, her part of the estate of the said Robert Deshazo, and for general relief

The answer admits the facts as set forth. The executor, Jones, states, that two years have not elapsed since he administered, and that there are a few debts still to pay—submits to an account and is willing to abide by and perform any order or decree that may be made.

The other defendants deny that Jones, as the executor of Deshazo, is bound to account with the plaintiff Drumright, as executor of H. Baily for any part of the property or money lent to the widow Mary, or is bound to give any security for its forthcoming on her death.

E. G. Reade, for the plaintiff.
Venable, for the defendants.

Nash, J. The case is before us on bill and answer, and the only contest is, as to the title to the $1,000 legacy. the negro Mary, and the negroes purchased by the plaintiff, Mary, at the sale of the property of her husband, H. Baily. There can be no doubt that under the will of H. Baily, his wife Mary took but a life estate in the property bequeathed her, and that upon her marriage with Robert Deshazo and his receipt of it from the executors, whatever legal estate was in her vested in him and that he holds it as she did for her life. In the hands of Jones, the executor of Deshazo, it constitutes a part of the estate of his testator, and to be held by him as he held it. There is no controversy, as to the power of the Court, at the instance of a person entitled to the ulterior interest of personal property, when a particular estate is carved out, to cause the immediate possessor to give security for its forthcoming—at the termination of the particular estate—and upon a proper case made out, it is the constant practice of the Courts to do so. But in this, it is the opinion of the Court, that a case, calling for the exercise of this power, is not stated in the bill. It is not alleged that Robert Jones, the executor of Robert Deshazo, is insolvent or in failing circumstances—nor is any fear expressed on that ground. He possesses the property, as his testator did, for the life of Mary Deshazo, and, upon her death, will be bound to have it ready to deliver over to the representatives of Henry Baily. It is his business then, to see that it is secure before he parts with its possession.

At the sale of the property of Henry Baily, the widow, Mary, purchased two negroes, Betty and Joe, and it was agreed between her and the executor, that they should go in part discharge of the pecuniary legacy. Afterwards, upon her marriage with Deshazo, the latter gave to the executors a receipt in the following terms: " Received from the executor of Henry Baily the sum of $1000 dollars, the amount of the legacy left my wife, Mary, according to the will." The Court is of opinion, that notwithstanding the agreement between the widow, Mary, and the executor of Henry Baily, this receipt establishes that the $1000 legacy was paid by the executors and received by Deshazo, and that the absolute title to the negroes Betty and Joe vested thereby in Deshazo.

The plaintiff, Mary Deshazo, is entitled to an account of the personal estate of her husband, Robert Deshazo, and to claim her portion thereof; the answer of the executor not pretending that it is necessary to keep it in possession for the payment of debt.

There must be a reference to the master to state the accounts.

PER CURIAM.   Decreed accordingly.

JOHN CLEMENTS, EX'R., &c. *vs.* PEARSON AND HARBIN.

It is not the usual course of a Court of equity to refer partnership accounts to the master, with a set of instructions from the Court. The accounts should first be reported, and the matters in contest between the parties be brought before the Court on exceptions.

Cause transmitted from the Court of Equity of Davie County, at the Spring Term, 1845.

The following case is presented by the pleadings:

The plaintiff states in his bill. that his testator and the two defendants were partners in trade and merchandize, under the firm and style of " Merony, Harbin & Co."; that the said firm was dissolved by the death of Merony, in the month of August, in the year 1837; that he is the executor of John A. Merony, and in that character he has called on the defendants, as surviving partners, to settle the accounts of the said partnership, and pay over to him the sums of money due the estate of his testator; that the defendants have refused to come to any settlement with him, unless he would allow them in the said account all the disputed items mentioned in the bill. All which demands, the plaintiff insists, are unjust and against law and equity. The bill then prays for an account of the partnership transactions, and a decree, &c.

The defendants, in their answers, admit the partnership, as stated in the bill, the death of John A. Merony at the time stated, and the qualification of the plaintiff as his executor. They admit that the partnership accounts have not been settled with the plaintiff. And they say, that the delay has been owing mainly to the difficulties and misunderstandings between the plaintiff and them, relative to the particular items of charge and discharge, mentioned in the bill. The defendants then answer, in detail, to each of the several disputed items of account, mentioned in the bill. There is a replication. Depositions have been taken and exhibits are filed.

Morehead, for the plaintiff.

No counsel for the defendants.

DANIEL, J.   Ordinarily, it is not the course of the Court to refer partnership accounts to the master to be reported on, with a set of instructions from the Court, as appears to have been desired by the parties, when the proceedings were drawn, but no motion was made to that effect. When the master's report comes in, if either party is dissatisfied with it, he may except to it or any part of it, and the exceptions thus made will thereafter be argued, and decided on by the Court.   We think that there must in the first place be a reference to the master, and a report by him on their account.   Let it be referred.

PER CURIAM.   Ordered accordingly.

JAMES B. BOWERS AND WIFE *vs.* THOMAS P. MATHEWS, EXECUTOR, & AL.

A testator devised to his wife M. certain lands, and the will then proceeds: " I also give her the negroes I got from John Knight's estate.   I also loan her $3000, and provided she has no child or children by me, that arrives to the age of twenty-one or dies under that age leaving lawful issue, I give her the said $3000.   I also lend her all my household and kitchen furniture during her life or widowhood.   It is also my will and desire, that the property I have given my wife and loaned her, with all the property I shall hereafter dispose of in this my will, remain together on my plantations, under the care of my executors and trustees, which I shall hereafter appoint, and the profits arising therefrom to go to the benefit of my mother and the education of my children, should I have any, until my oldest child, should I have any, arrives to the age of twenty-one years.   The balance of my property not already disposed of, both real and personal, together with the household and kitchen furniture loaned my wife, I leave in trust with my friends, A. B. and C. D., for the benefit of my child or children, should I have any to arrive to the age of twenty-one years, or the issue of such child or children at the age of twenty-one years—and for A. B., C. D and E. F. to deliver unto them the said property." The testator left surviving him a wife and daughter. *Held*, that by this will the testator has thrown his whole property, real and personal, into a joint fund, to be held by his executors in the manner specified in this will, the profits to be divided equally between his widow and her daughter; the division of this joint fund to be contingent, upon one of two events, either the arrival at age of her daughter or her death without issue before that period. *Held*, further, that the legacy of $3000 is still a loan; that it must be held by the executors, and the widow is only entitled to the interest on it, until the contingency happens of the daughter's dying under age and without issue, in which event it will be converted into an absolute gift to the widow. *Held*, further, that only the original stock of negroes from John Knight's estate passed under the bequest, and none of the increase before the making of the will.

This cause was transmitted by consent from the Court of Equity of Halifax County. at the Spring Term, 1846.

The bill sets out that Jeremiah Brinkley died in the year. 1840, seized of a large real and personal estate, having made and published in writing a last will and testament, which has been duly proven in the proper Court by the defendant, Thomas P. Mathews, one of the executors therein named. who qualified as such executor alone, the other persons appointed having renounced their right to do so: That the testator left surviving him a widow, the complainant Martha, since intermarried with James Bowers, the other plaintiff, and an only child, Mary P. Brinkly, the other defendant: That the said will is in the following words, to-wit: "I give to my wife, Martha Brinkly, the following property, that is to say, the land I purchased under a decree of the Halifax Superior Court; also all the land I obtained by her in marriage, that has not heretofore been disposed of; I also give her the negroes I got from John Knight's estate; I also leave her $3,000, and provided she has no child or children by me, that arrives to the age of twenty-one years or dies under that leaving lawful issue, I give her the said $3,000. I also lend her all my household and kitchen furniture during her life or widow-hood. It is is also my will and desire, that the property I have given my wife and loaned her, with all the property that I shall hereafter dispose of in this my will, remain together on my plantations, under the care of my executors and trustees, which I shall hereafter appoint, and the profits arising therefrom to go to the benefit of my wife Martha, my mother, Mary Brinkly, and the education of my children, should I have any, until my oldest child, should I have any, arrives to the age of twenty-one years. The balance of my property, not already disposed of, both real and personal, together with the household and kitchen furniture loaned to my wife, I leave in trust with my friends Isham Mathews and William Brinkly, for the benefit of my child or children, should I have any to arrive to the age of twenty-one years, or the issue of such child or children at the age of twenty-one years; and for Isham Mathews, Thomas P. Mathews, and William Brinkly, to deliver unto them the said property." The bill then sets out that, by his will, the testator had given to his mother, Mary Brinkly, property that belonged to her; and that after his death, she elected to hold and retain her own property, and shortly thereafter died. The plaintiffs claim the $3,000 legacy as a gift, and call upon the defendant to pay it over and account for the interest, and a general account, and state that the defendant, Mary Brinkly, was born soon after the making of the will and before the death of the testator.

The defendant, Mathews, admits the facts set forth in the bill, and prays the decision of the Court, in the construction of the several devises of the will—submits to an account, and avers his readiness and desire to discharge himself of the duties of his office. The answer of M. Brinkley is one of form.

No counsel in this Court for the plaintiffs.

B. Moore, for the defendants.

NASH, J. The construction of this will presents no

legal difficulty; it is one purely of intention. What did the testator intend? This is to be gathered from the paper itself. The plaintiffs claim the legacy of $3,000 as a gift *in solido*, and that they are entitled to its prompt payment by the defendant. In this we think they err. The testator had three individuals in view, as objects of his bounty—his wife, his mother, and such child as might be born to him thereafter. At the making of the will, he had no issue. His leading purpose seems to have been, to provide for the education of such child or children as he might have, and their maintenance, and that of his wife and mother, until his eldest child should arrive to the age of twenty-one years. With this view, he directs that the property he had previously, in the will, *given* and *loaned* to his wife, together with all the rest of his property, shall remain on his plantation under the care of his trustees and executors, " and the profits arising therefrom to go to the benefit of my wife Martha, my mother, Mary Brinkly, and the education of my children, should I have any, until my oldest child, should I have any, arrives at the age of twenty-one years." This is the general intention of the testator in the will, and is to govern in its construction; and other particular dispositions are to be construed in subordination to it, notwithstanding any apparent inconsistency with it. In the previous part of the will, the testator has given to his wife several tracts of land and certain negroes, and then says, "I also loan her $3,000." This loan is however accompanied by a proviso, by which it may be coneverted into an absolute gift. If she has by the testator no child or children, the loan becomes an absolute gift. But in the event of the testator's having children, the gift continues a loan, until the other contingency occurs—their death under age without issue. One of the contingencies pointed out by the testator has occurred, to-wit, the birth of a child, and that child is still alive, under the age of twenty-one years. The pecuniary legacy is still a loan, and will so continue until determined by the death of Mary Brinkly under age and without leaving lawful issue. What is to become of this legacy in the intermediate time? Is it to be taken into possession by the plaintiffs, and, if so, do they hold it as a loan to their separate use, or do they hold it burthened with a proportionate contribution, out of the interest, towards the education and maintenance of Mary Brinkley. The language of the will, in creating the fund for the joint interest of the legatees, is obscure, so far as the pecuniary legacy is concerned. All the property is to be *kept together on the plantations:* is the money to be kept there? No. In seeking into the intention of a testator, we are often compelled to transpose words and sentences, and always look to the whole of the clause and sometimes to the whole will. In this case, applying the rule *reddendo singula singulis,* rendering each according to the subject matter of each, there is no incongruity or obscurity in the clause. The property, which is to be kept together, is that which is given as well as loaned to the widow, and the money is the only loan. How remain together? as the testator had kept them. The negroes, and the horses and cattle in the cultivation of the soil, the household and kitchen furniture in the places appropriated to them, and the money in such place and used in such way as the executors or trustees might deem most advantageous to those interested in the fund. We are of opinion, then, that the plaintiffs are not entitled to have the pecuniary legacy raised at this time—that sum forms part of the joint fund of which the profits belong to the widow and child equally, until the period of division shall arrive, as provided for in the will. Should Mary Brinkly die under age and without leaving issue, the money becomes an absolute gift to the plaintiffs; or should she arrive at age or die leaving issue, and her mother surviving, the mother will then be entitled to the loan for life. The testator lends to his wife, all of his household and kitchen furniture, during her life or widowhood, and the defendant, the executor, asks the direction of the Court as to its fur-ther disposition. Mrs. Brinkly having married, her life estate in severalty in the furniture, in any event, can never arise. The furniture is however to be kept with the rest of the property, as a joint fund. The testator no doubt expected, that the mother and the child would live together and intended the furniture should continue in the house for their joint use. As to the third enquiry, we have in substance replied to it already, and cannot better express our opinion than in the language of the answer. So far as we are able to discover the general intention of the testator, it appears to be that all his pro-perty is to be held for the common use of his widow and his child, Mary Brinkly, until the latter shall arrive at age or die under age without leaving issue. And the testator directs that it shall be kept by the executor. The maintenance and education of Mary Brinkly is not a charge upon the property in the hands of the widow—but the latter is only entitled to receive from the executor her portion of the profits of it annually—it remains in the hands of the executor.

As to the negroes obtained by the testator from John Knight's estate, we are of opinion, that none of them, under the devise, pass to the plaintiff, Martha, but such as are of the original stock, and that the devise to her does not embrace any of those who were born before the date of the will, but that the plaintiffs are entitled to such as have been born of the original stock since, and such as may be born before the period of division may arrive. Our opinion upon the proper construction of this will may be summed up in a few words. The testator has thrown his whole property, real and personal, into a joint fund to be held by his executor, in the manner specified in the will, the profits to be divided equally between the plaintiff Martha and the defendant Mary. The division of this joint fund is contingent upon the happening of one or two events, either the arrival at age of Mary or her death before that period. Should the defendant Mary die under age and without leaving issue, the loan of the $3,000 becomes an absolute gift to the plaintiff Martha. But if Mary arrives at twenty-one years of age, or dies before that period and leaves issue, the legacy still continues a loan and the plaintiff will be entitled only to the interest on the whole sum.

The costs must be paid out of the fund, as the proceedings are manifestly instituted to procure directions to the executor as to the performance of his trust.

PER CURIAM.   Decree accordingly.

DAVID P. WEIR AND WIFE vs. THOMAS R. TATE & AL.

An executor cannot take land in the payment of debts due to his testator, and his purchases are on his own account, unless at the election of those entitled to the estate.

Until the parties so elect to take the land, the executor is chargeable for the price given for the land, or the land itself would, in a Court of Equity, have the character of personalty.

Where an executor sells land under a power contained in the will, the purchaser claims under the will, as if the devise had been to him; and therefore the widow of an heir of the testator has no right to dower in such land.

The wife of a mortgagee in fee, after forfeiture, may recover dower at law; but in equity she is subject to be redeemed as the husband's heir is, because equity considers the mortgagee as a trustee for the mortgagor from the first. Therefore, a Court of equity will not decree dower in such a case, when applied to in the first instance.

Where a husband is entitled only to a remainder in fee, after the termination of a life estate, which is existing at the time of his death, the wife cannot be endowed, for the right of dower only attaches to the immediate estate of freehold as well as the inheritance.

An estate for years, prior to the estate of inheritance limited to the husband, does not prevent the seizin of the immediate estate of inheritance by the husband, and the wife will be dowable of the land, subject to the term.

If rent be reserved on the term, the widow, endowed of the reversion, is entitled to her share of the rent.

Weir v. Humphries.

But if the preceding term yields no rent, as where there is a gift by will, for example, to one for a term, remainder to another in fee, the wife of the latter, though she has a right of dower and though it may be assigned her, takes subject to the term, and can neither enter nor receive any profits, until the termination of the term.

The same rules apply to all chattel interests in land, as well as to terms strictly speaking.

Thus, when a testator devised a cotton factory and all its appurtenances to his three children, to be equally divided among them as also the profits, when the youngest should arrive at twenty-one years of age, and in the meantime that the factory should be carried on under the sole management and direction of the executor, until such period of division, and the profits were to be suffered to accumulate; and one of the children died before such period, leaving a widow: *Held*, that this was such a chattel interest in the executor, as though it did not prevent the assignment of dower, yet postponed the enjoyment of it until the time appointed for the division.

A devise of land to " three children, to be kept together as *joint stock* until the youngest shall arrive to the age of twenty-one, and then the whole property and its increase to be divided equally between them, to each one third part," creates a tenancy in common and not a joint tenancy, being a gift of undivided property in joint shares.

The act of 1784, *Rev. St. ch.* 43, *sec.* 2, abolishes the right of survivorship, in the case of joint tenancy, and gives the share of the joint tenant, dying, to his heirs. But, when the heir takes *as heir*, the whole interest is necessarily in the ancestor, and he becomes absolutely tenant of the fee, to which dower is incident, and, so also, the power of devising.

The provision in the act of 1836, *Rev. Stat.* 121, *sec.* 1, which gives a right of dower to lands of which her husband died seized and possessed, is to receive the same construction as the act of 1784, which gives the dower in lands, of which the husband was " seized or possessed." The mistake is a clerical one, and none of the profession ever understood what was understood in the original law by the words " or possessed."

In point of law, too, the owner of the inheritance is not only seized, but is said to be possessed, for the purposes of dower and curtesy, when the reversion is not after a freehold, but after a term for years only. The possession of the tenant for years is the possession of the reversioner.

Cause transmitted by the Court of Equity of Guilford County, at the Spring Term 1846, to the Supreme Court, by consent of parties, the cause having been set down for hearing upon the bill, amended bill, answer and amended answer.

This is a bill for dower, filed by the widow of the late Absalom T. Humphries, and by her second husband, against the devisees of the first husband and others. The cause is set for hearing on bill and answer, and by them the case is as follows:

Henry Humphries, late of Greensborough, and the father of Absalom T. Humphries, made his will on the 18th of February, 1840, and died soon afterwards. He therein devised and bequeathed, amongst other things, as follows: " I give my cotton factory, with all the machinery thereto attached or belonging, together with all the lands and buildings of every description attached to or adjoining the factory, including the town lot, on which the old cotton gin (now converted into a lumber-house) and my stables stand: also all my negro slaves; also all the stock of cows, horses, wagons and other vehicles (excepting the family carriage); also the tract of land of 100 acres adjoining Crowson and others, which was bought of Washington Adams: also the tract of 55 acres purchased of the widow Forbes, adjoining John M. Morehead, to my three children, Nancy Tate, Absalom T. Humphries, and Sarah L. Humphries, for ever; but to be kept together, and managed as joint stock, for the benefit of all three, until my daughter Sarah L. shall arrive at the age of 21 years, or marry, and then, upon the happening of either event, the whole of said property and its increase and profits shall be equally divided between them—to each one-third part. I further give and bequeath to my said three children the stock on hand at my death belonging to the said factory, consisting of wood, yarn, raw cotton, cloth, paper, labels, twine, oil, &c. &c. &c. to be kept jointly and divided as the property mentioned in the foregoing clause. And that my children may know the amount of stock they commence with, I direct an inventory to be taken by my executor; and, further, it may not be amiss to let my children know, that the factory, land, and buildings, exclusive of the negroes, are worth under good management $100,000: The said stock, after the inventory is taken, is to be used to carry on the operations the operations of the factory. *Fourthly :* To my son in law, Thomas R. Tate, in whose prudence and honesty I have unbounded confidence, I leave the superintendence and management of the cotton factory and its operations until the time shall arrive for a division; and for his services in said management I give him $1,000 annually during his management out of the profits of the factory. *Fifthly :* I give to my son Absalom T. my large brick dwelling house in Greensborough, together with the lot on which it stands, and the other houses thereto attached, to him and his heirs. But I desire and direct my daughter Nancy Tate and her family, and my other two children, to have the use of the same, free of rent, until the division takes place, as mentioned in the foregoing clause ; and I also direct the store room, counting-room, and cellar, (in said house) to be rented out until the said division takes place, and the profits to be equally divided among my three children. *Sixthly :* I direct my executor to sell the house and lot in Greensborough, occupied by W. Woodburn ; the tract of land purchased of Mather Young, the tract of land deeded to me by William Slade, containing 50 or 60 acres, in Rutherford, and all my other real estate not herein mentioned: to be sold by him in such parcels, when and upon such credit and terms as he shall deem best. *Seventhly :* I give all the money belonging or due to me, and all moneys arising from the sale of any of my property, herein directed to be sold, to my said three children. I give to my son my clock and all furniture belonging to my hall-room ; and to my three children all the other household and kitchen furniture. Lastly, I appoint my said son-in-law, Thomas R. Tate, the sole executor of this my last will."

The testator had but the three children mentioned in his will. Up to 1835, he resided in the brick dwelling house mentioned in the will, and his daughter, Mrs. Tate, and her husband—who had then intermarried—resided with him. In that year Mrs. Humphries died, and the

63

testator then removed to a small house on his factory property, which was near to Greensborough, and thenceforward resided there for the convenience of attending to that property. He, however, left the brick dwelling-house in the occupation of Mr. Tate and Mrs. Tate, with whom Absalom T. then about 12 years of age, and Sarah L. then 7, lived; and this continued to be the state of things until the testator's death in 1840. After that event, the family continued to reside together as one family in the same house, and upon the marriage of Absalom T. at the age of 19, in 1842, he brought his wife to reside there and they lived as before, until, upon a difference between Absalom T. and his wife, they separated early in 1844, and she returned to her father and remained there until after the death of her husband. The other daughter, Sarah L., has lived with Mr. and Mrs. Tate at all times, until she was recently sent to a school in New Jersey, where she now is, and is about 18 years old.

The cotton factory is worked by steam power, and is situated on a piece of land adjoining Greensborough, containing about 25 acres, on which are the necessary houses for artificers and the other purposes of the factory; and the land, mentioned in that clause of the will, as purchased from Adams and from Forbes, were appendages of the factory and had been purchased and used solely for the purposes of getting wood, and are almost indispensable to it, as there is a daily consumption of five or six cords.

Of the land mentioned in the 6th clause, the defendant Tate, as executor, sold the house and lot occupied by Woodburn for $3,000 in 1842, before the marriage of Absalom T. Humphries, has recently sold for $500 the land in Rutherford which his testator purchased from Slade at $250, and it does not appear that any other profit has been derived from it. The other tract mentioned in this clause, as the tract purchased from Mather Young, has not been sold; and the answer states the title to be as follows. One Mitchell contracted for the purchase of it from Young at the price of $800, and paid $400 thereof, but was unable to pay the remaining $400; and at the request of Mitchell, the testator, H. Humphries, a number of years before his death, advanced the same upon a written and sealed contract between them to this effect, namely, that Young should convey the premises to Humphries in fee, (which he accordingly did,) and that whenever Mitchell should pay to Humphries the said sum of $400 with the interest thereon, the latter would convey in fee to the former; but, if he did not make such payment in Mitchell's life, that then the land should belong absolutely to Humphries, but that Mitchell and his wife should have the enjoyment thereof for their lives and that of the survivor; that, under that contract, Mitchell entered and has been in possession ever since, and he and his wife are both living, and will probably never call for a conveyance, as the principal and interest now considerably exceed the value of the land.

Absalom T. Humphries, just after coming of age, made his will, dated September 24th, 1844, and died in November following. By it he gave to his wife one-third of his personal estate, and also gave to her, for her life, one-third of his real estate. He gave to Absalom H. Tate, his nephew and the son of Thomas R. Tate, the dwelling-house and lot in Greensborough, which had been devised to him by his father, and the furniture therein; and, with one or two trivial exceptions, he gave the residue of his estates real and personal to Thomas R. Tate, whom he appointed executor. From the will, his widow, probably to entitle herself to a year's allowance under the late act, entered her dissent. The bill is filed against Mr. and Mrs. Tate and their infant son, Absalom H. Tate and Sarah L. Humphries; and it prays that dower may be immediately assigned specifically in the dwelling-house, in the factory and lands attached to it, and in the real estate ordered to be sold; or, if the plaintiff be not entitled to that, then that one-ninth part of a reasonable rent for the dwelling-house be annually paid to her until Sarah L. shall arrive to full age or marry, and, upon that event, that one-third of the rent thereof shall be thus paid to her; and that also proper accounts may be taken of the profits of the cotton factory, so as to ascertain whether it be necessary to retain, besides the original stock, all the profits now accruing in order to carry on the factory, (which the plaintiffs deny to be so,) and that dower may be assigned to her in the said lands and factory in metes and bounds, or that, until the marriage or full age of Sarah L., one-ninth part of the profits thereof accruing or that may accrue, since the death of her husband, may be paid to her annually; and also dower of one-third of the share of the other lands devised by H. Humphries to his son, or the interest on one-ninth of the purchase money obtained therefor.

The answers submit whether the plaintiffs can have dower in any of the lands devised by Henry Humphries; and they insist that, at all events, the son's widow is not entitled to have it assigned, until Sarah L. shall have arrived at full age or married, and that in the meanwhile Mrs. Tate and her children and Sarah L. are entitled to the exclusive use of the dwelling house for their residence; and that the profits arising from the rent of the store and counting-rooms and cellar, and the profits of the factory and the proceeds of the land directed to be sold, form a personal fund to accumulate or be divided among the three children or their representatives.

The defendant, Thomas R. Tate, states further, that a customer, who dealt largely for years on credit, before and after the death of the testator, became insolvent and made an assignment for the benefit of his creditors, including the testator's estate; and that at a sale of the property by the assignees, (during the life of Absalom T. Humphries, as we collect,) he, Tate, in order to make the effects bring a fair price and to save as much of the debt as he could, became a bidder, and purchased a tract of land containing 420 acres and took a conveyance to himself. He states, that the price was paid in the debt due to the estate, and that he considered himself acting exclusively for the benefit of the estate, and that the only reason why he took the conveyance to himself was for the convenience of making sale of the land and bringing the proceeds into the funds of the factory, to which they properly belong: that he has been as yet unable to sell it, though it is fully worth the price which he bid for it, and, in the mean while, he has had it cultivated by the factory hands, who used the crops for provisions.

Badger, for the plaintiffs.
Morehead, for the defendants.

Ruffin, C. J. With respect to the tract of land purchased by the executor, the Court can make no conclusive declaration in the present state of the case. We do not even understand the executor, as wishing it to be considered as real estate of the plaintiff's husband; but, rather, that it should be deemed a part of the factory property, and to be sold and accounted for as personalty, in the stead of the debt, which paid for it. Whether he would have a right to have it thus treated, might admit of doubt; for *prima facie* an executor cannot take land in the payment of debts and his purchases are upon his own account. unless at the election of those entitled to the estate. It does not appear that Absalom T. Humphries made an election, or that he knew the facts, in his life-time. The executor himself, who has since become the executor and residuary legatee of A. T. H. cannot elect to the prejudice of the widow. We cannot tell, what she will elect. This land is not mentioned in the bill at all, but the facts respecting it are found in the answer exclusively; and the plaintiff has not informed us, what she wishes. Unless she should choose to have it treated as a purchase for the benefit of her husband, and, further, to consider it as his land in equity, (so that under the statute she is entitled to dower therein,) no question can arise touching it in the present suit. For, unless she thus elects, then as between Mr. Tate, as the executor of H. Humphries, and her husband and herself, the executor is chargeable to the estate either for the price given by him for this land to his own use, or the land itself would in this Court have the character of personalty, as a part of the joint factory property. In either case, it would be taken out of this course, in which the plaintiff is seeking alone for dower out of the real estate. It is apparently so much more to the advantage of the plaintiff not to treat this interest as land vested in her husband, in which case she would have a life estate in one-third of her husband's third, but rather as personalty, or as a liability of the executor for the price he gave for it out of the joint funds, in which case she will have absolutely a third of her husband's third, that we do not anticipate, she will elect to treat it as real estate. But it is possible she may wish to do so; and if she should, it will be then time enough to determine whether she can make the election, and the effect of it in this suit. Until she shall elect or offer to elect to treat it as land, it is *prima facie* not so; and therefore the plaintiff cannot for the present be declared entitled to dower in it.

The proceeds of the lands sold by the executor, under a power for that purpose, go also, by the express provisions of the will, to swell the testator's personal estate, given to his three children. In that form the plaintiff will have the benefit of it in her suit for a distributive share of her late husband's estate. No profits were received since the death of Absalom T. Humphries from the two parcels sold; and, the purchaser, by the execution of the power, claims under the will, which created the power, in the same manner as if the devise had been to him; and therefore the legal title, which descended to the heirs from the testator, was superseded, and the right to dower therein, discharged even at law and much more in this Court.

The plaintiff cannot have dower in the land conveyed by Young, according to the agreement between Mitchell and H. Humphries, viewing it either in the light of a mortgage or security for that part of the purchase money which Humphries advanced, or as an estate in fee in H. Humphries subject to the life estate of Mitchell and his wife. It is true, the wife of a mortgagee in fee, after forfeiture, may recover dower at law; but in equity she is subject to be redeemed as the husband's heir is, because equity considers the mortgagee a trustee for the mortgagor or his personal representative. *Nash* v. *Preston,* Cro. Car. 190. Therefore, when the wife applies in the first instance to the Court of Equity for dower, it cannot be decreed to her upon the score of her legal right, when it is disclosed, that in conscience she cannot keep it. Neither can she have dower in this land in the other aspect in which it may be viewed. For if the instrument between Humphries and Mitchell, which is not laid before us, be a legal conveyance of a life estate to the latter, the wife cannot have dower for want of the seizin of the husband; for the right of dower only attaches to the immediate estate of freehold as well as the inheritance, and here the tenant for life was living at the death of the husband. But if the contract was executory, merely, still it would convert the vendor and his heirs into trustees for the vendee of a life estate; and that, in this Court, is deemed the ownership of the land, and, being outstanding, defeats the wife's dower, in equity.

But of the dwelling-house and lot, and the factory and the lands attached, the wife has, in the opinion of the Court, the right of dower, though she cannot be let into possession as yet, nor have a decree for a share of the profits or rents. An estate for years, prior to the estate of inheritance limited to the husband, does not prevent the seizin of the immediate estate of inheritance by the husband, and the wife will be dowable of the land, subject to the term. *Bates* v. *Bates*, 1 Ld. Ray. 326, Co. Lit. 29, b. 32, a. If rent be reserved on the term, the widow endowed of the reversion is entitled to her share of the rent. *Wheatly* v. *Best*, Cro. Eliz. 564. *Stoughton* v. *Leigh*, 1 Taunt. 402. But if the preceding term yields no rent, as when there is a gift by will, for example, to one for a term, remainder to another in fee, the wife of the latter, though she has a right of dower and though it may be assigned her, takes subject to the term, and can neither enter nor receive any profit, till the determination of the term. The same rule applies to all chattel interests in land as well as to terms, strictly speaking. *Park on Dower*, 78. Thus, where one devised, that, if his personal estate should not be sufficient for payment of his debts and legacies, his executors should pay them out of the profits of his real estate, and then to his son in *tail*, and the son married and died before the debts were paid; it was held that the executors had but a chattel interest, and that the wife had a right to dower. Co. Lit. 42, *Hitchen* v. *Hitchen*, 2 Vern. 403, Prec. in ch. 133. Similar to that is the case here, in respect of the factory and the real estate given with it. It is devised in fee to the testator's three children, two of whom are infants and were incapable of managing a property of this sort, of which the chief value consisted in the buildings and machinery of a very large cotton factory; and for that reason, the testator intercepted the immediate devise to them by placing the whole property, real and personal, as a joint stock, under the management and keeping of his executor, until his youngest child shall come of age or marry; and, upon either of those events, he directs the property and all the profits, then accumulated in the hands of the executor, to be divided equally among the children. The title of all the personalty included in this clause was legally in the executor *virtute officie;* and it is manifest that the interest and property of the realty

were intended likewise to be in him for the limited period mentioned, because it is necessary to the power,
which the testator bestows on him for conducting the business. It is impossible that it was meant the executor
should not have the right of entry and possession, or that
any one else, even one of the children, should have that
right in exclusion of the executor. In the executor then,
as executor, was vested a chattel interest, of which the
duration cannot extend beyond the full age or marriage
of the youngest child. Therefore the plaintiff has a right
of dower therein, but cannot come to the enjoyment for
the period prescribed, like it is in a recovery at law with
a *cesset execution*. *Co. Lit.* 208, *note,* 1 *P. Wil.* 137. Of
course she cannot claim, as dower, any of the profits in
the meanwhile, for they are not in the nature of rent, annexed in right to the reversion in the land, but they are
given directly, as profits in money or other personal form,
to the three children, and to be divided with the property
itself, and then the plaintiff will have the benefit thereof in a way fully as advantageous to her.

For a similar reason, the plaintiff has a title to dower
in the dwelling house and lot. Although the gift of that
property to the son in fee precedes, in the clause, the disposition in favor of the two daughters and the son himself for a residence, yet the intention requires that their
order should be transposed. Then the will would read,
that the testator gives his dwelling-house to his married
daughter and her family and to his own two infant children, who were then living with the elder sister, until the
youngest child shall come of age or marry; and upon
that event he gives the remainder in fee to the son, who
is dead, leaving a widow, and his youngest sister, of the
age of 18 now alive and unmarried. It is not stated what
family Mrs. Tate then had, further than that she certainly
had one son (to whom the plaintiff's husband devised this
house) and may have had others, as she had been married
several years; and, at all events, it was understood by

the testator that she might have more. These provisions, with the gifts of the furniture in the house, and the declaration that no rent shall be payable, create a strong probability, that the testator meant that his family should, during the minority of his younger children, live together as one family, and thence an implication that the gift was to them, and to the survivor of them, for their, his, or her personal use and enjoyment. But that need not be determined now, since, if such be not the construction, the gift to the three children and the family of one of them did not merge in the remainder given in fee to the son, because it was given as one term to them all. Therefore, if the interest of the son did not survive to his sisters by force of the testator's particular intention, it yet subsists in his executor, yielding no rent, and therefore the wife must await its expiration. It is true, that parts of the premises are to be let by the executor, but the rent to be reserved is not incident to the reversion, of which the plaintiff seeks to be endowed, but goes into the personal estate and is divisible among all the children.

The counsel for the defendants, however, took some other objections, deducible from two of our statutes. The one is, in reference to the devise of the factory property, that it is a devise in joint tenancy, and that the act of 1784 abolishes the *jus accrescendi* in favor only of the heir of the tenant first dying, and is silent as to his wife. To this there are two answers. The first is, that this is not a joint tenancy, but a tenancy in common. The devise is to the three children—" to be kept together as joint stock *until* Sarah L. shall arrive to 21, and *then* the whole property and its increase shall be *equally divided* between them—*to each one-third part*" : which is an express tenancy in common, being a gift of undivided property in distinct shares. The next answer is, that the act of 1784 has two clauses : one, that the part of any tenant dying shall *not* go to the surviving tenant; and the other, that it shall descend to the heir of the tenant so dying, in the same manner as estates in common. The first is the important provision, being in destruction of the previous right of the survivor; and the second is a natural and mere consequence from it, because the heir must take, if the other does not, since there is no one else on whom the law can throw the inheritance, unless under the operation of the odious principle of escheat—which was certainly not meant. Then, when the heir takes as heir, the whole interest is necessarily in the ancestor, and he becomes absolutely tenant of the fee; to which dower is incident and the power of devising. It is to be remarked, indeed, that the argument for the defendants excludes them in this case as well as the wife; for, while the act is silent as to the wife of the tenant dying, it is equally silent as to his devisees, and both Mr. Tate and his son must take in that character, because neither is an heir of the testator, Absalom T. Humphries. It is true, the act does not abolish joint tenancy, nor turn it into a tenancy in common. But it modifies it as far as this, that upon the death of one of the tenants, it prevents the survivor from taking any thing more than the share he before had, and makes what the dying tenant owned at his death descendible, as if it were a tenancy in common; which amounts to a several inheritance at his death in each tenant in his share, with all the rights and properties incident to that estate. Of consequence a title to dower arises to the wife, who is so much favored in the law, that her right of dower was put by an ancient maxim upon the same footing with life and liberty.

But another objection is taken, which applies equally to the factory property, and to the dwelling-house, which is, that the dower of the plaintiff is excluded by the previous chattel interests of the executor, and of the three children, which prevented her husband from being possessed. though seized, of the premises at the time of his death. This objection is founded on the *Revised Statute*, *c.* 121, *sec.* 1, which gives a right of dower, that is, "one third part of all the lands, tenements, and hereditaments of which her husband died seized and possessed": So that, it is said, there must have been both a seizin *and* possession of the husband, to entitle the wife to dower. In the act of 1784, c. 204, s. 8, the disjunctive *or* is used, the words being "seized *or* possessed." It was never understood in the profession, why the term "possessed" was introduced into that statute; as it certainly was not intended, that there should be dower of terms for years, or that the rule of the common law should be abrogated, which makes a legal seizin in the husband sufficient to support a title to dower. Such a construction was not given to the act on either point. On the contrary, it was always held, that the term "seized" was used in it in the same sense as in the common law touching dower, and that the only effect of the act was to change the extent of the right to dower from a third of the land, of which the husband was seized during the coverture, to a third of that of which he died seized. We cannot suppose the legislature intended in the *Revised Statutes* of 1836 to alter the act of '84 in this respect. The section is printed as being the 8th section of the act of '84, re-enacted without amendment; and, so far as it relates to dower, it is, leaving out the preamble, a copy from the act of '84, with the exception of the word *and* instead of *or* in the part designating the lands of which the wife shall be dowable. The natural conclusion then is, that it was a mere mistake in copying or printing; and the new act was not intended to be different in this respect from the former, especially in the very important point of excluding dower, where a term for years or any trivial chattel interest precedes the inheritance of the husband and subsists at his death. It cannot be possible, that the legislature, for example, meant to enable the husband to bar his wife's dower, by making a lease for a year, and keeping it on foot from year to year to his death: which would be a complete

destruction of the right, except at the will of the husband.
Therefore the Court holds, that, notwithstanding the use
of the copulative conjunction in the act of 1836, instead
of the disjunctive, as in the act of '84, the recent act
should receive the same construction in this respect that
was put on the former. In point of law, however, the
owner of the inheritance is not only seized, but is said to
be possessed, for the purposes of dower and courtesy,
when the reversion or remainder is not after a freehold,
but after a term for years only. The possession of the
tenant for years is the possession of the reversioner. At
the time that the titles by dower and courtesy were established, the interest of a termor was so little regarded,
as not to form an impediment to the rights or remedies
of the reversioner, to which he would be entitled if in the
actual possession. This was the foundation of the rule
originally, which let in dower and curtesy in such cases.
Park on Dower 78. But even now the possession of the
tenant is considered that of the reversioner for most purposes, but that of protecting the interest of the tenant, as
an estate, against the wrong of the reversioner. *Roper
on Husband and Wife* 861. As we have seen before, a
term did not impede dower; and that is not to be attrib-
uted to the rule, that the title to dower attaches to a
legal seizin. For, the same is true of curtesy, though to
that legal seizin is not sufficient, but actual seizin is requisite. If the wife be seized of the inheritance, subject
to a term for years, such chattel interest will not prevent
the wife's seizin of the freehold and inheritance, as required to found the right to curtesy; as the possession
of the lessee is the possession of the wife, as the owner of
the freehold and inheritance. *Co. Lit.* 29, *a. note* 1.
Where a woman inherited an estate tail, which was under leases for years, and died before she or her husband
had received rent, Lord HARDWICKE upon the bill of the
husband declared him entitled to the rents in arrear, and
also to curtesy in the estate; because he considered the

possession of the lessees to be that of the wife, and thus to give her for this purpose the actual, and not the mere legal, seizin. *De Grey* v. *Richardson*. 3 Atk. 469. If, then, the act of 1836 changed the preceding law, so as to require actual, and not legal, seizin, merely, to constitute a title to dower, there would in this case be that species of possession in the wife, which amounts to actual seizin, and complies with the letter of the act. But, for the reason before given, the Court entertains the opinion, that the one act was intended to be taken from the other, and therefore that, notwithstanding this accidental variance, they are to be received in the same sense.

The Court therefore holds, that Absalom T. Humphries' widow is entitled to dower in the dwelling-house, lot and out-houses, and in the factory land and tracts devised with it. mentioned in the pleadings; but as her husband could not have called for a division, and his enjoyment was temporarily suspended by his father's will, which gave the enjoyment to others, not rendering rent, she must also wait for the same period before she can have a decree for the enjoyment of her widow's estate.

It will be perceived, that the case has been treated as if the provision for the plaintiff in her husband's will had no effect whatever, after her dissent entered, and as if he had died intestate. It has been thus treated by the Court, because the counsel for the parties presented the case in that manner, and because, with the counsel, the Court has not perceived, that it would make any difference to these parties, whether the provision in a will for a wife is good *pro tanto*, notwithstanding her dissent, or is, upon her dissent, to be disregarded altogether. We have not thought it necessary, therefore, to give any opinion on that point.

PER CURIAM.   Decree accordingly.

JOSEPH J. EXUM & AL. *vs.* LEMUEL BOWDEN & AL.

Where a bond is, on its face, payable to a guardian for the benefit of his ward, this is *prima facie* notice to one, who takes an assignment of it, that it is the property of the ward and subject to his equities.

More especially is this the case, where the bond is taken in payment of the personal debt of the guardian, and where it is taken at an oppressive discount.

The case of a guardian disposing of securities for money belonging to his ward, is stronger against him than that of an executor disposing of the assets of the estate; for it is not so obviously necessary that the guardian should have such a power, as that the executor should, because infants usually come to their property, as the surplus of settled estates, and can hardly be properly in arrears to their guardian.

Yet in the case of an executor, if the person who takes a security from him, knows that the executor is raising money on it, for purposes not connected with the affairs of the estate, and more especially when the executor uses the testator's effects to pay his own antecedent debt to that person himself, it is deemed an act of concerted fraud between the two, and the owners of the property have a right to re-claim it.

The cases of *Fox* v. *Alexander*, 1 Ired. Eq. 340, *Bunting* v. *Ricks*, 2 Dev. and Bat. Eq. 130, and *Powell* v. *Jones*, 1 Ired. Eq. 387, cited and approved.

Cause removed from the Court of Equity of Northampton County, at the Spring Term 1846.

The following appeared, from the pleadings and proofs, to be the facts of the case.

In October, 1836, Samuel Spruill was appointed the guardian of Robert Cannon, an infant. He gave bond in the sum of $15,000 with the plaintiffs as his sureties, with three other persons, who have since become insolvent or removed out of the State. In a few days Spruill received about $3,500 for his ward; and on the 8th of March, 1837, he took from one Junius Amis a bond for the sum of $1,758 12 1-2, payable to Samuel B. Spruill, " guardian of Robert Cannon," and bearing interest from date. Spruill was indebted to the defendant, Bowden, on notes for about $1,200, and, upon being required to make payment, he agreed to let Bowden have the bond of Amis at 10 per cent. discount, in discharge of his notes to Bow-

· den as far as they went, he, Spruill, receiving the difference, between seven and eight hundred dollars, in cash.
Upon this agreement, Spruill endorsed the bond in blank
and delivered it to Bowden, who afterwards received the
money from Amis. Spruill was known to be embarrassed, and afterwards became insolvent and was removed;
and the succeeding guardian sued him and the present
plaintiffs on their bond, and recovered judgment in February, 1842, for $6,211 22, which the plaintiffs have
nearly paid. The plaintiffs then filed this bill against
Bowden, Spruill, and their three co-sureties, praying that
Bowden may be compelled to account for the money received from Amis, and apply it, as far as necessary, in
satisfaction of the sum still due the ward on the judgment, and the residue to reimbursing to the plaintiffs the
sum paid thereon by them. The bill states that the money, for which Amis gave his bond, belonged to the infant Cannon, and that Bowden knew that fact when he
took the bond, and that, in truth, the bond was the property of the ward.

Bowden answered and stated, that he did not know or
admit, that the bond of Amis was given in consideration
of money or effects, belonging to Robert Cannon; and, if
such was the fact, he denied, that he had such knowledge,
at the time he purchased and paid for the said bond.
"On the contrary," he says, "he then believed that the
bond was the property of Spruill, and that he was well-
authorized to sell and dispose of the same. It is true,
the bond was payable to said Spruill, as guardian of
Robt. Cannon, on its face; but it is, as this defendant
hath understood, a frequent practice of persons, who are
guardians, to take bonds for their personal claims in the
same way, and that was, as this defendant had understood from the said Spruill, the practice pursued by him.
Besides, the bond was executed by but one obligor, and
the defendant knew that, by law or uniform custom,
guardians take sureties for money due their wards. If

the face of the bond be sufficient in law to charge him
with notice, that it was the property of the ward, he must
submit to be thus charged; but no such notice was in
fact conveyed to this defendant thereby, nor did he have
such notice from any other source."

The defendant proved by a witness, that he enquired
of the witness, what the circumstances of Amis were,
and was told by him, that he was then surety for others,
and the witness also stated, that, on the same day on
which the defendant got the bond, Spruill wanted to sell
it to him, and that the witness asked 12 1-2 per cent. discount. And he proved by another witness, that, some
short time after Bowden got the bond, Spruill said that
although the bond was payable to him as guardian, he
had funds amply sufficient to pay his ward.

It appears by the accounts, returned by Spruill as guardian, to the County Court, in February 1837, that there
was then a balance of cash in his hands of $3,223 87,
and the sum was increased each year until his removal
in 1840.

B. *Moore*, for the plaintiffs.
Badger, for the defendants.

RUFFIN, C. J. The Court is of opinion, that the plaintiffs are entitled to the relief they ask. It is clear, that,
at the time Spruill let Amis have the money and took the
bond, he had in his hands a larger sum belonging to the
ward, which it was his duty to put out at interest. When
he lent the money and took a bond payable to him, as
guardian, it was an appropriation of this debt to the
ward; at all events, as against Spruill himself. It is
true, the bond does not appear in the guardian account
of February 1839; but that can make no difference, if it
really belonged to the ward, because in that case it was
the duty of the guardian to return it, as an investment
for the ward. The omission of the duty cannot injure the

ward. We think it cannot be doubted, if Spruill had died and left this bond payable to him as guardian, and he had been found to have been indebted to the ward at the time he took the bonds, at the time of his death and at every intermediate period, in a larger amount than that of the bond, that a Court of Equity would have compelled his executor to deliver it to the infant, as his property, in preference to applying it to the guardian's general creditors. Taking it payable to him, as guardian, could, *prima facie*, have no other object than to designate it as a portion of the ward's estate and set it apart accordingly. His subsequent declaration, that he had funds amply sufficient to pay the ward, has no effect against the ward's right. He did not mean, that he had never considered the bond as belonging to the ward. But we collect rather the reverse, from his reference to the form of the instrument. All he meant was, that notwithstanng he had made the bond the ward's, by the manner in which it was taken, and hence he might be supposed to have acted wrong in parting from it, as he had, and for the purposes he had, yet it would not really be to the prejudice of the ward, as he had other funds with which he could pay the ward. He was, in truth. apologising in a lame way for what appeared to be a breach of duty, and at the same time endeavoring to keep up his own credit, by holding out that the ward could not be hurt, because he had made the debt his own, and was able to pay it. If that had turned out to be true, all would have been well : for it is only when a trustee, who violates his trust, becomes insolvent, that a contest arises, by the necessity of the *cestui que trust* following his property into the hands, in which it was wrongfully put by the trustee, or submitting to the loss altogether. In this case it turned out to the contrary of Spruill's expectations, or, at least his declaration, and he proved unable to make the debt good. Would he therefore have the right to withold the bond from the ward? Certainly not. If he still had it, he would be decreed to deliver it to the ward. Then, *prima facie*, Bowden, who claims under it, cannot withold it. But he insists that he ought to be protected, for two reasons. The one is, that he had no knowledge nor just reasons to believe, at the time he took the bond, that it belonged to the ward; and the other, that, if the ward was the owner, yet a guardian has lawful authority to collect or dispose of debts to the ward, and that he is a purchaser for money paid, and securities surrendered.

Upon the first point the Court holds clearly, that Bowden is affected with notice. The bond, upon its face, disclosed the interest of the ward; told that he was the equitable owner, just as much as its being payable to the ward would have shown him to be the legal owner. But the defendant says, that, notwithstanding that circumstance, he did not in fact know it. The reason he gives, why the bond did not convey that information to him, is, not that the bond does not naturally import it, but that he had understood that some guardians had taken bonds payable to them, as guardians, for money that was their own, and that he had heard from Spruill that he had pursued such a practice. But that is a most illogical conclusion, and, if tolerated, would lead to serious mischief. It is an attempt to deny notice, which the instrument in its plain sense conveys, because it might be false. Although some persons might have corruptly endeavored to evade the statute of usury, and get compound interest by resorting to the device supposed, yet it did not follow, that this bond was not what it purported to be. It stated, that it was the equitable property of the ward, and, in dealing for it, he had to choose between the fact thus stated in it, and the opposite possibility or probability arising out of what he had heard some people had deceitfully practised. That was his risk; and it has happened that he reasoned falsely and came to a false conclusion, as it appears that the bond really belonged to the ward, as it purported on its face. In *Fox* v. *Alexander*, 1 Ired. Eq. 340, it was considered decisive, that the bond was payable " to R. D., guardian of R. R. D." Indeed, it was not a case, upon which the party was put upon enquiry merely; but in itself the bond contained full notice, and the only question was, whether it spoke the truth or falsehood. The most precise and circumstantial information would not amount to notice, if it could be got rid of by a person's declaration, that he did not believe it, because he had heard in other cases of such having been done colorably.

Upon the other point, it need not be denied, that a guardian has power to discount or otherwise dispose of a bond belonging to the ward, as well as to collect it. It is not so obviously necessary, that he should have that power, as that an executor should. The necessities of a testator's estate may often require the executor to raise money upon the securities belonging to the estate. But infants commonly come to their property as the surplus of settled estates, and can hardly be properly in arrear to the guardian. Therefore it is, at all events, more suspicious in a guardian than in an executor, to be found disposing of the securities; and one to whom they were offered, would naturally enquire for, at least, some apparently good reason for his doing so. But for the purposes of the case in hand, it may be admitted, that the two, a guardian and an executor, stand on the same footing. For it is well settled, that if the person who takes a security from an executor, knows that the executor is raising money on it for purposes not connected with the affairs of the estate, and especially when the executor uses the testator's effects to pay his own antecedent debt to that person himself, it is deemed an act of concerted fraud between the two, and the owners of the property have a right to reclaim it. For this position, we need go no farther back than the cases of *Scott* v. *Tyler*, 2 Dick. 712 and 2 Bro. C. C. 431, and *McLeod* v. *Drummond*, 17 Ves. 153, in the latter of which, Lord ELDON collects all the learning upon the point, and lays down

the rule distinctly. In conformity with the same principles, the cases were decided here of *Bunting* v. *Ricks*,
2 Dev. & Bat. Eq. 130. *Fox* v. *Alexander*, and *Powell*
v. *Jones*, 1 Ired. Eq. 337. And we then held, that the assignee of the bond was liable to the full amount of it,
though he paid for it partly in cash, because it was
originally the equitable property of the ward, or other
cestui que trust, and had not been transferred *bona fide*, and
therefore remained his property. Supposing the law
to be the same as to executors and guardians, then, if in
this case Bowden had done nothing more than advance
the $700 or $800 to Spruill, he might insist on holding
the bond as a security for it, although Spruill afterwards
converted the money to his own use ; for Bowden might
say, he thought he was advancing it for the benefit of the
ward. But he cannot say that now. The application, at
the time, of $1,200 of it, to the guardian's own debt to
Bowden, and the gross oppression to which the guardian
submitted, in order to get hold of the residue of the price
in cash, clearly proved, that both Spruill's integrity and
his prudence gave way under *his* necessities, and ought
to have led Bowden to expect, that Spruill would apply,
as he did apply, the whole to his own use. It is in that
point of view only, that the hard terms imposed on Spruill can be looked at in this case. The ward has no right
to complain of the oppression on his guardian. But the
guardian's agreeing to such terms, being 10 per cent. on
the whole bond of nearly $1,900 in order to get about
$700 in ready money, he remaining liable on his endorse-
ment, as he had been for his old debt, was enough to as-
sure Bowden, that Spruill was not raising the money for
his ward. No guardian ever raised money for a ward at
a loss of 25 per cent. or upwards. The truth is that the
transaction throughout was a breach of trust in Spruill,
and in the view of a Court of Equity, a fraud on the ward ;
and Bowden must have seen it, unless he was wilfully
blind, and therefore he must be regarded, as concurring

in it, and thereby to have lost the character of a *bona fide* purchaser to any purpose, and be accountable for the whole bond to the ward, and, by consequence, to the present plaintiffs, who have paid the ward and are entitled to stand in his place.

PER CURIAM.   Decree for the plaintiffs.

ABRAHAM SPENCER *vs.* FRANK HAWKINS & AL.

Where a series of executions issue on the same judgment, and have been *bona fide* acted on, the last of them relates to the teste of the first and binds the property of the defendant from that time.

But where the original, or any intermediate writ of execution, never was delivered to the sheriff, the lien is not carried back beyond the one on which the sheriff acted.

Where an original *fi. fa.* issues to one county, and an *alias* to another, a sale by the defendant of his property situated in the latter, while the *fi. fa.* was in the hands of the sheriff of the former, is good.

Whether a trustee had authority or not, under a deed of trust for the payment of debts, to make sale of personal property, his sale, acting in the capacity of trustee and in the presence and acquiescence of the *cestui que trust*, would give a good title, at least in equity.

Where an execution, though made out, does not appear to have been issued by the clerk, it creates no lien.

The cases of *Palmer* v. *Clark*, 2 Dev. 354, *Hardy* v. *Jasper*, 3 Dev. 158, and *Freeman* v. *Hill*, 1 Dev. and Bat. 9, cited and approved.

Cause transmitted by consent from Granville Court of Equity, at the Spring Term 1846.

The following facts appear upon the pleadings and proof:

The bill charges that the defendant. Hawkins, advertised for sale, as trustee of the other defendant, a number of negroes : that the plaintiff attended the sale, when a

negro woman named Daphne and her infant child were
offered : that he became the purchaser. That, when she
was put up, she was proclaimed by Hawkins in the presence of Jones, who was present assisting in the sale, to
be a healthy, sound negro : that he found that she was
unsound, with a chronic rheumatism, under which he
charges she has been laboring for many years, and which
was known to the defendant Jones, the owner, and that,
in consequence of such disease, she was utterly worthless. The bill further charges, that by the purchase of
the plaintiff from the defendant Hawkins, no title passed
to him as the negro Daphne and her child were not named
in the deed of trust ; and, further, that the negroes were
taken out of his possession by the sheriff of Granville,
and one G. C. Wiggins a constable of said county, as the
property of Jones and liable to his debts, and to satisfy
certain executions in their hands. One issued upon a
judgment in the County Court of Franklin, at December
term, 1841, of that Court, and which had been regularly
issued down to June term, 1843, and also upon a judgment
obtained in Granville County Court at August term, 1842,
upon which executions had been regularly issued, until
levied upon Daphne and her child, and who were sold
under them. The deed of trust was executed on the 19th
of February, 1842, and duly registered the 21st, two days
after, and the sale was made by Hawkins in March,
1842. The bill prays the contract may be rescinded.

The defendants severally answer, admitting the sale
of Daphne and her child by the defendant Hawkins, and
in the presence and with the approbation of the other defendant, Jones. They both deny that Daphne was unsound, but on the contrary, both aver, that at the time of
the sale and while in the possession of Jones, she was a
sound, healthy negro. They admit that Daphne and child
were not included in the deed of trust, but they were
both, at the time of the sale, under the full belief they
were included. But they aver that the sale, being made

by Hawkins in the presence of Jones and by his direc-rection, was made by the latter, and the plaintiff acquired by buying and securing the price, a good and valid title. They further deny, that, at the time of the sale by Hawkins, there were any executions against Jones which bound his property.

Replications were taken to the answers, and the cause set for hearing and transmitted to this Court.

Badger, for the plaintiff.
No counsel for the defendants.

NASH, J. Before proceeding to the main questions in the cause, we will dispose of the objections. made by the plaintiff, to the title from the executions, binding the property. It is admitted in the deed of trust, that up to the sale then made by Hawkins, the title to the property was in the defendant Jones, and liable to the payment of his debts. The sale by Hawkins was a sale by Jones; it was in his presence and by his directions. Had Jones the power at the time to make a valid sale of them? At December term, 1841, of Franklin County Court, a judgment was obtained against Jones and others, in favor of McIlvain and others, upon which an execution issued directed to the sheriff of Franklin, Jones being a citizen and resident in the county of Granville. This execution was returned to March term, 1842, of Franklin County Court, by the sheriff of that county, as "delayed by the plaintiff." From March an *alias fi. fa.* issued, directed to the sheriff of Granville, and returnable to the ensuing June term, but there is no evidence it ever was sent to the sheriff of Granville, or was ever in his hands. The record of Franklin Court states, "upon which there appears no indorsement by the sheriff." From June term, a *pluries fi. fa.* issued to the sheriff of Granville, which is returned "executed, &c." Before this last execution bears *teste*, the negroes had been sold by Hawkins, to-wit, on the 19th of March, 1842. When a series of executions issue on the same judgments, and have been *bona fide* acted on, the last of them relates to the *teste* of the first and binds the property of the defendant from that time. But when the original or any intermediate writ never was delivered to the sheriff, the lien is not carried back beyond the one on which the sheriff acted. *Palmer v. Clark*, 2 Dev. 354. And when an original *fi. fa.* issued to one county, and an *alias* to another, a sale by the defendant of his property, situated in the latter county, while the *fi. fa.* was in the hands of the sheriff of the former, is good. *Hardy v. Jasper*, 3 Dev. 158. Here there is no evidence that the *alias* ever left the clerk's office of Franklin—it was then, as to the question now before us, as if it never had been made out by the clerk. The first precept, that came to the sheriff of Granville, was the *pluries,* and that issued from the June term, 1842. In the March preceding the negroes had been sold. As to the execution in favor of Cooper, it bore *teste* of August term, 1842, subsequent to the sale by five months. These are the Court executions, under which the negro Daphne was taken out of the possession of the plaintiff and sold. The child of Daphne was taken by G. C. Wiggins, as a constable, under an execution in favor of one Gaylard, issued by a magistrate on the 3d of March, 1843. So far then as these executions were concerned, the sale under them did not divest the plaintiff, Spencer, of the title he had acquired by the sale to him. Hawkins professed to sell as a trustee of Jones, and in that character, conveyed the negroes to Spencer. Jones was present, assenting to and directing the sale. Under the deed of trust, Hawkins had no power to sell. If then, Spencer did not acquire a legal title, he acquired such an one as this Court would protect. Jones would not be permitted to set up any title in himself. If Jones still had the legal title, it was a title without an interest, and a Court of Equity would compel him to convey to the purchaser. The purchasers at

66

the sale made by the sheriff of Granville and the constable, Wiggins, acquired only the right which was in Jones
at the time of the sale with all his liabilities. *Freeman
v. Hill*, 1 Dev. & Bat. 9. The main question, however,
in this case, is as to the soundness of the negro Daphne
—alledged by the plaintiff and positively denied by the
defendants. Has the plaintiff made out his allegation?
The allegation in the bill is, that the negroe Daphne was,
at the time he purchased her, unsound, and that Jones
knew it. It is not sufficient for him to show her unsound.
The testimony, taken by the plaintiff, with the exception
of those witnesses, who speak of her in the year 1834,
while in the possession of Shelling Parish, consists prin-
cipally of opinion. In that year she was sick for a month,
and complained of pains in her limbs. Dr. Royster, who
attended her, thought at first it was a spinal affection,
but at length considered it rheumatic and chronic. Drs.
Herndon and Paschall, from her appearance and from a
scar on the back, which they considered the mark of an
abscess, are also of opinion she was afflicted with rheumatism of long standing. Dr. Paschall thinks the
scar on the back was the consequence of an abscess,
formed during her sickness at Shelling Parish's, and yet
neither he nor George Parish, nor Mr. Estis, who knew
her while sick there, knew any thing about it. Shelling
Parish says, after her return to his house, she was as
healthy as before she was taken sick. Opposed to this
testimony, inconclusive as it is, is the testimony on behalf
of the defendants. Willis Loyd knew Daphne from a
child and was overseer for the defendant, Jones, during
1835-7-8, and had been all "'38 and most of the time in
the preceding years." She was never sick during the
time, and did as much work as any hand he had—was
considered sound and healthy. Mrs. Estis lived near
Shelling Parish. The girl Daphne was carried to her
house—had a fever—no rheumatism; she has known her
from childhood up to 1842—never knew any thing the

matter—as sound and as likely as any other negro—the defect in her ankles belonged to her family—her mother the same. Mr. Abitt was an overseer of Jones, during the year 1839 and up to the end of 1842. Daphne was one of his hands, and as good a one as he had—never sick during that time. Several other witnesses testify the same. John B. Hicks' deposition was taken in August, 1844; he states that Daphne was then in his employment, having hired her for the year—that she is sound, healthy, and has not been sick during that time, and is an excellent hand and the strongest but one he saw in lifting. Mr. George Hicks states, that she was, at the time of taking his deposition, a sound healthy negro and an excellent hand. Other witnesses testify that they had seen her in May 1844 and she was apparently sound and healthy. The rest of the testimony for the defendant is of the same character.

The plaintiff's proofs do not sustain his allegations. It is not proved that the negro Daphne was, at the time of the sale, unsound. Nor is there the slightest testimony, that, if so, the defendant Jones knew it. We are, on the contrary, satisfied from all the proofs, that she was sound. The testimony of Mr. Estis, we think, accounts satisfactorily for the defect in her feet—her mother was so. The fact is proved by one of the witnesses of the plaintiff, Mr. G. Parish. The bill must be dismissed with costs.

PER CURIAM.   Decree accordingly.

MATTHEW R. MOORE vs. JOHN BANNER.

A plaintiff in a Court of Equity is bound to give security for costs, in the same manner as a plaintiff in a suit at law.

Appeal from an interlocutory order of the Court of Equity of Stokes County, at the Spring Term, 1846, his Honor Judge SETTLE presiding.

The following case appears from the record:

The plaintiff obtained a decree in the Court of Equity against William Moore for $3,285 08, and having made the requisite affidavit, he sued out a *scire facias* against Banner, suggesting therein, according to the act of 1806, that Banner was in possession of certain slaves, belonging to William Moore, and concealed them. and also that William Moore had fraudulently conveyed to Banner certain other slaves without any valuable consideration. for the purpose of delaying, hindering and avoiding the payment of the plaintiff's debt.

At the return of the writ, Banner's counsel moved the Court, that the plaintiff should be required to give security for the costs, he not having before given any. The Court refused a peremptory rule at that time, but granted a rule on the plaintiff to shew cause at the next term, why he should not give security for the costs, and, in the meantime, ordered the defendant, Banner, to make his declaration in writing and on oath, as required by the act, *Rev. St. ch.* 50, *sec.* 5, 6. He did so immediately, and therein stated, that in the year 1825 he married the daughter of William Moore, and that the said Moore did not then owe the plaintiff any debt, and was fully able to pay all his debts, and that, soon after his marriage, the said Moore transferred to him a negro woman, named Nancy, and he then took her into his, the defendant's, possession, and kept her about ten years, during which time she had issue two children, named Susan and Henry; and that the said Nancy then died, but the said two children are still in possession of him, Banner, and are claimed by him. He further states, that in 1843 he purchased from William Moore another negro, named Will, at the price of $676, and that the same was a full and fair price; and he avers, that he received the slave Nancy and purchased the slave Will, *bona fide* and without any intent to defraud the plaintiff or any creditor of William Moore.

The plaintiff did not require any issue to be made up on

the answer, nor make any motion that the Court should thereon order any of the negroes to be delivered up and made subject to his decree. At the next term, the counsel for the defendant moved the Court to make the rule of the preceding term absolute, so as to compel the plaintiff to give security for the costs or to dismiss his suit. But the Court refused the motion and discharged the rule; and thereupon the defendant, by leave of the Court, appealed.

Morehead and *Kerr*, for the plaintiff.
No counsel for the defendant.

RUFFIN, C. J. As the appeal is from an interlocutory order, our attention is restricted to it by the act allowing such appeals. We are to consider, then, that this is a proper proceeding in the Court of equity, and our only enquiry is, whether the plaintiff ought to be ruled to security for costs.

It has not been contended at the bar, that, generally speaking, plaintiffs in equity are not to give security for costs; but it was admitted to be the common course, and it seemed to be yielded that it was proper. The Masters and the Courts have acted, as if the act of 1787, c. 276 embraced as well the Courts of equity as the Courts of law, which last only are, properly speaking, Courts of record. But it does not seem material, whether Courts of equity are directly within the enactments of that statute, or not; for, if the statute *proprio vigore* does not embrace them, the rule ought to be adopted by the Court of equity, because it is prescribed to the Courts of law. The same reason extends to both Courts; and it is the course of the Courts of equity to follow the Courts of law in such matters. In England, the rule at law is to require security for costs from all plaintiffs without the jurisdiction, unless they be abroad temporarily, or involuntarily, as, for example, officers or privates in the army or navy, or otherwise in the public service. As a matter of course. the Court of equity adopted precisely the same rule And it is acted on, not as a thing in the discretion of the Court in each case, according to its circumstances; but as a thing of course, according to a settled law of the Court, corresponding with the rule at law, and embracing every person alike, rich and poor. *Beames on Costs*, 178. In the same manner, here the Court of equity has followed the Courts of law, and the practice of requiring security for costs has prevailed so universally as to establish it as a part of the law of that Court, whether it be strictly within the act of 1787 or not. So, indeed, it seems to have been regarded by the Legislature itself; for in the act of 1831, c. 46, the Courts of law and equity are expressly placed on the same footing, and are respectively required to give a judgment or decree, on motion, against the surety in the prosecution bond for the defendant's costs.

But it was supposed, that the present proceeding is not within the acts, because it is not an original suit, but a derivative and dependent proceeding. The answer to that is, that the statute expressly gives costs between the parties to the suits under it; and, as the defendant may thus have a decree for his costs, he is entitled to have them secured. It is true, that upon the face of the answer, the issue of the slave Nancy, whom the father-in-law "transferred," as the answer says, to the defendant at his marriage, but not stated to be for value or in writing, remains, apparently, the property of the donor. who is yet living; and, therefore, subject to be declared liable to execution for the plaintiff's debt. Therefore, supposing the act of 1806 to extend to the Court of Equity, there may be but a remote probability, that the plaintiff would be decreed to pay the costs. Yet as that question, as to the jurisdiction, is yet to be decided, and, indeed, as the plaintiff may, as he has hitherto done, decline making any motion on the defendant's declaration, we cannot foresee, that the decision may not be against the plaintiff. Consequently, we think, he ought to have been required to give security, as demanded : which will be certified accordingly to the Court of Equity. The appellant is entitled to his costs in this Court.

PER CURIAM.   Decreed accordingly.

WYNN NANCE & AL. *vs.* MARMADUKE POWELL & AL.

Legatees, next of kin, and creditors of a deceased person, can only file a bill against a debtor to the deceased or his trustee, by charging collusion between the debtor or trustee and the personal representatives, or some other peculiar circumstances, which give a right to the legatees, next of kin or creditors to bring that suit, which the personal representative might and ought to have brought.

Collusion is the usual foundation of such a bill, and without it, or some equivalent ground, as the insolvency of the executor or the like, it will not lie.

The facts, on which the allegation of collusion, &c. is made, ought to be stated in the bill, although the general allegation may be sufficient to prevent a demurrer, and they must be proved on the hearing.

Legatees, next of kin, and creditors of a deceased person, cannot bring a bill against a debtor to the deceased or his trustee, for the reason, that the executor could not, or that he could not prove the case, if the suit was brought by himself, but could, as a witness, prove it for the other parties.

The case of *Dameron v. Clay*, 2 Dev. Eq. 17, cited and approved.

Cause removed from the Court of Equity of Columbus County, at the Spring Term 1846.

The following case appears from the pleadings and proofs :

The bill states that Wynn Nance died intestate in 1815, leaving a widow, Dorothy, and four children, namely, Daniel H., Edward W., Betsey, intermarried with James Brown, and Lucy, intermarried with Jesse Foulk ;

that the two sons, Daniel H. and Edward W. administered on the estate, and that in 1815 a division of the estate was made by the widow, and the children, who were all of age; and in the division, several horses and other personal property were allotted to Mrs. Wynn: that in March 1819, the said Brown and Foulk being impatient to realize something immediately for their expectations from the reversion of what had passed to the widow, or their right as next of kin in the personal estate of the widow, respectively sold said expectations to the said Daniel and Edward. that is to say. Brown sold for the price of $450, and Foulk for the price of $500, which was paid to them respectively, and for which they gave several receipts, which are set out in the bill, and are expressed to be " given to Edward W. Nance and Daniel H. Nance, administrators of the estate of Wynn Nance, deceased," and to be "in full of all claims of every description against the estate of Wynn Nance, deceased." The bill then states, that, notwithstanding the form in which the receipts are expressed, the contracts were in fact for any claim Brown and wife and Foulk and wife then had or might have, " upon the portion of the estate of said Wynn Nance, which had gone into the hands of said Dorothy, with all the increase and profits," with the exception of a certain piece of land which belonged to Daniel H. Nance.

The bill then states that Dorothy, the widow, intermarried with Jethro Robins; that said Jethro subsequently died, leaving the said Dorothy surviving, and that she has since died in 1843, intestate, and leaving some personal estate, and the defendant, M. Powell, administered on it; and that Brown and wife and Foulk and wife now claim distributive shares of the estate as part of her next kin.

The bill also states, that Edward W. Nance died, having first made a will, and thereof appointed Moor Linnon the executor, who duly proved it and undertook its executions, and that Daniel H. Nance died intestate, and the same Moor Linnon administered on his estate.

The bill then states, that certain of the plaintiffs are the children of the testator, Edward Nance, and that the others are the children of Daniel H. Nance; and that the plaintiffs, Mrs. Brown and Mrs. Foulk are the rest of the kin of Dorothy Robins, deceased. The bill is filed against Brown and wife, Foulk and wife, Powell the administrator of Mrs. Robins, and Moor Linnon the executor of Edward W. and administrator of Daniel H. Nance. Besides the matters already set forth, it states that both the plaintiffs and Linnon had called on Powell to pay to the plaintiffs or Linnon the whole personal estate of Mrs. Robins, formerly Nance, and that he declined doing so without the consent of Brown and Foulk, and that those persons refuse to give such consent and demand of the administrator to pay them the distributive shares of their wives respectively, that is, to each, one fourth part.

The bill then states, that Linnon is an indispensable witness to establish the purchase, made by the fathers of the plaintiffs from Brown and Foulk: and that by reason thereof he could not bring a bill in his own name, as he could not give evidence for himself, and therefore the present plaintiffs have sued in their own names, and made the said Linnon one of the defendants, in order that, by leave of the Court, he might be examined against the other defendants.

The prayer is, that Brown and wife, and Foulk and wife may be compelled to perform their agreements with the fathers of the plaintiffs, "and relinquish all claim to any of the estate of the said Dorothy Robins, or such portion of the estate of Wynn Nance, deceased, as may have gone into her hands; and that the defendant, M. Powell, may account with and pay over to your orators and oratrixes the whole of the said fund; or that the said Powell may come to an account with your orator and oratrixes, and with the defendant Brown and Foulk, and thereupon be decreed to pay to the plaintiffs the sums of $500 and $450, received by them, Brown and Foulk on the contract aforesaid, and which, from want of proof and lapse of time, neither the plaintiffs nor the said Linnon, as executor and administrator, as aforesaid, would be able to recover at law;" and for general relief.

The answers of Brown and Foulk admit the execution of the receipts by them respectively; but they deny that there was any such contract, as alleged in the bill, for the sale of any reversion in the estate allotted to the widow, or of their expectations from her as her next of kin or otherwise: and they aver that the receipts were for sums paid to them by the administrator, for a surplus of money which remained in their hands, after the payment of the debts of the father, Wynn Nance, for distribution under the statute. They insist, therefore, that they are entitled to full distributive shares of the estate of Mrs. Robins without any abatement. The administrator Powell denies all knowledge of the contracts alleged in the bill. He states that he is ready to account for the personal estate of his intestate, Mrs. Robins, when properly required; but he insists, that if, under the alleged contracts, Edward W. Nance and Daniel H. Nance became entitled to the shares of the said estate, that would have belonged to Mrs. Brown and Mrs. Foulk, he is not bound nor at liberty to account therefor to the plaintiffs, but to Moor Linnon as the executor and administrator of the said Edward W. and Daniel H. He admits that the plaintiffs are the children of those two persons, as stated in the bill, and their next of kin respectively.

Under an order, the deposition of Moor Linnon was taken, subject to just exceptions. He states, that Daniel H. Nance agreed to give Brown $450 for his right of inheritance to the property then in the hands of Dorothy Nance, widow of Wynn Nance, deceased, which she received in the division of the estate of her husband, and the witness saw Brown give the receipt, as set forth in the bill, and take the bónds of Nance for the money.

Another witness states, that he was present at the contract with Brown and Foulk, and wrote their receipts, and that he understood it to be a final settlement, between the administrator of Wynn Nance and Brown and Foulk against all further claims on the estate, and "to the property that went into the hands of the widow of the deceased."

Strange, for the plaintiffs.

J. H. Bryan, for the defendants.

RUFFIN, C. J.   There are several objections to the plaintiffs' case, which are fatal to it.   The principal object of the bill is, to set up the alledged agreement of Brown and Foulk, to sell to the fathers of the plaintiffs some interest, it was supposed they had in the property that fell to Mrs. Nance in the distribution of her first husband's estate ; and to have it specifically executed, or in some way to have a decree for the payment of the sums which were given as the price of that interest.   Now, the rule is clear, that a suit against Brown and Foulk, for those purposes ought to be brought by Linnon, the executor of Edward W. Nance, one of the supposed purchasers, and the administrator of Daniel H. Nance, the other of such purchasers.   Instead of that, it has been brought by the children of those persons, as being entitled as their next of kin.   In the first place the remark occurs, that the bill states that one of those persons, Edward W. Nance, made a will—and that puts an end at once to the rights of his children in this fund, as next of kin, and makes it necessary that they should show a title under the will, if it gives any thing to them.   But the bill states no part of the will, except that it appoints Linnon executor, which is certainly insufficient, as the Court cannot decree, upon a presumption that the instrument contains no disposing clause. when it was so easy to state its provisions in the bill, and produce the will in evidence. Supposing, then, that a bill could be brought in this case by the legatees and children of those purchasers respectively against the vendors, making the executor and administrator and the purchasers, a defendant; this bill at all events cannot be sustained, because none of the plaintiffs legally represent Edward W. Nance, whose interest must be before us in some way. But if that difficulty was removed, and Edward W. had died intestate as well as Daniel H. Nance, we should hold, that the bill, as it is framed, will not lie. It charges no collusion, either in detail as to its circumstances, or even generally, between Linnon and the other defendant. It does not implicate that person, even in the formal charge of combination and confederacy, but restricts that to the other parties, Brown and wife, Foulk and wife, and Powell. Indeed, the bill expressly repels any such imputation against Linnon, by assigning, as the reason why he did not sue and why the plaintiffs did, that Linnon's evidence was indispensable to establish the alleged contract between his testator and intestate and the other parties; and not that the plaintiffs had applied to Linnon to sue, and that, by collusion with the other defendants or for some other insufficient reason, he refused to do so. It is plain, therefore, that Linnon's unfaithful conduct has not compelled the plaintiffs to resort to this mode of seeking redress: but that the suit has assumed its present form by concert between Linnon and the plaintiffs, because it was supposed that by that means he might be made a witness in the case, in which he regularly ought to have been the plaintiff. We are not aware of any such precedent, nor any principle upon which such a proceeding could be upheld. There is no privity between the plaintiff and Brown and Foulk, in respect of this part of the claim between them and Powell, the administrator of Mrs. Robins, which can make those persons answerable to the plaintiffs. Those persons are answerable, not to the next of kin, but to the personal representatives of the two purchasers. Legatees, next of kin and creditors of a deceased person can only file a bill against a debtor to the deceased, or his trustee, by charging collusion between the debtor or trustee and the personal representative, or some other peculiar circumstances. which give a right to the legatees, next of kin or creditors, to bring that suit which the personal representative might and ought to have brought. Collusion is the usual foundation of such a bill, and without it or some equivalent ground, as the insolvency of the executor or the like, it will not lie. *Mit. Pl.* 158. *Doran* v. *Simpson,* 4 Ves. 665. *Troughton* v. *Binks,* 6 Ves. 572. *Alsager* v. *Rowley,* Idem. 748. And although in such cases the general allegation of collusion may be sufficient to shut out a demurrer, yet it is most proper to state the facts, on which the allegation is made; and, very clearly, when the cause is brought on to a hearing they must be proved, since the collusion is a material ingredient in the jurisdiction. *Benfield* v. *Solomons,* 9 Ves. 77, 86. *Dameron* v. *Clay,* 2 Dev. Eq. 17. But there never has been an idea, that legatees and creditors can bring such a bill. for the reason, that the executor could not, or that he would not prove the case, if the suit was brought by himself, but could, as a witness, prove it for the other parties. It would reverse the whole rule that is founded on collusion. This, therefore, is another conclusive objection to the bill. It, however, would not have been adverted to thus particularly, had it not been material to another part of the bill, which will be presently considered and to which it is equally applicable, as it is to the claim under consideration: For, independent of all legal impediments to this part of the plaintiffs' demand, there is a clear answer to it on the merits, as proved by the witnesses, or admitted in the bill, as a little attention to facts will show. The statement of the bill, as to the subject of the alledged contract, is vague, and perhaps might

be properly objected to as destructive of the bill altogether, as every bill ought, at least, to state with precision a contract, which it seeks to enforce.   Here the language of the bill is, that Brown and Foulk sold to their
brothers-in-law, " their expectations from the reversion
of what had passed to the widow in the said division, or
their right as next of kin in the personal estate of the
widow." Those defendants deny any such contract as
either of those alleged, and say that the receipts they
gave plainly and correctly express the transaction to
have been the payment to them of the several sums remaining due for the distributive shares of their wives;
and there is no evidence of any mistake in drawing those
instruments.   But passing that by, and proceeding to the
fact as stated by the plaintiffs' witness, we find that the
contract between the parties was, that the sums paid to
Brown and Foulk were in satisfaction of their wives'
shares of the estate of the father then in the hands of
the administrators, and also as the price for their shares
in " the property that went into, and was then in the
hands of Dorothy, the widow, which she received in the
division of the estate of her husband." This agreement,
therefore, was not for the sale of the daughters' expec-
tancies, generally, from their mother, but for their ex-
pectancies in reference to the slaves and other property
which she received as her distributive share, as widow
of Wynn Nance, and then had in her hands. From the
very nature of such a purchase, admitting the terms of
this contract to have been sufficiently specific to admit
of execution in this Court, it is subject to the contingencies, that Mrs. Nance did not dispose of that particular property in her life-time, or by her will in favor of
some other person, but that she either should give it to
Brown and Foulk and their wives, or die entitled to that
property and intestate, whereby distributive shares of it
would come to those persons. Thus viewed, the whole
subject of the agreement was lost to Mrs. Nance and to

her first children by her subsequent intermarriage with
Robins, which is stated in the bill; for, by that event, all
that property, thus being at the time in her possession,
vested in her second husband and could never again vest
in her, as her distributive share of Nance's estate. But
it was contended at the bar, that the plaintiffs were, at
all events, and laying aside all agreements, entitled to an
account from Powell, as administrator of Mrs. Robins,
and distribution of the property as her estate. That depends upon the enquiry, whether they are to be taken as
her next of kin at her death, or some of them. The
plaintiffs are the children and next of kin respectively of
Edward W. and Daniel H. Nance, who were, [we suppose, though it is not stated,] the sons of Dorothy Nance,
as well as of her first husband. The death of Dorothy
is stated to have been in March 1843, but it does not appear at what time either Edward W. or Daniel H. died;
whether before or after their mother, supposing her to be
their mother. The bill, indeed, alleges that the plaintiffs
are, with Mrs. Brown and Mrs. Foulk, the next kin of
Mrs. Robins; but the answers admit only that the plaintiffs are the children and next of kin of their respective
fathers, and not that they are some of the next of kin of
the widow; and there is no evidence upon the point.
Since, then, the plaintiffs do not establish, nor even state,
that their father died before their grand-mother; the bill
cannot be supported upon any such presumption; for the
Court cannot declare the fact, and that is indispensable
to enable them to sue in the character of next of kin of
the grand-mother. Of course, it lies on every plaintiff
to shew his title upon the record. If the bill be considered as being brought by the children and next of kin of
the deceased sons, Edward W. and Daniel H. Nance, .
·then the objections recur with still more force, which
have been already under discussion: that one of those
persons made a will, and that Linonn is the proper person to claim their shares. and that no reason whatever

is given why, in respect to this part of the case, he should be made a defendant. The bill must, therefore. be necessarily dismissed with costs ; but it will be without prejudice to the rights of the plaintiffs as some of the next of kin of Mrs. Robins, (if they be so,) to bring any other proper suits for their shares of her estate.

PER CURIAM.   Bill dismissed with costs.

REUBEN WASHBURN & AL. vs. ABRAHAM WASHBURN.

Two brothers proved the will of their father in common form. Afterwards, this probate was set aside at the instance of the widow, and an issue of *devisavit vel non* was made up. While this was pending, one of the sons acting for the other, as he alleged, as well as for himself, entered into a written compromise with the widow, by which the property was agreed to be divided in a particular manner. Both the sons took the property assigned to them by the compromise and held it for eleven years. *Held*, that after this act and long acquiescence, they cannot now repudiate the compromise and be permitted to claim under the provisions of the will.

Our act of Assembly, *Rev. Stat. c. 50, s. 8*, which makes void all contracts for the sale of slaves not reduced to writing and signed, does not require, when the contract is by an agent, that it should be signed by the principal or by the agent in the name of the principal.

The statute of limitations does not apply in the case of a vendee bringing a bill for the specific performance of a contract. The only question, as to time, is a question of diligence.

The case of *Oliver v. Dix*, 1 Dev. and Bat. Eq. 165, cited and approved.

Cause transmitted from the Court of Equity of Cleaveland County. at the Spring Term, 1846.

This case was formerly before this Court upon an interlocutory order made in the Court of Equity of Cleveland County. Upon that occasion, it was declared that, from the bill and the answers, the Court could not say, that Abraham Washburn, one of the defendants, was not a party to the compromise, set out in the bill, and decreed that the injunction previously granted, should be continued until the final hearing. Upon being certified of this opinion, the parties proceeded to take the necessary steps in the Court below, to prepare the cause for a decision. Replication was taken to the answer, and the testimony and exhibits filed, and the cause is now here for hearing. The facts are shortly these : Gabriel Washburn died in the year 1825, and the plaintiffs and defendants are his next of kin or their proper representatives, and who, together with his widow, were entitled to his personal estate. At the February term, 1826, of Rutherford County Court, the defendant offered for probate, a paper purporting to be the last will and testament of Gabriel Washburn. This paper was admitted to probate in common form and the defendants were qualified as executors thereof, being, with their mother Priscilla Washburn, the widow, appointed to execute the same, at the succeeding July term of the County Court of Rutherford. The plaintiffs filed a petition to set aside the probate, and the Court ordered an issue to be made, to try the validity of the will. The issue continued untried until July term, 1827, when the following entries appear upon the records: "Gilbert Harrell, in right of his wife, *against* Abraham Washburn and Josiah Washburn, Ex'rs. &c. Will caveated, *devisavit vel non*, compromised. Terms filed." And an instrument was filed in the following terms:— " North Carolina, Court of Pleas and Quarter Sessions, July term, 1827. Gilbert Harrell *vs.* Abraham Washburn and Josiah Washburn, Executors of G. Washburn, dec'd. Petition to set aside a will. This suit is compromised on the following terms—Priscilla Washburn is to remain in possession of the whole estate, both real and personal, during her life, and at her death the land is to be divided between Abraham and Josiah Washburn, and all the personal property to be equally divided between the bal-

67

ance of the heirs of Gabriel Washburn, dec'd. The costs of this suit to be paid out of the personal estate." Signed by Gilbert Harrell and Josiah Washburn. Priscilla Washburn, the widow, at the March term, 1828 of Rutherford County Court, was appointed administratrix of her deceased husband, and Abraham Washburn, Josiah Washburn, John Harrell and Martin S. Elliott were his sureties. Soon after this compromise, the defendants divided between themselves the land belonging to the estate, and one of them took a portion of the negroes into his possession with the consent of the widow, who died in 1839—upon which event the defendants possessed themselves of the rest of the negroes in dispute, and again propounded for probate the script, the subject of the previous compromise. What has become of this second attempt to prove that paper, no where appears.

The defendants deny that the first probate was ever set aside, and admit, that a petition for that purpose was filed by the plaintiffs, in the proper Court, and that during its pending, the compromise set forth in the bill was made, but deny that any person was bound by it, but the immediate parties who signed it, to-wit, Gilbert Harrell and his wife and Josiah Washburn. The latter admits he signed it, but averred it was not to be binding on him, unless Abraham agreed to it and signed it also; neither of which he ever did. Abraham also denies that he was any party to it; but avers, that, as soon as he heard of it, he refused to become a party, or to accede to it; and that, in taking possession of the land and negroes, they were acting under the will of Gabriel Washburn, as devisees and legatees.

Alexander and *J. H. Bryan,* for the plaintiff.
No counsel for the defendant.

NASH, J. The object of the bill is to set up and enforce the compromise set forth in it. There is no dis-

pute as to the fact of the compromise, nor its terms. The
only controversy is as to its effect. Josiah alleges, it
never bound him, because Abraham never acceded to it,
and the latter denies he ever was a party to it. The
same questions presented themselves, when the case was
upon a former occasion, before us, and we then declared
that the facts admitted by the answers were sufficient to
continue the injunction, previously granted to the hearing, and to put the parties to their proofs. The testimony
filed has not in any respect altered the view then taken
of the equities of the parties. Josiah and Abraham
Washburn, as two of the executors of the last will and
testament of Gabriel Washburn and devisees under it,
caused it to be proved in common form, without giving
to the other parties interested any notice. A petition
was filed by Gilbert Harrell and his wife, for the pur pose
of setting aside the probate. An issue of *devisavit vel
non* was made up, to which the defendants were parties;
and, during its pendency, the compromise now in dispute
was effected, and entered upon the records of the Court.
This took place at July term, 1827, of Rutherford County
Court, after which time there were no further proceedings in the case. In pursuance, however, it would appear, of the compromise, the widow at the March term
following is, by the same Court, appointed administratrix
of her deceased husband, and the plaintiff Harrell and
the defendant executed her bond as sureties for the faithful discharge of her duties. From March 1825, until her
death in 1833, she remained in undisturbed possession of
the whole of the property, except so far as she permitted
the defendants to take into their occupancy portions of
it. No attempts were made by any of the next of kin,
to disturb her, or to call her to account to obtain a
distribution of what might be due and coming to them.
Eleven years she enjoyed the property—in a manner perfectly consistent with the terms of the compromise, and
her possession is acquiesced in by all the parties in-

terested in the distribution of G. Washburn's estate. It
is impossible to believe under these circumstances, that
the compromise was effected by Harrell and Josiah Washburn alone, and for their sole benefit; but it is evident it
was so intended and so understood at the time, by all
the parties, that it was made by them all. As to the allegations of the defendant Abraham, it is painful to remark upon them. He would have us believe, that a proceeding instituted by himself to establish the last will
and testament of his father, in which he was deeply interested, had been stopped in its progress without his
knowledge and consent—without eliciting from him any
enquiries—any expression of discontent—or any effort,
until eleven years thereafter, to cause the will to be
proved. But more than this: immediately after the compromise, he not only acquiesces in the appointment of his
mother as administratrix, but aids and assists her in her
application, by burdening himself as one of her sureties,
and signing the bond as such. In swearing to the answer
filed by him, he has encountered a painful responsibility.

The defendants admit they took possession of the property as charged, but aver they did so in the character of
devisees and legatees, and not under the compromise;
and that the original probate never was set aside. The
record sets out enough to satisfy us that the probate was
called in; for it shews, that after the petition was filed
and notice served on the defendants, an issue of *devisavit
vel non* was ordered by the Court. But we are not left
to deductions drawn from the fact admitted by the answers. The testimony in the cause fully sustains the
charge in the bill, as to the compromise. Mrs. Langford
testifies that she heard Abraham Washburn say, that he
had agreed to the compromise. The testimony of this
witness is assailed by several witnesses on behalf of the
defendant, but her character is sustained by others as
many in number, and is supported by the attendant circumstances. It is true, a Court of equity will not decree

against the positive averment of an answer, upon the testimony of one witness, unless there are circumstances proved by other witnesses, which sustain it. Such is the case here. She is strongly corroborated by Major R. Alexander, a witness on behalf of the defendant; he is the surveyor who divided the land between the defendants, and states that the division was made after the compromise, and that he understood, from the defendants, that they were to take the land for their part of the estate of Gabriel Washburn. Another witness, Hosea Harrell, avers the same. We have, then, no hesitation in saying the compromise is established to our entire satisfaction. But it is said, if that be so, the Court cannot grant to the plaintiffs the relief they seek against Abraham Washburn. The act of 1819, *Rev. St. ch.* 50, *s.* 8, is relied on. The act provides, " that all contracts to sell any slave or slaves shall be void, unless such contract, or some memorandum thereof, shall be put in writing, signed by the party to be charged therewith, or by some other person, by him thereto lawfully authorized, &c."

The objection is, that Josiah Washburn was not lawfully authorized by Abraham to act as his agent in making the contract; and, if he were such agent, he has not signed the name of Abraham Washburn, nor his own as such agent. The difficulty raised in this part of the case is, we think, answered by the Court, in the case of *Oliver* v. *Dix*, 1 Dev. & Bat. Eq. 165. It is there said— " The transaction was prior to the statute of Frauds, and a contract of James, by parol, made by his agent, was good. But it would be equally so now, for the statute requires a writing, to be signed by the party to be charged therewith, or some other person, thereto by him lawfully authorized. Within the statute, the signature need not be that of the principal, nor in his name, but that of the agent is sufficient." We are of opinion, then, that the plaintiffs are entitled to the relief they seek—that Josiah Washburn, in signing the contract of compromise, was the agent of his brother Abraham Washburn, and the latter is bound by it as well as Josiah. Although the appointment of Josiah as agent of his brother is not expressly proved, yet the repeated acts of Abraham, recognizing and adopting the terms of the compromise, and his long acquiescence under it, put it beyond his power successfully to deny it. 2 *Kent Com.* 613. As to the statute of limitations, we think it has no operation upon the rights of the plaintiffs. This is a bill for a specific performance of a contract—by the vendee against the vendors. As to diligence, it is obvious that the plaintiffs have been constantly urging their claims, either at law or in equity. It is a question of diligence.

PER CURIAM.   Decree for the plaintiff with costs.

JOHN NEWLIN vs. RICHARD FREEMAN & AL.

A power to the wife created by marriage articles will, though only an equitable one, bind the estate to which it refers and be supported in Equity, in the same manner as if proper legal conveyances had been made.

Where land is conveyed to a married woman, or to a trustee, for her separate use, she has no ability to dispose of that land by will, nor otherwise, than by the ordinary mode prescribed for the conveyance of land by *femes coverts*, unless a power to that effect has been expressly given to her in the deed of conveyance. It is otherwise in respect to personal property.

Where by marriage articles *the land, which the wife should have at the time of the marriage* and other property were agreed to be reserved to the separate use of the wife, with a power to dispose by will or otherwise of the *said land* and other property, and the wife, after the marriage, purchased, out of the proceeds of her separate estate, other land. *Held,* that she had no more right under the marriage articles to dispose of this land than if the marriage articles did not exist, the deed of conveyance not giving her any power to dispose of it.

Cause transmitted by consent from the Court of Equity of Orange county, at the Spring term, 1846.

The following from the pleadings appears to be the case :

Sarah Foust was entitled to several slaves and sums of money and debts due to her, and also to a tract of land in fee, on which she resided in Orange county, and being about to intermarry with the defendant, Freeman. then entered into articles, whereby it was provided that each should keep his and her own property after the marriage, and she renounced all right to dower in the intended husband's lands and to a distributive share of his personalty, and he also renounced all interest and right that he might acquire in her estate by the marriage. After providing that she should have her personal property to her separate use, it was further agreed, that she should have full power and authority, during coverture, to dispose of the same by deed or will. The articles then provided, that, upon the marriage, Freeman might enter into the tract of land and cultivate and enjoy it during the coverture, and it is then added, "that the said Sarah Foust shall have full power and authority, during the coverture, by her last will and testament, to dispose of the said land to whomsoever she may choose, and, in case of failure by the said Sarah to make such disposition by her last will and testament, such land, upon her death, shall descend to her heirs." The marriage took effect; and, during the coverture, the wife purchased from her husband a tract of land containing 200 acres, situate on Rocky River in Chatham county, and paid for the same out of the money, which formed a part of her separate personal estate, and took a conveyance in fee to the present plaintiff in trust, as the bill alleges, for her separate use, but in point of fact, in trust merely for her. By her will, dated May the 20th, 1835, and attested by two witnesses, Sarah Freeman devised to her husband for life, her land on Rocky River, and after his death she devised the same to the plaintiff Newlin, in fee, and also devised to him all her other land in fee, and gave him her whole personal estate of every kind, and made him the executor. After her death, the plaintiff propounded the instrument in the County Court, as Mrs. Freeman's will, to pass both real and personal estate, and, upon the caveat of the husband and of the heirs at law and next of kin, (who are the defendants in this suit,) it was tried upon an issue of *devisavit vel non*, and after a verdict in favor of the will, the defendants took the case by appeal to the Superior Court, where it was again tried and a second verdict found for the plaintiff. The Court thereupon pronounced for the instrument as a will of personalty, but notwithstanding the verdict the Court pronounced against it as a devise, upon the ground that a *feme covert* had no capacity to devise land and could not acquire it by articles with her husband, and upon appeal to this Court that judgment was affirmed, *Newlin* v. *Freeman*, 1 Ired. 514.

Newlin then filed this bill against the husband and the heirs at law, setting out the foregoing facts and seeking that the will may be declared sufficient as an appointment of the real estate, in execution of the powers reserved to Mrs. Freeman over her estate in the articles—the same made effectual by proper conveyances from the heirs at law—the husband not being tenant by the curtesy, as there was no issue of the marriage.

The answer of Freeman states circumstances of fraud and imposition on him by Newlin, in inducing him to enter into the articles, and at the same time concealing from him the facts, that Mrs. Foust had before executed a will of her whole property in favor of Newlin, and then intended to do so again, as was known to Newlin, while they held out to him that she would under the power make a disposition of the land or a part of it in his, Freeman's, favor. All the answers state and insist upon many circumstances of circumvention and undue influence, practised by Newlin upon the testatrix, in order to obtain the will from her, while she had not mental capacity to make a will. And the heirs insist that the articles are not binding upon them, upon the ground that they were not parties to them, and that as the instrument is ineffectual at law, this Court will not supply its defects as against them.

Waddell and *J. H. Bryan,* for the plaintiff.
Badger and *Norwood,* for the defendants.

RUFFIN, C. J. A mass of depositions has been filed in the case. which it is unnecessary to set forth particularly, as they leave no such doubt as to the fact, as to call for a discussion in detail of the testimony of the witnesses. The due execution of the articles before the marriage is established; and the defendant, Freeman, has entirely failed to establish any imposition by either the intended wife or the plaintiff, or any representation from either of them to him of an intention of the wife to make any disposition in his favor, as an inducement to him to enter into the agreement. The due execution of the will is proved by the subscribing witnesses, and by them and many other witnesses, it is shewn that the testatrix had full capacity to do so, and that she executed it in pursuance of a deliberate purpose, long entertained by her, with a view to the emancipation of her slaves.

The probate of a will in the ecclesiastical Court, does not preclude the necessity of proving it as an appointment for the purpose of claiming under it in a Court of equity: for the Court of probate only declares the instrument to be testamentary, but cannot judge of it as the execution of a power. Therefore, it is to be proved again in a Court of chancery, in such manner as the Chancellor shall direct, either by witnesses or upon an issue, so as to shew that it is, both in form and substance, such an instrument as will be a due execution of the power, according to the provisions in the instrument creating the power. Whether, when it appears, as in this case, that the instrument has the requisite form, namely, that it purports to be a will of real estate, duly

attested by two witnesses, and, thus, sufficient in law as
a will of land, if the testatrix were sole, the Court would
require it to be re-proved in the cause in the Court of
equity, after two verdicts in its favor on an issue *devisavit vel non*, between the very same persons who are parties in the cause, is made a question in the pleadings
before us, and perhaps deserves some consideration. But
we are not disposed unnecessarily to discuss it ; and here
it will not be done, as the proof of the execution of the
will, the proper state of mind of the testatrix, and every
thing requisite to shew that it was a voluntary and deliberate act of this lady, is fully made in this Court, independent of the findings of the jury upon the issue in
the former proceedings, and the judgment of the Court
thereon. It remains, therefore, only to consider the effect
of this instrument. The heirs object, that it is not obligatory on them, because the power was not created in a
proper legal conveyance of the estates, limiting them to
such uses or in trust for such persons as the wife should
appoint by will, but was reserved in a mere agreement
between the husband and wife. This notion seems once
to have been entertained by eminent lawyers. Lord
HARDWICKE expressed a doubt on the point in *Peacock* v.
Monk, 2 Ves. 191. But it was held by Lord NORTHING-
TON, in *Wright* v. *Englefield*, Ambler 468, and affirmed
by the House of Lords, 1 *Brow. P. C.* 486, that, under
marriage articles, a *feme covert* may execute her power
in the same manner as if she had a power over a legal
estate as above supposed. In *Rippon* v. *Dawding*, Ambl.
565, Lord CAMDEN held, that equity would sustain the
execution of a power in articles, upon the ground, that
the appointee was not a volunteer, but came in under
articles made on the consideration of marriage, which,
therefore, equity would compel the husband to execute
by joining in a legal conveyance, containing a regular
and proper power to the wife. And in *Dillon* v. *Grace*,
2 Sch. & Lef. 456, Lord REDESDALE said, that when the

wife did not actually convey her estate, but only entered into articles before marriage, yet the contract, even so far as it was a stipulation for her own benefit, was binding as against her heirs, as in the case of any other contract, upon the principle, that the agreement bound her, and that when an agreement respecting land bound the ancestor, it must bind the heir also. So that it now appears to be settled, that such a power, though only an equitable one, binds the estate to which it refers, and will be supported in equity.

The next question is upon the extent of the power reserved in the articles. They speak only of one parcel of land—that on which the lady resided at the time of the marriage ; and the power is to dispose of " said land" by will. That land therefore is undoubtedly comprised in the power, and is well appointed in the will. But we think the land, bought from the husband after the marriage, does not pass by the will, but is vested in the plaintiff, by the conveyance to him, and is now held by him in trust for the wife's heirs at law. It is true, the articles are explicit, that neither party was to have any interest whatever in the property of the other, and therefore the husband is excluded from this land, even had there been issue of the marriage. But that does not enable the wife to dispose of it as a *feme sole*, which she can only do when she has a power to that effect. Here the power expressed in the articles is restrained to " the said land," which she then owned. Therefore the plaintiff is obliged to rely on something else as the source of the requisite power over this land ; and he says, first, that it arises out of the circumstance, that the land was purchased with her separate property, over which the articles gave her the power of disposition ; and, secondly, that she had it also conveyed to a trustee for her separate use. With respect to the latter point, it is sufficient to say, that it is not true in fact, for the deed to the plaintiff is but an ordinary deed of bargain and sale in fee, upon a general trust for the wife, without saying for her separate use. Mr. Roper lays it down, that, without expressing more, it will not enable her to dispose of the real estate during the marriage, otherwise than by fine and recovery—or with us, by the deed of husband and wife, according to the statute—because no power having been given to her by the instrument to make any disposition of the property, she can only do so by the mode prescribed by the general law, and, if she omit that, her heirs must take. 2 *Roper on Husband and Wife*, 182. In this respect, real and personal property differ; for as to the latter, the separate estate of the wife includes the *ius disponendi*, as held in *Fettiplace* v. *Georges*, 1 Ves. Jr. 46, and 3 Bro. C. C. 8, in which Lord Thurlow explicitly states the distinction between the two kinds of property, by saying, that where the wife makes a voluntary disposition of an estate held to her separate use, against the heir, it cannot be carried into execution; but with respect to personal property, her gift is good.

Then as to the further circumstance, that the land is the produce of the wife's separate property, it can have no effect, but the land is to be treated as if it had been devised by her in any other manner. In the case of *Peacock* v. *Monk*, Mrs. Lestock bought the house after the marriage, with her separate personal property, and the agreement between the husband and wife, as here, was only as to real estate she had at the marriage, and Lord Hardwicke held, that it could not be considered as part of her separate estate, in respect of the money laid out in it, and so go to the executor, as between him and the heir; and, therefore, that it would not pass by the will of the wife; for she had made her money realty, and made a purchase to go to her heirs. It is true, that there the conveyance was taken to the wife herself, and that might be supposed to denote some intent to give up her power to dispose further of so much of her separate estate. But, as far as the question is affected by the

quarter from which the purchase money comes, the form
in which she takes the conveyance cannot be material,
provided the conveyance itself vests no power to dispose
of that land by will; for the omission of such a clause in
the deed, whether taken to herself or to a trustee for her,
or for her separate use, equally imports that, as to that
part of her property, she did not wish to retain or possess
any power of disposition as a *feme covert.* For in another case, *Churchill* v. *Dibben,* a report of which has
recently been published in 3 Lord KENYON's cases. 85, and
is found also in a note to *Curtis* v. *Kenrick,* 9 Sim. 443,
as extracted from a manuscript of Sergeant Hills, the
wife, with the savings of her separate property, purchased, during the coverture, several freehold lands, and
took conveyances to herself; and she contracted for the
purchase of other freehold lands from one Saunders, but
no deed had been executed : and by a will, she gave some
of those lands to her husband, and some to other persons ; and Lord HARDWICKE held, that neither passed.
After admitting that a *feme covert,* having a separate
personal estate, or the produce of a separate real estate,
may dispose of the same by will, he proceeds to shew,
that if it be laid out in land and a conveyance taken to
herself, she cannot devise that land, and then adds, "that
the land contracted for with Saunders, and devised to the
husband, must be considered as if the conveyance had
been executed. The vendor, who has still the legal title,
may indeed, to some purposes, be considered a trustee ;
but that will not give her any power of devising. for a
feme covert can no more dispose of a trust than of a legal
estate, without a particular power of appointment" : and
all those lands went alike to the wife's heir at law.

As there was, therefore, no power in the marriage
articles. which comprised after purchased lands and no
power of devising it newly reserved to the wife in the
deed, which she took to her trustee, we can only look
to this, as to any other ordinary trust of real property

for a married woman, and she can convey the land only by the ordinary means by which she can convey her legal estates, for as to that, equity follows the law.

It must be declared, therefore, that the plaintiff is entitled to relief in respect of the land which the wife had at the marriage, and a decree for a proper conveyance to him from the heirs at law, to be settled by the master; and that he is entitled to no relief in respect to the other land mentioned in the pleadings as having been conveyed by the defendant Freeman to the plaintiff in trust for Mrs. Freeman, because the plaintiff became upon the death of Mrs. F. a trustee in respect thereof, for the defendants, who are her heirs at law. Each of the parties must pay his or her own costs up to this time; and the parties may have any enquiries as to the profits, &c. which they may desire.

PER CURIAM.   Decreed accordingly.

ALEXANDER H LINDSAY *vs.* STEPHEN PLEASANTS & AL.

A devise or legacy to a child, not *in esse* at the time the will was made, does not come within the provisions of the act of assembly, Rev. Stat. ch. 122, sec. 15, in relation to children, who have died in the life-time of their parents.

That act has relation only to legacies which, but for its provisions, would have lapsed; but when the child or children were not in existence at the time the will was made, the devise or legacy was void *ab initio.*

The personal property therefore bequeathed by the will to such children goes into the undisposed of fund and must be divided among the next of kin, of which the widow by the act of 1835, ch. 10, Rev. Stat. ch. 121, sec. 12, is one.

By the will in this case the real property was directed to be sold and the proceeds divided among the testator's widow and children, naming them, and the property was sold accordingly. *Held* that, three of the children being dead at the time the will was made, the proportions of the proceeds of such sale, which would have gone to such children, if they had been living when the will was made, are still to be considered as real estate and go to the testator's heirs as real estate.

Where a testator directs his land to be turned into personalty, for particular objects, and some of those objects fail, his intention is presumed, *pro tanto*, to be defeated, and the money raised out of the lands for those objects, shall not be considered to belong to his personal estate, but is, in this Court, considered as land, and will result to the heirs at law of the testator.

It is a clear rule in Equity, that where real estate is directed to be converted into personal, for an express purpose, which fails, to consider the disappointed interest (although the land has been sold,) as realty and resulting to the heirs.

This rule equally applies, where the proceeds of the real and personal property are blended in the devise or legacy.

Cause removed from the Court of Equity of Guilford County, at the Fall Term, 1846.

The facts of the case are stated in the opinion delivered in this Court.

Morehead, for the plaintiff.
Mendenhall, for the defendant.

DANIEL, J.. David Archer, late of Guilford county, in the year 1835, made his will in manner following: "I David Archer, of the county of Guilford, &c. being weak in body but of sound mind and memory, do make and ordain this my last will and testament, in the following manner and form, to-wit: *First.* I give and bequeath unto my beloved wife, Sarah, all the use and profit of my home plantation during her widowhood; and it is my will, that all my household and kitchen furniture be continued in the possession of my beloved wife, and hereafter to be equally divided between her and my daughter, Sarah Ann Archer, and my daughter, Frances Archer. It is my will that my daughter, Sarah Ann, and my daughter, Frances, and my son, Washington D. Archer, have one hundred dollars each out of my personal estate. It is my will that my Jack, Green, be sold, and the money arising from said sale to be put to the use and benefit of raising and educating my son, Washington D. Archer. It is my will, that all my negro slaves should be continued in the possession of my beloved wife during her widowhood, or until my son, Washington D. Archer, arrives at the age of eighteen years. It is my will that all my negro slaves be sold or equally divided, and all the residue of my estate between my dear wife and all my children, namely. James, William, Elizabeth, Mary, Daniel, Abel, Sarah Ann, Frances, and my son, Washington D. Archer. I appoint my trusty son-in-law, Daniel Howren and Ithama Hunt my executors, and my will is that all my just debts and formal expenses be paid by my executors. In witness whereof, &c." (dated the 1st of September, 1835.) "On consideration I further add, that it is my will that my negro man Bob be free and at full liberty to go where and when he pleases at the death or marriage of my beloved wife. It is my will that my negro man Bob have the use and profit of ten acres of my land in the east corner adjoining Morris' land. In. witness whereof, &c." duly signed and attested by the same witnesses, but without date. His executors proved the will and qualified. The testator's widow died in the year 1842; and, upon that event, the residue of the estate, both real and personal, became liable to be converted into money by the executors, according to the direction of the will. The testator directs this fund to be equally divided between his wife and all his children, namely, James, William, Elizabeth, Mary, Daniel, Abel, Sarah Ann, Frances and Washington. At the time the will was made, three of the above-named children were dead, namely, Elizabeth, William and David, and that fact was known to the testator. The question asked of the Court is, how is this fund to be divided? The answer is, that seven-tenth parts of it are to be divided equally among the children that were alive at the death of the testator and the administrator of the widow. The legacies and devises to the three dead children of the testator were void. And the children of such deceased children cannot take, by force of the act of Assembly, *Rev. Stat. ch.* 122, *s.* 15. That section of the statute declares, that, when any person shall bequeath or devise to his *child or children*, and *such* child or children shall have died in the *life-time* of the testator, the said legacy or devise shall take effect and vest a title to the property described and mentioned in the issue of *such* child or children. Such a testamentary disposition must have lapsed, by the death of the legatee or devisee, during the life of the testator, were it not for the statute, 1 *Roper on Leg.* 320. The case before us is not within the definition of a lapsed legacy or devise, and therefore it is not aided by the above statute. The Legislature never thought of a case like this, and has not provided for it. It is a devise and bequest to no one *in esse*, or that can ever come *in esse*. It is a void devise and bequest, *ab initio*, of three-tenths of the residuum of the slaves and land and other property, directed to be turned into money, and divided among the widow and the afore-named children. Three-tenths of the real estate, directed to be sold by the will, will therefore descend to the heirs at law of the testator; or, rather, three-tenths of the money, which shall be raised by the sale of the land, is to be considered in this Court as land, and will go to the heirs. because, the objects of the devise failing, the said money results to the heirs of the testator, as if it were land. It is apparent that the testator did not mean to have his lands turned into money, out and out. He had particular objects in view, when he directed his land to be turned into money. Some of those objects failing, his intention is presumed, *pro tanto*, to be defeated, and the money raised out of the land for those objects, shall not be considered to belong to his personal estate, but is, in this Court, considered as land, and shall result to the heirs at law of the testator.

It is a clear rule in equity, that, where real estate is

directed to be converted into personal, for an *express* purpose, which fails, to consider the disappointed interest as realty (although the land has been sold,) and resulting to the heir.   The rule equally applies to cases, where the real proceeds are blended and bequeathed with the personalty (after answering particular objects) ; and the context of the will affords no manifestation of the testator's intention to convert the real into personal estate, *out and out.* 1 *Roper on Leg.* 363, 364, and the cases there cited.

Three-tenths of the money arising from the sale of the slaves and other personal things, mentioned in the residuary legacy to his wife and nine named children, will be assets undisposed of, and, as the debts are paid, will go, according to the statute of distributions, to the testator's next of kin.   The residue was given by the will, to the testator's wife and nine named children, that were alive at the testator's death, and they took, as tenants in common, each his or her *aliquot* part of the fund.   And that portion of the said fund, produced by the personal estate, which shall remain after the widow's administrator and the six children, living at the death of the testator, or their representatives, or their assignees, have got their *aliquot* parts, must go to the next of kin.   *Roper on Leg.* 493 ; and this will include the widow, under the act of 1835, *ch.* 10, *Rev. Stat. ch,* 121, *sec.* 12.

PER CURIAM.   Decree accordingly.

WILLIAM ALLEN, Adm'r. &c. *vs.* DUNCAN McRAE'S, Adm'a. & AL.

In a suit for redemption, an absolute deed is not conclusive, but it can be shewn to be a mortgage by some admissions of the defendant in his answer, or by a chain of circumstances, that render it almost as certain, that it was intended as a security, as if it had been expressed in the deed: such as the disparity between the sum advanced and the value of the property—the continued possession of the former owner—written admissions, for example, in stating accounts as for mortgage money. But there is no case, in which relief has been given, upon mere proof by witnesses of declarations by the party, in opposition to the deed and the answer.

Cause removed to this Court by consent from the Court of Equity of Anson County, at the Spring Term, 1845.

This is a bill to redeem a mortgage, and for an account. It was filed the 13th of January, 1843, and it states: That in 1822, Dennis Ingram obtained a grant from the State for a tract of land, containing 20 acres situate on Pedee river, which was then in the adverse possession of C. Watkins and G. Colson, and was of the value of about $200; that, being insolvent, Ingram was unable to give security for the prosecution of an eject-ment, or to raise money to defray the expenses of the suit, without mortgaging the land; and, that in order to induce Duncan McRae to become surety in the premises, he agreed to convey the land to him as a security against any loss he might incur by becoming surety for the prose-cution of the suit, or for any money he might expend or become in any manner bound for in and about the suit; That accordingly a deed of conveyance was made in the year 1823 by Ingram to McRae. and that the same was intended and understood by both of the parties to be in trust, solely for the purpose aforesaid. The bill states, that the plaintiffs are ignorant, whether the deed con-tained any declaration of trust, or proviso for redemption; and charges, if it did not, that it was omitted either by mistake or inadvertence, or by the fraudulent contrivance of McRae—for that the same was fully intended to be inserted. The bill then states, that no money was paid by McRae, or secured to be paid, or other property exchanged for the land so conveyed; but that the only consideration therefor was the liabilities to be incurred by him as Ingram's surety as aforesaid: That an ejectment was then brought against Williams and Colson, on the demise of Ingram, for the prosecution of which, McRae was surety, and that it was prosecuted by Ingram exclusively as his own suit throughout, he employing counsel, binding himself to pay their fees, and doing all the other acts usually done by those who prosecute suits for their own benefit; and that McRae became liable only for parts of the fees of counsel and other expenses, not exceeding in amount $300, as Ingram's surety, and in that character paid them: That in 1830 a recovery was finally effected in the action, and a writ of possession issued; and that before the execution, viz, on the 13th day of September 1836, McRae procured Ingram to execute to him another deed, reciting that he had, by the deed dated May 30th, 1823, conveyed this land to him in fee simple, and conveyed the land and confirmed the same in fee: That this second deed contains no condition or defeazance, and declares no trust; but, nevertheless, that it was then expressly agreed or understood, that it should have no other effect or operation than the former one: that it was executed without any new consideration, (though the sum of $10 is falsely stated therein to have been paid as the consideration,) except that at the same time McRae became security for Ingram in a bond for $100, to a gentleman who had been of counsel in the suit, and that the reason for giving that deed was only because the parties supposed the first deed was void, on account of its being made when Ingram was out of possession of the land, and others held adversely to him: That in fact the last deed, as well as the first, was intended only as a security for the money paid or that might be paid by McRae for Ingram, and that the omission of a clause of redemption happened by mistake or accident, or by the fraudulent design of McRae : And, besides the other circumstances as already mentioned, the bill further states. in support of· that allegation, that, on the same day, Sept. 13th, 1830, McRae accepted a power of attorney from Ingram to receive possession of the land in Ingram's name and stead, and "to settle and compromise as he thought proper for the mesne profits of the said land or sue for the same in Ingram's name, and apply the same when received to the payment of the expenses and charges of the suit about said lands :" And that, in pursuance thereof, McRae, Watkins and Colson, referred the amount of damages to arbitrators, and McRae acted therein " as agent of Dennis Ingram," and then declared to the arbitrators, and also to divers persons at other times, " that the land belonged to Ingram, and that he, McRae, held it only as a surety for the money he had advanced for Ingram in prosecuting the suit, and that in the same way he only claimed to retain as much of the rents and profits, as would discharge his advances and liabilities aforesaid."

The bill then insists, " that, if the deed of September 13th, 1836, was intended as a release of Ingram's equity of redemption. the same could not in equity so operate, because there was no adequate, and, in truth, no consideration for it." And it states that Ingram was so poor as not to be able to assert his rights against McRae, and was needy and dependent upon McRae, so as to be compelled to submit to his demands. It then states the entry of McRae into the land, and an award in March for the mesne profits ; the death of McRae in 1837 intestate— the grant of administration of his intestate to two of the defendants, and the receipt by them in 1837 and early in 1838 of the $890 and interest—the death of Dennis Ingram subsequently in 1838 intestate, and administration granted of his estate to the plaintiff, Allen ; and that the other plaintiffs are his heirs at law. The land was sold by a decree of the Court of Equity upon a bill by McRae's heirs at law for the purposes of partition, and was purchased by Daniel McRae at the price of $18 per acre. The bill is brought by the heirs and administrator of Ingram against McRae's heirs and administrator, and against Daniel McRae, and prays redemption of the land and a re conveyance to the heirs and an account of the profits since Duncan McRae entered, and also an account of the sums received for the mesne profits and how the same have been applied, and payment of the residue of them to Allen, the administrator.

The answer admits that Ingram was poor, and that during the pendency of the suit, or the greater part of the time, he was dependent upon and chiefly supported by McRae. They state that the defendants have no personal knowledge of the transaction, but that they believe that the agreement between McRae and Ingram was not for a conveyance of the land as a security against loss by McRae by becoming Ingram's surety, but was for an absolute purchase, with the risk on McRae's part of losing all the costs and expenses in the suit in case of failure, as the land could only be recovered by suit, and, from Ingram's insolvency, the whole responsibility was in fact on McRae, although the proceedings were in Ingram's name. The defendants say, that they found their belief as to the nature of the agreement on several circumstances: That McRae would not have incurred the risk of the costs and expenses, and the trouble of the tedious litigation without having any interest in the subject, as would be the case, if he was to have a mortgage only as security, not for other demands against Ingram, but for those arising out of the suit for the land; since in case of failure, he would be liable for all those sums, without any recourse whatever. And that the deed which was made on the 30th of May, 1823, is absolute in its terms, as a conveyance in fee: And, further, that at the time of the execution of the said deed, McRae gave to Ingram his covenant in the following words: " May 30th, 1823. This is to certify that this day Dennis Ingram has made me a deed to 20 acres of land in Colson's Island, which said land is now under some embarrassment by being in the possession of Colson and Watkins. Now, if the said land should be recovered, and I obtain a lawful and peaceable possession. I will be accountable to said Dennis on settlement for the sum of three hundred dollars, but am to be allowed all reasonable expenses that may ensue on the same: 20 acres at $15 per acre." The defendants say they believe the said covenant was given for the price agreed to be given for the land, and that it was fully the value thereof at the time, as it was situated. The answers admit that Ingram attended to the suit, but say that McRae did also, and that he alone advanced the sums to defray the expenses, and was indeed the only person really responsible for them. They deny that, to their knowledge or belief, there was any agreement or understanding between the said parties on the 13th of Sept. 1836, or before or afterwards, touching the deed of that date, that it should be different from what it was on its face, or that the same was not absolute; and they say that they are informed and believe that it was given after the recovery in the ejectment, from the apprehension of the first being defective by reason of the adverse possession, and expressly, if it should be so, to supply the defect and confirm the land to McRae absolutely in fee: and the defendants insist on the deed as being conclusive on its face of the nature of the agreement and transaction between the parties. The answers admit the power of attorney from Ingram to McRae on the 13th of September 1836, the reference and the award as stated in the bill, and also the deaths of McRae and Ingram, and administrations on their estates at the periods mentioned, and the receipt by McRae's administrators of the sum awarded between the death of McRae and that of Ingram. The defendants insist, that the money belonged to McRae as he was, as between him and Ingram, the owner of the land, though he had to use Ingram's name to recover the land and the mesne profits, and to enable him readily to do so, was the only motive for making the power of attorney; and though not bound in law therefore. that McRae, in consideration of the large sum that would probably be recovered for the mesne profits, agreed to pay thereout costs and expenses of the suit, over and above the purchase money. And in respect of the sum so received by the administrators of McRae after his death for the mesne profits, those defendants insist that, if the said Ingram was entitled thereto at all. it was as for money had and received to his use, and that therefore he and his administrator could have had an action at law, and therefore ought not to proceed for the same in this Court; and they further insist, in respect thereof, upon the statute of limitations, barring actions of account and on the case within three years, as a bar to the plaintiff's bill.

Winston and *Mendenhall*, for the plaintiff.
Strange, for the defendant.

RUFFIN, C. J. The two deeds are exhibited and their date and contents are as stated in the pleadings. That of the 30th day of May, 1823, is expressed to be for the consideration of $300 then paid, and is for the fee unconditionally. and with covenants of general warranty and quiet possession. That of September 13th, 1836, recites that Ingram by deed conveyed the land to McRae on the 30th of May, 1823, and "that the same had been in contest for many years with C. Watkins and others, and has been recovered by judgment of the Supreme Court. and a writ of possession is now to issue and to be executed *for the benefit of* said McRae," and then it witnesses, "that the said Dennis, in whose name said suit has been

carried on, and said writ is to be issued, in consideration
of the premises and of the sum of $10 in hand paid to
him by said McRae, hath granted, bargained, sold and
confirmed, and doth grant, bargain and sell, and now actually confirm the said land to the said McRae and his
heirs : And the said Dennis doth authorize and empower
said McRae to have the said writ of possession sued out
and executed in said Ingram's name, and the possession
of said land to be delivered to him by the sheriff of
Anson, and when so delivered, the said McRae is *to retain and hold the same to himself and his heirs in his, the
said McRae's own right.*"

The power of attorney is of the same date, and authorizes McRae to sue out a writ of possession, "for a
tract of land recovered in my name against C. Watkins
and others, on Pedee, and containing about 20 acres, and
to have said writ executed in my name, for said McRae
to take actual possession of said tract and retain the
same ; and also to settle and compromise, as he may
deem proper, for the mesne profits of the said land, or
sue and recover the same in my name, and apply the
same, when recovered and received, to the payment
and expenses and charges of the suit about said land.
And the said McRae is hereby empowered to do all acts
necessary to be done about recovering and taking possession of the said land and receiving and settling for
the mesne profits."

The plaintiff examined a gentleman of the bar, who
conducted the action of ejectment against Colson and
Watkins, and who states that in July 1823, McRae and
Ingram applied to him to bring suit for the land, and
that McRae then showed him the deed from Ingram, and
said he had taken it "to make himself safe," or "to save
himself;" that the witness brought the suit on the demise
of Ingram, and it pended in various Courts until June
1836, when the plaintiff recovered : That, after the recovery, the witness advised McRae to take another deed,

70

which Ingram agreed to give, and that the witness prepared the deed and power of attorney, bearing date September 13th, 1836, and Ingram executed them and the witness attested them. At that time, the witness took a note from Ingram and McRae for $100, as a fee in the suit, but Ingram was known to be insolvent and the note was paid by McRae's administrator. McRae, pending the suit, had paid the witness $120 on account of the fee, and also to two other gentlemen of the bar $150 as a fee—as the case was one of much doubt and had become of consequence to the parties, by the accumulation of a large amount of costs. He states that he relied on McRae almost entirely for the management of the suit, and that he attended to it throughout.

The sheriff of Anson states, that when he put McRae in possession about the middle of Sept. 1836, he then mentioned to him, that after all the trouble in law, Ingram would get nothing. but that he, McRae, would get it and all the profit, and that McRae replied, " that there would be a good deal coming to Dennis, but there was a long settlement to make, and his lawyers' fees and expenses in attending Court were to come out of them."

Another witness states, that Ingram owed him a debt, and in March 1837 he applied to McRae to settle it, and McRae replied, " Ingram owes me about $100, and also for what I have paid as lawyers' fees and expenses about $400 more ; and that they had not yet settled, but expected to do so before long ; and I wish you would come when we settle, for after paying me there will be a balance going to Dennis, sufficient to pay his debts, unless he owes more than I think." McRae also said he thought he ought to have something for his own trouble. He died about a month after the conversation.

Another witness, Barnawell, states, that, about a month before McRae's death, Ingram told McRae he wished their business arranged ; that he wished the land sold

and whatever he owed McRae paid out of the proceeds;
and that McRae answered, that whatever remained
after paying the debt to him belonged to Ingram. Mc-
Rae also said he had paid all the expenses of the suit,
and Ingram had not paid a dollar. Ingram stated that
he intended to give McRae $100 extra for his services.
McRae made no further reply.

The defendants exhibited the covenant of McRae of
May 20th, binding himself to pay Ingram $300, for the
land upon being let into possession. It is of the tenor before set forth.

They also proved by another gentleman of the bar,
that, after the action of ejectment had been pending
a considerable time, Ingram applied to him to appear for
him, and the witness assented, provided the fee was secured. Ingram then said he had sold the land to McRae,
who was to pay the lawyers' fees and the other expenses,
and also, in case the land should be recovered, was to pay
him $500 for the price of the land. Ingram then requested
McRae to be responsible for the fee, but he refused, saying that he would not employ any other lawyer, as he
already had employed enough and had paid or agreed to
pay more fees than the land was worth. The witness
understood from both parties that the contract between
them was in writing: That Ingram had made McRae
an absolute deed for the land, and McRae had given him
a paper to show what he was to pay upon a recovery.

The bill states with great clearness a case for redemption. notwithstanding the conveyance was by an absolute
deed. It states a fit occasion for the execution of some
deed, as a security from one of the parties to the other;
and, besides the direct averment of the intention, that it
should operate only as a security, and that it should contain a clause to that effect, and that the omission of such
a clause was occasioned by fraud or accident, it states
positively the very material circumstance, that McRae
neither paid nor secured any price for the land. Upon

that supposition, there would be a strong ground for saying, that the deed was given in the form it was, by surprise; and the bill then uses the subsequent events with much skill, in order to shew that they are consistent with the idea, that a security and not a sale was intended. But the misfortune is, that the facts stated in the bill are not all the facts, and that others appear in the answer and proofs, which make a case very different from that which is so well told in the bill. The deed of May 1823 is not only absolute, but it appears to be founded on the consideration of $300 paid; and, cotemporaneously with the execution of the deed, McRae, who is admitted to be a man of wealth, gave his obligation to Ingram for the sum of $300 therein expressed to be the purchase money for this land, and made payable whenever the purchaser should be let into possession. Of that part of the case the bill takes no notice whatever, but assumes the contrary. One cannot see how it is possible to get over that fact, in pursuing the enquiry, whether that deed was intended to be a security for a debt or by way of indemnity for responsibilities about to be assumed by the bargainee for the bargainor, unless it was given colorably for the purpose of deceiving Ingram's creditors and that is not asserted. The obligation for the price, made at the same time with the deed and attested by the same witnesses, is as conclusive that the transaction was a purchase, as the most direct and credible evidence of the actual payment of the money would be. Nay, more so; for if the money had been paid, there might have been a doubt, whether it was paid as a price, or advanced as a loan, and then leave the mind uncertain as to the character of the deed. But it is impossible to suppose, that the deed could be executed as a security for a sum to be advanced at an uncertain future day. Such a thing was never done, unless where a person wants an open credit with a banker, and to that end gives a security for all advances to cover whatever balances may be due from time to time. But a needy and insolvent man would never bind his estate with a mortgage upon such terms, though he might sell it to one, who was able and willing to support a law suit for the recovery of it, and agree to wait until the result of the suit for the payment of the price. An absolute deed is not indeed conclusive, that there was an absolute purchase. But it is almost so: and can only be avoided by some admissions of the defendant in his answer, or by a chain of circumstances that render it almost as certain, that it was intended as a security as if it had been expressed in the deed: such as the disparity between the sum advanced and the value of the property—the continued possession of the former owner—written admissions, for example, in stating accounts as for mortgage money, and repeated and explicit declarations. But there is no case, we believe, in which relief has been given upon mere proof by witnesses of declarations by the party, in opposition to the deed and the answer. Here, there is nothing else, and the declarations themselves, far from being clear and satisfactory to that point, but rather leading the other way. The bill, indeed, charges a great disparity between the value of the land and the price agreed to be paid. But the plaintiffs do not support that by proof, and it is hardly to be expected they could, as very little land in this State is worth $60 an acre throughout for agriculture. Besides, the same land, when sold 20 years afterwards, on a credit, for partition, appears to have brought only $18 an acre, and McRae agreed to give $15 and be at much trouble to get it. The expression of McRae, that he took the conveyance from Ingram, "to make himself safe" or "to save himself" is very unsatisfactory. The witness is uncertain, indeed, which was the expression, and that may be material, for he might have meant, that he had saved a debt by buying the land, which would be consistent with the covenant, that he was "to be accountable for the sum of $300 in settlement." Or it might mean, that by buying the land he had saved himself from the danger of losing what he might advance in the suit, by some other creditor of Ingram selling the land as soon. or even before the recovery. It would seem scarcely credible, if this had been intended as a mortgage, that the counsel of the parties should not have been able to state it explicitly, or that a respectable member of the profession should have permitted, much less advised the parties—both his clients —that it was proper, after the recovery, that the mortgagor should, without any new consideration. execute a new deed, confirming the title under the former one, as if it were intended to be, as it is, absolute. Both of the parties attended to the suit, because both had an interest in it: McRae to get the land, and Ingram to get the price. The form in which the devise was laid was the only one in which it could have been laid, and therefore proves nothing, as to the intention. Then to another gentleman of the bar, both of the parties stated explicitly, that it was a sale, and indeed they gave an account of the transaction exactly in accordance with that appearing on the papers, except in mistaking the amount of the purchase money. The declarations spoken of by the other witnesses only shew, that money would be coming to Ingram, which might be either as the price to be paid by McRae, or out of the rents, and do not shew any acknowledgement by McRae, that Ingram was entitled to the land. The only exception is in the testimony of Barnawell, from which it may be collected, there was some confidential understanding between the parties, without our being able to say what it was. But that cannot shake the deeds, and the other consistent circumstances.

It was argued at the bar, that, even if the transaction was intended to be as the defendants insist it was, it ought to be relieved against, upon the ground that it was tainted with champerty. and was oppressive on the seller. But to that it must be answered, that no such ground is taken in the bill. As before remarked, the bill states with uncommon precision a case for redemption, as of a mortgage, and confines itself to that case. Now that is inconsistent with the idea of champerty; for what part of the land is he to have, who only claims a security on it for money actually advanced? The bill alleges no oppression on Ingram or undue advantage taken of him, except in omitting the clause of redemption in the deed, as agreed for; and that is not established. It is true, that in respect of the second deed, the plaintiffs say, that Ingram was in McRae's power and obliged to submit to his demands. But the bill thus speaks of that transaction, upon the supposition, that, under the first contract, Ingram had a right of redemption, and that the second deed was " a release of the equity of redemption," obtained without any consideration. Now, that view wholly fails, if the sale was intended to be absolute in the beginning, as it seems clearly to have been. Then, supposing that the bill might have impeached that dealing upon the ground of champerty, and that the Court of equity would relieve upon that ground merely, yet the bill has not raised that equity at all, and it cannot now be taken. But if it had been raised in the bill, the objection is clearly obviated by the deed of Sept. 1836; for, certainly, when a vendor has actually recovered the land which he had sold when out of possession, there can be no objection to his completing his contract by executing a conveyance that will be valid. There needs no new consideration, because he has already received the price, or, which is the same thing, had it secured. The very purpose of the second deed was to confirm McRae's title to the land, and entitle Ingram to the purchase money agreed on. There was no longer champerty, if there was at first. Whether Ingram has received the purchase money, or may still be entitled to it, is not the subject of enquiry in this suit. He has other remedy for what may be due on that score. The claim to the sum received for mesne profits, as stated in the bill, is incidental to Ingram's right to the land as mortgagor; and what is said about the form of the power, is not said with a view to assert a right to that money as an independent right, but for the purpose of proving that McRae did not claim them, and therefore that he had not purchased the land. When he is declared to have purchased the land in 1823, the mesne profits follow the title in this Court, though at law Ingram's name was necessary to the recovery. So, we regard the power of attorney merely as authorizing the use of Ingram's name for the benefit of McRae, in respect as well of the profits, as of the land itself—specifying only that McRae is thereout to reimburse himself for his advances in the suit, and not still claim them from Ingram. But, if that were otherwise, and Ingram became entitled to them, they were recovered in his name and received under his authority; then, that is a mere legal demand not incident to the equity of redemption claimed in the bill, and therefore might have been recovered at law. For that reason, this Court ought not to take jurisdiction of it, after objection distinctly taken in the answer. But if the Court would relieve at all, it cannot in this case, after a lapse of five years between the receipt of the money and the filing of the bill, and the statute of limitations insisted on in the answer, as to that part of the demand. *Hamilton* v. *Skepard*, 3 Murp. 115. *Bell* v. *Beeman*, Idem, 273.

Upon the whole, therefore, the plaintiff can have no relief, and the bill must be dismissed with costs.

Per Curiam.   Bill dismissed with costs.

JOSEPH MEDLEY *vs.* JOHN H MASK & AL.

In a suit brought against a mortgagor and mortgagee by one claiming to be an assignee of the mortgagor, for the purpose of setting up the assignment and redeeming, it is necessary to prove that the assignment was for a valuable consideration.

If the suit had been against the mortgagor alone, it would have been sufficient to prove the assignment without proving any consideration.

Although equity does not interfere with the legal operation of instruments, merely upon the want of consideration, where there is no fraud nor imposition, but leaves the parties to the law ; it will, yet, not afford relief upon a voluntary executory contract, which passed nothing and created no right at law. Equity in such a case does not act for a mere volunteer, but only for a real purchaser at a fair price.

The mere general, formal words in a deed of assignment, declaring that the assignor had been fully paid and satisfied, are not conclusive evidence that any consideration has been paid, much less an adequate consideration.

The case of *Thorpe* v. *Ricks*, 1 D. & B. Eq. 613, cited and approved.

Cause removed to this Court from the Court of Equity of Anson County, at the Spring Term, 1846.

The pleadings and proofs presented the following case. On the 1st of December, 1834, the defendant, Hough, borrowed from the other defendant, Mask, the sum of $400, and as a security therefor he conveyed to Mask 100 acres of land on Pedee river in fee, by a deed absolute on its face. At the same time, however, Mask gave Hough an obligation under a penalty, and, thereby, (after reciting that he, Mask, had purchased the land and paid the consideration of $400 and received a deed from Hough,) he bound himself to re-convey the land to Hough upon the payment of the said sum of $400 with lawful interest thereon within two years thereafter, or during the life of Hough. On the 7th October 1840, Hough assigned Mask's obligation to the plaintiff by an endorsement thereon under his hand and seal, but not attested. After an assignment of the land in terms, it adds, " I now give and grant to the said Joseph Medley the right of redeeming the said land within-mentioned, as he has

71

fully paid and satisfied me for my interest in the said land." The bill states, " that the said William Hough. having in the course of dealings between them running through several years, fallen in debt to your orator, in a sum between two and three hundred dollars, the exact amount of which your orator does not recollect, in consideration thereof executed the assignment to him." The bill was brought in September 1841, to set up the contract between the plaintiff and Hough as an assignment of the equity of redemption, and to redeem and obtain a conveyance from Mask to the plaintiff upon payment of the debt and interest, which the plaintiff had before offered to make.

The answer of Hough states, that he has no recollection of having executed the assignment on the bond; and it denies that it was executed upon the consideration stated in the bill, or was intended as a sale of the land to the plaintiff, or an assignment of his equity of redemption. It denies that he then owed the plaintiff any debts, but such as had been amply secured by a mortgage of other land to the plaintiff. The answer then states the occasion on which Mask's bond was transferred to the plaintiff to have been as follows: That Mask had need of the sum of $80, and applied to him, Hough, for it, and requested him, if he had it not of his own, to endeavor to borrow it for him; and that, for that purpose, he, Hough, applied to the plaintiff to advance that sum to Mask by way of loan, and the plaintiff agreed to do so, provided this defendant would deposit the bond in question as a security therefor; and that to that Hough assented, and thereupon he delivered the bond to the plaintiff, and, it seems, executed a written assignment on it. The answer avers positively, that this was the only purpose for which the bond was placed in the plaintiff's hands, and that nothing whatever was said respecting any debts or other transactions between the plaintiff and Hough. The answer further states, that this defendant informed Mask, that the plaintiff had agreed to advance him the sum he needed, and told him to apply to the plaintiff for it ; and that he was afterwards informed by Mask that he applied accordingly, but that the plaintiff refused to lend him the money, unless, upon his doing so and paying the original advance by Mask of $400 and the interest thereon, Mask would convey the land to the plaintiff in fee ; which Mask refused to do, and, consequently, that the plaintiff gave nothing for the assignment to either of the defendants.

The answer of Mask contains the like statement of his request to Hough to borrow the money for him, and that Hough informed him, that the plaintiff had agreed to lend him $30 upon the security of the bond, which Hough said he had placed in the plaintiff's hands. This defendant then states, that, in consequence of the information thus received from Hough, he applied to the plaintiff for the said sum, but the plaintiff refused it, except upon the terms of receiving an absolute conveyance of the land, as stated in Hough's answer ; and the defendant Mask avers, that he received nothing from the plaintiff upon the transaction

The plaintiff has filed several exhibits besides Mask's bond and Hough's assignment of it to him. One is a deed of trust for another tract of land " containing three or four hundred acres on Pedee river" made by Hough to the plaintiff on the 17th of November 1838, reciting that " said Hough is indebted to the said Medley in the sum of $700, for moneys had and received of him to pay and discharge said Hough's just debts," and conveying the said land in fee as a surety therefor, and in trust to sell it at any time after the 1st of February 1840. On the deed is an entry by the plaintiff, that the debt was satisfied by a sale of the land by the sheriff of Anson on the 15th of September 1840 on execution, subject to that deed of trust.

The other exhibits by the plaintiff are of evidences of

debts from Hough to himself of the following dates and sums :

1820—April 20. Bond payable to plaintiff one day after
date, $8 86
1840—March 28. Bond to plaintiff, payable 1st
January, 1841,   464 87
                                                          ———————
Oct. 13. Bond of Hough to Horn, and paid   473 73
by plaintiff on this day $136 83
Degernette's judgment paid this day by
plaintiff.   8 63
Habbinds' judgment paid this day by
plaintiff,   6 50
Myers' judgment paid this day by pl'tiff,   6 02
Threadgill's judgment paid this day by
plaintiff,   45 66   203 65
                                              ———————
                                              $677 37
1841—April 5. Bond of Hough to plaintiff for
this sum borrowed, $40 00
1842—Feb. 5. Paid balance of Horn's judgm't.   13 88
  " 24. Liles' judgment paid by pl'ntiff.   24 52
  " "   Bond to Bogan paid by plaintiff,   23 90
                                              ———————
                                              $779 67

The plaintiff likewise proved by the sheriff of Anson,
that, on the 14th of March 1839, the plaintiff paid him
on an execution against Hough the further sum of $65 :
and that, under another execution against Hough, the
plaintiff on the 15th of September 1840 purchased the
land mortgaged to the plaintiff, and subject to that mortgage, at the price of $1200 ; of which he paid the sheriff
the sum of $66 only, in discharge of the said execution.
The plaintiff further proved, that the debts paid by him,
as aforesaid, on the 13th of October 1840, and in February 1842, were paid at the request of Hough, or were
debts for which the plaintiff was his surety. It is also

proved that the land mortgaged to the plaintiff is worth from $1,500 to $2,000, and the tract conveyed by Hough to Mask is as valuable as any land in the county, and is worth $1,500.

Strange, for the plaintiff.
Iredell, for the defendants.

RUFFIN, C. J. There is no doubt that the transaction between Hough and Mask, though not strictly a mortgage, in point of form, was substantially so, and is to be treated but as a security in this Court. Neither of those persons raise a question upon the right of Hough to redeem. The only dispute is, whether the plaintiff has that right; and that depends upon the question, whether he has such an assignment of the equity of redemption, as is effectual and sufficient in a Court of Equity. Upon that question the opinion of the Court is against the plaintiff. If this had been the case of an ordinary mortgage upon its face, and Hough had made a formal deed of assignment of the equity of redemption to the plaintiff, he might have filed a bill against Mask for redemption, without bringing Hough into the cause, or proving the consideration moving from himself to Hough, as the price of the equity of redemption. For a plaintiff need not make a person a party, who, according to the facts alleged in the bill, has no interest in the subject, and, although it requires a consideration to raise a trust, yet, after it is well raised, it may be transferred, as against the trustee, voluntarily. To Mask it would be immaterial upon what consideration Hough might have assigned to the plaintiff; and it would therefore be sufficient, in the case supposed, for the plaintiff to prove the assignment, on the hearing. *Thorpe* v. *Ricks*, 1 Dev. & Bat. Eq. 613. We do not say, that it would be so in this case, since it is, in form, not an assignment of a clear and admitted equity of redemption, but an assignment of a covenant or executory agreement from Mask to Hough to convey the land to him upon the payment of a certain sum. Perhaps, therefore, it was indispensable in this case, that the plaintiff should bring in Hough, as well as the mortgagee. But, admitting that it was not, and that the plaintiff might have had a decree upon a bill against Mask alone, yet he has not thought proper to proceed in that way and claim a decree against the mortgagee upon the apparent assignment to him, leaving it to the assignor to assert his right afterwards in a bill of his own, denying the assignment or its legal efficacy. On the contrary, the plaintiff has chosen to proceed against both the mortgagee and mortgagor; and thus he puts, himself, in issue, the assignment in respect of both of those parties, and is, consequently, bound to shew one which is efficacious, and which the Court will specifically uphold against the assignor, so as to conclude him by a declaration of the assignment in the decree in this suit. Hence it became necessary in the bill to set out not only the naked fact of the assignment from Hough to Medley, but also that it was made on a valuable consideration. For, although equity does not interfere with the legal operation of instruments, merely upon the want of consideration, where there is no fraud or imposition, but leaves the parties to the law · it will, yet, not afford relief upon a voluntary executory contract, which passed nothing and created no right at law. Equity in such a case does not act for a mere volunteer, but only for a real purchaser, at a fair price. The plaintiff has endeavored to appear to be such a purchaser. But he entirely fails in the attempt. It is urged for him, that the assignment itself states, that he had fully paid and satisfied Hough for his interest in the land; and that such an acknowledgement is not to be disregarded. but must be deemed sufficient evidence *prima facie* of a valuable consideration. Upon the same technical reasoning, it might be insisted that the seal imported a consideration

in this Court, because at law it precludes an enquiry as
to the consideration. But, in equity, there must be proof
of an actual consideration; and, therefore, while a receipt from a party for a certain sum of money is evidence of the payment, these general words, inserted
merely as formal parts of an instrument and declaring
no particulars, can by no means be admitted as conclusive, that some valuable consideration was actually
paid or secured, much less that an adequate consideration was paid or secured. Those words, respecting the
consideration, would, for example, be equally true, whether
the assignment was upon a sale, as alleged by the plaintiff, or upon a pledge, as declared by the defendants. The
assignment, therefore, cannot supply the place of all other
proof of a consideration paid or secured. Indeed, the
plaintiff has not relied on it in the bill for that purpose.
On the contrary, the bill professes to set forth the actual
consideration, and the plaintiff has gone into evidence,
apparently, with the view to the proof of it. The statement of the bill is, that in fact the consideration was a
sum due from Hough to the plaintiff on dealings, running through several previous years; the amount of
which the plaintiff does not recollect, further than that
it was between two and three hundred dollars. This
statement is singularly loose and unsatisfactory. It sets
forth no particular sum, either as the amount or the
balance of the account, and gives no items; and the
only excuse for the omission is, that the plaintiff's recollection failed him, although the bill was filed in less than
a year after the assignment, and although it would have
been easy to refer to the settlement of accounts, which
it is to be supposed must have been made, if the balance
on it was to be paid by the sale of this land. But the
very inadequacy of that consideration, taking it at the
larger sum, makes it difficult to credit the statement.
The value of the land is fixed at $1500; and in October
1840, the principal and interest due to Mask, supposing

him not to have been in possession amounted to $540. The value of the equity of redemption was, then, about $960, while the price at which Hough is supposed to have agreed to sell it, was at the utmost only $300; which is not one-third of its value. Thus, any presumption of a fair price, to be inferred from the general expressions of the assignment, is confined by the bill to a sum, as the actual price, so totally inadequate as to render it almost incredible. that a contract of sale was made or intended, notwithstanding the form into which the transaction was moulded. It is, indeed possible, that a man may agree to take less than one-third of the value of his land; and, if he did. the Court would not be at liberty, merely for that reason, to set aside his conveyance. But equity would not lean to enforcing, by specific performance. a contract for the sale upon such a consideration, but, rather, leave the case to its fate at law. At all events, without good proof of the fact of sale at that price, the Court would not incline to the conclusion, that one was intended, especially when there is a fair ground for thinking, that the contract might have been in the nature of a security or for some other purpose. Now, the defendant here, in answer to those allegations in the bill and its interrogations, denies most positively that he contracted to sell the land or his equity of redemption at any price; and he avers that the bond was not even deposited with the plaintiff as a surety for any debt of his own, but exclusively as a security for the small sum of $80, which the plaintiff agreed to lend to Mask, but which, as the answers state, after getting the bond, he refused to advance. If this account of the transaction were less probable in itself than that given in the bill, though it would seem quite the contrary, yet, upon a law of evidence in this Court. it is to be received as true, as far as it is responsive to the bill, unless shaken by other credible evidence. There is no other evidence here, which can have that effect. If a sale had been intended, and the mortgagor had, as is usual, continued in possession, he would have let the plaintiff into the possession, as the owner after his purchase. But nothing of the sort appears. It is not shown that there was any treaty for a sale and purchase; that there was any acknowledgement by Hough, even in an unguarded moment, that he had made a sale upon any terms, or that he ever represented the transaction differently from what it appears in his answer. The answer is in no way brought into doubt. On the contrary, it is sustained by the evidence which the plaintiff adduces in order to shew Hough's indebtedness. The deed of trust recites a debt of $700, which is said to be for advances of money at different times to pay Hough's debts. It is not stated to be due on bond, nor when it was or would be payable. And it looks, therefore, very much as if that sum were not an ascertained debt, but was inserted in the deed to cover all advances. That, however, need not be insisted on. The plaintiff also produces bonds and judgments against Hough to the amount of $779 67, and proves that he paid for him another sum of $65—in all, $844. Of that sum, $538 73 appears to have been due before and at the 15th of September 1840. As there is no evidence of the consideration of the bond for $464 87, which Hough gave the plaintiff March 28th, 1840, it might, if necessary, be proper to enquire, whether that bond was not given on a settlement for the advances secured by the deed of trust. But, for purposes now in view, it may be assumed, that both of the debts of $700 and $464 87 were subsisting. Still, Hough would not have been indebted to the plaintiff in $300, or any other sum on the 7th of October, 1840. For, on the 15th of September 1840, the land that had been mortgaged for the debt of $700, was sold under a *fieri facias* at the instance of another creditor, subject to that mortgage: in other words, the equity of redemption was sold, and was purchased by the plaintiff at the price of $1,200. That,

72

The following case is presented by the pleadings and proofs.

In 1772 Frederick Michael purchased from Henry Eustace McCulloch, a tract of land in Rowan, containing 300 acres, at the price of £200 : of which he paid £23 and McCulloch gave a bond to convey in fee upon the payment of the residue of the purchase money. Frederick Michael entered into possession and levied on the land until he died in 1780 intestate, leaving several children ; of whom Barna and Nicholas were two, the former being the eldest son and heir at law of the father. The two brothers continued in possession until 1787. In that year Barna left Nicholas in the sole possession and removed to Orange, a distance of about 50 miles, and resided there until his death, intestate, in 1794. He left a daughter, Elizabeth, and an only son, David, the present plaintiff, who was then about a year old.

The estates of Henry E. McCulloch were included in the confiscation acts ; and one Joseph Cunningham purchased this land, as part of his estate, and took a deed from the commissioners ; and he afterwards conveyed a part, containing 162 acres, to John Allen, who evicted Nicholas Michael therefrom about 1801 or 1802. In 1805 a bill was filed by Nicholas Michael, in the names of Elizabeth and David Michael, infants, by himself as their next friend, against Allen and others, setting up the purchase from McCulloch and claiming the land as belonging to the plaintiffs therein, as the infant heirs of Barna Michael, and in April 1817 there was a decree that the defendants in the suit should convey the land, 162 acres, to the plaintiffs, David and Elizabeth, and pay them the sum of $250 for profits.

In 1803 Hugh Cunningham, claiming also under Joseph Cunningham, entered into another part of the land containing about 120 acres.

The present bill was filed by David Michael, in July 1834, against Nicholas Michael originally. It states.

that, soon after obtaining the decree against Allen, (who never conveyed under the decree,) Nicholas Michael sent to Orange for the plaintiff and one Willis, who had married Elizabeth, and informed them of the recovery; and represented, as it had been effected, that it would be necessary to pay McCulloch's representatives the residue of the purchase money and interest, then amounting to some large sum. It states further, that the plaintiff and Willis were unable to pay the same, as Nicholas well knew; and that he, Nicholas, then offered to do so, and also to prosecute for their benefit a suit against Hugh Cunningham for the tract of 120 acres, if they would convey to him the land which had been recovered from Allen: insisting that they ought to do so, as he had been at much trouble and expense in conducting the suit. The bill states, that, believing those representations, the plaintiff and Willis assented to those propositions; and that it was agreed, that they should, on some appointed day, go to Salisbury and have the deed there prepared by the Clerk and Master of the Court, in which the decree had been rendered: That in some short time they did so, and that the Clerk and Master, Mr. Charles Fisher, readily agreed to prepare a deed, and immediately, on the 21st of November, 1817, wrote it in the presence of the parties; and the plaintiff and Willis, having unbounded confidence in their uncle Nicholas, and believing that he had properly instructed Mr. Fisher as to the land, which was to be conveyed, executed the deed forthwith, without reading or hearing it read, and in the belief, that it was for the 162 acres only, which had been recovered from Allen. The bill states positively, that the deed was not, by the agreement, to include the 120 acres in possession of Hugh Cunningham's heirs; and that Nicholas Michael engaged, if they would convey to him the 162 acres, that he would institute a suit in the Court of Equity for the other tract of 120 acres, in their names and prosecute it for their benefit. The bill then avers, that the plaintiff had not the

slightest suspicion that the deed included any but the 162
acres, and that Mr. Fisher, acting under the belief that
the subject was properly understood by the parties, did
not offer to read the deed, and that the plaintiff and Willis, being young and inexperienced and confiding fully in
their uncle, did not request to have it read.

Elizabeth Willis afterwards executed the deed, but
was never privily examined. In 1818, Nicholas Michael
filed a bill in the names of David Michael and Willis
and wife in Rowan, against Hugh Cunningham's heirs,
setting up for the 120 acres the same title, and in October 1831. (it having been noticed, that Elizabeth was not
an heir of her father,) a decree was made therein, that
the defendant should deliver possession and convey the
land in fee to the plaintiff, and also pay him $700 for
the profits.

The bill states further, that, with the view of throwing
the costs of that suit upon the plaintiff and Willis, in
case the decree should be for the defendants, and also to
prevent them from discovering the contents of the deed,
Nicholas Michael did not make himself a party to that
suit, nor register his deed, but kept it secret until August
1831. after the rights of the parties had been declared in
the suit ; and that, until that time, the plaintiff had no
knowledge that the deed included, as in fact it did, the
whole tract purchased from McCulloch. The bill further
states, that the land recovered from Allen was worth
$1.600 ; that the rent of the land occupied by Nicholas
from 1787 up to the period at which he was ejected, was
worth $100 a year ; that Nicholas received the sum of
$250 decreed to be paid by Allen, and applied it to his
own use, and that he took possession in 1831 of the land
recovered in the suit against Cunningham, and also received the $700 and applied the same to his own use ;
and that those sums greatly exceed the sum paid by
him to McCulloch, which the bill states to have been
only $600.

The bill thereupon charges, that the plaintiff was deceived into the execution of the deed, under the belief that it conveyed the tract of 162 acres only, and also that he was induced to convey that tract without any consideration, and was so induced by an uncle, professing to act as a parent and protector, and in fact acting as his agent and next friend, but who availed himself of the advantages of the relation between them to obtain the conveyance upon those terms; and therefore it insists that the deed should be declared fraudulent and wholly void, as against the plaintiff; and it prays a decree, accordingly, for a conveyance of the whole tract, and that the defendant should come to an account of the sums received by him, and also for the profits while he occupied the premises. The answer states, that, shortly after the death of Frederick Michael, the agents of McCulloch recovered a judgment against his administrator for the residue of the purchase money of the land, but the same remained wholly unsatisfied for the want of personal assets; and that application was then made to Barna, the heir-at-law, for payment, who said the land was not worth the money, and refused; but he told the defendant that, if he chose, he might pay for the land and have it, and delivered to him the plots of survey and McCulloch's bond. It being then uncertain, as he was advised by counsel, what was the effect of the sale of the land as confiscated property, the defendant says he declined paying the purchase money, either to McCulloch or to Joseph Cunningham, the purchaser from the commissioners, and in 1791 Cunningham instituted an ejectment against him, for the 162 acres, which he defended at his own expense, without aid from his brother Barna. In 1801 that suit at law was decided against him; and a year or two afterwards Hugh Cunningham evicted him from the residue of the tract.

.The defendant further states, that he instituted the suit in equity against Allen in 1805 for his own benefit, though, from necessity, in the names of his brother's infant heirs, as his brother, though not setting up any claim nor advancing any money, had died without executing an assignment of McCulloch's bond to him. During the twelve years it was pending, neither the plaintiff nor his sister, (then supposed to be an heir,) nor her husband set up any claim to the land or any part of it, nor advanced anything toward the expenses, or interfered in the suit in any way, nor had any communication whatever with the defendant or with the counsel on the subject of the suit. But, after the recovery in their names, it was found indispensable, that the plaintiff and his sister should act in some way in the business; and the defendant admits that he sent for them to Orange, and, when the plaintiff and Willis arrived at his house, that he made the representations respecting the debt, then ascertained to be going to McCulloch, and respecting the trouble and expense which he had borne in the business, as stated in the bill.

The defendant says, that in fact he disclosed the truth of the whole transaction to them and the understanding which had existed with his brother, and stated to them that he thought himself justly entitled to the land, upon paying the sum due to McCulloch; but at the same time he explained to them fully the advantage they had in the case, and their power of denying him the justice he thought they owed him; and left it to them to determine, whether they would pay him for his trouble and expenses and time, and pay McCulloch and take the land, or let him pay McCulloch and have the land. The defendant avers, that both the plaintiff and Willis fully understood the subject, and preferred giving up the contract, with all its benefits and burdens, to the defendant, with liberty to him to sue for the other part of the land, then claimed by the heirs of Hugh Cunningham; and upon those representations and that understanding, those two persons executed the deed to the defendant, and subsequently induced Mrs. Willis also to execute it. The defendant denies explicitly, that the plaintiff and Willis executed the deed without its being read, and affirms that Mr. Fisher, as soon as he had written it, read it plainly and distinctly in the hearing of all the said parties, and that the plaintiff, as he believes, knew the contents of the deed as well as the writer of it did ; and he says that in fact the deed is perfectly conformable to the agreement that was made, and also that the plaintiff is able to read writing very well.　The defendant denies that, in either of the suits in equity, he professed to be acting for the benefit of the plaintiff or his sister, although he admits, as the suits were in their names, he styled himself "agent" in affidavits, notices, and other proceedings in the cases in which he acted personally. On the contrary, he says he acted throughout, as if the suits were his own, and he so considered them, and so did the plaintiff in respect to the last suit, which, indeed, was the only one he knew of until after their decision.　The defendant states, that the balance, due to McCulloch on the judgment, was about $1900, and that he applied the sum of $250 recovered from Allen, toward the payment thereof, and that he paid the residue out of his other property or cash.　He also says, that besides giving his personal attention to one suit after another about the land, for upwards of forty years, he paid more than $300 to the counsel in the causes at different times; and he avers, that from the execution of the deed to him until the final determination of the suit against Cunningham in 1831, the plaintiffs took no part in the suit and put up no claim to what might be recovered in it.　He denies that he concealed the existence of the deed to him, and says that it was known, though he admits that he did not register it until August 1831 ; and says the reason thereof was, that until that time he had not discovered that Mrs. Willis was not an heir of her father, and he was waiting to have her privy examination taken.　After answering. Nicholas Michael died, and in 1839 the suit was

73

revived against his heirs, and by an amendment it was also charged, that, in February 1827, he had conveyed the land to one of his sons. That son in his answer sets up title under the deed from his father; and all the others disclaim any interest.

After replication, the parties proceeded to proofs. Elisha Willis and Elizabeth Willis were examined for the plaintiff. The former states, that when the plaintiff and he reached Nicholas Michael's, he informed them, that the balance of the debt to McCulloch was $1,600, and that he had paid it and required them to refund it, and said, if they did not, he would have the land sold for it, and if the land did not pay him, he would have David Michael and the witness put in jail. Nicholas Michael offered to give them $1,300 for the 162 acres, that had been then recovered. He states that the three went to Salisbury, and David Michael and he "executed the deed to Nicholas Michael in Mr. Fisher's office for, as he understood, the one hundred and sixty-two acres of land, but at the time the deed was not read over to David Michael or himself."

Mrs. Willis states, that, sometime after her husband and brother returned from Rowan, Nicholas Michael and his son John came to her house to get her signature to the deed, saying that he had paid for the land and wanted to be made safe. She stated to him, that she did not like to sign the paper, unless she could hear it read and explained by some person who understood it: That John Michael then began to read it, when his father said it was not worth while and stopped him, and said if she did not sign it he would have the land sold, and if that would not do he would put her in jail—whereupon she executed the deed. Her husband was present at the time. Both of these witnesses make a mark.

It appears in the cause, that while the second suit was pending against Cunningham, Elizabeth Willis went on a part of the land under Cunningham, and after the decree, refused to give up the possession to Nicholas Michael. A witness states, that the present plaintiff told Nicholas Michael to turn Willis off, as he had no right. In January 1832, Nicholas Michael brought ejectment upon his own demise against Willis, which was pending when the present bill was filed. In March 1835, the plaintiff got an injunction in this suit against further prosecuting the ejectment, upon the ground, that Willis was his tenant and ought not to be evicted until the right was determined in the cause. The injunction was dissolved in September 1835, and in the succeeding month judgment was obtained by the plaintiff in the suit at law and Willis was evicted. It was pending the injunction, namely, on the 14th of May, 1835, that the plaintiff took the depositions of Willis and his wife.

Several witnesses prove, that, while Nicholas Michael was carrying on the suit against the Cunninghams, he said that he was the agent of his brother's orphans. One witness, Philip Berner, states, that he mentioned to him, that he had recovered a part of Barna Michael's land from Allen. and he intended to bring suit against Hugh Cunningham's heirs for the other part—for the land belonged to Barna Michael's heirs, and they had been up a short time before and employed him to act as their agent and bring suit. This witness says that he knew, that David Michael came up to Rowan to sell the land, and agreed to let Nicholas Michael have it, and they went over to Salisbury to have a conveyance made, which was sometime before the conversation between N. Michael and the witness. He says, he never understood that the plaintiff and Willis conveyed the whole tract, but understood that they conveyed the part recovered from Allen; and that he had lived within about a mile from the land and from Nicholas Michael, about thirty-five years. He says the land would now be worth $10 an acre, if it was in the condition it was in, when he first knew it. Other witnesses prove that when the suit was brought, the average value of the tract was $5 50 an acre.

On the part of the original defendant were examined the two subscribing witnesses to the deed from the plaintiff. John Michael states, that he was sent by his father to Orange, for the plaintiff and Willis; and that after getting up and hearing from his father the circumstances of the case, they came to an arrangement with him to take the land and pay McCulloch; and the next day they went to Salisbury to execute the contract, and the witness went with them: that at Salisbury they met Mc-Culloch's agent and settled with him; and that Mr. Charles Fisher wrote a deed according to the direction of the parties, and he read it over to all of them, and the plaintiff himself also read it over, and then he and Willis executed it, and Mr. Fisher attested it. Afterwards, Mrs. Willis executed it in Orange and this witness attested it as to her.

The other witness is Mr. Fisher. He says, he wrote the deed, he is sure, as he finds it in his hand-writing and he has an indistinct recollection of having written it. His recollection is not sufficient to enable him to state positively from memory, that, after having written the deed, he read it; but he has no doubt that he either read it to the parties or that they read it themselves, as he is confident, from long habit, that he would not have witnessed it, (as he did as to David Michael and Elisha Willis,) if he had not known of his own knowledge, or heard them acknowledge, that they knew its contents. He states further, that on the day the deed was made, he understood from the plaintiff, Willis, and Nicholas Michael, that Nicholas was to pay McCulloch for the land and take it; that the debt was a considerable sum, though he cannot recollect the amount, and that it was either then paid or in a short time afterwards, as he heard Mc-Culloch and his agent say it was discharged—who have both been dead many years. He states that Nicholas was the manager and conductor of the suit, and the whole business connected with the land, and that in conducting it he was called agent.

The deed itself is annexed to those two depositions. It is a printed deed of bargain and sale, except as to the date, names of the parties, consideration, and description of the land. It is dated November 21st, 1817, and the consideration set forth is $1900, paid. The written parts of the deed are in large, legible, and uncommonly plain hand-writing; and David Michael's signature purports to be written by himself, and is distinctly written in a good though stiff hand. Willis and his wife made marks. A witness proves, however, that the plaintiff, who is of a German family, has but a defective English education, and does not read writing with ease.

W. H. Haywood, Norwood and *J. H. Bryan,* for the plaintiff.

No counsel for the defendants.

RUFFIN, C. J. The bill raises two points of equity. They are combined in some confusion in the bill; but, as they are in their nature entirely distinct, they ought to be disposed of, each by itself. The first is, that the deed by mistake of the writer, or the contrivance of the purchaser, was drawn so as to cover more land than was agreed to be conveyed, and the plaintiff executed it without a knowledge of the error, and fully believi covered only the tract of 162 acres. But, the plaintiff says that he ought, at all ever lieved against the deed, upon the ground, th him to have known the contents, and to hav willingly at the time, it is one of those cont the policy of the law forbids, because it w obtained from an inexperienced young man, just f age, by one standing *in loco parentis.* and acting as his guardian and agent about this property. The natural order of treating the subject is to ascertain, first, what really was the contract, before we consider whether it be obligatory in law or not. There is, in the first place, a presumption that the dealings are fair, and that the deed conforms to the agreement of the parties, unless the contrary is made to appear by satisfactory proof, direct or circumstantial The allegation in the bill is, that the defendant agreed to take the land then recovered, which was 162 acres, and the sum of $250 decreed for the profits, and pay the purchase money to McCulloch, give up any demand for previous expenditures in the various suits, and, at his own expense, prosecute a suit for the other tract of 120 acres and the profits, in the name of the plaintiff and Willis, and for their benefit. Now, this is positively denied in the answer; and the defendant avers, that his expenses and the payment to McCulloch amounted to more than the full value of the land and the profits, and that, although he claimed the land by contract with his brother, yet he offered the other parties their choice, either to reimburse to him his expenses and take the land to themselves, subject to the debt to McCulloch and the contest as to part with Hugh Cunningham's heirs, or let him have their claim. The defendant says, that, without hesitation, they preferred the latter, and that the deed, as drawn, was but in completion of the agreement.

Against those statements in the answer, thus responsive and directly contradictory to the bill, the plaintiff cannot have a declaration of facts in his favor, unless upon very clear proof, that the contract, as made, was different from these representations of the answer, and that the contents of the deed were concealed from, or, at the least, unknown to the plaintiff, when he executed it. Generally, when a person makes a deed, who is able to read it, the presumption is, that he did read it, and, if he did not, it is an instance of such consummate folly to act upon so blind a confidence in a bargain, when each party is supposed to take care of himself, that it would be dangerous to relieve upon the mere ground of a party's negligence to inform himself, as he so easily might, of what he was doing. Therefore, commonly, the Court ought not to act on the mere ignorance of the contents of the deed ; but there should be evidence of a contrivance in the opposite party to have the instrument drawn wrong and to keep the maker in the dark. In this case, however, it may be yielded, that from the confidence arising out of their near blood relationship and from the apparent candor, with which his uncle had commnicated the information of his rights, and the fairness with which he seemed to deal with his nephews, that the plaintiff might have executed the deed, prepared under his uncle's directions, without being so culpable for not reading it or having it read, as to preclude him from being relieved against so much of it as may not accord with the bargain as made. Then, we are to enquire what is the evidence opposed to or in support of the representations of the answer. There are but two witnesses who professed to have been present at the making of the contract. The one is Elisha Willis, a party to it, and the other is the defendant's son, John, who now claims part of the land ; both of whose depositions have been taken and read without objection. The account of each is very barren of details : so much so, as to lead to some suspicion, that they might be afraid to trust themselves to entering on them, or do more than depose to what they thought the main fact, lest they might be exposed to contradiction. Willis, however, says, that Nicholas Michael agreed to give $1,300 for the tract of 162 acres then recovered, and that the deed executed in Fisher's office was, "as he nnderstood it," for that tract, but that it was not read. He says also, that the debt due to McCulloch then was $1,600. On the other hand, John Michael says, that the plaintiff and Willis, after hearing from his father the circumstances of the case, came to an arrangement with him to pay McCulloch and "take the land," without positively specifying what land, whether the whole tract purchased from McCulloch, or the part recovered from Allen, though the former must be supposed to have been meant. Upon these two statements, by themselves, no one could say he had a clear belief as to the actual agreement; and therefore, upon them it would be impossible to declare, that the deed was different from the agreement. For, in such a case, in order to determine which of the two witnesses is entitled to the more confidence in his memory and integrity, one naturally enquires whether the executory contract was about the time executed by making a deed; and, if it was, one looks at once at the deed, as the best evidence which is right. Instead of such evidence controlling the deed, that instrument is decisive between the witnesses. But here, it is said, the deed was not read, and the execution of it, when the party was ignorant of its contents, takes away all its force, as evidence of the terms of the original contract, and that it is not pretended in the case, that those terms were intended to be varied by any second contract. That brings us down to an enquiry into that single question of fact, whether the deed was read or not. The bill says it was not. The answer is positive, that it was. Willis supports the bill, and John Michael as directly supports the answer. If the matter rested there, the decree must be for the defendant, without taking any notice of the circumstances under which Willis gave his deposition; for the *onus* is on the plaintiff, not only to produce a preponderance of proof, but a plain preponderance, leaving no doubt in the mind as to the fact of the case. But the evidence does not stop there, for, besides the presumption that the contents of the deed were known to the parties before they would execute it, there are the testimony of Mr. Fisher, and the circumstances under which the deed was prepared, and also the probability, as will be presently pointed out, that the bargain would have been as the defendant says it was. There is nothing to induce a suspicion that the instructions to Mr. Fisher, respecting the land to be described and conveyed in the deed, were not given by both of the parties, or, at all events, by Nicholas Michael in the presence of the others. The bargain was made in the country on one day, and the parties all went together the next day to the office of the Clerk and Master, where the boundaries of the land could be ascertained, to have the deed drawn. Willis does not suggest, nor is John Michael or Mr. Fisher examined to show, that Nicholas Michael alone gave the instructions or had any private interview with Mr. Fisher, and, without particular instructions from some one, that gentleman could not have known at all, how the deed was to be drawn. The open manner then, in which the instructions must have been given, and the perfect indifference of the writer between the parties, and the capacity of the plaintiff to read the deed, and the impossibility of knowing before hand that he would not read it or have it read, all go to show, that there was no intentional departure from the instructions, and also the extreme probability that the instructions were agreeable to the bargain. It is to be remembered, that there is no pretence that the deed was read falsely. The allegation is, that it was not read at all, as an excuse for executing it, notwithstanding its variance from the agreement. Now, how should it happen, that Mr. Fisher should write the deed variant from the bargain? What motive had he to do so? How could he have made such a mistake? But Mr. Fisher says, that he is confident, that either the plaintiff read the deed or that he read it to all the parties. Not that he remembers it absolutely, though he has some recollection of the transaction. But he knows certainly from his habits, as a man of business, that he would not have attested the instrument as a subscribing witness, unless the contents had been known to the parties. Here, then, is direct proof of a very satisfactory kind, supported too, by the circumstances. under which the deed must have been drawn, to establish, that the plaintiff knew the contents of the deed, and by consequence, that the contents were according to the intention of the parties. But the plaintiff meets this argument by the observation, that it is only an inference from Mr. Fisher's testimony, that the plaintiff knew the deed covered more than the 162 acres, and that such inference is met and repelled by the opposite inferences, to be deduced from the facts, that the sums paid and to be paid by the purchaser were much less, than the value of the whole tract; that he did not register his deed, but kept the contents concealed; and that afterwards the defendant instituted a suit for the 120 acres, in the name of the plaintiff and his sister, and put up no claim to it for himself, but declared he was prosecuting it as agent for their benefit.

As to the relative amount of the value and the price, the inference is clearly the other way. even upon Willis' testimony. The plaintiff does not examine a witness, as to the value of the land, except one, who says, that, if the land was as he knew it thirty-five years before this suit —meaning, we suppose when nearly all uncleared and with its virgin soil—it would now be worth $8 per acre. But other witnesses prove the actual value of one half to be $5, and of the other half $4 an acre, making an average of $4 50. Now, Willis says, that the debt to McCulloch was $1.600, as he understood, and this was to be paid off by Nicholas Michael, out of the price of the land, which was sold to him—which, he understood, was the 152 acres, taken at $1,300. In the first place, it is to be noted, that he does not say one word about what was to become of the remaining 120 acres, or that any suit was to be brought for it by Nicholas Michael for his benefit and the plaintiff's. That statement is found in the bill, but not in the deposition of the witness, and is denied in the answer. But it is clear. that the witness must also be mistaken, as to the price of the parcel of land pur-

chased by the defendant. For, to make the 162 acres
bring $1,300. it must be valued at upwards of $8 per
acre; and, if that was all the purchaser was to have, in
cluding even the $250 then in the office for profits, there
would still remain unpaid $50 of the debt to McCulloch,
and Nicholas Michael be out of pocket all his expenses,
besides the loss of time and trouble. If to that be added
(as must be according to the allegation of the bill) the
expense and further loss of time and trouble of carrying
on the projected controversy with the Cunninghams, it
would appear to have been one of the most disadvanta-
geous bargains, that a silly old man ever made. One cannot readily contradict a tale, if there were precise evidence
to the several circumstances supposed. But when the
computation is made, upon the basis of the true value of
the land, it is seen, that it would be utterly impossible it
could be true, if Nicholas Michael had any sense at all.
The 162 acres, at the actual value, $4 50 an acre,
came only to $729, and the profits of $250 added,
only made $979; and it is pretended, that for that land
and money the purchaser was to pay McCulloch upon
the spot $1600, and pay himself for all his outlays. Even
if the other 120 acres be added at $4 50, making $540,
and an aggregate of $1519, there would be left $81 due
to McCulloch, and all that the uncle had, himself, been
out of pocket; which the parties might expect to be covered by the profits to be recovered from Cunningham, but
which was not thus covered; for, at the end of fourteen
years more, only the sum of $700 was received therefor.
But, computing the debt to McCulloch at $1900, as the
defendant swears it was, and as is rendered probable by
that sum being inserted in the deed as the consideration,
the badness of the bargain is so palpable, that, on the
part of the purchaser, we can only account for his making it by the attachment to the property, which might
have arisen from his long contests for it, and the final
triumph as to the most important portion of it. Thus

we should suppose, if the transaction had been considered by the parties as really a purchase, upon a new contract then made. But upon the footing upon which the answer puts it, we readily understand why the business should have taken that course. The answer says, that the defendant and his brother had, thirty years before, understood each other, that the defendant was to pay for the land and have it; and therefore, that he had been contending all along for himself, though in the names of his brother's children, and hence he felt bound to treat the land as his own, and, of course, to bear the whole burden.

The deed is, therefore, not impeached by the least probability from the price, that the purchase was of less land than was conveyed, but, on the contrary, the circumstances most strongly sustain it in that point of view. Then, as to the circumstances, that the defendant did not register the deed until 1831, and called himself "agent," and said he had been employed to sue for the land for those parties: they furnish, at best, but feeble and inconclusive arguments, in opposition to the other circumstances and to the allegation of the bill, that the contents of the deed were not known to the plaintiff. But the answer gives a reasonable explanation, why the deed was not registered sooner, which removes the inference from that; and to the other part of the argument, it is plain, as the answer states, that the defendant would naturally hold himself out as agent, when suing in the names of the others, though to his own use. But whatever weight there might be in those circumstances and in the testimony of Willis, the whole is completely overthrown by the deductions necessarily to be made from a few other undisputed and indispensable facts. One is the fact, that, pending the suit with Cunningham, Willis entered into a part of the land under Cunningham and as his tenant. Now, if it had been understood, that Nicholas Michael was suing for the benefit of Willis and his wife, would he have attempted to defeat his own bill by becoming the tenant of his adversary? Undoubtedly not. The other is, that the suit against Cunningham pended fourteen years, and, during the whole time and for three years afterwards—until this bill was filed—the plaintiff did not look after it at all, made no enquiries as to its progress or result, and had, indeed, no communication whatever with the defendant, or with the solicitor or counsel in the cause, except that he once expressed his indignation that Willis should pretend any right to the land, or go in under the opposite title. If the suit had been for his benefit—as he says he understood it—it cannot be believed, that he should have been so totally regardless of his own interest, as not to have opened his mouth about it, for upwards of seventeen years. On the opposite supposition, that he had agreed, that his uncle should take the whole of the land, and that he had conveyed his claim to him, and that the uncle was carrying on the suit for his own benefit, every thing is consistent.

The Court has no doubt, therefore, that the plaintiff well knew, when he executed the deed to his uncle, that it included the whole of the land, which had been purchased from McCulloch: as well that then in the possession of Hugh Cunningham's heirs, as that which had been recovered from Allen. And we are well satisfied, that this pretence would never have been set up, if the plaintiff had not hoped, that he might have had some ground of relief in the doctrine of the Court of Equity, which forbids undue advantages being made in contracts between persons standing in confidential relations.

There is no doubt about the rule of the Court. If a guardian, agent, or other person standing in a confidential relation, avail himself of information, which his situation puts him in possession of, or of the influence, which is the natural consequence of habitual authority or confidence, to gain an undue advantage by getting obligations or con-

veyances without adequate consideration, they cannot
stand. The Court regards such transactions as extremely
dangerous, and sets them aside, except as securities for
what may have been done under them. Even if that
were done here, the plaintiff, it would seem, would not
profit by it, as it is fully clear, the land cost the defendant
the value to the last farthing. But the difficulty is, to
make the principle of equity reach this case, by finding
such a confidential relation between the parties as comes
within the sense of the rule, or, if there was, that any
undue advantage was taken of the defendant. It may,
however, be remarked, in the first place, that the plaintiff's witnesses, Willis and wife, completely disprove the
statements of the bill, as to the pretended professions of
paternal regard on the part of the uncle, and the compliance with the demands on the part of the plaintiff being
the effect of confidence or induced by personal influence:
They make out a case, in which the defendant insisted
upon his rights, and threatened to enforce them against
the properties and bodies of the plaintiffs, and his witnesses. But, passing by that contradiction, we will come
to the other point. There was no guardianship in fact of
the plaintiff by his uncle, nor any agency constituted by the
contract. The whole matter is, that the uncle had been
suing for the land for his own benefit, in the names of
the infant heirs of a former equitable owner. Whether
his claim of a purchase or donation from a former owner
was well or ill founded, makes no difference to this purpose. He represented a case to the plaintiff, in which, if
true, he had really been suing for himself and not for the
plaintiff, though he had been proceeding in the plaintiff's
name. Now, he candidly told the plaintiff, that he could
not establish the contract with the plaintiff's father; and
therefore it was at the plaintiff's option to claim the land
and take it under certain known incumbrances, or let the
defendant have it as his own, under those encumbrances,
according to the alleged understanding with the plain-

tiff's father. The latter arrangement the plaintiff preferred, and very properly, if he had any faith in the assurance of his uncle, because he was but fulfilling the engagement of his father, under which his uncle had incurred much expense, and had vast trouble. Thus viewed, the transaction was not a sale of the plaintiff's property. Neither party so regarded it, for not a cent was offered by the one or received by the other. It was a mere surrender of a legal title, and, as it were, to the equitable owner of the land—a title which an honest man could not have withheld. The bill puts the case upon the assumption by the defendant of the title of next friend of the plaintiff, in the bill filed in his name, and calling himself agent in conducting the business. But that is a poor quibble; for those titles the defendant was obliged to assume, because he had to sue in the plaintiff's name, and he was at the time an infant. The question is, for whose benefit he was suing. Was he really endeavoring to recover the land, as land equitably belonging to the plaintiff or himself. Upon the record, he said, necessarily, that it was the plaintiff's; but every body understood, as Mr. Fisher states, that the defendant was the sole manager, and conducted the case as if it was his own. If the defendant had meant anything unfair, and his object had been to make a profitable bargain out of his nephew, he would have made his proposals before the suit was decided, when he might have expected an advantage. But, instead of that, he waited until the decision, and then made a representation to the plaintiff and his sister, which does not appear to have been in any respect unfounded, except in a mistake as to her being an heir; and, under the influence of the representation, they agreed to convey their formal title, and the plaintiff has acquiesced in that arrangement seventeen years without a murmur—while the defendant was prosecuting a doubtful litigation at great expense for nearly half of the property. It is as clear,

that the defendant prosecuted the first suit upon a claim
of his own to the land, as that he did the second, though
his title in the first instance was not established by such
apparent proof as it was in the second, when he had obtained a deed from the plaintiff for the whole of the
land. It is a total perversion of the rule of equity, to
apply it to such a case. There had in fact been no confidential relation between the parties, nor any previous
communications even; and there was no purchase, as of
the plaintiff's right in the land. He simply gave up a
nominal claim to it, as all the parties understood. Besides, if it had been a sale, it would have been one, as
we have already seen in considering the other point, in
which the land stood the defendant in the fullest value.

Upon the whole, therefore, the Court deems the suit
to be entirely groundless, and dismisses the bill with costs.

Per Curiam.   Bill dismissed with costs.

GEORGE W. LOGAN & AL. vs. PETER GREEN & AL.

Per Daniel, J. Merger never takes place, when it would have the effect to
destroy intermediate *vested* estates in third persons.

When there is an outstanding lease for a number of years, and the reversioner
makes a new lease to third persons to commence immediately, this is a
vested estate; and, although the second lessees could not take possession of
their term, inasmuch as the possession belonged to the first lessee, they would
have a *concurrent* lease and be entitled to all the rents issuing out of the
term of the first lessee, and on the expiration of that term, they could legally enter and possess the land for the residue of their own term. This
estate would prevent a merger when the first lessee became entitled to the
reversion.

But, if the deed, conveying this second interest, created only what is sometimes called a future lease, that is, a contract to have a lease to commence
after the expiration of the first lease, then it conveyed no present *estate* in

the land, either in interest or possession. It would be only an *interesse termini*, which neither makes a merger, nor prevents one, but may be accelerated in the time of its becoming an estate in the land by possession, by the merger of an antecedent vested term by the termor's purchasing in the next immediate estate in reversion.

Cause removed from the Court of Equity of Rutherford County, at the Spring Term, 1846.

Thomas Hall was seized in fee of a tract of land, containing about 100 acres, in Rutherford, and on the 24th of September 1823, leased it to William Owens for the term of thirty years thereafter rendering rent, and Owens entered into the premises. The bill charges, that the land consisted partly of cultivated and partly of wood land, and that the lease was for the purposes of farming only. In 1824, Hall devised the reversion to Thomas Coggin, and on the 11th of July 1831, Coggin made to Thomas Dews, John McEntire and John Logan, a lease for thirty years, (expressed to be,) " to a certain extent, and for certain purposes thereinafter to be named, of a certain tract of land, on which William Owens now lives, lying, &c., on the conditions following, viz. for the special and sole purpose of digging and searching for, and extracting the precious metals, if any be there found, on or from any and every part of the said premises"; and granting also such ways, woods, water, stone and timber for machinery, building, and other purposes, as might be found necessary and useful for prosecuting the business of opening and working mines on the premises. In consideration whereof, it was agreed between the parties, that Coggins should be entitled, equally with the three lessees, to the privilege of working in the mines so opened, and using the machinery so to be erected and draw a proportion of the metals according to the number of hands furnished by each, provided that the number furnished by Coggins should not exceed one fourth—the whole, however, subject to the understanding and proviso, that it should be at the option of the lessees to erect such ma-

75

chinery as they thought requisite, or none at all, and to
work or not to work mines on the premises, as they might
please.   The bill states that the foregoing lease was made
with the privity and consent of Owens; and that, shortly
thereafter, the lessees entered on the premises and commenced working for gold, Owens then living on the land,
and knowing of their operations and making no objection
thereto, nor setting up any claim to the minerals in the
land.   The bill further states, that on the 19th of September, 1831, Logan purchased from Coggins the interest in
the minerals, and right of working for gold and other
metals to him reserved or secured by the previous lease
of July; and that Owens was also present at that time,
and made no objection to the contract, but, on the contrary, then contracted with Coggin for the purchase of the
reversion in the premises, and took from him a covenant
to convey the land to him in fee, expressly, however, subject to the rights of Logan, Dews, and McEntire, under
the said lease and contract; and that, on the same day,
Owens agreed in writing with Logan, that he might erect
on the premises a grist-mill and use it for the term of
thirty years, and at the end thereof remove the stones.

The bill then states, "that the said company soon ceased
to work the mines; and it so remained until about the
year 1840, when the defendants, Green, McDowell, and
Lord, pretending some right so to do, opened mines on the
land and took thereout four or five penny weights of
gold."   It is then stated, that Dews, one of the lessees,
died in 1838, having made a will and given all his estate
to his father, Thomas Dews the elder, one of the plaintiffs; and that John Logan died in 1842, having made a
will, in which he gave his interest in the premises to
George W. Logan, and appointed him and John W. Logan
the executors, who are the other plaintiffs.

The bill was filed in 1843 against McIntire, Green,
McDowell, and Ford, and prays that the three latter may
discover what gold they have collected on the premises,

and may be decreed to pay to the plaintiffs " such damages, rents and profits, as may be just."

The defendant, Green, states that in 1840 he took a lease of the premises from William B. Owens, a son of William Owens, to whom the latter had made a deed in fee for them; that his lease was for the purposes of mining and was for five years, paying a rent of one-sixth part of the gold found; and that he admitted McDowell and Ford under him. The three then state, that they have paid the rent to Owens, and set forth the amount of the gold found, which, they say, will not more than compensate for the expenses of working. Green states, that before he took the lease, he had heard, that some contract had been made by Coggins and Dews, Logan and McEntire, respecting the premises, and that he applied to McEntire to know what it was, and whether it was still in force, and was informed by him that there had been such a lease as is stated in the bill, but that, soon afterwards, the lessees, having commenced operations, found the business unprofitable, and abandoned the lease. The defendants deny, that as far as they are informed and believe, William Owens was privy to the making of the lease or contract from Coggins and Dews, Logan and McEntire, or assented to the same before or afterwards, or agreed that they might open or work any mines under the same. The answer also states, that the defendants believe, that Logan did make some verbal contract with Coggins for the purchase of his interest in the metals on the premises, under the previous lease, for some small price, which was paid in a barrel of flour and 70 gallons of whiskey; but that, after the mines had been found not to be worth working as aforesaid, Logan rescinded the contract with Coggins, and took Coggins' bond for the value of the flour and whiskey, and afterwards received the money thereon.

The plaintiffs took the deposition of James Walker, who says that he knows nothing of the lease to Dews,

Logan and McEntire; but that he was present when Logan and Coggins made a verbal agreement for the sale of Coggins' mineral interest to Logan. which was afterwards to be reduced to writing. The witness says he cannot state the time, farther than that it was between 1828 and 1831; but that William Owens was present, and made no objection; and that, sometime afterwards, Logan called on him in Rutherfordton to witness that he was then paying Coggins for his interest in the mine, and let him have some liquor and flour.

All the other testimony for the plaintiffs relates to the proceeds of the mines worked by the defendants Green, McDowell and Ford.

The other defendants, under an order, took the deposition of the defendant McEntire. He says, that after the lease from Coggins, he and Logan worked on the land "two or three days, for the purpose of testing it": that Owens was opposed to it, but after a while consented that they might test outside of his field, and, after they had done so, he consented for them to test it inside of the field: that for that purpose they sunk six or seven pits and found but little gold, and then abandoned all idea of working farther, and never went back: that he gave this information to the other defendants, and gave his consent that they should take a lease from Owens in 1840, but told them he would not act for Logan, who, he believed, still set up some claim.

It is further proved by two witnesses, Cole and Owens, that William Owens, when informed that the lease had been made by Coggins to Dews, Logan and McEntire, expressed much dissatisfaction and would not agree that they should work on the premises even for the purpose of "testing" the mines; that those persons did, nevertheless, go on for a short time, until they became satisfied that there were no mines worth working, and then abandoned the premises; that Logan informed Coggins that they could make nothing, and insisted that he should

rescind the contract, and that finally it was agreed to
rescind, and that Coggins should pay Logan for certain
flour and whiskey which Logan had paid him on the
contracts respecting the mines; that, in a few days afterwards, Coggins agreed to sell the premises in fee to
Owens, and made him a deed, which appears to be dated
September 28th, 1831, and that Logan, when he heard
of it, applied to Owens to secure in his hands Logan's
demand against Coggins for the flour and whiskey, but
was informed that Owens had fully satisfied Coggins for
the purchase money, and thereupon he, Logan, took
Coggins' own bond to himself for the amount.

No counsel for the plaintiffs.
Badger, for the defendants.

RUFFIN, C. J. This is a singular bill, seeking merely
an account of the profits of working the mines by some
of the defendants, and payment of shares thereof to the
plaintiffs, without asking any relief in respect of the title
of the land, and without bringing before the Court Coggins, under a contract with whom the plaintiffs claim,
and under whom also the defendants claim; and without
bringing in William Owens, on whose consent to their
lease and contract they rely to give them efficacy, and
under whom also the defendants claim, who have worked
the mines. But, without noticing any objections arising
from these circumstances, there are others upon the
facts which are decisive against the bill.

It is objected, first, by the defendants' counsel, that
the plaintiffs have failed to establish their title, as set
forth, under the wills of Dews and Logan, two of the
lessees; as they are not admitted in the answers, nor
copies of them exhibited. This objection is, of course,
fatal; but if there were nothing more in the cause,
the Court would be disposed to consider it a case of
surprise, and allow the proofs to be completed by ex-

hibiting copies of the wills now. It would, however, be of no avail to do so, as there are other grounds, on which all relief to the plaintiffs must be denied. In the first place, as far as the assent of W. Owens, (who was in possession under a previous lease for a term, of which 22 years were unexpired) is material to the validity of the subsequent lease, under which the plaintiffs claim, on which assent, indeed, the bill rests entirely the efficacy of that lease as against Owens, the evidence directly contradicts the statements of the bill. There is no proof whatever of such assent. Although Mr. McEntire, one of the parties to that lease is examined, the plaintiffs do not even ask him a question upon the point; and it is clear from what he and the witnesses, Cole and Mrs. Owens, all say, that W. Owens did not know of the lease until after it had been made. and that he never did agree to it. It is true, Walker says, that Owens was present when Logan made a verbal agreement with Coggins, and made no objection. But that clearly relates to the agreement, subsequent and distinct from the lease between Coggins and Logan alone, for the sale of Coggin's mineral interest, as it is called, under the lease itself: for Walker speaks of the whiskey and flour, as being paid on the contract to which he deposes, which must refer to the subsequent transaction, since, for the original lease itself there was no such consideration as appears upon its face. McEntire says, indeed, that, after at first refusing, Owens consented to let them "test" the mines; which, we suppose, means that he allowed them to make some examinations with the view simply to ascertain, whether the land contained gold, or enough of it to be worth working. This he might have done, and, as we think, did, as one mode, and perhaps the easiest, of preventing disputes between the parties, as he would naturally expect, if it should turn out there was little gold, that he would have no more trouble upon the subject That is very different from his yielding to them, as a matter of right under their

lease, ingress upon the premises for the purpose of opening and working mines where they pleased.

But, secondly, McEntire says, that, after they had satisfied themselves by " tests." that there was too little gold
to make the business worth pursuing, the lessees from
Coggins abandoned all idea of it; and there can be little
doubt that they so informed Owens. It is natural to suppose so, after what had passed between them, as stated
by this witness. But the other two, Cole and Mrs. Owens, state that Logan and Coggins expressly agreed to
rescind. Whether they did it effectually or not, as between themselves, is not material. It is sufficient, that
Logan and Coggins so represented to Owens, and that,
under that belief, he purchased the premises from Coggins
as unincumbered and unaffected by either of the previous
contracts with Logan, or with him and his associates.
Certainly contracts cannot afterwards be set up with good
faith against W. Owens, or any persons claiming under
him; and especially after lying by, without once setting
up the claim, for nine years or thereabouts.

DANIEL, J. When William Owen, the tenant under
Hall, purchased from Coggins the reversion in fee on the
land, the two estates, to-wit, his term and his reversion
in fee then meeting in the same person, would have had
the effect of merging the precedent lesser estate in the
fee, if there had been no intermediate estate, outstanding
in a third person. But merger never takes place, when
it would have the effect to destroy intermediate *vested*
estates in third persons. If Coggins' lessees had been
the owners of their term in all the land, and the lease
was to have commenced immediately, it would in law
have been a vested estate in interest for the term of
thirty years. And, although they could not have taken
possession of their term, inasmuch as the possession belonged to Owen, the first lessee, they would, however.
have had a *concurrent* lease, and have been entitled to

all the rents issuing out of Owen's term; and, on the expiration of that term, they could have legally entered, and possessed the land for the residue of their own term. If the deed from Coggins to Logan and others created only what is sometimes called a future lease, to-wit, a contract to have a lease for thirty years, to commence after the lease to Owen, then it would have conveyed no present *estate* in the land, either in interest or in possession. It would have been only an *interesse termini*, which neither makes a merger nor prevents one, but may be accelerated, in the time of its becoming an estate in the land by possession, by the merger of an antecedent vested term by the termor purchasing in the next immediate estate in reversion. *Whitechurch* v. *Whitechurch*. 2 Peere W. 236. Dyer 112 (a.) 10 Vin. Ab. 204, vol. 3 and 264 pl. 3. Sheph. Touch. 106. Preston on Estates, 208 to 212 (new pages). The deed from Coggins to Logan & al. cannot be construed an estate or lease of the land for thirty years, concurrent with the lease to Owen; because the things, attempted to be leased in that deed, to-wit, minerals, timber and fire-wood, were not in law capable of being *leased*, so as to enable the lessee to have a *concurrent* lease with Owen, in those things. Coggins, at the date of his deed to Logan and others, could not himself have entered upon Owen, and opened the mines, cut timber or fire-wood, without the permission of Owen. And if *he* could not do such things himself, it is certain, that he could not assign to Logan and others the right to do them   This deed, therefore, conveyed no present estate, out of the reversion. It is then to be considered by us, as a contract only, to have the mineral ores, timber, fire-wood, &c. at the time of the expiration of the term of Owen. It then is an *interesse termini*, and, coming in between Owen's term and reversion, it cannot prevent a merger of his term in his reversion. By that reversion, this *interesse termini* was accelerated, in the time it was to become an estate.

For it was to become an estate. as soon as the thirty years' lease of Owen ceased to exist; and it did cease to exist, as soon as it was merged, to-wit, on the very day Owen purchased the fee from Coggins. The instant Owen's term merged in his reversion, that instant the *interesse termini* of Logan and others sprung into an *estate*, coupled with a right of entry into the possession of the things leased. They had never alienated their interest in the land by any writing. It, therefore, by the statute of frauds, still remained in them. But Owen and his son, William B. Owen, and the defendants, have continued in the adverse possession of the land, ever since Coggins sold the reversion to Owen, to-wit, ever since September 1831. This bill is an ejectment bill, brought to have an account of the profits of land, which has been, and now is, in the possession of William Owen and his assignees for many years. This Court never relieves in such a case, before the plaintiffs recover possession of their term at law. And, *secondly*, the answer of neither of the defendants admits that the two plaintiffs, George W. Logan and John W. Logan are the executors of John Logan, dec'd., or that the said John Logan died testate. The defendants do not admit. that Thomas Dews, Jun. is dead testate; and, if that fact appeared, his executor ought certainly to sue, and not his legatee, Thomas Dews, Sen. as he is described in the bill. There is a replication to all the answers, and there is neither any probate nor any copies of the wills of John Logan or Thomas Dews, Jun. We must, for the reasons above mentioned, dimiss the bill, with costs to be taxed against the plaintiffs.

PER CURIAM.   Bill dismissed with costs.

TO SUBSCRIBERS.

The undersigned, having become Proprietor, since June Term, 1845, of the Supreme Court Reports, respectfully requests Subscribers thereto, to make payment to him, for the numbers published since that date. The price of the Number for December Term 1845, was $4 50; and of that for June Term 1846, (the present,) $4.

The present Number finishes the 6th Volume of Law, the Index to which is now in Press, and will be forwarded in a few days to Subscribers.

WESTON R. GALES.

November 2, 1846.

EQUITY CASES

ARGUED AND DETERMINED IN

THE SUPREME COURT

OF

NORTH CAROLINA.

———

DECEMBER TERM, 1846.

———

JOHN MORRISON *vs.* JAMES MEACHAM.

In a suit in Equity to recover upon a lost bond, when the answer denies that there was a bond, the same degree of proof is requisite, which a Court of law would call for, to be laid before the jury upon *non est factum* pleaded to a declaration on a lost bond.

As the declaration would have been to aver the sealing of the obligation, and identify it by its date, day of payment and the sum mentioned in it, so the proof would have to come up to that description.

Cause transmitted by consent of the parties from the Court of Equity of Richmond County, at the Fall Term, 1846.

The bill was filed in August, 1843, and prays the payment of a lost bond. It states that previous to the month of December, 1836, the defendant was indebted to the plaintiff in the sum of $60, and, for the purpose of securing the same, executed to the plaintiff a bond for that sum, with another person as his surety, who has removed from this State. The bill states, that the plaintiff is unable to remember the date of the bond, or who was the subscribing witness to it; but it avers that it was payable on some day in December 1836. The bill further states, that in 1839, the plaintiff lost his pocket book. which contained that bond and several others, and that he has never been able to recover this or any other of those papers; but that they are certainly lost: That the plaintiff never received from the defendant, nor the other obligor, nor any other person, payment of the debt, or any part of it, but that the whole sum together with interest thereon is due to him: And, after a tender of indemnity, the bill prays payment. The bill is verified by the affidavit of the plaintiff.

The answer denies, that the defendant ever gave the plaintiff a bond by himself, or with any other person, for the sum of $60, or any other sum, during the year 1836, or any subsequent period; and it avers that the defendant paid every debt which he had contracted to the plaintiff at any time before 1836.

There is evidence that, in January 1836, the plaintiff held a bond of the defendant to him for $100, which the defendant paid and took up; and there is no evidence of subsequent dealings between them. But a son of the plaintiff states, that in 1842 or 1843, in a conversation with the witness respecting the bonds of some other persons, which the plaintiff had stated he had lost, the defendant remarked, " your father had a note against me for about sixty dollars, and it is gone as well as the rest; and I am not willing to pay it, unless it be produced." The wife of the last witness states, that, about the same period, she heard a conversation between the plaintiff's wife and the defendant, in the course of which the former said, " I have no harm against you, Mr. Meacham, if you would pay my husband the money you borrowed of him;"

and he replied : " well, if he will bring me my note, I will pay him ; but he has lost my note, and I do not want to pay it twice." The witness states, that she knew nothing of the debt, and that neither of the other persons mentioned what money was alluded to, nor what sum was due or alleged to be due from the defendant.

Strange, for the plaintiff.
No counsel for the defendant.

RUFFIN, C. J. The evidence is not sufficient to authorize a decree for the plaintiff, in opposition to the answer, which peremtorily denies the execution of any such bond, or the existence of any debt whatever. Without stopping to consider, whether any proof of the loss of the bond is necessary upon the hearing, and admitting some to be requisite, it seems pretty certain, that very slight evidence answers on that point ; and we should be satisfied with that before us, supposing it, however, to be first admitted or established, that the bond once actually subsisted, which it is alleged has been lost. Upon that question there is nothing in the nature of the jurisdiction of a Court of Equity, when the answer denies that there was a bond, to dispense with the degree of proof, which a Court of law would call for, to be laid before a jury on *non est factum* pleaded to a declaration on a lost bond. As the declaration would have to aver the sealing of the obligation, and identify it by its date, day of payment, and the sum mentioned in it, so the proof would have to come up to that description. Upon evidence so vague as not to fix any date, day of payment, or certain sum mentioned in it, and leaving it doubtful whether the instrument was a bond or note, a verdict could not be expected for the plaintiff on such declaration. Much less can a decree here, since the defendant's answer is by the rules of equity evidence for him. Here no date or day of payment is specified by either witness. One of them is unable to mention any sum, as acknowledged or claimed ; and both call the instrument a note, instead of a bond. The plaintiff's son says, indeed, that the defendant admitted the amount to be " about sixty dollars." That is the only evidence to the fact. It is possible, perhaps probable, that the plaintiff had the defendant's note for that amount, and we rather believe, that he had a bond or note for some amount; but the Court cannot declare that to be the fact in a decree, upon so vague a statement from one witness, in opposition to the positive oath of the defendant, especially when the bill states that another person executed the instrument as a surety, and the plaintiff has not called for an answer from that person by making him a defendant, nor attempted to examine him as a witness. Under such circumstances the Court is obliged to declare, that the plaintiff has not established, that the defendant executed to him a bond for the sum of $60, payable in December 1836, as alleged by him ; and therefore his bill must be dismissed. But the Court does not deem it a proper case for costs.

PER CURIÁM.   Bill dismissed.

JOHN J. ROGERS vs. JOHN BUMPASS & WIFE.

A Clerk and Master ought not to refer back to the Court a point, which the Court has expressly referred to him, or which is necessarily involved in the enquiry, which he was directed to make. The clerk and master should decide every question directly, and leave it to the parties, if dissatisfied, to bring the matter up for the decision of the Court by an exception.

A debt, legacy or distributive share of the wife is under the control of the husband, so far as to empower him to release, assign or receive them. But if, in his lifetime, he neither releases, conveys nor receives her choses in action, but leaves them outstanding, they belong to the surviving wife.

Therefore, where a husband gave his bonds to the executor or administrator of the father of the wife, of whose estate she was a legatee or distributee, and the husband gave his bonds to the administrator for certain purchases he made at the administrator's sale, and also for money loaned to him out of the funds of the estate, there being no agreement that these were to be regarded as payments of the distributive share of the wife; *Held,* that, after the death of the husband, the wife was entitled to recover the whole of her distributive share.

Cause transmitted by consent from the Court of Equity of Person County, at the Spring Term, 1846.

The bill is filed by some of the residuary legatees of Simon Clement, deceased, against his widow and her second husband ; she being the executrix of the will and one of the residuary legatees. The prayer is for the usual accounts of the estate, and payment of the plaintiff's shares. After an answer, there was a reference to the master to take the accounts. A report has been made, to which neither party has excepted. But the master has, in the report itself, submitted a question for the decision of the Court upon certain facts stated by him, as follows :

The testator married Nancy, the daughter of Hubbard Cozort. He, Cozort, died intestate in 1836, and William Clement administered on his estate. On the 31st of May, 1836, the administrator made sale of the property, and Simon Clement purchased to the amount of $270 75 : for which he then gave the administrator his bond payable nine months after date. On the 31st of July, 1837, Simon

Clement borrowed from the administrator the sum of $442, of the money belonging to the estate, and gave therefor a bond payable to the administrator one day after date. And on the 6th of 1837, he borrowed from the administrator the further sum of $30: for which he also gave a bond payable in like manner. On the 15th of November, 1837, Simon Clements made a payment of $100, on the bond for $442, and made no other payment on either of the bonds before his death; which happened early in the year 1838, and before the estate of Hubbard Cozort had been settled or the expiration of two years from the grant of administration on that estate. After the death of Simon Clement, his widow, whom he appointed executrix, proved his will; and subsequently, viz: on the 28th of May. 1838, she came to an account with William Clement, the administrator of her father's estate, and found her distributive share thereof to be the sum of $1,085 00, and on that day received the same. The sum then due on the three bonds of her late husband, was $685 34; and she received those bonds in part payment of her distributive share as so much cash, taking thereon the receipts of the administrator, William Clement, to her as executrix. At the same time the administrator took from her a refunding bond, in the condition of which it was recited, "that the above bound Nancy Clement, executrix of Simon Clement deceased, has received from William Clement administrator, &c., the sum of $1085, in full of the distributive share of the said Simon Clement in right of his wife Nancy in the personal estate of Hubbard Cozort deceased."

Upon the reference, the defendants carried the three bonds of the testator into the Master's office, as vouchers of disbursements by them. The Master neither allowed nor disallowed them; but he stated an account of the estate, shewing the balance in the hands of the defendants if those vouchers should be allowed to them, and also stated a second account, shewing the balance in their hands, if those bonds should not be allowed. The Master then refers it to the Court to decide which is the proper balance upon the foregoing facts.

Venable, for the plaintiff.
Norwood and *E. G. Reade*, for the defendants.

RUFFIN, C. J. The Court has several times expressed disapprobation of the manner of reporting adopted in this case. The Master ought not to refer back to the Court a point, which the Court has expressly referred to him, or which is necessarily involved in the enquiry he was directed to make. It is much more convenient and renders the proceedings more direct and concise, that the Master should decide every question directly, and leave it to the parties, if dissatisfied, to bring the matter up for the decision of the Court by an exception. If, therefore, this were a report made by our own officer, under a reference in this Court, we would not act on it, but direct it to be put into the proper form. But, as the report was made in the Court below and was received there, and the case sent here upon the single point raised in the report, and has been brought on by counsel for a decision without objection, we think it best, perhaps, to proceed in the case in its present shape, especially as the point itself seems to be so plain, that it is not necessary to put the parties to further expense about it.

The Court is opinion, that the three defendants are entitled to credit in their administration account for the amount of the three bonds in question. The objection to it is founded upon the notion, that the distributive share of Mrs. Clement in her father's estate vested in the testator, as her husband: at least, to the extent of his debts to the estate or to the administrator. But that is a mistake. A debt, legacy, or distributive share of the wife is under the control of the husband, so far as to empower him to release, assign, or receive them. His release ex-

tinguishes them, and the collection of the money vests it
in him as his absolute property. But if, in his life-time,
he neither releases, conveys, nor receives her choses in
action, but leaves them outstanding, they belong to the
surviving wife. If, therefore, the testator, in this case,
had not owed the debts in question, it could not be argued,
that the wife, on the death of her husband, was not entitled to the distributive share of her father's personalty.
That he owed those debts can make no difference. It is
probable the husband might have formed an expectation,
that, in settling with Cozort's administrator for his wife's
distributive share, his own debts would be discharged by
their being discounted or set off in such settlement. But
that was a mere expectation in the testator's own mind,
dependent upon the events, that he should not otherwise
have paid the residue of those debts, as he had a part,
and that he should live to make the settlement. It is
certain, that he did not consider his bonds paid *in presenti*, by being set off against so much of his wife's distributive share. Indeed, it does not appear, that any
arrangement whatever, had even been talked of between
the administrator or himself on that subject, or that the
testator had expressed an opinion on purpose to appropriate to the discharge of those debts an equal sum out
of the distributive share. It was not known what the
distributive share would be or any thing near it, when
the debts were contracted, nor even at the death of
Simon Clement, which happened before the estate was
settled or the time for making a settlement of it had
arrived. There was, then, nothing done by the testator,
or that occurred in his life time, that could affect the
operation of the rule of law, by which a distributive share
outstanding survives to a wife. The circumstances that
the widow herself received the money and her husband's
bonds afterwards, and gave a refunding bond in which it
is stated, that she received them as executrix of her late
husband, does not change the right. It does not appear,

that the husband professed to dispose of that interest in his will, or that there was any thing else to put Mrs. Clement to an election, by which she should give up her distributive share. Without something of that sort, it is apparent that it was a mere mistake to suppose, that the share belonged to the husband, instead of herself; and that mistake cannot preclude her, upon its discovery, from claiming her real rights.

Upon the question submitted by the Master, it must therefore be declared, that the defendants are entitled to credit for the amount due on the testator's bonds at the time they were taken up by Mrs. Clement, and interest thereon from that time, according to the first account anexed to the report.

There will be a decree for the plaintiffs according to that amount. The decree will be with costs against the defendants, because the executrix returned no inventory, amount of sales, nor accounts of the administration, before the bill filed, which was upwards of four years after the testator's death.

Per Curiam. Decree accordingly.

WILLIAM THOMPSON *vs.* MARVIL MILLS.

When a defendant asks the Court to act on his answer, as he does, when he moves to dissolve an injunction, it is not sufficient that he should make an answer, which merely does not admit the ground of the plaintiff's equity, but it must set forth a full and fair discovery of all the matters within his knowledge or in his power to discover, and then deny the material grounds, upon which the plaintiff's equity is founded.

An answer, that is evasive, that declines admitting or denying a fact positively, when it is in the party's power, if he will, to obtain information, that will enable him to admit or deny the fact ; and, much more, an answer, that keeps back information that is possessed by a party upon a material fact, on the pretence, that the defendant cannot give the information with all the minuteness of which the subject is susceptible, such an answer ought not to entitle the person, who makes it, to any favor.

Appeal from an interlocutory order, made in the Court of Equity of Rutherford County. at the Fall Term 1846, his Honor Judge CALDWELL presiding.

The object of the bill is to obtain an injunction and relief against a judgment at law. The parties reside in Rutherford, and the defendant kept a retail shop, in which the plaintiff had dealt for several years. The bill states, that on the 27th of January, 1841, the plaintiff paid the defendant all he then owed him on account, and took a receipt in full. It is annexed to the bill as an exhibit A, and is in the following words : "January 27th, 1841. Received of William Thompson in full for a judgment and all accounts up to this date." (Signed,) "M. Mills." The bill further states, that the plaintiff then went to Henderson County, and worked there about 18 months, having left his wife and family at his residence in Rutherford ; and that, upon his return home, the defendant demanded from him a debt of $120 70, for dealings which he alleged the plaintiff's family had in his store during the plaintiff's absence : that the plaintiff was very drunk at the time, and that the defendant availed himself of that opportunity to obtain an undue advantage of him, and insisted that the plaintiff should give his bond for the said sum; and that he did so, while drunk, and under the belief, from the defendant's representations, that the demand was just.

The bill further states, that, becoming sober, the plaintiff enquired of his family, what dealings they had, during his absence with the defendant; and was informed by them and believes, that not an article was purchased by any member of his family, excepting only two pieces of tobacco; and that, in a short time afterwards, he went to the defendant and informed him of what his family had told the plaintiff, and requested him to produce his books containing the account, so that he might see the items and the amount of it; but that the defendant refused to let him see his books. or to give him any satisfaction upon the subject, pretending however, at some times, that the bond was taken for the dealings of the plaintiff's family as aforesaid, whereas they had no such dealings; and at other times pretending that it was taken, partly, for a book account, and partly, for a balance due on a note for $100, which the plaintiff had given the defendant for the price of a mare, whereas, the plaintiff had discharged the note by paying on it, at one time $85, and at another $90; and also, he had paid $10 on account, and had received no credit therefor.

The bill then contains several interrogatories; particularly, whether the parties did not settle all accounts on the 27th of January, 1841; and whether the defendant did not give the plaintiff the receipt or acquittance of that date exhibited with the bill: whether the defendant did not demand the bond for dealings of the plaintiff's family subsequent to the said settlement of January 1841, or for what other cause. And it calls on the defendant to set forth a copy of his account, for which the bond was taken.

The answer admits that the plaintiff made the payment of $35, on the note for $100 given for the mare, and denies that he made any other. It states, that the plaintiff had been dealing with the defendant for ten or twelve years, and was generally in his debt, and that he may have made payments of $20, and $10, though the defendant says he has no recollection of any such, and that, if they were made, they were credited on accounts existing at the time.

The answer states, that on the 1st of August, 1842, the plaintiff was indebted to the defendant in the sum of $120 70, upon accounts, in part for dealings of the plaintiff, and in part of his wife and family, and including a a balance of $15, due on the note for the mare, and interest thereon; and that the settlement was made and the bond given of that date, when the plaintiff was not in the least drunk, and "with a full knowledge of all the facts." The defendant denies, that the plaintiff ever applied for an inspection of the defendant's books; and states, that on all occasions the defendant declared the consideration of the bond to have been as herein set forth.

The answer then proceeds: "Respondent doth not know, whether exhibit A, is a copy of a receipt executed by him to complainant, as he had no opportunity of seeing the original, and has no recollection of giving a receipt of that date. Since the last settlement with complainant, respondent did not deem it necessary to preserve the accounts, for which the said bond was given; and, consequently he cannot now set out an exact statement of all the articles furnished complainant; but he recollects, that the same was for a variety of articles of merchandize, and for work in a blacksmith's shop, and for the balance of the note and interest, as aforesaid."

An injunction was granted on the bill, while. on the answer, the defendant moved to dissolve. But the Court refused the motion, and ordered the injunction to stand to the hearing, but allowed the defendant an appeal.

Woodfin, for the plaintiff.
Baxter, for the defendant.

RUFFIN, C. J. The Court of equity compels an answer on oath, to enable the plaintiff to get a discovery of facts, which he cannot prove by indifferent witnesses, or to save him from the trouble and expense of thus proving them. The defendant is turned into a witness in the cause ; and as a witness he ought honestly and explicitly to set forth every thing he knows, or has the means of knowing and believes, that is material to the plaintiff's case, as well as such matters as constitute his own defence. But, judging from many answers that come up here, and, especially, in injunction causes, the purposes for which the answer is required, and the nature of the jurisdiction are often almost entirely overlooked. Answers are drawn for the sole benefit of the defendant, apparently, and not to disclose the truth and justice of the case. It is true, that often the bill is so defectively framed as not to compel a full discovery in the answer. And it is likewise true, that by not excepting to an insufficient answer, and replying to it, the plaintiff may be put to great disadvantage at the hearing, as the truth of a matter, charged in the bill, cannot upon that occasion be inferred from the silence of the answer as to it, or the omission merely of a denial. But when the defendant asks the Court to act on his answer, as he does when he moves to dissolve an injunction, it is not sufficient that he should make an answer, which merely does not admit the grounds of the plaintiff's equity, but it must set forth a full and fair discovery of all the matters within his knowledge, or in his power to discover, and then deny the material grounds upon which the plaintiff's equity is founded. An answer that is evasive, that declines admitting or denying a fact positively, when it is in the party's power, if he will, to obtain information that will enable him thus to admit or deny the fact ; and much more, an answer that keeps back information that is possessed by the party upon a material fact, on the pretence, that the defendant cannot give the information with all the minuteness, of which the subject is susceptible ; such an answer ought not to entitle the person, who makes it, to any favour. Of that character is the answer in this case. Either from carelessness in the writer, or want of explicitness and candour in the party, this answer is grossly evasive. The equity of the plaintiff is, that the defendant obtained a bond from him for $120 70, on the misrepresentation, that he was indebted to him in that sum on account, for dealings by the plaintiff's family after the 27th of January, 1841. The bill adds, indeed, that the plaintiff was drunk, when he gave the bond, and that is denied distinctly enough. But that is material in the present state of the case, since the defendant admits that the bond was not intended as a voluntary bond, but was understood to be founded on existing debts. Now, it is obviously, an important part of the plaintiff's case, that the period of the alleged dealings should be precisely fixed, in order to confine the account to the particular transactions included in the settlement. For that purpose the bill charges, that it must have been for dealings after January 29th, 1841, forasmuch, as on that day the parties settled for all previous dealings, and the defendant gave a receipt to that effect ; and that receipt was filed in the office with the bill as an exhibit, and the defendant interrogated as to its genuineness. Instead of answering directly to the interrogatory, the defendant says, he "does not know." Why? because in the copy of the bill sent to him, only a copy of the receipt was annexed, and he had no opportunity of seeing the original. But, if he had forgotten giving the paper, and wished to know the truth or to make it known to the Court, nothing was easier than to have gone to the office and seen the original. Instead of that, he merely answers at large, that the account was for dealings of both the plaintiff and his family, without specifying any periods for such dealings, or denying that for 18 months the plaintiff had been out of the county, and thus leaving it to be inferred that the dealing had run through the 10 or 12 years, spoken of in another part of the answer.

Besides, though expressly called on to set out a copy of the account on which the bond was given. and though the defendant says it was for merchandize sold, in a country store, to the plaintiff and to his family, and for blacksmith's work, the defendant wholly omits to give any account. The reason given is, that " he cannot *now* set out an *exact* account of *all* the articles furnished complainant," forasmuch, as " since the settlement he did not deem it necessary to preserve the accounts." It will be observed, that the defendant does not pretend, that copies of the accounts were delivered to the plaintiff nor that his books containing the original entries have been destroyed, nor that any book or paper *has* in fact been lost or destroyed, nor that he cannot state the articles the plaintiff's family purchased. He says only, that he did not deem it necessary to preserve the accounts, for which the bond was given and consequently that he cannot furnish an *exact* settlement of *all* the articles furnished to the plaintiff himself. From this we collect that the defendant probably meant, without directly averring it, that the Court should understand or infer, that the particular papers, containing the computations and calculations at the settlement, were mislaid. But suppose the answer could be taken in that sense. yet the defendant gives no reason for not annexing copies of the accounts as they stand in his books; which ought to shew the different settlements, and the several items. And although he might not be able to give an *exact* account of *all* the articles, yet he was bound to give the accounts as far as he could; and, if he could give no account, he was bound to say so, and give the plaintiff the full benefit of that singular circumstance.

It is clear, therefore, that the defendant has not given the answer that was called for, and that he might and ought to have given, but has evaded it in several essential points. Therefore, the injunction was properly continued

Rogers v. Bumpass.

to the hearing ; and it must be so certified to the Court
below.   The defendant must pay the costs in this Court.

PER CURIAM.   Certificate ordered accordingly.

EZEKIEL RICH vs. ALFRED H. MARSH & AL.

A suppression of competition at an execution sale by the representatives of
the defendant, that he was buying for the plaintiff, by means of which he
purchased the land of a distressed man for a very inadequate price, will
authorize a decree for the plaintiff, on a bill to redeem the land on paying
the sum for which it was sold, on the ground of an undue advantage taken
of his necessities, and a fraud practised in getting the title in that way,
and then claiming it for his own benefit.

The cases of *Neely* v. *Torian*, 1 Dev. and Bat. 410, and *Turner* v. *King*, 2
Ired. Eq. 132, cited and approved.

The bill is for the redemption and reconveyance of a
tract of land.   In 1837 there were several judgments and
executions against the plaintiff, under which the premises
were about to be sold ; and he applied to the defendant,
Davis, to lend him money to discharge them, and take a
deed of trust to secure the same.   But Davis declined
doing so, as he states in the answer, because he feared
the incumbrances of other judgments ; and they came
to another agreement : which was, " that this defendant
(he not having the ready money) should borrow money
and bid off the land at the sheriff's sale, and take the
conveyance to himself, and that the plaintiff might redeem
the land upon re-paying the purchase money, by the time
the borrowed money became due."   The answer further
states, that Davis borrowed the money in November 1837,

and agreed to re-pay it and did re-pay it in September following. The land is charged in the bill and proved to have been worth about $400; but Davis purchased it at the Sheriff's sale for $36, and took a deed. At the sale several persons were present with the intention of bidding for the land, but were prevented from doing so by Davis, who informed them that he had agreed to buy it for the benefit of the plaintiff, and allow him to redeem it. After the sale, the plaintiff continued to occupy the land and Davis took annually from him a note for about $5, for the rent, as he states, of the land; but a witness states it to have been for the interest of the sum advanced and the taxes on the land, which Davis paid. In 1842, Davis executed a deed of trust for the land and other property to the defendant Elliott to secure a debt he owed the defendant Marsh, and in 1843 the land was offered at public sale under the deed of trust by the defendant Marsh, acting as the agent of the trustee, Elliott, and was bid off by Marsh. At that time the plaintiff was still living on the land, and, when it was put up for sale, he forbid the sale and claimed the land.

No counsel for the plaintiff.
Winston, for the defendant.

RUFFIN, C. J. The plaintiff is clearly entitled to the relief he seeks. Independent of the express agreement for redemption, and the right to have that executed upon the admission of it in the answer. the suppression of competition at the sale by the representations of Davis, that he was buying for the plaintiff, by means of which he purchased the land of a distressed man for $36, which was worth $400 or more, would authorize a decree for the plaintiff upon the ground of an undue advantage taken of his necessities and a fraud practiced in getting the title in that way and claiming it for his own benefit. This has been already decided in several cases. *Neely*

79

v. *Torian*, 1 Dev. & Bat. Eq. 410. *Turner* v. *King*, 2 Ired. Eq. 132. To such cases the statute of frauds, 1819, has no application; for, besides the agreement for redemption, there is the additional circumstance of the suppression of competition at the sale, and it is a fraud to bring that about or to take advantage of it under those circumstances. However, in the present case there can be no doubt of the agreement for redemption, as the answer explicitly admits it. It is said, indeed, in the argument, that it was an agreement for redemption by a particular day, so as in effect to be an agreement for a conditional sale; and that it was lost for non-performance at the day. But the law is clearly otherwise.

There cannot be a doubt, that Davis was to take the legal title *as a security* for the money advanced; so that in fact, to use the word in the answer, it was intended, that the plaintiff might "redeem" the land; and when the agreement is for redemption, it confers the right to it with all its incidents as to time and circumstances.

The decree must be against the defendants Elliott and Marsh as well as Davis; for there is nothing to protect them. They were not purchasers for value and without notice. Elliott gave nothing for the land; indeed, the conveyance was taken to him without his knowledge by Marsh, as a security for a previous debt to himself. And it was necessary to make Elliott a party, as it does not appear that he had conveyed to Marsh under his purchase at the sale made for the trustee. Besides, the plaintiff was living on the land at the time, and that was notice of his title, because it made it the duty of the other parties to make the enquiry of him. And that was not all, but he gave express notice of his claim, when the land was offered under the deed of trust.

It must be declared, therefore, that the plaintiff is entitled to redeem upon payment of the sum advanced by Davis and the interest thereon, or the balance due therefor; and it must be referred to the Clerk to take the usual accounts, and state the balance due on either side, as upon the foot of a mortgage of the premises from the plaintiff to the defendant Davis.

PER CURIAM.   Decreed accordingly.

NATHANIEL C. GORDON vs. HAMILTON BROWN.

Equity disregards penalties.

A penalty limits the sum which may be recovered in an action of debt for a breach of a contract.

The party who claims for the breach of a contract is not restricted to his legal remedy by an action for the penalty, but may claim an execution of the contract, as it is understood in a Court of Equity; that is, as a stipulation, without reference to the penalty, to do the several things stated in the condition.

Cause transmitted to this Court by consent of the parties from the Court of Equity of Wilkes County at the Fall Term, 1846.

The facts of this case seem to be these, as collected from the pleadings and exhibits. Sarah Gordon was in 1834 of an advanced age and owned some slaves and other property; and among them was a negro man, named Jim, and a woman named Harriett. She had a numerous family of descendants. Two of her sons were then dead, namely, Nathaniel and John. The former left several infant children, of whom the present defendant was the guardian and step-father. The latter left a son, who is the present plaintiff and was then of full age and resided in Mississippi. John Gordon was, at the time of

.his death, indebted to one Thomas Brown on a judgment
in a Court of Tennessee for the sum of $550; and the
present defendant was the agent of the creditor to collect
or secure the debt.   In that state of things, Mrs. Gordon .
was desirous of making some immediate advancement for
the children of her deceased son Nathaniel, and provide
for the payment of the debt of her late son John, and also
make some prospective provision for the present plaintiff;
and she determined to give to Nathaniel's children the
use of the negro Jim during her own life, and to give the
remainder in him after her death, and also the other
negro Harriett to her grand son, the plaintiff, subject,
nevertheless, to the payment at her death of what should
be then due for principal and interest upon the judgment
of Thomas Brown against his father; and to that arrangement the defendant, as the agent of Thomas Brown, assented.   In order to carry it into effect the parties adopted
this method.   Sarah Gordon and Nathaniel C. Gordon,
the plaintiff, made an absolute bill of sale to the defendant for the two negroes, bearing date March 13th, 1834;
and at the same time he, with a surety executed to them
a bond in the penal sum of $1000, with a condition, re-
citing that, whereas Sarah Gordon and Nathaniel C.
Gordon, had sold to H. B., the defendant, the two slaves
Jim and Harriett, and for the purpose of re-purchasing
them had agreed to pay him at the death of Sarah Gordon the sum of $550 and interest thereon, to be applied
to the judgment in favour of Thomas Brown against John
Gordon, and then providing that the bond shall be void.
if during the life of Sarah Gordon H. B. shall allow her
to have the use and possession of Harriett, and, during
the same term, shall hold the slave Jim for the benefit of
the infant children of Nathaniel Gordon deceased, and,
upon the death of the said Sarah, shall convey the said
two slaves Jim and Harriett to Nathaniel C. Gordon;
(the plaintiff) he, the said Nathaniel C. first paying to
H. B. the said sum of $550, with the interest thereon.

On the 15th of March, 1834, the bond was proved before a Judge and registered.

In March 1842, Sarah Gordon died, having made a will, in which the defendant is appointed executor. In October 1843, this bill was filed by Nathaniel C. Gordon against Hamilton Brown, to obtain the conveyance of the two slaves and an account and payment of their profits. since the death of Sarah Gordon, the plaintiff offering to pay the principal and interest of the debt of his father to Thomas Brown   The bill charges, however, that the defendant was unable to convey the negroes, because he had sold them in the life time of Mrs. Gordon ; that is to say, Jim for the price of $637 to a person in this State, who has since carried him to parts unknown, and Harriett to some person in Georgia for $1000: that those sums were less than the value of the slaves, but that the plaintiff was willing and had offered to accept them instead of the slaves, and, after deducting the sum due on Thomas Brown's judgment, to receive the residue and interest thereon from the death of Mrs. Gordon ; but that the defendant refused to settle on that principle or any other, except that of accounting to the plaintiff for the penalty of $1000, named in his bond, by deducting therefrom $814 for the debt to Thomas Brown, and paying the balance of $186 to the plaintiff.   The prayer is for a conveyance and delivery of the slaves, and the increase of Harriett, or payment of the sums for which they were sold, or payment of their present values.

The bill states that the original bond was in the possession of Sarah Gordon, and has been lost, and a copy from the Register's books is annexed as an exhibit.

The answer admits the execution of a bond in the penalty of $1,000 and that "it was not materially variant from the copy annexed to the bill; but "the defendant upon the best of his recollection does not admit, and does not deny, that the paper, annexed as a copy, is a true copy of the bond."

The answer states, that the bond was executed with the understanding, that Sarah Gordon might, nevertheless, at her will and pleasure, dispose of the negroes, provided she should pay the debts to Thomas Brown: that in 1836 Sarah Gordon, on account of the bad qualities of the negro, sent Harriett to Georgia, and had her sold there on a credit for $1,000, for which a note was taken payable in Georgia bank notes to one Gwyn, her agent. The defendant admits that Sarah Gordon made known to him her wish to dispose of Harriett, and her intention to appropriate a part of the price to making a further provision for the children of Nathaniel Gordon, who were the wards of the defendant; and that the defendant did not interfere to prevent her, but advanced the money for the expenses of carrying the slave to Georgia. The answer states that in 1839 the defendant received $300 on the note for the price of Harriett: and that no other part of the debt has as yet been collected, though he thinks that, after a short delay. the residue may be collected. He says that the reason he did not receive the money before, was the depreciation of Georgia notes, being as much at one time as 16 per cent. below those of this State; and therefore he let the debt continue outstanding, until the circumstances of the debtor became doubtful: but that in doing so and in all his other conduct, he acted upon the best of his judgment for the interests of those concerned as he would for himself. He furthermore states, that Sarah Gordon afterwards made her will, and therein bequeathed divers legacies, which will be defeated by reason of a deficiency of assets, unless a part of the price of Harriett be applied to their satisfaction.

The answer states the reason for the sale of Jim to have been, his insubordination and the apprehension, on certain circumstances mentioned, that he designed an escape into Canada or a north-western State. It admits the price to have been $637, which it says was the full value: and states the defendant's ignorance, whether Jim or Harriett be living or dead, or what is their present value, or whether Harriett had any children. It also admits that the defendant hath kept out at interest the said sums of $637, and $300, and states that he paid the interest to Mrs. Gordon during her life, and is ready to account for the principal and interest since her death to the plaintiff, if he be entitled thereto. The defendant states, that when he executed the bond, his understanding was, that the demand of the plaintiff for a breach of the condition was limited to the penalty of $1,000; and he insists on that, as the law of their contract. Moreover the answer insists, that, as the bond was payable to Sarah Gordon and the plaintiff, he is bound by the acts of his co-obligee, and that, as she sold the negro Harriett and directed the disposition of part of the proceeds, and therefore could not complain thereof, so neither can the plaintiff. The defendant then submits to pay the plaintiff the penalty of $1,000, deducting therefrom the debt to Thomas Brown.

The plaintiff put in as evidence two letters written to him by the defendant. One dated April 29th, 1842, in which he advises him of the death of Mrs. Gordon, and that he was desirous that the plaintiff should come in and settle the business between them. He then states, that he had sold Jim for $637, and then proceeds: "I sent Harriett to Georgia and sold her for $1,000 in Georgia money. I have paid the interest annually to Mrs. Gordon. As there was and now is a large discount between Georgia and North Carolina money, I let it remain in Georgia, with the expectation that Georgia money would get better. I was there last January and had the misfortune to lose $700 of that money." The other is dated November 18th, 1842, and appears to be in answer to one from the plaintiff, in which he claims the negroes or their value, and his unwillingness to bear the loss of any part of the price of Harriett. The letter then says: "I intended, after Brown's claim was settled, to pay you the balance of the sale of the two negroes; but I was unfortunate and lost in Georgia $700 of the price of Harriett. If I had been unfortunate and both of the negroes had run or died, I still would have expected to pay you the amount of the bond at Mrs. Gordon's death. As I was unfortunate in losing a part of the price of Harriett, I must fall back on the amount of my bond."

Dodge, for the plaintiff.
Bynum, for the defendant.

Ruffin, C. J. The plaintiff would be entitled to a decree for a conveyance of the slaves, if the defendant had them in possession. It is true, as the defendant says, the penalty was *the law* of their contract, limiting the sum which could have been recovered from the defendant in an action of debt. But equity disregards penalties. If the penalty here had been ten times as much, the defendant would have then thought it reasonable and equitable, that he should be relieved from it by performance of the act, upon the non-performance of which the penalty accrued by strict law. So, the other side is not restricted to his legal remedy by an action for the penalty, but may claim an execution of the contract, as it is understood in this Court; that is, as a stipulation, without reference to the penalty, to do the several things stated in the condition.

The negroes, however, have been sold; and several questions are made, how far the defendant is thereby discharged. As to Jim, there is no allegation in the answer that Mrs. Gordon directed or even assented to the sale made by the defendant, and therefore the defendant is undoubtedly liable for him. The defences as to Harriett must also, we think, all fail. In the first place, it is clear that Mrs. Gordon had parted from all control over her, except for the term of her life. Her conveyance was by deed, in part for a valuable consideration in respect of Thomas Brown's debt; and, moreover, good without that circumstance, inasmuch as the *St. 27 Eliz.* (*Rev. Stat. ch.* 50, *sec.* 2,) in favour of purchasers, does not embrace personal chattels. *McKee* v. *Houston.* 3 *Murp.* 429. Still less can a sale to raise a fund for the payment of legacies defeat a *bona fide* voluntary conveyance to or for a grand-son. For the same reason that in this Court the penalty is not respected, the acts of Mrs. Gordon in making or assenting to a sale of the negroes cannot affect the interest of the plaintiff. The form of the contract is nothing. The substance is, that upon the death of that lady, the defendant became the trustee of the slaves for the plaintiff, subject to the incumbrance of Thomas Brown's debt.

But, setting aside all those considerations, the defence fails for want of proof. There is no evidence, that Mrs. Gordon sold or agreed to the sale of either of the negroes. On the contrary the only evidence upon the point, except the answer, are the letters of the defendant, in which he assumes the act, as exclusively his own. Then, it is the common case of a trustee undertaking of his own head, and without the concurrence or knowledge of the *cestui que trust*, to dispose of the trust property; and he must undoubtedly make it good, by answering for the value, at the least. If the *cestui que trust* chooses, he may claim the price got by the trustee, however far above the value; for a trustee can make no profit for himself, though he may lose by a breach of trust. But if the *cestui que trust* claim the price, he must take it in its actual state; for when he follows the fund, he gets it as it is. Therefore the plaintiff cannot charge the defendant with $1000 for Harriett (if that exceeds her value) without accepting the money collected by the defendant and the sureties held by him for the residue. But he has the right to take the sum of $637, received for Jim, as his counsel says, he is content to do; and, at his election, to have a decree for the present value of Harriett and her issue, if any, or

for the sum received by the defendant and the securities
for the residue of the price ; and to those ends he may
have all necessary enquiries.

PER CURIAM.   Decreed accordingly.

JOEL MERRITT vs. JAMES HUNT.

Where there was a public sale of lands, where the vendor gave notice at the
sale that there were doubts as to the title, but that he would give a warranty deed, being a man of undoubted ability to answer the warranty, and
where such deed was accordingly given and the purchaser gave his bond
for the purchase money, upon which the vendor afterwards obtained judgment ; *Held,* that the purchaser had no right to an injunction against
this judgment, that the Court of Equity would not look into the title, but
would leave the purchaser to his remedy at law upon the warranty.

Cause removed from the Court of Equity of Granville
County, at the Fall Term, 1846.

In December 1841, the defendant, the executor of Mary
Jones, deceased, offered at public sale two tracts of land,
as having been the property in fee of the testator, which
he was authorized to sell. As to one of the tracts, the
bill states that the defendant declared, that he would sell
only such interest as his testatrix had, and at the risk of
the purchaser. As to the other, containing 100 acres, the
defendant announced, that it was the property of the testatrix, although he had been unable to find any deed for
it, and that he would warrant it to the purchaser. This
latter piece, the plaintiff purchased at the price of $303,
and he immediately gave his bond therefor and took a

conveyance and entered into possession of the land. The bill states that in the course of the next summer, further doubts arose as to the title to the land, and that there was some negotiation between the parties about rescinding the contract; but that, finally, the defendant, in November 1842, declined doing any thing further, and thereupon, the plaintiff offered to surrender the deed and demanded his bond, and abandoned the premises. The defendant afterwards took a judgment on the plaintiff's bond, and he then filed the bill to have the contract rescinded and the judgment perpetually enjoined.

The bill states, that search has been made, in the Register's office, and that no evidence of any title in the testatrix can be found, and that the plaintiff believes none exists.

It further states, that upon consulting counsel upon the question of title, it was discovered, that the deed, which the defendant made, conveyed but an estate for the plaintiff's life, although the defendant contracted to convey in fee, and the warranty is to the plaintiff and his heirs. The bill charges, that the plaintiff is an illiterate man, and that the deed was prepared by the defendant or under his direction, and was accepted by the plaintiff, not knowing the deficiency therein and in the confidence that it was according to the contract.

The answer denies, that the defendant undertook to covenant, that the land had belonged to his testatrix. On the contrary, the defendant says, that, in respect to a small tract, he refused to make any covenant, because he could not discover any trace of right in the testatrix except possession; and the purchaser was to take a conveyance without warranty. With respect to the other tract, which the plaintiff purchased, the defendant admits it was otherwise. He says that he discovered that his testatrix never had a deed for it; but that, understanding that one William Jones had taken a conveyance for it from a former owner upon some trust for the testatrix, he had applied to him to know how the truth was; and that William Jones admitted that he held the title under an engagement to convey it to Mary Jones, and accordingly he executed a deed to the defendant, as the executor and devisee of Mary Jones. Believing, from those circumstances, that the land really belonged to his testatrix, and that the purchaser would never be disturbed, although he was unable to trace the title back beyond William Jones, the defendant states, that he publicly made known to the plaintiff and other persons present, the state of the title, and in order to enhance the price by satisfying bidders of their security, he agreed that he would make a deed for the fee and give therein his own covenant of warranty, binding him and his heirs to indemnify the purchaser, if he should be disturbed in the possession. And the answer positively avers, that it was understood that the purchaser was to have no other security for the title, but the conveyance of the defendant in fee, with his covenant against an eviction by superior title.

The defendant admits, that, as he is advised, the deed made by him, is only for a life estate, and that, by the terms of the sale, he was to make one purporting to convey a fee, with general warranty. But he says that neither the plaintiff nor he being versed in drawing conveyances, application was made to a merchant, residing at the place of sale, and supposed to be competent thereto, and that the deed was drawn by him as the friend of the parties; and that it was executed by the defendant in the belief, that it was a deed for the fee simple: that he had no suspicion to the contrary, until the plaintiff, after the judgment at law, informed him of the defect: and that then the defendant offered to make any deed plaintiff might wish, which would carry out the agreement between them, but the plaintiff declared that he would not take one.

The answer further states, that the plaintiff had sold

and conveyed a part of the land, about five acres, to Benjamin Sims, who claims and occupies it.

The defendant filed, with his answer, the deed to him by William Jones; and also another deed to the plaintiff, and submits to be bound by it or to make a conveyance in fee with any covenants, to which the Court shall declare the plaintiff entitled.

Badger, for the plaintiff.
Gilliam and *Husted*, for the defendant.

RUFFIN, C. J. The parties have taken much testimony; and the substance of it is clearly in support of the answer. There were no written articles, but the crier at the sale and several of the bidders prove, that the defendant gave distinct notice, that doubts rested upon the title, as he was unable to trace it or find any evidence of it upon the Register's books; and that the defendant, in order to induce persons to bid a fair price for the land, said that he would warrant the title. The witnesses all understood that the purchaser was to take a conveyance for the land at all events, whether the defendant could shew a good title or not in his testatrix or himself, provided he would bind himself by a general warranty in the deed. They state that the defendant was known to be a man of substantial and independent property, and that the bidders considered the title good to them by his agreement to make it good in case of an eviction. It is evident, that the plaintiff, also, had the same impression and understanding, For, after he was declared the purchaser, he made no enquiry as to the title, nor asked any delay for the purpose of looking into it; but was satisfied to give his bond for the price immediately, and take a deed, purporting, as was then thought, to convey a fee, and containing a general warranty, binding the defendant and his heirs. He also sold a part to another person, and conveyed it in fee. If there be a defect in the title, therefore, it cannot affect the contract these persons made: for the contract, in terms provided for such a possible or probable defect, and for the consequences of it. If a person chooses to buy a doubtful or bad title with his eyes open, and at his own risk, he is as much bound by that, as by any other contract fairly made. So, if he buy such a title with a guaranty of the seller against eviction or disturbance, he must take the title, and look to the vendor's covenants for his security or indemnity. He cannot complain of any injury: for he gets precisely what he bargained for, namely, a conveyance with the warranty of the vendor. In such a case the Court will not look into the title at all; because the bargain was, that it was immaterial whether it was good or bad, provided the vendee had a covenant of indemnity. The plaintiff, therefore, would have been clearly bound to pay the purchase money, had the deed, that was made to him, been for a fee. That it was not, was merely by the mistake of the writer, and of the parties—as much of the one as of the other—as is proved by the writer of the deed and the subscribing witnesses. All thought it to be for the fee. The defect cannot excuse the refusal of the plaintiff to fulfil his part of the contract, inasmuch as the defendant, as soon as he had notice of it, offered to supply it by making another deed, and now submits to convey under the direction of the Court. The injunction ought, therefore, to be dissolved with full costs up to this time, and the plaintiff declared entitled to a deed from the defendant for the premises, which shall purport to convey the fee simple, and contain a general warranty or covenant of quiet possession, binding the defendant and his heirs, to be approved of by the Clerk.

PER CURIAM. Decree accordingly.

ANTHONY R. MARKHAM & AL. *vs.* ELIZABETH SHANNON-HOUSE & AL.

A. purchased at execution sale a tract of land belonging to B.; afterwards the same tract of land was levied upon and set up for sale under another execution against B. posterior in its lien. A. forbid the sale and then bid for the land and it was struck off to him. *Held,* that, in so doing, A. was guilty of no fraud upon B.

Cause removed from the Court of Equity of Pasquotank, County at the Fall Term, 1846.

The plaintiffs state that they are the children and heirs at law of Anthony Markham, and that a judgment was rendered at June Term, 1828, of Pasquotank County Court, and the land, the subject in controversy, sold under the execution issued thereon and purchased by Thomas L. Shannonhouse, the father of the defendants, who are his heirs at law. They charge that at the sale by the Sheriff, Thomas L. Shannonhouse was present and forbid the sale, alleging that the title of the land was in him. That the land was bid off by one Ambrose Knox, who was acting as the secret agent of said Shannonhouse, who immediately directed the sheriff to make the deed of the land to him, as he had bought it for him. The bill prays that the defendants may be compelled to re-convey the land, &c.

The defendants in their answer state that in the year 1825, one William C. Banks obtained a judgment, in the Court of Pleas and Quarter Sessions, against Demarcus Markham and Anthony R. Markham, the father of complainants, upon which an execution issued and was levied on the land in question, which was sold at the Court house door, and he became the purchaser, and took a deed therefor from the sheriff on the 7th day of December, 1825, and that under that deed he claimed the land as his.

A copy of the record of the suit of Banks against Demarcus Markham and Anthony R. Markham, and the sheriff's deed of December 1825, to Thomas L. Shannon-house are filed as exhibits in the case. The deed bears date as set forth in the answer and is proved and registered at March term, 1826, of Pasquotank Court of Pleas and Quarter Sessions.

No counsel for the plaintiffs.
A. Moore, for the defendants.

NASH, J. The bill sets forth that the land claimed by the plaintiff, and for the re-conveyance of which it is filed, is the land sold under Banks' execution. There is then no question as to the identity of the land. The only ground, upon which the plaintiffs seek a re-conveyance, is the fraud, it is alleged, perpetrated by Shannonhouse in forbidding the sale, at which he purchased. To this allegation of fraud the defendants reply, that the land, at the time of that sale, did actually belong to Thomas L. Shannonhouse and the exhibits prove it. The title being in him, he could perpetrate no fraud upon the plaintiffs by forbidding the sale and afterwards purchasing himself. The plaintiffs do not allege in their bill any fraud in the first sale, or that Thomas L. Shannonhouse held under any trust for their father Anthony Markham. That sale they do not impeach any farther than to allege, that Thomas L. Shannonhouse forbid the sale under a pretended title. The defendants have shown a title in their father, upon its face good and perfect. Under a different form of the bill, the facts alleged might become important. In the present case they are not. Thomas L. Shannonhouse had a right to forbid the sale of his own land and then to purchase, if he chose. In so doing he did no injury to the complainants, and committed no fraud upon them.

PER CURIAM.   Bill dismissed with costs.

PURVIS vs. BROWN.

A person, who had no title to property which he mortgaged, has no right to a decree for redemption.

A right to redeem property may be reserved to a stranger to the contract, but then it must be an express reservation.

Cause removed from the Court of Equity of Randolph County, at the Fall Term, 1846.

The facts on which this Court pronounced its decision are fully set forth in the opinion here delivered.

J. H. Bryan and *H. Waddell*, for the plaintiff.
Winston, for the defendant.

NASH, J. The bill is filed to redeem a negro named Travis, mortgaged, it is alleged, by Susan Purvis, one of the complainants, and William Purvis, her father, to the defendant. The case stated in the bill is as follows: The mother of the complainants was the daughter of John Lane, who, upon her intermarriage with William Purvis, their father, put into her possession a negro woman named Penny, who so remained up to the death of their mother and their grand-father, who died intestate. Penny is the mother of the boy Travis, born while in the possession of their mother and father. After the death of their grand-father, John Lane, a bill in equity was filed by his next of kin, to procure a division of his personal estate, and by a decree obtained thereon, the negroes Penny and Travis, were assigned to the plaintiffs. The bill then alleges, that William Purvis, their father, borrowed of the defendant Brown $100, and to secure the payment thereof, the negro Travis was mortgaged to the defendant by William Purvis, and that the plaintiff, Susan Purvis, joined in the mortgage. It then avers the tender of the money borrowed and the demand for the negro Travis, and the refusal of the defendant to receive the money or deliver up the boy. It prays a redemption of the negro, and a sequestration, &c.

From the view we have taken of the case, it is not necessary to say any thing further of the answer, than that it denies, that Travis was mortgaged, but alleges he was purchased by the defendant, and further, it denies, that the plaintiffs have any right to redeem the negro if he was mortgaged, as the title to him was in William Purvis, and not in them.

Among the exhibits filed in the cause, is the record of the suit in the Court of Equity for Randolph County, to which the plaintiffs refer in their bill. They were parties complainants. Upon the hearing of the cause, an account was decreed, and a reference made to the master to take an account of the estate of John Lane, sr. in the hands of his administrator, and make report thereof. The master made a report, and in it states that the negro woman Penny was an advancement to Sally Purvis, the mother of the plaintiff, by her father, John Lane. In ascertaining the distributive share of the children of Sally Purvis, who were parties plaintiffs, the master deducted from their share the sum of $821 68, the amount of the advancement made their mother: leaving the sum of $359 72, as the balance coming to them from their grand-father's estate. There was a decree for that sum, in their favor, in conformity with the report. It appears then, that the negro Penny was an advancement to Sally Purvis and became the property of William Purvis, her husband, who is still alive. The plaintiffs have failed to show any title to the negro Travis, and therefore have no right to the equity of redemption, claimed by them, if he was mortgaged to the defendant. We do not deny, that a right to redeem property may be reserved to a stranger to the contract, but then it must be an express reservation, which is not pretended here in favor of these plaintiffs. In truth, the bill is framed under an entire

different statement of facts, which is denied in the answer, and not proved, but contradicted by the proofs.

PER CURIAM.   Bill dismissed with costs.

———

WILLIAM MILTON & AL. vs. DAVID HOGUE & AL.

Where a bill is amended, and the amendment filed contains allegation
directly contrary to those made in the original bill, the Court can make no
decree, because they must look into all the pleadings and cannot act upon
such contradictory statements.

The proper way in such a case is strike out so much of the original bill as is
contradicted by the allegations in the amended bill.

Without a contract between the parties, the sale of the whole tract of land
and receipt of the price by one tenant in common, does not turn him into
a trustee for a co-tenant, as the latter still has the legal title to his own
share and can have redress on it at law.

Cause removed from the Court of Equity of Rutherford
County, at the Spring Term, 1846.

The plaintiffs filed an original bill against David
Hogue in September 1841, and therein charged, that
Stephen Hogue was seized in fee of a tract of land in
Rutherford, containing 100 acres, and devised the same
to his wife for life, with remainder over to his children
—of whom the plaintiff, Mrs. Milton, was one: That
the testator died and his widow entered into the premises,
and died in the year 1830; and that then the plaintiffs,
the defendant David Hogue, and the other children of the
testator, entered. The bill states that in 1832 a gold
mine of great value was discovered on the land; and

that it was then agreed between the plaintiffs and the defendant. David, (who alleged that he owned the shares of the other remaindermen) that they would not make partition of the land, but that instead thereof the defendant David should sell the whole of it, including the undivided share of the plaintiffs ; and that, in pursuance of that agreement, David Hogue, in a short time thereafter, sold the whole tract to William McGee for the price of $8500 paid to him.   The bill states, that the plaintiffs are entitled to one sixth part thereof; but that David hath heretofore paid them only $200, and for that took the notes of the plaintiff William ; he agreeing, however, that the same should be taken into account in settling for his wife's share of the purchase money.   The bill further states that David Hogue conveyed the land to McGee in his own name alone, as if he claimed the whole and were the sole owner; but that the same was done by the assent of the plaintiffs and that they were ready to convey to David Hogue or to McGee, a good title to their share, upon the receipt of their share of the purchase money. The prayer is, that David Hogue come to an account with the plaintiffs for their share of the purchase money and the interest thereon, and be decreed, after deducting the principal and interest of the notes for $200, to pay the plaintiffs what may be found due to them.

David Hogue answered, that Stephen Hogue did not make a will, but died intestate, seized of the tract of land mentioned in the bill and other land, and leaving a widow and nine children, of whom the defendant and the plaintiff Zilphia were two ; and that the tract containing 100 acres was allotted to the widow as dower and she occupied it until her death in 1830.

The answer denies that it was ever agreed between the plaintiffs and the defendant, that he should sell the land or any part of it for them or on their account, or divide the proceeds of the sale with them in any manner. On the contrary the defendant says that in 1831 (before the discovery of gold) the plaintiff sold to him the share of Zilphia in this and another tract of land, at the price of $500, and by a deed bearing date April 29th, 1831, conveyed the same to him. The deed is exhibited with the answer. and purports to be a bargain and sale made between the plaintiff William Melton and David Hogue, and, for the consideration of $500, to convey "his undivided share" of the two tracts of land in fee. It is, however, signed and sealed by the plaintiff Zilphia also ; but she has never acknowledged it on privy examination. The defendant admits, that, in the latter part of 1831, he discovered gold on the land and sold it to McGee for $8500 ; but he says he sold it as his own property and not as agent for the plaintiffs. and conveyed it, with warranty, in his own name. He denies any payment to the plaintiffs or either of them of any part of the purchase money, and says that the note he took from the plaintiff William was for the sum of $200, lent to him in 1840.

Upon the foregoing answer being put in, the plaintiffs obtained leave to amend their bill. They then filed an amended bill as it is called, against David Hogue, William McGee and John J. Price, in which they state, that Stephen Hogue did not devise the land in question, but that he died intestate, leaving "seven or eight children." to whom the land descended, and of whom one was named Delpha and that she died intestate and without issue : That partition was made of all the other land that descended, except the tract containing 100 acres, which was allotted to the widow for dower and was never divided. This bill then states, that the defendant David, having in 1831 or 1832, discovered a gold mine on the land, and having previously, as he alleged, purchased the shares of some of the other children, sold the 100 acre tract to the defendant McGee, for the sum of $8500, paid down ; and that McGee then entered and opened gold mines, and, by exhausting them, obtained $20,000 clear profit from them, and has destroyed the value of the land.

This bill farther alleges, that the plaintiffs never contracted for the sale of their share of the land, nor authorized a sale thereof; but that, after the sale had been made, they thought it a good one, and were willing to abide by it, and informed David Hogue that they would accede to the sale and confirm the title, if he would pay them their share of the purchase money, and he promised the plaintiffs that he would; but that he never paid any part of it until 1839 or 1840, and then he only paid the sum of $200, and took notes therefor as mentioned in the original bill.

This bill then states that in 1831, the plaintiffs contracted with David Hogue to sell him the share of the *feme* plaintiff in that part of the land, which descended from their father, which belonged to her as one of the heirs of their deceased sister Delpha, at the price of $15, which he paid then; and that afterwards he presented to them for execution a deed therefor, as he represented, and they, upon the faith of his representation and in the belief that it included the share so agreed to be sold and no more, executed without reading it; and they aver that the same was the only deed at any time made by them or either of them to David Hogue, and that the deed exhibited by the defendant with his former answer, is the one so executed by them. The bill charges that the deed was obtained from the plaintiffs under a mistake as to the contents of it, which was caused by the fraudulent contrivance and false representations of David Hogue, as before mentioned, and also in setting out therein as the consideration the sum of $500, whereas he only paid them $15 or thereabouts, and the plaintiffs never at any time intended or treated for a sale of their share in the gold mine tract.

The bill further charges that the land is now occupied by John I. Price, claiming under McGee. And the prayer is, as before, for a decree against David Hogue for a share of the purchase money, received from McGee, upon the plaintiff's executing proper assurances for the land, which they offer to do; or that the deed to David Hogue be declared to have been obtained by fraud and cancelled; or that the defendants Hogue, McGee, and Price, re-convey to the plaintiffs a share of the land, and account with them for the profits of the same.

David Hogue put in another answer, in which he denies positively that he ever promised to pay or account with the plaintiffs or either of them for any part of the purchase money received for the land, or had any treaty with them on the subject. He avers, that it is not true, that he contracted with the plaintiffs for a share of their deceased sister Delpha's land; but that he contracted with them for all the interest of the plaintiff Zilphia and of the plaintiff William, as her husband, in the lands which descended from their father and are described in the deed dated April 29th. 1831, and that the deed was rightly drawn according to the contract, both in respect of the land sold and the price; for he states, that he, the defendant, had made advances for the support of the family to a greater amount than $500, and was induced to take the land at that price, though more than its value, because it was all that he could get. The answer further states, as evidence that no fraud was practised on the plaintiffs, that the plaintiffs knew of the sale to McGee in 1832, and that the price was then paid, and that McGee was making large profits, and that the parties have lived near each other ever since, and the plaintiffs have been in needy circumstances, and yet that no demand was made or complaint in the premises, until the filing of the bill in 1841.

McGee put in no answer, having left the State; and the answer of Price states nothing of importance.

The material evidence is that of the person, who wrote and attested the deed. He was examined in September 1844, and says, that he understood that the deed was made for the undivided portion of Zilphia in the lands,

which fell into possession upon the death of her father,
and that he did not think the gold mine tract was included. He did not, however, hear either of the parties
say so, but he understood it from another person, who
was present when he wrote the deed, and who married
one of the daughters of Stephen Hogue and produced the
deeds, from which the boundaries in this deed were taken. The witness is unable to remember, whether the
parties read the deed or whether it was read to them, or
not, before it was executed; but he thinks he never wrote
and witnessed a deed unless he knew the parties were
acquainted with the contents. He states that the parties
were all present when he wrote the deed, and that he
perceived nothing unfair in the conduct of David Hogue;
and that he was at the time in possession of the gold
mine tract.

Several witnesses prove that the plaintiffs have always
been in straitened circumstances and lived in the same
neighborhood with the defendant, David. Other witnesses prove, that, pending this suit, David Hogue said,
that his sister, Mrs. Milton, had a claim on him, and that
he loved her and would pay her $500, and others say,
that he said he had offered to give William Milton $750
to compromise the controversy.

Bynum and *Guion*, for the plaintiffs.
Alexander and *J. H. Bryan*, for the defendants.

RUFFIN, C. J. The plaintiffs have entirely failed to
establish those parts of their case, which depend on an
agreement of David Hogue to sell their share of the
land for them with his own, or an agreement after the
sale, that they should confirm it by a conveyance of their
share, and thereupon receive a due proportion of the purchase money. The answer directly denies any such
agreements, and the plaintiffs have not given any evidence of either. If there had been evidence upon either

of those heads, the Court would have been at much loss, upon these pleadings, how to give the plaintiffs the benefit of it. The bill, as at first framed, states a title in the plaintiffs under a devise from the former owner, Stephen Hogue, and then an authority from them by parol to David Hogue, to sell their share, and an agreement on his part to do so on their behalf. Afterwards upon leave to amend their bill, the plaintiffs, without striking out those allegations, allege as new matter, that Stephen Hogue did not devise the land, but that it descended from him to them, and that they did not authorize David Hogue to sell their share, but that he sold it without their consent or knowledge, though they were willing, after the sale was made, to abide by it, because the price was a good one, provided they got their share of the price. It seems not to have been considered, that the bill was thus rendered contradictory in its state of events, or not remembered that the party is bound by every part of his pleadings, and that the Court can no more decree for him against the allegations in one part of them than those in another. In such a case an amendment must be made by striking out the portions in which a mistake has been made, and then adding the allegations according to the truth, as the party means to make it appear. Instead of the pleadings being amended by such means as those here used, they are perplexed and rendered absurd by containing contradictory allegations from the same party. It is true there is no harm done here, because the defendant agrees, that he did not act upon an authority from the plaintiffs ; and they have offered no evidence that they came to an agreement, after the sale, that the plaintiffs should have a part of the price got for the land.

The case therefore turns entirely upon the part of the bill, which seeks to set aside the deed to David Hogue, upon the ground that it was obtained from the plaintiffs by fraud or surprise, being for different or more land than that contracted for.   The first observation upon this point is, that the interests of Mrs. Milton are not all involved in it; for the instrument has no operation as to her, as upon its face it is an indenture between her husband and brother alone, and, even if that were otherwise, it would still be void as to her, for want of execution in the manner necessary to give efficacy to the deed of a married woman.   In due time, therefore, she will have her remedy at law upon her legal title by ejectment and partition; and she has no ground for relief here.   For, without a contract between the parties, the sale of the whole tract of land and receipt of the price by one tenant in common, does not turn him into a trustee for a co-tenant; as the latter still has the legal title to his own share and can have redress on it at law.   It is not like a sale by one, of the personal property of another, in which case the owner may waive the tort and treat it as a sale made for him, and recover the price as money had and received to his use; because the property passes by parol.   But it is otherwise in respect to land: for that can pass only by deed, and the purchaser may refuse to accept it.

Then, in regard to the deed, as the deed of the husband alone, the question is, whether a sufficient ground is laid for holding it to have been obtained by fraud or surprise.

There is no doubt, that there was a mistake in it in one respect; which was in drawing it as the deed of the husband alone " for his undivided share" of the two tracts of land described in it.   For it was the intention that the husband and wife should unite in conveying both his right as tenant by the curtesy, and also her right to the inheritance in some land.   But that mistake is one, which is not to the prejudice of the plaintiff and of which he does not complain.   The ground of surprise on him he alleges in the bill to be, that he and his wife agreed to sell to David Hogue other land, namely, the share of the wife in the lands that had been allotted to her deceased sister Delpha, as her part of her father's estate. That lot did not, according to the bill, include any part of the gold mine tract; for the bill alleges, first, that partition had not been made of that tract, and consequently no part of it had been assigned in severalty to Delpha: and, secondly, that partition had been made of all the lands descended, except the 100 acres, which is the subject of this controversy, and consequently Delpha's share of the other lands was held by her in severalty. The subject of the sale to David Hogue was, therefore, according to the bill, Mrs. Milton's undivided share of the land, that had been allotted in severalty to Delpha Hogue in a division of a part of the land descended from the father—which part included all the land descended, excepting only the 100 acres held by the widow as dower, and on which gold was afterwards found. Now, that statement the answer distinctly and positively denies; and it states that the defendant purchased all the interests which Milton and his wife then had in any of the lands, which had descended from the father. Stephen Hogue, including the 100 acres, whether the interest was derived by her directly from the father as one of his heirs, or through Delpha as one of her heirs. Between the parties thus at issue, the Court is obliged to decide on the greater credit due to the sworn answer of the defendant, unless it be overborne by the evidence to the contrary of indifferent witnesses. But there is not such evidence in this case. There is but one witness who says any thing material on the subject, namely, the writer and witness to the deed; and his testimony is very unsatisfactory. To say nothing of the distant period from the transaction at which he gave his testimony, it is obvious that his means of information, as to the subject of the contract, were very imperfect, and that, in truth, according to both the bill and answers, his statement of it, even as far as it goes, is quite erroneous. He was not present at the bargain, and did not hear the terms, nor the subject of it described by the parties or either of them; but learnt all he knows from a third person, who, he says, furnished him with the title papers in order to get the boundaries of the land for which the deed was to be written, and yet told him that no part of one of the tracts, therein conveyed, had been sold. He, however, does say distinctly, that he did not understand the gold mine tract was to be included, but understood from that person, that it was not to be. Let us see, then, what, according to his understanding, was to be conveyed. He does not mention *Delpha* at all, nor allude to her share. He says, he understood that the deed was to be for "the undivided portion of *Zilphia* (the plaintiff) in the lands which fell into possession on the death of her father." He obviously means thereby all the land descended from the father, except the 100 acres which was assigned to the widow as dower, and therefore was not considered as having fallen into possession immediately after the father's death. Now, undoubtedly, the witness is entirely mistaken in this part of his evidence: for of the land, that fell into possession at the death of the father, there was, at that time, none undivided. The bill itself states, that all the land descended had been divided, except the widow's dower. Consequently, the plaintiff Zilphia had then no "undivided portion" in the lands of the father, except in the gold mine tract. All this goes to shew, that the witness had no accurate knowledge on the subject of the contract— much less that he could give such a statement of it as would repel the credit due to the answer, and the presumption from the execution of the deed itself, that it correctly sets forth the subject of the sale. That presumption is much fortified by the just inference from the silence of the plaintiffs, under much necessity, for so long a period (upwards of nine years,) with respect to the rights and grievances set forth in this bill.   No regard can be paid to the offers of compromise, upon the principle of the law of evidence which excludes them.   But, besides, there was a plain motive for the offers of the defendant, independent of an acknowledgement of any of the wrongs to the plaintiffs alleged in the suit: which was to obtain a proper deed for the inheritance belonging to the plaintiff Zilphia, as some day it may be very important to him to have that title.   The Court must therefore declare, that the plaintiffs have not established, that the deed in question was obtained by the defendant by fraud or surprise, or that it conveys any land which the parties thereto did not intend at the time should be conveyed.

PER CURIAM.   The bill dismissed with costs.

☞ At the session of the General Assembly in 1846–'47, EDWARD STANLY, Esquire, was elected ATTORNEY GENERAL, in the place of SPIER WHITAKER, Esquire, whose term of office had expired, and was thereupon commissioned by the Governor.

EQUITY CASES

ARGUED AND DETERMINED IN

THE SUPREME COURT

OF

NORTH CAROLINA.

———

JUNE TERM, 1847.

———

JAMES E. KEA vs. JOHN A. ROBESON, Ex'r. &c.

A notice to take a number of depositions, on the 1st, 2d, 3rd, 4th, 5th, 6th, 7th, 8th, 9th and 10th, of a particular month, does not, of itself, furnish a ground for suppressing the depositions.

Where, under this notice, the plaintiff took twenty-six depositions on the 1st and 2nd of that month, and the only one of the defendants, who complained, was present on those days, there can be no reason whatever fo suppressing those depositions on the ground of the indefiniteness of the notice.

Appeal from an interlocutory order, made in the Court of Equity of Bladen County, at the Fall Term 1846, his Honor Judge Settle, presiding.

This is an appeal from an order suppressing depositions in a suit in Bladen Court of Equity, against John A. Robeson and several other defendants. The plaintiff gave the defendants notice, that he would take the depositions of Joseph M. Gillespie and many other persons therein named at L. MacLeod's store in Bladen on the 1st, 2nd, 3rd, 4th, 5th, 6th, 7th, 8th, 9th, and 10th, days of June, 1846. On the 1st and 2nd days of June the plaintiff took depositions, to the number of twenty-six, before the Clerk and Master at the place mentioned. One of the defendants was an infant, and one James Robeson was his guardian *ad litem ;* and he resided about thirty miles from MacLeod's and did not attend. Josiah Maultsby, another defendant, resided about twenty miles off, and did not attend on the 1st, but did on the 2nd day of June. The defendant John A. Robeson resided two miles from MacLeod's, and was present at the taking of all the depositions.

When the Master was passing on the depositions in the cause, the defendants objected to those twenty-six upon the ground of the number of days specified in the notice. But the Master allowed them to be read ; and the defendant, John A. Robeson, appealed to the Court. The Master then reported the facts ; and upon his report the Court reversed the Master's decision and suppressed those depositions, but allowed the plaintiff an appeal to this Court.

Strange, for the plaintiff.
Badger, and *Warren Winslow*, for the defendants.

RUFFIN, C. J. The Court is of opinion, that the depositions ought not to have been suppressed. It is true, that, under the notice, it might be possible for the plaintiff to impose on the defendants the necessity of an inconvenient detention, or practise a surprise on them, as by not obtaining the attendance of the witnesses or not proceeding to examine them, until the term of nine days, embraced in the notice, was near expiring, or when the opposite parties happened not to be present. It need not be said, if such appeared to have been the course of the plaintiff, or if there were any just grounds for suspecting that he intended such abuses, this Court would at once concur with his Honor. But we do not perceive any such ground of suspicion. The number of witnesses was considerable, and it could not easily be anticipated how long it might require, under prolix cross-examinations, to take the depositions, or that some of the witnesses might not be able to attend on the earlier of the days. It would have been quite proper for the plaintiff, as is common, to have given the notice, that he would take the depositions on a particular day, and from day to day thereafter, until completed. As acted on, this was in substance a notice of that kind, and was intended so to be, as far as we can see. For the plaintiff collected his witnesses on the first day and proceeded immediately to examine them to the large number of twenty-six; thus shewing an intention to take his evidence in good faith and without imposing any unnecessary or avoidable inconvenience on the defendants. The objection could not, therefore, have been sustained, if it had been taken by a defendant, who was not present at the taking of the depositions. But neither the infant defendant, nor Maultsby, complained of the Master's order, and the appeal, therefore, was taken by John A. Robeson alone, who lived within two miles of the place of taking the depositions, and was present during the whole time of taking them. The pleadings are not before us on the present appeal, and we are not informed of any interest of that defendant in the attendance of the others, which can give him a right to insist on an error against them, which they think proper to acquiesce in. At all events, then, it was erroneous to reverse the decision of the Master at the instance of that defendant by himself.

Braddy v. Parker.

The opinion of the Court, therefore, is, that the order of his Honor must be reversed, and that of the Master, allowing the depositions to be read, affirmed, with costs in this Court.

PER CURIAM.   Ordered accordingly.

SOLOMON T. BRADY, ADM'R, vs. HARDY PARKER & AL.

Wherever a written contract contains, by mistake, less than the parties intended, or more, and the mistake is clearly established, a Court of Equity will reform it, so as to make it conform to the precise intentions of the parties.

The case of *Harrison* v. *Howard*, 1 Ired. Eq. 409, cited and approved.

Cause transferred to the Supreme Court by consent, from the Court of Equity of Edgecomb County.

The facts of the case are stated in the Opinion delivered in this Court.

B. F. Moore, for the plaintiff.
Mordecai, for the defendants.

NASH, J. We presume this case has been brought here, for the purpose of obtaining a decree, which, being made in the highest Judicial tribunal, known to the law, will quiet all disputes for the future, as to the title to the negroes in question. There can be no doubt, that the plaintiff is entitled to the relief he seeks. All the facts are admitted, and are as follows: In the year 1830, Solomon T. Braddy purchased from Kader Parker a negro girl, named Phillis, at the price of fifty pounds, and, a short time thereafter, re-sold her to Kader Parker. the latter paying him the sum of £18 3, in part of the purchase money. Before the balance remaining due was paid, Parker died, leaving a widow and several children, among whom was the wife of Solomon Braddy and to whom he was married before he purchased the negro Phillis. The defendant, Hardy Parker, administered on the estate of Kader Parker, and refused to complete the bargain made by his intestate, with the intestate Solomon Braddy. At the sale, made by the administrator, Hardy Parker, the widow was a large purchaser, and it was agreed by all the parties concerned, that she should pay to Solomon Braddy, what remained due of the purchase money of Phillis, out of what she owed the estate, upon condition, that she should retain the negro during her life. Accordingly. she did so make payment to Solomon Braddy and took the girl into her possession, and so kept her until her death in the year ——. Upon the payment of the money by the widow. the intestate Braddy, made the conveyance, set forth in the bill, by which he conveyed Phillis and her children, "to the heirs and claimants" of Hardy Parker; and the bill charges expressly, that the said conveyance was intended, to complete the bargain made by Braddy with Kader Parker and vest the title of the negroes in those who were entitled as his distributors. Solomon Braddy and his wife are both dead and the plaintiff has administered on their estates. These facts are admitted, but the defendants say, that, at law, the title of the negroes in controversy is conveyed to them, and that Solomon Braddy is not entitled to any of them. Certainly the legal title is in the defendants, and it is equally certain, that it was not intended by the parties to be so, to the exclusion of Elizabeth Braddy, the wife of the intestate. It could not have been the intention of Solomon Braddy to exclude his wife or himself from a due share of Phillis and her children ; for in re-selling her to Kader Parker, he merely got back the money he had paid for her. Such could not have been his intention, and the defendants themselves admit, that the intention was to re-invest the estate with the negroes, as if no sale from Parker ever had been made; and finally it is manifest, from the deed of conveyance, that such was not the intention of the parties. In the recital of the deed is contained a brief statement of the inducement for making it. In the conveying part, after conveying Phillis and her children to the widow and the heirs and claimants of said deceased, it proceeds, " as fully, clearly, amply, as if no contract had ever been made, or bill of sale given by the said deceased." It is very clear, then, that it was the intention of the parties to place Phillis and her children, precisely as she would have been, if Kader Parker had died leaving a clear title to them. Wherever a written contract contains, by mistake, less than the parties intended, or more, and the mistake is clearly established, a Court of Equity will reform it, so as to make it conform to the precise intention of the parties. *Durant* v. *Durant*, 1 Cox R. 58. *Calverly* v. *Williams*, 1st Vez. Id. 210. *Harrison* v. *Howard*, 1st Ired. Eq. 409. The plaintiff is entitled to have said deed reformed, in accordance with the true intent of the parties, and, as his wife, Elizabeth survived her father, Kader Parker, she was entitled, as one of his next of kin, to a distributive share in the negro Phillis and her children. This was a vested interest and upon her death passed to her personal representative, who held it in trust for her husband, Solomon Braddy. And the plaintiff is entitled, as the representative of Solomon Braddy, to partition of the said negroes.

PER CURIAM.   Decreed accordingly.

MARY R. SMITH *vs.* JOSIAH TURNER & AL.

A Court of Equity does not like to entertain bills to perpetuate testimony, except in cases of plain necessity.

If the object of a bill is to perpetuate the testimony of witnesses to a deed respecting lands, the deed must be properly described, and the names of the witnesses, who are to prove it, be set forth, and also the facts, to which they are to give evidence, be specially stated.

Such a bill must shew the interest of the plaintiff in the subject, and, in stating it, should, though succinctly, set it forth plainly and with convenient certainty as to the material facts, so that, on the bill itself, some certain interest in the plaintiff shall appear; which, indeed, is sufficient, however minute the interest may be.

In a bill of this kind a Court of Equity only assists a Court of law by preserving testimony, where the plaintiff's right is purely a legal one.

But a Court of Equity will not entertain a bill to perpetuate testimony, touching a subject of its own jurisdiction, because the party can always, though in possession, file a bill for relief, and the Court can, in its discretion, make the proper orders upon an emergency, for speeding the taking of the testimony of old, infirm, or removing witnesses.

Appeal from an interlocutory order of the Court of Equity of Orange County, at the Fall Term, 1846, his Honor Judge BATTLE presiding.

The bill states, "that, by deed bearing date the 10th day of December, 1840, J. S. Smith, the father of the plaintiff, did convey and assign to her, the plaintiff, in remainder, certain lands lying on Price's creek in Orange county, which will more fully appear, reference being had to the said deed, registered in book D, page 396, in the Register's office of Orange; that the land designated in said deed, as the Price's creek tract, was once owned by Francis Jones, the grand-father of the plaintiff; and that, by deed bearing date March 19th, 1819, Francis Jones conveyed to J. S. Smith, his son in-law, the said tract; that by the said deed, bearing date the 19th day of January, 1825, the said Francis Jones conveyed to J. S. Smith other lands, called the Park's Neck lands, for the sum of $7,000, and also, upon an express agreement between the said parties, that the said Smith should re-convey to the said Francis Jones the lands on Price's creek; that, as she is informed, and believes, a deed was accordingly executed by her father to the said Francis Jones for the said lands, bearing even date with that made by Francis Jones to him for the Park's Neck lands, to-wit. the 19th of January, 1825; that this deed, as ex-ecuted. was delivered to the said Jones, and was seen at the time of delivery or afterwards, by sundry persons, some of whom are advanced in years, others have left the State, and recently departed this life; that the said deed remained in possession of Francis Jones many years, but, as your oratrix is informed and believes, was taken from his possession by Ruffin Jones, his only son, and was by him destroyed; and that the said Ruffin Jones died many years since.

"Further complaining your oratrix shews, that her said grand-father Jones avowed his intention, after his reception of said deed, of giving said lands on Price's creek to your oratrix at his death; and she further shews, that in accordance with that purpose. which was fre-quently declared, he made and published his last will in writing in the year 1840, in and by which, among other things, he did devise to your oratrix the said lands, di-recting his executor in what manner his said purpose should be carried into effect; that some months after the publication of the said will, and in the life-time of the said Francis Jones, her father, not only in obedience to the direction and devise in said will contained, but also in compliance with a promise long before made by him to the said Jones, did convey by deed, lands on Price's creek, in remainder to your oratrix, reserving life estates therein, as well to himself as to his wife, the mother of your oratrix: all of which will appear by reference to the said deed, registered in book D, as heretofore stated; that your oratrix accepted the said deed at the time of its execution, and because, as she is advised, entitled absolutely to a vested remainder in said lands; that in the year 1844, her grand-father Jones departed this life, leaving his said will unaltered and unrevoked, and that said will was admitted to probate at May Sessions of Orange Court of Pleas and Quarter Sessions 1844, and her father, J. S. Smith, the executor therein named, was qualified as such (a certified copy of which she hath ready to produce when required by the Court,) and took upon himself the burden of executing the same; that on the 21st day of November, 1845, she purchased of her said father his life estate in the Price's creek lands, at and for the price of $1,000, and he executed and delivered to her a deed for the said lands, bearing date on that day, which will more fully appear by reference to the same as registered in book D, page 398, in the Register's office of Orange. Your oratrix shews that she has become the owner in remainder, of the said land on Price's creek, and also of the life estate of her father in the same, and is in possession of said land under and by virtue of the said several conveyances, subject, nevertheless, to the life estate of her mother in the event of her surviving the father of your oratrix; and your oratrix had well hoped that she would have enjoyed her said estates quietly, and without interruption or doubt as to her titles to the same."

The bill then states, that the defendant, Turner, " although her deed had been registered as aforesaid, and thus he had notice of her said title," yet had an execution against Turner and J. S. Smith levied on said lands as the property of J. S. Smith, and at a sale by the sheriff he, Turner, became the purchaser, and had received or would receive the sheriff's deed therefor."

The bill then proceeds, " that she, being thus in possession of said lands, has no means of having her title to said lands established, and that, as the witnesses to the existence of the deed from Dr. J. S. Smith to Francis

Jones, re-conveying the lands in question, are some of them advanced in years. and others have left the State, and that one of them in particular hath recently died, and that said deed is lost or destroyed, she hath good reason to fear that, hereafter, in the event of the death of the said witnesses, it would be impossible to establish her title to the said lands : that from the course taken by the said Turner, she doth believe that, perhaps at some distant day, he means to institute proceedings in regard to these lands, which may be injurious to her, if the testimony of the said witnesses cannot now be perpetuated, the more especially as she has no means of trying the question of title by any act of hers, and there is no reasonable probability that there will be any immediate action by others to try the said question ; that she is informed that the said Turner hath charged that your oratrix hath no good title to the said lands ; that no deed was ever made by the said Dr. J. S. Smith to Francis Jones, re-conveying the said lands, and that the said lands therefore were not the property of the said Jones or conveyed by his will to your oratrix." The prayer is, "that your oratrix may be at liberty to examine her said witnesses, touching said deed, lost or destroyed as aforesaid, and touching her title to the said lands in every particular, so that their testimony may be perpetuated and preserved ;" and for process of subpœna commanding Turner to appear and answer, "and to stand to, abide by, and perform such decree as to your Honor may seem meet."

The defendant answered, and admits that he purchased the same land under an execution against J. S. Smith, which the plaintiff claims, and that he meant to contest her title, and states that he had already commenced an action of ejectment against her. The answer takes several objections to the bill for certain imputed defects, in not being supported by any affidavit, and in having a prayer for relief, and in various other particulars.

At the first term, the Court of Equity "on the motion of the plaintiff, ordered that the complainant have leave to examine witnesses and take testimony as prayed in the bill without prejudice, and that the Clerk and Master issue Commissions accordingly." Upon an affidavit of the plaintiff, that two persons, M. S. and C. Y. were, the one about to leave the State, and the other confined by sickness, the Court further ordered, that the depositions of those two persons might be taken on three days notice. From those orders the defendant appealed.

Norwood, Waddell, and *W. H. Haywood,* for the plaintiff. *J. H. Bryan,* for the defendant.

RUFFIN, C. J. The primary object of the bill appears to be, and we are told at the bar that the sole object of it is, to perpetuate the testimony of witnesses. It is a kind of bill that is not of frequent occurrence and, indeed, one that the Court of Equity does not, for very good reasons, like to entertain except in cases of plain necessity. *Angel* v. *Angel,* 1 Sim. & Stu. 83. It so seldom occurs in practice. that the profession is probably not familiar with it. Yet the jurisdiction is well settled, and the cases in which such bills will lie, and the proper form of the bill and of the orders on it, are clearly enough stated in the books. The frame of the bill before us is, however, thoroughly defective. In the first place every bill should describe a subject of controversy so as to identify it. This is absolutely necessary in order to enable the Court to decree on the rights of the parties to the thing, or, in this proceeding, to direct the interrogatories or specify the matter to which the witnesses are to be examined. Now, all we learn of the subject of this dispute is, that it is, " certain lands lying on Price's Creek in Orange County," without any further description. It is true, that the bill says that those lands were conveyed by J. S. Smith to the plaintiff in remainder, by a deed dated, December 10th, 1841, and registered in Orange in a certain book. But that is not a description of the land upon this record, but only a reference to another paper as evidence of the plaintiff's title; and it would be impossible, without bringing into the cause that deed—a thing not in the contemplation of a mere bill *in perpetuum rei memoriam*—to make an order as to the subject touching which the witnesses should be examined. Look upon the order that was made, and see how indefinite, and necessarily indefinite, it is; being, that the plaintiff " may examine witnesses and take testimony as prayed for in the bill," and the prayer is for the examination of witnesses at large, "touching her title to said lands in every particular," as well as touching a deed, alleged to be lost. We suppose, however, that it was mainly the object to establish the execution, existence and validity of a deed for certain lands from J. S. Smith to F. Jones; about which the allegation is, that it was seen "by sundry persons," and that Turner denies that such a deed was ever made. But it is laid down, that, if the object of the bill is to perpetuate the testimony of witnesses to a deed respecting land, the deed must be properly described and the names of the witnesses, who are to prove it, be set forth; and also the facts to which they are to give evidence be specially stated. *Mason* v. *Goodburn,* Finch's Rep. 391. *Knight* v. *Knight,* 4 Madd. Rep. 8. In each of those particulars the bill is defective. This kind of bill, too, like every other, must shew the interest of the plaintiff in the subject. *Mitf. Pl.* 51. And in stating the plaintiff's title, the bill should, though succinctly, set it forth plainly and with convenient certainty as to the material facts—so that on the bill itself some certain interest in the plaintiff shall appear; which, indeed, is sufficient, however minute the interest may be. In applying this rule to a bill to perpetuate evidence in regard to a title to a tract of land, which stated only that on a certain day A. executed a deed to the plaintiff, whereby the land was conveyed to the plaintiff, and that thereupon the plaintiff executed to A. a lease of the premises during his life, it was held that it was fatally defective, both as to the matter and the manner of treating the plaintiff's title, because it did not set out the contents of the deed nor state what species of estate or quantity of interest was granted. *Jerome* v. *Jerome*, 5 Conn. Rep. 352. Now, the bill here omits every thing of that sort as respects the deed from J. S. Smith to F. Jones—not stating whether it conveyed a present or future interest, or a fee, or life estate, or term for years. We cannot tell, whether any thing could now be claimed under that deed, if it ever existed. The same observation extends to the manner of setting forth all the other title papers. The bill begins by stating that J. S. Smith, by a deed dated December 10th, 1841, conveyed to the plaintiff the premises " in remainder ;" but after what particular estate, or what the interest in remainder was, whether in fee, for life, or otherwise, contingent, or absolute, we are not told. In subsequently stating the will of the grand-father, the same vagueness is displayed, and even more. It sets out, that the land was devised thereby to the plaintiff ; and, if it had stopped there, perhaps it might be taken to be a devise in fee, under our Statute. But it goes on to state, that the testator therein " directed his executor in what manner his said purpose should be carried into effect, without setting out that part of the will *hæc verba*, or as much as mentioning the manner in which the purpose was to be effected : which, we suppose, must mean, the manner in which the estate in the land should be passed to or vested in the plaintiff. Something of that sort was indispensably necessary in the bill to make it intelligible ; for the executor, *virtute officii*, would have nothing to do with the conveyance of land to a person, to whom the testator devised it, and could only have a power, touching the land, specially conferred by the will ; and that does not appear here.

But a more important objection to the bill, arises from the manner in which the plaintiff states her title, from which it follows, that the question, touching which she prays to perpetuate testimony, or, rather, the only question which is specifically stated, is one, that can never arise in a Court of law, and therefore the Court will not perpetuate evidence to it. This is one of that kind of bills, on which the Court of Equity does not decide on rights, but assists a Court of Law in doing so, by preserving evidence. *Mitf. Pl.* 148. The Court will not do a useless thing. As if a bill be to perpetuate evidence against a tenant in tail, who may immediately bar the estate, the Court will make no order, inasmuch as it would be fruitless. *Dursby* v. *Fitzhardinge,* 6 Ves. 260. So, if this plaintiff can never set up the title, stated in her bill, as a legal title, on which she can defend her possession, it is in vain to perpetuate the evidence. For, if her redress upon that title, must be in a Court of Equity at last, then her proper course is to file a bill for relief at once, and not a bill of this kind. The Court of Equity will not entertain a bill *in perpetuam rei memoriam,* touching a subject of its own jurisdiction, because the party can always, though in possession, file a bill for relief, and the Court can, in its discretion, make the proper orders upon an emergency for speeding the taking the testimony of old, infirm or removing witnesses; which, indeed is, in this State, specially provided for by statute. *Rev. St.* c. 32, *s.* 4. Now, it is very plain that the plaintiff cannot assert the title, which she sets up under Francis Jones, at law, and that it is material to her to rely on that title. She states, indeed, that J. S. Smith became seised of the land under a conveyance from Jones, and that by two deeds from Smith she has the legal title for the life of her father, upon a purchase for $1,000, and for the remainder after the deaths of her father and mother. But this latter conveyance would not be good as against the father's creditors, because it was upon no consideration, moving from the plaintiff, unless she can connect herself with the title Jones derived by the deed, alleged to have been made to him by J. S. Smith and to have been lost. That she does through the devise by Jones to herself—supposing that to be sufficiently stated in the bill. But, as appearing in the bill, it will not support the deed from her father to the plaintiff, because that deed could not have been made to the plaintiff as the devisee of Jones, since it was executed before the death of Jones. If it be said, the bill states, that the conveyance was made in compliance with a promise of Smith to Jones, the answer is, that, whether the interest of Jones be regarded as legal or equitable in its nature, it could not be passed by even an express act by parol, much less by implication in the manner charged. Therefore the plaintiff is obliged to resort to her grand-father's will to sustain her title. But after she shall have done so, she still cannot shew a good title in a Court of Law, because the deed to Jones was not registered, as far as appears, and therefore could not be given in evidence at law. It is very singular, upon the statements in the bill, that, upon the loss of that deed, a new one had not been executed from J. S. Smith to Jones. However, Jones had a clear right to call for another deed in this Court and it would have been decreed to him. *Tolor* v. *Tolor,* 1 Dev. Eq. 456. *Plummer* v. *Baskerville,* 1 Ired. Eq. 252. In like manner the plaintiff, as his devisee, can call for a conveyance from her father, or from the present defendant, as having succeeded to the legal title, that rested in the father, in consequence of the loss of his deed to the grand-father before registration. If, in fact, J. S. Smith made the deed to Jones *bona fide,* and for the consideration alleged in the bill, and Jones did devise the land to the plaintiff in possession, or in remainder in fee, after the death of her father and mother, (as we suppose it was intended to be charged,) her title to relief here will be clear; and so far as her right is derived from the grand-father, that is the only mode in which she can assert it.

It is plain, therefore, that in no point of view, and to no extent, is this bill sufficient to entitle the plaintiff to the assistance of the Court, if it had been demurred to. That would have been the most correct course; for no discovery was sought from the defendant, and there was no occasion for an answer. But the mere circumstance, that the defendant put in a needless answer, not called for, but not admitting any part of the plaintiff's title, nor any fact on which she grounds her claim on the Court for aid, cannot dispense with a statement of some case in the bill, apparently proper for the interposition of the Court, or cure a bill so radically deficient as the present both in form and substance. And, finally, the Court is of opinion, that the orders appealed from were erroneous and ought to be reversed, and of course if any commissions issued thereon, they ought to be called in and cancelled, so as in effect to suppress the depositions, if any have been taken. The appellant is entitled to his costs in this Court.

PER CURIAM.   Decreed accordingly.

An inquisition of lunacy, if properly taken, is, when offered in evidence, but presumptive proof against persons not parties or privies.

If not a lunatic, yet equity will grant the plaintiff relief, if his mind was so weak, that he was unable to guard himself against imposition, or to resist importunity, or the use of undue influence, if he has been imposed upon by either of these means.

Mere weakness will not be sufficient.

Where there is a legal capacity, there cannot be an equitable incapacity, apart from fraud.

Cause transmitted by consent from the Court of Equity of Orange County, at the Spring Term 1847.

The bill charges, that the defendant is a very old man, and his mind, very feeble ; so much so, as to subject him to the influence and control of any person, in whom he had confidence ; that the defendant expressed great commiseration for his situation, and particularly, as regarded a sale he had made of a negro girl, named Milly, and offered his services to get her back for the plaintiff; that, accordingly, by threatening the purchaser with a suit, he induced him to return Milly to the plaintiff, and then availing himself of the influence he had over him, he prevailed on him to sell Milly to him for $175, for which he gave his note, payable on demand, without interest, and that he gave the former purchaser $25 to reconvey the negro, and that Milly was about ten years of age and worth $400. The bill further states, that the family of the plaintiff, becoming uneasy, applied to the County Court of Orange to have a guardian appointed for him, and, a commission of lunacy being ordered, the jury found that he was a lunatic and the Court appointed John Roney his guardian, who instituted this suit.

The bill prays for a reconveyance of the negro Milly. The defendant admits the purchase, by him, of the girl

Milly, from the plaintiff, and states that he gave for her not $175, as alleged, but $215, which was her full value. He admits, the plaintiff was an aged man and infirm, but denies he was a lunatic at the time of the sale, or at any other, and avers that, at the time he executed the bill of sale, he was entirely of sound mind and capable of transacting ordinary business ; that the plaintiff has been declared by a jury of the County a lunatic, but that was after his purchase. He denies that he ever exercised or attempted to exercise any undue influence over the plaintiff, who was his Uncle, and for whom he entertained a deep regard ; that he purchased Milly at the instance and by the request of the plaintiff.

Replication is taken to the answer and the parties have produced much testimony on both sides.

Mebane and *Norwood*, for the plaintiff.
E. G. Reade, for the defendant.

NASH, J. The bill claims the interference of this Court upon two grounds : first, that, at the time of the sale of the negro Milly to the defendant, the plaintiff was a lunatic ; and secondly, if not a lunatic, his mind was so weak, as to disqualify him from making a valid contract, and that the defendant obtained the conveyance from him by the exercise of an undue influence, and an inadequate price.

We are of opinion that the plaintiff has failed in establishing either proposition. It is true, a jury of inquest have, by their verdict, returned to May Term 1845, of Orange County Court, declared that he was at that time, " incapable of managing his affairs from want of understanding or mental capacity." The bill of sale for Milly to the defendant bears date the 8th of April 1844 ; thirteen months before. But the inquest does not say how far back his want of capacity extended, and is confined to the time at which it speaks. An inquisition of lunacy, however, if properly taken is, when offered in evidence, but presumptive proof against persons not parties or privies. The evidence taken in the cause, so far from showing that he was a lunatic, establishes fully that he was not. Although, however, the plaintiff be not a lunatic or insane, yet, if his mind was so weak, that he was unable to guard himself against imposition, or to resist importunity, or the use of undue influence, equity will grant him the relief he seeks, provided it be shown that he has been imposed upon by the use of either of the means enumerated. Mere weakness, however, will not be sufficient. A Court of Equity can not measure the understandings or capacities of individuals. Where there is a legal capacity, there cannot be an equitable incapacity, apart from fraud. 1 *Fonbl. Eq. B.* 1, *M.* 2, *S.* 3. If he be of sane mind, he has a right to dispose of his property, and his will stands in place of a reason, provided the contract or act justify the conclusion, that he has exercised a deliberate judgment such as it is, and has not been circumvented, or imposed on by cunning, artifice, or undue influence, means abhorrent to equity, and constituting fraud. Let us bring this case to the test of these principles. The testimony shows that the plaintiff was at all times a man of weak mind, but also that he was legally competent to make a contract. Do the circumstances evidence that he was imposed on by the plaintiff, or that he was circumvented by cunning or artifice, or that he was induced to make the contract by any undue influence of the defendant. We think not. The plaintiff had sold the negro girl Milly to a man by the name of Freeland, and he told Thomas Hodge, a witness for the plaintiff, that his reason was, that he was indebted, occasioned by his manager George, one of his negroes, in clearing too much land, and running too often to the Smith's shop; that Milly was a mulatto, and that he hated mulattoes, and would sell Milly if he did not get $25 for her; much or little, he would keep her no longer, she "should go." The deposition of John Freeland, to whom Milly had been sold by the plaintiff, was taken by him, and he deposes to the same reason, given by the plaintiff for selling Milly. He is asked by the defendant, what was the plaintiff's reason for selling Milly. He stated, the old man said he wanted money, and he would sell Milly; she was a mulatto and he despised them in his sight, and he would not sell one of his little blacks.

Henry Stanly, another witness for the plaintiff, is asked on his examination in chief, "what did Gant tell you was the reason of the plaintiff's wish to sell Milly;" his answer is, he told me Thomas Rippy wished to sell Milly because she was a mulatto; and this was at the time of the sale to Gant. These witnesses show that the plaintiff was self-moved in his wish to sell the girl; it was his own motion, and upon sufficient ground. He was obliged to pay some of his debts; he selected the girl in controversy, and gave, as his reason for so doing, what many men of much sounder minds think a sufficient objection to the owning of such property. Did the defendant possess influence with the plaintiff, and did he use it unduly and fraudulently in procuring a sale of the girl? Henry Stanly is the only witness, who speaks directly to the point. He is asked by the plaintiff, did you think that Thomas Rippy was much under the influence of Col. Gant? His answer is "Yes." He is asked on his cross-examination by the defendant, in what way was Thomas Rippy under the influence of Gant? He answered, "because he was capable of doing business for him;" a very insufficient reason.

There is no doubt, the defendant had influence, and much influence with the plaintiff. He was his nephew, and a man of business, and did much of his business for him; but that is not the question. Did he possess over the old man an undue influence, and did he make an undue or fraudulent use of it? The testimony of this witness does not prove it. Stanly, in answer to another

question of the plaintiff, states, that before Gant got
Milly into possession, he asked the witness what he
thought she was worth, and he told him $300; when
Gant replied, she will not bring that at private sale.
Very likely, if she had been offered to the highest bidder.
being a likely mulatto, some speculator would have given
for her $300. Mr. Hurdle, one of the witnesses, thinks
she might have brought that sum at public sale. I see
nothing in this testimony to impeach the integrity of the
transaction. But it is alleged in the bill, as an evidence
of fraud, that Milly was worth much more than Gant gave
for her. This certainly is a legitimate ground, upon
which to charge fraud, particularly in a transaction
such as this; a nephew purchasing from an old and
weak-minded uncle. The witnesses for the plaintiff
vary in their estimate of the value of Milly at the time
of sale. One values her as high as $400, the others
from $300 to $350. The defendant's witnesses, generally,
place her value at $250. Among the plaintiff's witnesses
the only negro trader is Jacob O. Hurdle. He states her
then value to be $400, but at the time Gant purchased
her, she was not worth that sum by $150, which would
make it $250, agreeing with the defendant's witnesses.
John Trollinger states that in the latter part of '43, he
purchased negro girls and boys from nine to ten years of
age at $200, but that they were worth $225; and that in
the same year he was called on to value a great many
negroes, preparatory to dividing them, among those entitled to them, and that negro girls of ten were valued
at $225. We think the weight of testimony is decidedly
in favor of $250, as being the value of Milly, at the time
of the sale. The defendant, as is proved by the bill of
sale, and other testimony, gave for her $215, less by $35,
than the full value; a difference too small, under the circumstances of the case, to authorise the Court to interfere
with the contract on that ground. We cannot say, the
plaintiff acted without judgment in the matter, for he

gave reasons for selling Milly, which are entirely satisfactory. We cannot say that the defendant, in purchasing the girl, used any trick or contrivance, or exerted any undue influence. Much testimony has been taken, and much difference of opinion expressed, as to the ability of the plaintiff to manage his own business or take proper care of his property. All agree, that he is a weak-minded man, and all agree, to whom the question was put, that his property was received by him from his father, and was then worth $1000, and that it is now worth $2500, or $2600, and that he has, in the mean time, raised a large family of children and grand-children, upon a small and poor piece of land. He must, through life, have been frugal, careful, and industrious, and most certainly showed, he knew how to take care of, and manage his little property. There is no evidence of any decay of intellect, at the time of the contract. He seems to have had as much capacity as he ever possessed. He did, what many a man of far brighter intellect has failed to do, preserve and improve the substance, which a father's labour had prepared for him.

PER CURIAM.   The Bill dismissed with costs.

JOHN BALLINGER *vs.* WILLIAM E. EDWARDS.

The purchase of a negotiable security for less than the real value is valid.

But that is subject to this qualification, that it must be merely a purchase of the security and at the risk of the purchaser; and, therefore, if the person, who claims to be such purchaser, holds the person, to whom the money is advanced, responsible for the payment of the debt, it is not, in law and fact, a purchase of the security, but a loan of money upon the security, and, if the sum advanced be less than the amount of it, deducting the legal interest for the time until maturity, the loan is usurious.

The Statute of Usury is as binding in a Court of Equity as at law, except in cases were the borrower asks the assistance of a Court of Equity, and then the Court will compel him to do equity, by paying the principal and the legal interest.

Cause transmitted by consent from the Court of Equity of Guilford County, at the Fall Term, 1846.

The bill was filed in October 1843, and states, that in November 1842, the defendant Lane, purchased from the defendant Edwards, a bond given him by the defendant Boykin, for $175, payable on the 1st of January 1843, and that Edwards transferred it to Lane by delivery only; that afterwards, Lane transferred and delivered the bond to the plaintiff, in satisfaction of a debt to a larger amount, which he owed to the plaintiff. It is further stated, that Lane was unacquainted with Boykin, who resided in a distant county, and was unwilling to take the bond without the endorsement of Edwards, and that Edwards, under the pretence of not wishing to offend Boykin, was unwilling to endorse the bond; but, instead thereof, he, with another person as his surety, executed to Lane a bond for the sum of $175, which was accepted by Lane as collateral security for the payment of Boykin's bond, and that, in like manner, Lane had transferred to the plaintiff the latter bond also. The plaintiff instituted an action at law in the name of Edwards to his use against Boykin and Edwards, dismissed it, and claimed Boykin's bond as his own. The prayer of the bill is, that the plaintiff's right to Boykin's bond may be established and that Edwards may be restrained from receiving the money or releasing the debt and Boykin decreed to pay it to plaintiff.

The answer of Edwards states, that, being in want of money, he applied to Lane to lend him the sum of $175, on the bond of himself and another person as his surety payable to Lane, and that after some treaty Lane agreed to advance to him, and did advance, the sum of $120 and that sum only, and took therefor the said bond of Edwards for $175.

He further states, that, after the transaction was closed, Lane mentioned to him, that he was going down the country on business and would pass near the residence of Boykin, and that Edwards then requested Lane to take Boykin's bond and present it for him, in the hope that, although it lacked a few weeks of being due, Boykin might have the money and be willing to accomodate him by then making payment, in part at least, and Lane agreed to oblige him by doing so ; and he avers that, in that manner and for that purpose only. did he put Boykin's bond into the hands of Lane, and he positively denies that he sold it to Lane, or transferred, or intended to transfer, any interest whatever in the same to Lane.

Boykin answers, that, in December 1842, Lane presented the bond for payment, and that he declined making any payment as it was not due, and it was not convenient to him. He says that Lane professed to act as the agent of Edwards, and did not intimate that he had himself any interest in the debt, and that afterwards, Edwards gave him notice that the bond belonged to him, and forbade him from paying it to Lane.

Lane's answer admits the transfer of the two bonds to the plaintiff as stated in the bill. It also sets forth, that he purchased Boykin's bond from Edwards, and paid him therefor the sum of $120, and required Edwards to assign the bond to him by endorsement, but that Edwards preferred guaranteeing the payment by giving a bond made by himself, and his father a surety to Lane for $175 as collatteral security, for the payment of the sum mentioned in Boykin's bond, and that finally he acceded to Edwards' proposition, and took Boykin's bond, without endorsement as his own property, and the other bond as collateral security. The plaintiff, in support of the bill, took the depositions of Lane and of an attesting witness to the bond of Edwards to Lane ; and they state the contract and transaction to have been as they are set forth in Lane's answer.

Morehead, for the plaintiff.
No counsel for the defendant.

RUFFIN, C. J. The difference between the accounts given by Lane and Edwards of their dealings is not material to the determination of the present suit. The latter says the advance of money to him was by way of loan, secured exclusively by the bond of himself and his father to Lane for $175, and that Boykin's bond was delivered to Lane, upon a distinct agreement for collection for him, Edwards : while Lane states the money to have been advanced upon and for Boykin's bond and the payment of that bond, instead of being secured by Edwards' endorsement, was secured by the bond to Lane of Edwards and his father. as a collateral engagement, but they agree in this, that Lane advanced to Edwards upon these papers only the sum of $120, instead of that of $175, less the interest for the time the bond of Boykin had to run. Now that is a case of plain usury, and the contracts of Edwards touching it are void by the statute. The bill indeed does not enter into the particulars of the contract, but the plaintiff is content to state. in general. that Lane "purchased" Boykin's bond and it is laid down that a purchase of a negotiable security for less than the

real value is valid.   But that is subject to this qualification that it must be merely a purchase of the security and
at the risk of the purchaser, and therefore if the person,
who claims to be such purchaser, holds the person to
whom the money is advanced responsible for the payment
of the debt, it is not in law and fact a purchase of the
security, but a loan of money upon the security ; and if
the sum advanced be less than the amount of it, deducting
the legal interest for the time until maturity, the loan is
usurious.   *Collier* v. *Neville*, 3 Dev. 30.   *McElwee &
Collins*, 4 Dev. & Bat. 209.   The latter case expressly and
correctly lays down the rule that the ordinary case of
discounting a note, with an endorsement or guaranty of
the receiver of the usury is a lending within the statute.

Now according to the plaintiff's own proof and taking
the case most strongly for him, Lane took an obligation
of Edwards and his father to himself for $175, as a col-
lateral security and guaranty of the payment of the
whole sum due on Boykin's bond, and that constituted
usury.

Such being the nature of the contract, as established
by the plaintiff himself, he can have no relief in this Court.
The statute is as binding in this Court as at law.   If indeed the borrower asks for assistance from equity, it may
be referred, unless he deal equitably by paying the principal money borrowed and legal interest.   But the lender
has no ground on which he can come into and stand in
a Court of Equity.   He cannot ask this Court to restrain
the other party from taking advantage of the statute at
law, for example, by pleading it to an action against him
for usury.   And the borrower has just the same right to
insist on the statute in any other form as in that.   This
defendant Edwards says, that the transfer of Boykin's
bond to Lane, as claimed by the plaintiff, was void at
law upon the ground of usury, and therefore that he has
a right to treat the bond still as his own, as in law it is,
and receive the money on it from Boykin, or release it

and dismiss all suits brought in his name on it.   That is just as true, at law, as that he might plead the statute of usury to a suit brought by Lane against him for the money on his bond or his guaranty of Boykin's bond.   Lane, in whose shoes the plaintiff stands, has no equity, on which he can ask this Court to enjoin Edwards from asserting his legal rights; for the equitable assignment, on which the plaintiff insists, being founded on usurious lending, gives him no right to assistance here.   *McBrayer* v. *Roberts,* 2 Dev. Eq. 75.   *State Bank* v. *Knox,* 1 Dev. & Bat. Eq. 50.

The bill must therefore be dismissed with costs.

PER CURIAM.   Bill dismissed with costs.

CASES IN EQUITY

ARGUED AND DETERMINED IN

THE SUPREME COURT

OF

NORTH CAROLINA,

AT

THE TOWN OF MORGANTON.

———

AUGUST TERM, 1847.

———

MICHAEL FILHOUR vs. JOHN GIBSON & AL.

Where an administrator files a bill to recover back a chose in action, which
he had assigned before administration was granted to him, when it appears that there was no creditor of the intestate and that the next of kin
had assented to the contract of assignment, a Court of Equity will grant
him no relief.

The case of Love v. Love, 3 Ired. Eq. 104, cited and approved.

Cause removed by consent from the Court of Equity of
Rowan County, at the Spring Term, 1847.

———

MEMORANDUM.—By an Act of the General Assembly, passed at
the Session of 1846-7, the Judges of the Supreme Court were directed to
hold an annual term of the said Court, at the Town of Morganton, on the
first Monday of August.

James R. Dodge, Esquire, of Surry County, was appointed by the
Judges Clerk of that Court in May 1847.

The Attorney General and the Reporter both attended at this Term.

On the 26th of March, 1839, William D. Crawford, for a debt which he then contracted, executed to Thomas A. Hague three bonds, each for the sum of $1873 and payable, with interest from date, in one, two and three years. The bonds were also executed by Christian Bringle, Charles Fisher and William Watson, as Crawford's sureties. The bond payable in 1840, was assigned, by Hague, to the defendant John Gibson, after it became due; and he instituted a suit on it against the obligors, in which the defendants pleaded certain payments made to Hague and set offs, for the residue. Hague also transferred to Gibson and one Waddell, or to Waddell alone, the bond that was made payable in March 1842; and before it fell due they, Gibson and Waddell, or Waddell, sold this last bond to Adam Filhour, for less than the sum due on it and transferred it to him by delivery only and without recourse on them or him. Adam Filhour died intestate in December 1841, out of debt and entitled to a considerable personal estate and leaving a widow and a son, the present plaintiff, and two daughters, the next of kin; and the plaintiff obtained administration of the estate in February 1842. The bill states that in January 1842, Gibson came to the late residence of the intestate, where all the family resided together, and, after transacting some trivial business, on pretence of which, he came there, Gibson told the plaintiff privately, that he had understood from an authentic source, that Crawford had become insolvent, and that his sureties had determined to plead usury, against the bond that belonged to his father's estate, because he had purchased it for less than its nominal value: and suggested, that, as they could only prove the usury, by Gibson and Waddell, it would be best to transfer that bond to him, Gibson, in exchange for the other bond, which Gibson then held upon the same parties. The bill then further states, that the proposition was communicated to the plaintiff's mother and sisters, all of whom were exceedingly ignorant, in matters of law, and that, after some deliberation, all four of them, in confidence of the truth of Gibson's representations, that the obligors, in the bond could avail themselves of the defence of usury and were disposed to take all advantages, agreed to Gibson's proposal and they exchanged the bonds, by mutual delivery only.

The bill then charges, that it was entirely untrue, that the obligors ever intended, or could have been allowed to set up such a defence, as the plaintiff has since discovered and been advised ; and that it was a device of Gibson's, to practice on the ignorance and inexperience of the plaintiff and his mother and sisters and obtain their bond, which was not yet due and against which, there were no counter-claims, for the one then held by himself, against which there were. to his knowledge, alleged payments and counter-demands to the full amount thereof or nearly so.   And. as evidence thereof, the bill further charges that the suit, which Gibson had instituted on the bond, due in March 1840, and held by him, was at that time, January 1842, still pending and had been for a considerable time, on the pleas of payment and set off ; and that Gibson knew the defendants were ready to support their pleas by proof, which would have left nothing or very nearly nothing due on the bond, and therefore he did not bring the suit to trial, but carefully concealed all those facts, from the plaintiff, his mother and sister, and passed the bond off to them as before mentioned, and then dismissed the suit he had brought on it.

The bill further charges, that Gibson refused to rescind the exchange of the bonds, but obtained from Hague an endorsement of the bond he got from the plaintiff, and claims it as his absolute property at law.

The bill was filed against Gibson and Crawford and his sureties, and prays that it may be declared, that Gibson effected the exchange of the bonds, by fraud, and thereon got from the plaintiff the bond due in March 1842 without any adequate consideration ; and that the contract may be rescinded and Gibson restrained from disposing of the bond, and that, upon the surrender by the plaintiff of the bond now held by him, (which he submits to make,) the obligors may be decreed to make payment to the plaintiff of the whole principal and interest due on the bond of March 1842, or to pay him what may still be due, if any thing, on the bond of 1840. and that Gibson may be compelled to make good the residue, for which no recovery ought to be had thereon, against the obligors, and for general relief.

Two of the obligors, Fisher and Bringle, answer, that there was never any intention to plead usury against the bond which Adam Filhour first purchased, or to set up any objection to the payment of it. They state, however, as to the other bond, which Filhour now holds, that, after it fell due and before it was passed to Gibson by Hague, their principal, Crawford, had discharged it, either by payments or by set-offs and settlements between Crawford and Hague; and that to the action, which Gibson brought thereon, they made that defence, and believe they could have proved it, and that Gibson became satisfied they could and withdrew his suit for that reason. They insist, that there is nothing due on the bond now held by the plaintiff, and state that on the other bond a suit has been commenced against them by Gibson, the indorsee of Hague, to the use of Thomas Smith, who claims the money; and they submit to pay that debt to whomsoever it may be decreed they ought.

Gibson's answer admits that he brought suit against Crawford and his sureties ou the first bond that fell due, and that the debtors insisted and pleaded, that it was discharged by payments and set-offs. This defendant further admits, that " he exchanged notes with the plaintiff;" but expressly denies all fraud in obtaining the note from the plaintiff. On the contrary he alleges, that the said Michael was willing and anxious to make the exchange. He admits that he ol d said Michael, that his father Adam had purchased the note, for less than its nominal value, but he did not assert, that the principal or sureties in said note were determined to plead usury to it, or advise or request the plaintiff to transfer the same to this defendant to avoid the effects of such plea. He admits that "after he obtained the note from the plaintiff he dismissed the suit, he had before brought on the other note, which he had then transferred to the plaintiff." But he denies "that the obligors had made payments or had any set offs, to the amount of said bond or any considerable part thereof. On the contrary, the claims, as he understands and believes, which they pretended to have against said bond, were neither payments or set offs —being notes or other claims, obtained by the obligors or some of them, from third persons, to whom Hague was indebted, and therefore not mutual debts between the said Crawford and Hague. Defendant did not conceal from plaintiff the fact, that a defence of this kind was set-up; but on the contrary informed him, that it was insisted on, but that the defendant did not believe it would be available. He denies that Hague authorized the obligors or any of them, to procure debts, which he owed to third persons, and agreed to allow them as payments or set offs to this bond."

The answer then states, that before this suit was brought the defendant " transferred the bond *bona fide*, for a full and valuable consideration to Thomas Smith."

By an amended and supplemental bill Smith is made a party and it is charged, that he is the brother-in-law of Gibson, and took the bond with knowledge, that it had belonged to Adam Filhour and of the manner in which Gibson had obtained it from the present plaintiff, and of the circumstances charged in the original bill; and also, that he had obtained judgment on the bond and was about to collect the money, and prayed that he should be enjoined therefrom.

88

The answer of Smith states, that, before the filing of the bill, he purchased the bond from Gibson *bona fide* and for full value paid, and that he had no knowledge of any defence to it either in law or equity, nor of any claim of the plaintiff or of any other person to the bond, except that of Gibson himself, and insists that he has a right to collect the judgment to his own use.

Upon the answers the injunction, prayed and granted on the bill, was dissolved ; and after replication to the answers the cause was set for hearing and sent to this Court, without further evidence.

Alexander and *Craige*, for the plaintiff.
Boyden and *Iredell*, for the defendants.

RUFFIN, C. J.   The Court does not accede to the argument for the plaintiff, that he has a right to relief upon the ground merely, that his contract with Gibson was before administration granted and without authority, and that the subsequent administration vested the property in him, as administrator, and entitled him to recover the bond.   For however that may be at law, yet relief can not be granted in this Court, in a case like this—in which the bill admits, that there were no creditors of the intestate, who owned the bond, and therefore shews, that the suit is prosecuted solely for the benefit of the next of kin, who were the equitable owners, and who, as appears in the bill, all united in, or consented to the contract with Gibson.   If the plaintiff had recovered at law, as administrator, equity would, at the instance of the defendant, restrain him from collecting the money, because it would be held by him for the persons, who had assigned their interest—which was the whole equitable interest—to the defendant at law ; and of consequence, the Court of equity can not give original relief in such a case to a mere administrator, in trust for the next of kin.   *Love* v. *Love*, 3 Ired. Eq. 104.

But we are of opinion, that the plaintiff is entitled to a decree upon the merits of the case. Not being the legal assignee, by endorsement, of either of the bonds, he had no action at law in respect of them. His only remedy was in equity, by a decree for payment by either the obligors in the bond, or by the person, Gibson, who passed it to him, as a subsisting security for the principal and interest appearing to be due on it, or out of the funds received or due upon the bond, which was obtained from the plaintiff without adequate consideration.

Here it may be observed, in the first place, that the last bond, in the hand of Smith, is, for the purpose of this cause, subject to be dealt with, as if it were still in the hands of Gibson, because it was not endorsed to Smith, and also because Smith's answer is not supported by any evidence, that he paid any thing for the bond, so as to make him a purchaser. He is therefore a volunteer, and the fund in his hands is liable, as if it had remained in the hands of Gibson. Thus considered there is a plain equity for the plaintiff against it, if the bond was improperly obtained from him, and if, by reason of the insolvency of the parties, it should turn out, that the plaintiff should be unable to raise the money upon personal decrees against the obligors or Gibson. The question is, whether the plaintiff is entitled to such personal decree, for what amount and against whom? We think he undoubtedly is entitled to it for his whole debt and costs, against either Crawford and his sureties, or against Gibson. Crawford and one of the sureties suffered the bill to be taken for confessed, and the other sureties say that all or nearly all the money has been paid on the bond passed by Gibson to the plaintiff, and they submit to pay any balance that may be due thereon. The only question, as to them, is, then, as to the sum, if any, remaining due on this bond; which will, according to the course of the Court, be the subject of an inquiry before the master. The only remaining question is, whether the plaintiff has not also a right to a decree against Gibson and the fund accruing from the other bond ; and we hold clearly that he has.

The defendant's answer is an extraordinary and not a fair one, as to the circumstances which led to the exchange of bonds. The account given in the bill is a natural and probable one, and the answer does not meet it, but equivocates. It denies indeed " all fraud in obtaining the bond." But how? Because, it says, " the plaintiff was willing and anxious to make the exchange." That was never denied by the plaintiff. But the question is, why he became thus anxious—at whose instance, and upon what inducements or representations? The bill tells the reasons : but the answer, though admitting the fact of the exchange, assigns no consideration whatever, that could have moved either party to it, that is, if the answer be taken. according to its generalities as it was probably intended to be understood, and without adverting to the cautious and special pleading manner in which it is expressed. The defendant says " that he did not assert that the principal or his sureties were determined to plead usury," and that " he did not advise or request the plaintiff to transfer the bond to him, *to avoid the effect* of such plea." But at the same time he admits, " that he informed the plaintiff, that his father bought it for less than its nominal value," and he gives no reason, why he was led to make that communication, nor tells of its effect on the plaintiff and his mother and sisters, nor denies that those persons made the exchange, under the influence of that communication, nor gives any other fact or reason, that could have induced it, but that suggestion of this defendant's. It is impossible not to see, that the answer keeps back much and material parts of what passed, and well deserves to be called a dishonest answer—such as ought not to be put into any bill. For without some such inducement as that stated in the bill, the transaction is the most unaccountable, that men in their

senses ever made. Gibson had already a suit pending
on the bond of March 1840, and it had been standing for
trial on "payment and set-off" for a considerable time.
Now, both of the bonds were for precisely the same sum,
with interest from the same day. Why then should
either party wish to exchange? Why does not the defendant inform us of *his* reason for wishing or consenting
to it? He does not intimate that it was to oblige his
friend, Filhour, though, he represents the latter as so
anxious for the bargain. The defendant then acted, not
from a disposition to serve the plaintiff, but to serve himself. It is to be remembered, that by the exchange Gibson not only got but a bond for the same sum, which,
upon its face, was due on the other bond, but also that
he would thereby be put to the delay of a new suit on
the bond, and have to pay the costs of the suit, which he
had brought on the other bond. We should have liked
this party to have told us, how he could have made such
a bargain as this : and we doubt not he would have told
it distinctly enough, if, as the bill states, he had not believed, that the defendants, in the suit he had brought,
would, to some extent, at least, make good their defence,
and, in order to shift that loss from himself, procured an
exchange of bonds with the family of Filhour, by hints
and innuendos, that induced them to expect a defence,
which would defeat their suit, on the bond which they
held, and to think they might recover the same sum on
the other bond. It is true, the answer denies that the
defendant concealed that the obligor insisted on the discharge of the bond he was to let him have, but he was
obliged to admit, that he told the plaintiff, that there
were in fact no payments or set-offs, that would or could
legally be allowed, and indeed, he insists in his answer
that there are none, for the reasons therein assigned. It
is clear, therefore, that Gibson passed this bond as one,
on which the whole sum mentioned in it and the interest
were then due, and ought to be recovered by the plaintiff;

and therefore, that if it should turn out to the contrary, on the inquiry ordered, he ought in conscience, to make it good, for what the plaintiff received it. At present we need not carry the decree to Smith, because, if the plaintiff can get the money decreed to him from the obligor and Gibson, that will satisfy him; and there is no suggestion of the insolvency of either of those persons. If, however, they should be insolvent, then certainly Smith, if he has received the money, must answer the decree against Gibson; and perhaps also that against the other parties, if they have become insolvent pending the present proceedings. As to the last point though, there is no occasion to give any opinion, as it will stand over as one of the equities reserved for further directions. There must accordingly be a reference to ascertain what sum is due upon the bond, held by the plaintiff, from the obligors, after deducting all payments and set-offs, legal and equitable, against the same; and whether the obligors are now able to pay the same, or if not, when they became unable.

PER CURIAM.   Decree accordingly.

AMBROSE J. EDNEY, EX'R. & AL. vs. ELISHA KING, AD'R. & AL.

Every person, who claims to recover, either at law or in equity, must shew a title in the pleadings, and that ought to be done by distinct averments or plain affirmative statements.

The title of a bill is no part of it. It is merely a mode of conveniently denominating a bill or cause, and it cannot be deemed a part of the statements of the bill, either as to the title or the parties.

Where a bill of injunction is filed to stay the execution of a judgment, it is improper to make the clerk, who issues the execution, and the sheriff who has received it, parties defendant. They are mere ministers of the law, and have no interest in the controversy.

If the sheriff has notice of the injunction, it is a contempt in him to proceed with execution; but to that purpose a notice is sufficient, and a subpœna should not be served on him.

Appeal from an interlocutory order in this case dissolving the injunction, which had before been granted, made at the Fall Term, 1846, of Henderson Court of Equity, his Honor Judge CALDWELL, presiding.

This was an injunction bill. The bill states, that William Mills died intestate, " leaving seven children." and that "the said heirs met, and by common consent divided the personal estate of said intestate, by which division a boy, named George, and a girl, named Nelly, fell to the share of Asa Edney: that the value thereof exceeded one seventh part of the said personal estate, and that " the said Edney then executed four forty-five dollar bonds to the other heirs for the overplus, and that all of them have been paid by said Edney's Executor, namely, the plaintiff, Ambrose J. Edney." The bill further states, that "sometime thereafter, Elisha King and Benjamin King obtained letters of administration of the estate of the intestate, William Mills, and thereupon required all the heirs to bring forward the property of the estate and have it sold; upon which the said Nelly was surrendered by the said

Asa Edney (the boy George having been sold by him,)
and the said Nelly was then sold by the administrators
and bought by the said Asa, he being the highest bidder,
at the price of $362, for which he gave his bond, with
Samuel J. Edney, one of the plaintiffs, as his surety."
The bill further states, that "at the execution of the said
bond, the administrators, to whom it was payable, expressly agreed, that, if the division, as made by the heirs,
was ever rendered valid by common consent or otherwise, then the said bond should be cancelled," and that
it was upon that agreement and condition the said bond
was given. The bill further states, that "afterwards
Elisha King, surviving administrator, agreed, together
with the heirs and distributees of William Mills, to refer
the whole matter to B. Shipp and Joshua Roberts, and
that said award has been made and confirmed, without
allowing a credit of the said $362, and, if so, that they
have failed to allow said Edney credit for the four $45
bonds, which he had long ago paid for said girl." The
bill then charges that "the said award was a final settlement of said estate, and that, upon said settlement, the
said bond for $362 should have been surrendered," as the
estate of said William Mills is freed from debt, and there
is no necessity for collecting it, and that it ought not to
be collected, because the said girl Nelly was the absolute
property of the said Asa Edney, and therefore he received no value for the said bond, but making the sale
and taking the bond by the administrators was a fraud
upon the said Asa." The bill then states, that judgment
at law had been obtained on the bond, by the surviving
administrator against the plaintiff, Ambrose J. Edney,
the executor of the principal obligor, Asa Edney, and
against the surety, Samuel Edney, who is the other plaintiff, upon which the plaintiff at law threatens to levy the
debt and costs. Thereupon it prays process of subpœna,
"to the said defendants, together with the sheriff and the
clerk of the Superior Court of Henderson County, com-

manding them to be and appear, &c., and that the said clerk and sheriff be injoined from all further attempts to collect said iniquitous judgment," and for further relief. An injunction was granted by a Judge out of Court, as prayed in the bill.

The clerk and the sheriff put in answers, in which they state, that they have no interest in the subject matter of the controversy, nor any agency touching the same, except only in their official capacities to issue and execute the process of the Court.

Elisha King, the surviving administrator of the intestate, William Mills, appeared as a defendant in the cause, and put in an answer. It states, that "after the death of the intestate, his children or a part of them supposed, that a paper writing, which purported so to be, was his last will and testament, and that they met, and made a partial division of the estate among themselves, but that, afterwards, the paper was offered for probate, as a will, and, upon a caveat, such proceedings were had, that the said paper was duly found not to be the will or testament of the said William Mills, deceased, and the Court pronounced that he died intestate, and thereupon granted administration to this defendant and to one Benjamin King, since deceased." The answer further states, that the administrators demanded different parts of the personal estate of the intestate from the persons who had the same in possession ; but that several of them refused to surrender the negroes they had received ; that Asa Edney had sold the negro George for $1200, and, of course, did not surrender him, but did surrender Nelly ; and that, at a sale made by the administrators, he purchased her and gave the bond for the price stated in the bill. But the answer denies, that the bond was given on any condition or agreement, other than what appears on its face. It states further, that, at the request of the next of kin of the intestate, and to save the expenses of many suits, which the administrators were about to bring for the property not surrendered to them, they agreed to a reference, proposed by the next of kin, to Messrs. Shipp and Roberts, to make a full and final settlement and division of the estate amongst the next of kin; and that it is true, that the said arbitrators made a settlement and division amongst the next of kin and awarded accordingly; and that by the said award this defendant was charged with the payment of certain sums of money, and that the fund for the payment thereof consisted of this bond of Asa Edney and of others, which were taken at the sale, and remained in his hands, uncollected. The defendant states, that he is informed by the arbitrators, that they did take into their consideration the four notes or bonds for $45 each, given by the said Asa, that are mentioned in the bill, and gave him credit therefor in making the award; and the defendant believes it to be true, and avers that the plaintiffs have no just claim to any credit on the bond and judgment, but that the whole debt is justly due."

Isaac B. Sawyer and his wife Mary and several other persons put in answers, in which they state themselves to be grand-children of William Mills, deceased, or otherwise related to him; but they do not set forth any thing material in other respects.

Upon the answers being put in, the defendants moved to dissolve the injunction; and, thereupon, by leave of the Court, the plaintiff filed, as an exhibit, a copy of an award by the arbitrators, named in the pleadings. It recites, that E. King, the administrator of William Mills, and John Mills, Marvell Mills, Samuel Edney and wife, Asa Edney and wife, George Jones and wife, P. Myers and the heirs of Mourning Lewis had referred to them to settle the said estate and to make an award upon the same; and thereupon they award as follows, to-wit:

" That there is found in the hands of E. King, administrator, the sum of $678 93
In the hands of M. M. Edney, former adm'r.   435 00

Amount against P. Brittain, for which we have awarded	901 00
George Jones, on which judgment is recovered,	106 19
A. J. Edney, administrator of A. Edney,	14 48
Marvel Mills, on which judgment has been recovered,	12 71
Amounting altogether to the sum of	$2,145 51

Out of which we have allowed the administrator, as follows :

His commissions,	$125 00
Attorney, N. W. W.	50 00
Attorney, A. L. W.	25 00
Other vouchers,	100 40
	$300 40

Leaving in the hands of the administrator for distribution, the sum of $1,845 11

Which sum of $1,845 11, we direct and award that he pay to the following distributees, to-wit :

To the heirs of Mourning Lewis, the sum of	$912 66
To P. Myers, the sum of	740 46
To the representatives of John Mills. the sum of	173 68
To Samuel Edney, the sum of	8 61

Upon the pleadings and exhibit, the Court allowed the defendant's motion and dissolved the injunction with costs to the defendant, E. King, reserving the question of costs, as to the other defendants, until the hearing. From this decree an appeal was allowed to the plaintiffs.

Edney, for the plaintiffs.
Francis, and *N. W. Woodfin*, for the defendants.

Ruffin, C. J. If the plaintiffs had merits, the bill is so imperfectly framed, that the Court could not afford them the relief they ask, or any part of it. The supposed testator, Asa Edney, (for neither his death nor will are stated in the bill,) purchased from the defendant King, the administrator of William Mills, a negro belonging to the estate and gave his bond for the price: and the plaintiffs in this suit seek to be relieved from paying it. On what ground they consider themselves entitled to the relief. it is not easy to say upon their bill. It may be supposed, perhaps, that Asa Edney is entitled to a part of the estate of the intestate, William Mills, and we conjecture that it was intended so to state in the bill. But there is no such statement in it. The bill begins by shewing, that the intestate died, " leaving seven children ;" but who they were. or that Asa Edney was one of them, no where appears. From the difference in the names, the presumption is, that Asa Edney was not one of the seven children. Then, it may be, that he married a daughter of the intestate, and that is probably the truth, and we would so presume, if the Court could proceed to determine rights upon such loose guesses. But that cannot be done ; and, therefore, every person, who claims to recover either at law or in equity, must shew a title in the pleadings, and that ought to be done by distinct averments or plain affirmative statements. It cannot be assumed, that Asa Edney was one of the intestate's seven children, or entitled in right of one of those children, or otherwise, to a share of his estate ; since there is no such allegation in the bill. It is true, that the bill is entitled "the bill of complaint of Ambrose J. Edney, executor of Asa Edney deceased, and of Samuel J. Edney against Elisha King, administrator of William Mills deceased, and Marvell Mills, P. Myers, William S. Mills, George Mills, Louisa Camp, John Camp, John Dillen, Winsom Edney, Sarah Edney, William J. Lewis, (and upwards of twenty other persons of different names,) heirs at law and legal representatives, of William Mills deceased." But that in no degree helps the plaintiff's case. For, in the first place, the title of a bill is no part of it. It is merely a mode of conveniently denominating a bill or cause, and it cannot be deemed a part of the statements of the bill, either as to the title or the parties. But if it were otherwise, still no title would appear in Asa Edney, because the persons, named in the title of the bill as defendants, are called " heirs at law and legal representatives of William Mills deceased," thus excluding Asa Edney from that character. Moreover, instead of seven next of kin, there are here upwards of thirty named as such. The bill, therefore, clearly could not be maintained for any purpose, as this objection goes to the whole foundation of the plaintiff's equity. For it does not appear to what share Asa Edney was entitled, nor, with any certainty, that he was entitled to any, and if he was not, as one of the intestate's next of kin, entitled to a seventh part of the estate, there is no ground whatever for the title set up for him to the negro girl, Nelly, nor any reason why he should not pay the sum bid for her. But if the allegations of the bill upon that point had been formal and distinct, and it were admitted that Asa Edney was, as one of the next of kin, entitled to one seventh part of the estate of the intestate, yet the plaintiffs can have no relief on this bill, because it in no manner appears upon it, either by particular or even general allegations, that he did not receive his seventh part, over and above the amount of the bond given for the price of Nelly. It is admitted that he got George (of the value as stated in the answer of $1200) and that he paid $180 to some persons claiming to be of the next of kin, which left $1020 in his hands; and there is no allegation that a full share amounted to more than that sum. Indeed there is no statement of the particulars or value of the estate, nor, consequently, of the amount of a distributive share. It is said, indeed, that the two negroes, George and Nelly, exceeded a seventh part by the sum of $180, but no value is set upon Nelly, and therefore the whole matter is still left in obscurity. If, however, it be taken as an inference from the statements of the bill, that George and Nelly, after deducting $180 from their value, were equal to a share of one seventh, and that Nelly was estimated in the division at the sum of $362, for which she was afterwards sold; still the matter of the bill is too defective to authorize any decree for the plaintiffs. For the share of Edney, for which he received those negroes, was calcula·ted according to the estimate of the estate, as made by the parties to that division. Now it is plain that objections were raised to that by the other persons interested, either because the estate was erroneously estimated, or because the division ought to have been made as upon an intestacy, whereas it was made upon the footing of a will, or for some other reason; and that a controversy existed in the family as to the proper principle of division, in consequence of which an administration was taken on the estate, that it might be distributed according to the due course of law. Under that administration Nelly was sold and purchased by Asa Edney; and the administrator was about to bring suits, for other property not delivered to him by the several next of kin, including, no doubt, the negro George, which Edney had converted. Under these circumstances, the bill states, that, when Edney gave his bond, the administrator agreed, that, if the previous division was valid or should ever be rendered so by the general consent of the next of kin or otherwise, then the bond for the price of Nelly should be cancelled. If this agreement be relied on as the ground of relief, it behooves the plaintiff to shew, either that the division was in truth according to the rights of all the next of kin; or that it was subsequently confirmed or made valid by an agreement of the next of kin, or in some other manner. To shew the first no attempt is made, and we are at much loss to determine whether

.the,bill meant to charge the latter. It states, that the administrator and the next of kin—called in the bill "heirs
and distributees"—agreed to refer " the whole matter" to
two arbitrators. What the "whole matter," thus submitted,
was, we are not told, but are left to conjecture. Certainly,
however, that reference cannot be construed into "a
general consent" of the next of kin " to render the previous division valid ;" because, if the reference related
to this estate at all, it must have involved a settlement
of the administrator's accounts, and the proper distribution of the estate among the next of kin. Therefore the
plaintiff's rights, if an award was made, must depend
upon the award in his favor. In other words, when he
calls upon the administrator to deliver his bond or discharge him from the payment of it, he must shew, as the
ground of that relief and upon the agreement, which the
bill states to have been made when the bond was given,
that the arbitrators awarded expressly, that the administrator should deliver up the bond, or, at the least, that
they confirmed the division which had been made, or
awarded that Nelly belonged to Asa Edney, and that, by
mistake, he bought his own property. Now the bill states
not an award to that effect; and, indeed, although it
says " an award was made and confirmed, and that it
was a final settlement of the estate," no part of its contents is set forth in the bill, as awarding any thing to the
plaintiffs touching the subject of this suit. On the contrary it rather complains of the award, because, in making it, the arbitrators did not allow Edney a credit for
the $362, and also (as we suppose the bill to have meant)
because they did not allow him a credit for the $180.
The bill, therefore, instead of setting up a title under the
award, rather impeaches it by insinuation. But as a bill
to impeach an award, it is entirely defective; for it
neither states the award, nor any particular error therein,
nor any fraud in the arbitrators, nor mistake by them,
either as to matter of law or fact—not even alleging that

these claims were set before the arbitrators, or made
known to them, nor assigning any reason, why they were
not. Upon the face of the bill, therefore, the plaintiffs
have no case for relief. But, if the bill had properly
charged the matter, which. perhaps, the party wished to
set forth, the merits of even that case are completely
disposed of in the answers.   The administrator positively
denies, that there was any condition or agreement, that
the bond should be surrendered in any event; and, moreover, he states, that the arbitrators did take into consideration the $180, which Edney paid, and also charged the
administrator with Edney's bond for $362, and it was a
part of the fund in his hands, which he was required by
the award to distribute among the other next of kin.

So, in every point of view, the dissolution of the injunction with costs was right; and we can only express
our regret, that costs had not been given immediately to
the sheriff and clerk. Those persons were most improperly made defendants, as they are merely ministers of
the law, and have no interest whatever in the controversy.
Upon notice of the injunction it would, it is true, have
been a contempt in the sheriff to proceed on the execution; but to that purpose notice would have been sufficient, and it was very wrong to serve a subpœna on them
and put them to the expense of appearing in the cause,
and putting in answers as defendants.

The interlocutory decree is affirmed with costs in this
Court, and this must be certified to the Court of Equity
of Henderson County.

 PER CURIAM.   Ordered accordingly.

JAMES R. LOVE vs. THOMAS RAPER & AL.

Where a person receives a foreign bill of exchange, in payment of certain
negroes sold, and on presentation of the bill the drawee refuses to pay,
and there is no protest for non-acceptance nor notice to the drawee, nor
proof that the drawee had no funds of the drawer in his possession at the
time, the payee of the bill has by his negligence made the bill his own,
and can have no claim in equity against the purchaser of the negroes,
either for the negroes themselves or for the price for which they were sold.
The cases of *Austin* v. *Rodman*, 1 Hawks 194, and *Yancy* v. *Littlejohn*, 2
Hawks 525, cited and approved.

Appeal from an interlocutory order, dissolving the injunction which had before been made in this cause at
the Spring Term, 1847, his Honor Judge DICK presiding.

The bill charges, that the plaintiff entered into an agreement to sell to the defendant, Raper, three negroes, for
the sum of $2,000, to be paid by an order on one W. H.
Thomas, out of funds then in his hands, belonging to
Raper ; and articles of agreement were executed by the
parties on the 18th of March, 1844. In them it was set
forth, that the order was drawn on funds of Raper, *then*
in the hands of Thomas : and it was stipulated as follows,
"Now if the said Thomas Raper will, by any means, with
or without suit, either in law or equity, enable the above
named James R. Love to recover from the said William
H. Thomas the above named sum of $2000, with lawful
interest thereon from this date, then the said James R.
Love binds himself, &c., that the above Bill of Sale shall
be absolute, &c., otherwise to be void and of no effect."
The bill states that on the same day the order was drawn
on Thomas, and was by Thomas L. Clingman, presented
to William H. Thomas, at the City of Washington, where
he lived, on the 29th of April, 1844, and that he refused
to pay it for want of funds. The order is set out, and

the endorsement by Clingman, the plaintiff's agent, as follows: " The above order was presented, this April 29th, 1844, to Wm. H. Thomas, and he declined to pay it." The bill then charges, that, shortly after the refusal of Thomas to pay the order, the plaintiff communicated the fact to the defendant, Raper, who promised, that, if he did not get the money from Thomas, he would return the negroes and pay him, &c.—that shortly thereafter the plaintiff was informed by letter from Thomas, that he had in his hands large claims in favor of Raper against the United States, which he had no doubt would be paid, and that he would retain a sum sufficient to pay off the order. The bill then charges, that, a few weeks since, Raper had sold the negroes to James H. Bryson and Daniel Ramsour, for $2000, secured by bonds payable at different times, who have run them out of the State, and that Thomas has lately become insolvent, and Raper is also insolvent. The bill prays an injunction restraining the defendants Bryson and Ramsour from paying to Raper the amount of the bonds—that a receiver may be appointed, and the amount when received paid to him, &c. The bill was filed the 4th Monday of March, 1847.

The answer of Thomas Raper admits the sale of the negroes and the mode of payment, as set forth in the plaintiff's bill, and that the paper marked "A." appended thereto, is a correct copy of the agreement between the parties. He further alleges, that it was expressly agreed and understood between them, that. if the order was not paid by Thomas on presentment, it should be returned to the defendant, Raper, who was in that case to give up the negroes to the plaintiff; it further alleges that Thomas was indebted in large sums to the defendant, on account of money received by him from the United States to his use, and that this was well known to the plaintiff. It denies that Raper ever received any notice whatever, that Thomas had not paid the order, until the March or September term, 1846, of the Superior Court of Cherokee

County, when he was called on by the attorney of the plaintiff to confess a judgment for the amount claimed by the plaintiff: which he refused, but proffered to give up the negroes, even then, if he would return the order —but denies he promised to pay the money to him. It avers that the defendant heard nothing further of the business until served with process in this suit—and that believing, either that the plaintiff had received the money from Thomas, or had made the order his own property, he sold the negroes to James H. Bryson and Jesse Brooks ; that the order was drawn in good faith upon funds then in the hands of Thomas, which have never been drawn out by the defendant, and that Thomas is now insolvent. The answer of Ramsour denies he had any concern in the purchase of the negroes by Bryson. The latter admits the purchase by himself and Brooks, and states that they purchased without any knowledge of the plaintiff's claim, or of the contract between the plaintiff and Raper.

Upon the filing of the answers, the presiding Judge dissolved the injunction, and the plaintiff, by leave, appealed to the Supreme Court.

Francis, for the plaintiff.
Gaither, for the defendants.

NASH, J. In the opinion of his Honor below we entirely concur. If any doubt rested upon our minds as to the facts of this case, and as to the legal and equitable principles resulting from them, we should continue the injunction to the hearing. But we have no such doubt. To us it is clear the plaintiff is not entitled to the aid of this Court. The plaintiff's claim to come into a Court of Equity rests upon the grounds, that the title to the negroes is still in him, because the order was not paid by Thomas, agreeably to the contract, and the insolvency of Raper and the danger of permitting the proceeds of the sale of the negroes to get into his, Raper's, hands. Whether he can ultimately, either at law or in equity, recover from Raper the price of the negroes, does not now come before us. Our only enquiry is, as to the correctness of the interlocutory order made by the presiding Judge, and of this we must judge from the bill and answer and exhibits.

The case is simply this. The defendant Raper, on the 18th of March, 1844, made a conditional bargain with the plaintiff for the purchase of three negroes—a man and his wife and their child, about ten years of age, for which he was to give the large sum of $2,000. Raper drew an order of the same date upon William H. Thomas, who lived at the city of Washington, for that amount. Upon its presentment on the 29th of April succeeding, Thomas declined paying it. In the written agreement between the parties, it was stipulated, that, if Raper would by any means enable the plaintiff Love to recover the sum of $2,000 from Thomas, the negroes should be his; if not, that the sale should be void and of no effect. That is, as we understand it, if he should furnish Love with evidence sufficient to compel Thomas to pay it, the sale should be valid. The agreement is evidently drawn by one little conversant with legal proceedings, and we are in no manner sure we have put upon it a proper construction. If so, the sale became absolute, and the legal title to the negroes vested in the defendant, by the subsequent *laches* of the plaintiff, as every thing had been done by the defendant which it was necessary for him to do. But the plaintiff says the order was not paid by Thomas, who had no funds of the defendant, wherewith to discharge it, and that it was received by him conditionally. All this is true, as admitted by the defendant, except as to the want of funds by Thomas. The enquiry remains, whether, under the fact disclosed in the bill and answers, the defendant has not a right to consider the bill of exchange, which was the price of the negroes, as paid, and, so, the conditional sale become absolute.

Thomas was the agent of Raper to receive, from the Government of the United States, moneys due to him; and the written agreement states, that the fund, upon which the order was drawn was "*part* of an amount of money *received* by Wm. H. Thomas from the United States" for Raper. The bill charges that Thomas refused to accept the bill, because he had no funds of Raper's in his hands. The endorsement of Mr. Clingman upon the order, which is by the plaintiff made a part of his bill, simply states that he declined paying it, without assigning any reason, and the answer avers that he had ample funds of the defendant in his hands. It was the duty of the plaintiff, as soon as he could, conveniently after receiving the order, to have it presented to Thomas for his acceptance, and upon his refusal to do so, it being a foreign bill, to have it protested, and within a reasonable time to notify the drawer, and that he looked to him for the payment of it. This is said to be a part of the constitution of a foreign bill, that is, according to the law merchant, it is a part of the contract, *Chitty on Bills* 339; and a consequence of a failure to have the bill protested, and giving notice in due time to the person entitled to object to the want of it, is, that he is discharged from his liability on it, *Chitty* 248. *Austin* v. *Rodman*, 1 Hawks 194. *Yancy* v. *Littlejohn*, 2nd Hawks 525. It is not pretended that the bill was protested; and, as to notice of non-acceptance, the plaintiff charges, that, shortly after the refusal of Thomas he gave Raper notice—within what time he does not state. The answer alleges that notice was not given until the Spring or Fall Term, 1846, of Cherokee Superior Court, two years after the order was drawn. If this be so, and for the purposes of our present enquiry we must consider it true, then, most unquestionably, the plaintiff has by his *laches* discharged the defendant, Raper, from all liability on the order, and this upon the ground, that, by his negligence, he has made the order his own, and taken Thomas for his paymaster in the place of Raper ;

of this, the non-protesting of the bill is strong evidence. By so doing he has made the sale absolute. The answer is strengthened by the statement of the bill. It alleges, that, shortly after the plaintiff had given notice to the defendant, he received a letter from Thomas, that he had in his hands large claims against the United States in behalf of the defendant, which he had no doubt he should receive, and when received he would retain a sum sufficient to pay the order. It was this letter, doubtless, which caused the plaintiff to rest so long upon his claim. The refusal of Thomas to pay the order entitled the plaintiff to rescind the contract, but that he did not desire. The price to be given for the negroes was a very large one, and he chose to run the risque of getting his money from Thomas; in other words, to take him for the debt; and, not until Thomas became insolvent, did he notify the defendant that he was looked to for payment. Having made his choice, he must abide by it. All this we gather from the bill and answers, and the plaintiff is not entitled to the equitable relief he seeks.

There is no error in the interlocutory decree appealed from. This opinion must be certified to the Court of Equity of Haywood County.

PER CURIAM.   Ordered accordingly.

EPHRAIM M. GREENLEE vs CHARLES McDOWELL.

An injunction to restrain the execution of a decree in equity cannot be granted.

But, though an injunction cannot issue, the Court of Equity may, upon a proper case, supported by affidavits, withdraw any process it has issued, or stay an execution by granting a supersedeas.

When a record of a bill, &c. has been lost and destroyed, the Court has full power to order a copy or the original bill to be filed.

A party to a suit is bound by the acts and agreements, made by his counsel in the management of his cause.

A bill of review, to rehear and set aside a decree, upon the ground of newly discovered testimony, cannot not be sustained, if it appears, that the testimony, though unknown to the plaintiff, was known to his attorney, solicitor or agent, in time to have been used, notice to either of them being notice to the principal.

The cases of *Reynolds* v. *Harshaw*, 2 Ire. Eq. 196. *Harris* v. *McRee*, 4 Ire. 81, and *Grice* v. *Rix*, 3 Dev. 62, cited and approved.

Appeal from the Court of Equity of Burke County, upon an interlocutory order dissolving the injunction in this case, made at the Spring Term, 1846, his Honor Judge PEARSON, presiding.

The plaintiff alleges in his bill, that Charles McDowell and Thomas Butler, as administrators of William C. Butler, dec'd. filed their bill in equity against him and John H. Greenlee, returnable to the Fall term, 1843, of the Court of Equity for Burke County; that a copy and subpœna were served upon him, returnable to the succeeding Spring Term, 1844, at which time he appeared, and employed as his solicitor, W. J. Alexander, Esquire. Time was given him until the Fall Term ensuing to file his answer; before which time all the papers and most of the records in the suit were lost or destroyed. At Fall Term 1844, when he attended to file his answer, being informed of the loss or destruction of the record of the suit, it was proposed to him to suffer a copy of the bill to be filed in the place of the original, to which he objected and refused his assent. By the direction of Mr. Alexander he returned home, believing that nothing further could or would be done in the cause ; and heard nothing more of it, until informed by the sheriff, that he had an execution against him, in favor of Charles McDowell alone, for the sum of $318 11, upon a decree obtained at Spring-Term, 1846, of Burke Court of Equity. The plaintiff then states, that " upon examining the records of the Court, he finds that, at Spring Term, 1845, a copy of the said bill. certified by the former clerk as a true copy, was filed by the plaintiff and the case entered on the appearance docket of that term—that, at the same time, the following entry appears on the docket, to-wit, " Bill amended by consent of parties, by substitution of complainant, copies served and answers to be filed at the next Court ;" that the following entry was likewise made, upon the copy of the bill filed as aforesaid, to-wit, " By consent of the parties this bill amended, by striking out altogether the claims of Butler's administrators and their names, and substituting the name of Charles McDowell for the following claims, &c." At the succeeding Fall Term, 1845, the bill was taken *pro confesso* against the defendant, and set for hearing at the next term : when a decree was rendered against him for $318 11 in favor of the plaintiff, Charles McDowell, and was duly enrolled—upon which decree an execution was issued. The present plaintiff then avers, that the copy of the original bill, with the indorsed amendments, was filed at the Spring Term, 1845, and the entries upon the records were made without his knowledge or consent, and that no copy of the bill, as amended, was ever served upon him. He prays, for these reasons, that the decree *pro confesso* may be reviewed, and he be permitted to file an answer in the original cause ; and that, in the mean time, an injunction may issue to restrain the collection of the money.

The defendant answers, that two bills in equity were filed in the Court of Equity for Burke County, at the same time, against the present plaintiff, John H. Greenlee, the one on behalf of Charles McDowell and Thomas Butler, as stated in the plaintiff's bill, and the other by Charles McDowell to recover debts due to him alone ; that copies of these bills were served on the defendant, and, at the return term, he appeared and employed Mr. Alexander to appear as his counsel. Before that time, however, the records and papers of the Court of Equity of Burke County had been stolen ; and, the Butler claim being abandoned, it was agreed by the defendant and his counsel, that the copy of the Butler bill, which was furnished by the defendant, should be amended as set forth in the records and as stated and filed in this bill ; and, that the defendant stated, he had, by mistake, left behind him at home the copy of the McDowell bill, which was in all respects like to the Butler bill, except as to the claims of Butler and those of McDowell. The answer further states, that it was expressly agreed between the parties, that no other copies should issue ; and that no alteration was made in the Butler bill or entries made on the records relative thereto, without the express consent of the plaintiff, who was present at the time.

Upon the coming in of the answer, the injunction previously granted, was dissolved and the bill dismissed. From this decree the plaintiff appealed.

Avery, for the plaintiff.
N. W. Woodfin, for the defendant.

NASH, J. The bill is filed to set aside the decree, obtained by Charles McDowell against the present plaintiff, and for an injunction to stay proceedings under it.

An application to a Court of Equity to restrain its own proceedings is certainly a novelty. We are not apprized of any precedent for such a bill. The process prayed for

91

and granted in this case is to enjoin a decree in Equity.
The principle, upon which injunctions are granted to stay
the proceedings of other Courts, is, that, from their organization, they cannot take effectual notice of the circumstances, which render *their* proceedings wrongful.
But such is not the case with a Court of Equity.   When
it is called on to injoin its own proceedings, it is asked
to pronounce, that to be iniquitous and wrong, which it
has already declared to be right and proper.   And when
it made this latter declaration, it was perfectly competent to declare it wrong, if it were so.   *Reynolds* v. *Harshaw,* 2 Ired. Eq. 196.   But, although a Court of Equity
cannot with propriety be asked to injoin the use of its
own process, which it has previously granted to execute
its own orders or decrees, yet a party grieved or supposing
himself to be so, by its use, is not without redress.   The
Court can, and, upon a proper case made, supported by
affidavits, will withdraw the process itself, or stay an
execution by granting a supersedeas.   2 *Mad. Ch.* 375.

The bill in this case is called a bill of review ; but it
is not in reality so.   It is admitted, there is in the original
suit no error in law, of which the plaintiff can avail himself in this proceeding, for the bill does not even intimate
an error in the decree.   But the object is, to set aside the
interlocutory decree, taking the bill in the former suit
pro confesso, and to allow the plaintiff to file an answer
to it.   The application is made on the ground of surprise.
If, therefore, the bill and answer are considered as affidavits, upon which the motion is made, do they exhibit such
a state of facts, as would justify the Court in granting
the relief asked for ?   We think not.   The plaintiff's allegation is, that, upon the loss of the records of the former
suit, a copy of the original bill, properly certified by the
clerk, was filed without and against his consent ; and
that no copy has been served upon him.   He further alleges, that the amendments upon it, and the entries upon
the record, were made without his knowledge or consent.

That the records and papers had been lost or destroyed, is stated by the plaintiff; and, in that case, it cannot be doubted, that the Court, without or against the will of the plaintiff, had full power to order a copy of the original bill to be filed. That the copy filed was a correct one is not questioned. *Harris* v. *McRea*, 4 Ired. 81. But it is a sufficient answer to all these grounds of complaint by the plaintiff, that the records he sets forth shew that they were all done by consent of the parties, and the counter allegations of the defendant sustain them. The plaintiff's own statements satisfy us the facts were so. Although the plaintiff avers, that the copy of the original bill was amended and filed, and the entries on the record made, without his knowledge or consent, he no where alleges that they were done without the knowledge and consent of his counsel. On the contrary, it is in substance admitted, by denying his power and authority to do so. Mr. Alexander was employed by the plaintiff, as his counsel in the case, at the return term; and it is not alleged, that he had been discharged, at the time the transactions took place. By his acts and agreement, made in the management of the cause, the plaintiff was bound, *Grice* v. *Rix*, 3 Dev. 64; and by his knowledge also of facts. If this were a bill of review to re-hear or set aside the decree, upon the ground of newly discovered testimony, it could not be sustained, if it appeared, that the testimony, though unknown to the plaintiff, was known to his attorney, solicitor or agent, in time to have been used; notice to either of them being notice to the principal. 2 *Mad. Ch.* 411. Much stronger is the application of the principle to the acts of a solicitor, done within the scope of his authority in the management of the suit. The plaintiff further alleges, that no copy of the amended bill was served upon him. The record shews that it was agreed no copy should issue; and there was a propriety in the agreement. For it is alleged by the defendant, in his answer, that the copy was furnished by the plaintiff himself, being the one which had been served on him. The answer also avers, that the plaintiff was present, when all the transactions took place, of which he now complains; and that he assented to them all. And we are entirely satisfied that such was the fact.

PER CURIAM.　　　　　　Bill dismissed with costs.

JAMES M SMITH vs. THOMAS HARKINS & AL.

After an injunction has been ordered to stand to the hearing, it seems to be irregular, in effect to reverse that order, by dissolving the injunction, or motion, before the hearing.

Where an appeal has been taken from a County to a Superior Court of Law, a Court of Equity has no right to decide whether the appeal was properly allowed or not. That is a question of law, which can only be decided by a Court of Law.

An appeal from an order of the County Court, establishing a road or bridge, will lie for any person aggrieved thereby, either as it may affect his franchises or other property, or on the ground that he is subject to pay taxes in that County.

The cases of *Atkinson* v. *Foreman*, 2 Mur. 55, and *Hawkins* v. *Randolph*, 1 Mur. 118, cited and approved.

Appeal from an interlocutory order of the Court of Equity of Buncombe County, dissolving an injunction which had been theretofore granted, made at Spring Term, 1846, his Honor Judge PEARSON presiding.

This cause was before the Court in June 1845, and is reported 3 Ired. Eq. 613. The decree made on the circuit, which continued the injunction to the hearing, was

there affirmed and the cause remanded for further proceedings.   It comes back upon an appeal from a subsequent decree, dissolving the injunction.

Besides the matters appearing upon the pleadings
formerly, the following facts appear by a supplemental
answer, exhibits and a case agreed between the parties.
In October 1845, the present defendants, with many other
inhabitants of the County, petitioned the County Court of
Buncombe to establish a ferry or bridge across the French
Broad river, at the place mentioned in the pleadings, and
the persons, who owned the bridge, against which the
injunction was granted in this cause, tendered it to the
Court, by way of donation to the public, as a free County
bridge, and bound themselves by an obligation in the
penalty of $5000, payable to the Chairman of the Court,
to keep it in repair for ten years, without any charge on
the County.

The plaintiff opposed the application, upon the grounds
of his previous right to keep a bridge over the river, and
the sufficiency of his bridge for the convenient passing of
all persons—so that there was no necessity for a new
bridge within two miles or a little more.   But in March,
1846, upon hearing the allegations of the parties and
without other evidence, the County Court made an order
declaring a bridge necessary at this point and accepting
from the proprietors that already built, as a donation
upon the terms above mentioned, and therefore establishing it as a free bridge, for the passage of all persons, until that Court should further order.   From that order the
present plaintiff prayed an appeal, which was allowed
him by the Court ; and it is now pending in the Superior
Court.

It is admitted by the parties, that the County Court established a road leading from Asheville towards Haywood
County and crossing the French Broad at or near the
point, where the bridge is erected, by a ford, which is at
all times deep, and frequently too deep to be forded ; and

that the river there is so large, deep, and rapid, as to render it too burdensome to build a bridge there and keep it in repair, by a tax on the inhabitants.

Upon the original pleadings and these additional facts, the counsel for the defendants in April 1846, moved for a dissolution of the injunction, and his Honor declared his opinion, that the order of the Justices accepting and establishing the bridge was conclusive and could not be appealed from; and thereupon he dissolved the injunction, upon the payment of all the costs by the defendants up to that time. But from that decree the plaintiff was allowed to appeal to this Court.

N. W. Woodfin, for the plaintiff.
Francis, and *Edney,* for the defendants.

RUFFIN, C. J. After the injunction had been ordered to stand to the hearing, it strikes one as irregular, in effect to reverse that order before the hearing and on motion. But although it be proper to notice the point, we do not stop to investigate it, as there appear to the Court to be strong objections to the substance of the decree under review.

If there could be an appeal from the order of the County Court, that order was vacated by the appeal, and the case stood in Equity, as if no such order had been made, and the then injunction should have been retained, upon the principles of the decision, when the case was formerly before this Court. His Honor however held, that the jurisdiction of the County Court is exclusive, and that there can be no appeal from an order of this kind by that Court. We think it was erroneous in the Court of Equity to undertake to decide that point, at all, under the circumstances of this case; and likewise, that the opinion given on the question of jurisdiction was, in itself, erroneous. The question is one respecting the jurisdiction of two Courts of Law, and is purely a legal ques-

tion, and peculiarly fit for the decision of the Courts of
Law alone.   As far as the Judge in Equity had the means
of forming an opinion from the acts of the legal tribunals, the order was the subject of appeal : for the County
Court had granted it, and thus, in form at least, admitted
its own order and the Superior Court had, thus far, entertained the appeal.   As the point was still *sub judice*
at law, the Court of Equity ought not to undertake, before
hand, to determine, that the Superior Court could not or
would not entertain the appeal fully, and decide the controversy on its merits.   One may be sure, that the Chancellor, in England would await the judgment of the law
Courts upon a question of legal jurisdiction, then pending in those Courts, and would not proceed to give relief
in Equity, upon an assumption, that a higher Court at
Law had not a jurisdiction, which it was at the time
exercising.   As far as the rights of the parties depended
in Equity upon that point, the Chancellor would say they
must abide the decision, that would be made at law, and
that, until that decision, things must remain as they were,
without disturbing the state or relation of the parties or
altering the subject of the controversy.   It is true that
the same Judge sits, with us, on both the Law and Equity
side of the Court on the circuit ; and at the first blush it
may seem immaterial in what form, or in which forum,
he gave his opinion of the law ; and so it would be, if
his opinion were final.   But the right of appeal makes
an essential difference, and replaces the point upon the
same ground here, that it rests on in England.   If it were
true, that there lies no appeal from an order for a bridge,
the obvious method of having a speedy and conclusive
decision on it, was for the Judge to have ordered these
defendants to bring on the case at law, on a motion simply to dismiss the appeal, as having been imprudently
granted.   He would have granted the motion, and then
the appellant would have again appealed upon that single question, to this Court ; and thus the matter would

be conclusively settled—leaving all things, in the interim, *in statu quo*, as they ought to be, and without exposing the plaintiff to the illegal encroachments of the defendants, or what might turn out to be such encroachments, in case it should be finally held that the appeal does lie. The difference in the two modes of proceeding is obvious and important. As this matter has been transacted, that is, by the Judge sitting in Equity, deciding that point in law, and, on the foundation of that decision, dissolving the injunction, which the plaintiff, as the owner and in the enjoyment of a franchise, had obtained against the invasion of it, this plaintiff suffers severely by the liberty allowed to the defendants actively to violate the franchise, before the defendants' right is established at law, and during the whole time required for a decision upon it. For it must be remembered, that an appeal from an interlocutory decree is in the discretion of the Judge on the circuit, and moreover, that it does not remove the cause into this Court, and these defendants, by the method here taken, may have been enabled to keep open their bridge for eighteen months, while the correctness of the legal opinion has been in review; and thus in truth the natural order of things has been reversed. It ought to have been remembered, that it might possibly be held by the Court of the last resort, that the appeal did lie; and therefore the decision on the circuit ought to have been so given, that no prejudice could arise from it before a final adjudication upon it. It would not only be more conformable to the distinct functions of Courts of Law and Equity, but more consonant to the justice due the parties, to have the legal question decided at law; which could have been rendered without any intermediate change in the condition of things; and we think it was erroneous to have made the decree in equity upon that basis, before its correctness had been duly pronounced at law. This opinion would be sufficient to reverse the decree. But the Court likewise holds that the appeal was properly granted, and that the effect of it, in this, as in other cases, was to vacate the order appealed from.

Under the Act of 1777, it is true, that the jurisdiction of the County Court, in laying out public roads and establishing ferries, was exclusive. It concerned the local police, and the justices were supposed to be the most competent judges of the local necessity. Therefore no appeal would lie from that Court. *Hawkins* v. *Randolph*, 1 Mur. 118. *Atkinson* v. *Foreman*, 2 Mur. 55. But that led to such abuses and oppressions of individuals, that in 1813 an act was passed, expressly to give the right of appeal "to any person dissatisfied with the judgment, the County Court may pronounce." These broad words, it is, insisted for the defendant, should, by construction, be confined to those persons, to whom, by the previous section, the notice of twenty days must be given—namely, the persons over whose lands a proposed road is to run, or whose ferry is within two miles of the place, at which it is proposed to establish another. *Rev. St. ch.* 4, *sec.* 2, and *ch.* 104, *sec.* 283. But that construction cannot be admitted, as is very clear; because it would take away an appeal in every case of an order for discontinuing a road, although plainly within the mischief and the words of the act. We suppose, indeed, that a mere stranger, who cannot, in any way, be affected by the order, as the inhabitant of another State or County, not having lands or property within the jurisdiction, can not appeal and officiously frustrate a measure, which the authorities and all the people of a County desire. But one affected in his income and property by an order of this kind is as much within the reason of the law, as those persons, who, upon the construction of the defendant's counsel, can appeal; and, as the words are large enough to embrace him, he can not be excluded. Indeed in respect to roads and bridges, there is an interest in every inhabitant of a county, who may be required to work on the former, or, by taxation, to contribute to building or repairing the latter, which is sufficient to entitle him to an appeal, at the risk, it must be remembered, of such costs, as may be adjudged against him, if unsuccessful. It is true the act does not speak expressly of bridges, as well as ferries. But they stand on the same ground of necessity and are pretty much identified in other Statutes. By the Act of 1806, Rev. St. ch. 104, sec. 28, instead of keeping a ferry, the proprietors of it may build a bridge, under the same right and in the same manner, by which the ferry is claimed and held. Upon this ground and on the principle that appeals are favored, this seems to be a case clearly within the equity of the act. Besides the bridge, when erected, will, strictly speaking, be a part of the highway; and, as such, the order for it is the subject of appeal. These reasons require a reversal of the decree and enable the Court to pronounce it without taking into consideration an interesting question, which would have been presented by the facts, had the opinion of the Court been different on the other points. It is whether the Court of Equity could interpose and ought not to interpose, by injunction, against an order, by which, it is admitted, the value of the plaintiff's property is impaired one-half, until some reasonable compensation be made. The statute confers the whole jurisdiction of roads, ferries, and bridges, on the County Court, subject, of course, to appeal; and therefore it was unquestionably competent to that Court, to establish this, as a free bridge. But still it is to be enquired, on what terms ought that Court to accept and establish the bridge, or rather, on what terms, ought the Court of Equity to allow the bridge to be opened thus, to the detriment of the plaintiff. The point is mentioned, merely that it may be seen, that it has not been overlooked nor regarded as of no consequence, and not for the purpose of deciding or discussing it. There is no necessity to do so on this appeal, and we do not mean an opinion on it, for we have really formed none. We can only say that there ought to be a plain public utility, in the new bridge thus interfering with a franchise, previously granted and on which much money has been spent, to justify its establishment, on any terms; and the very highest public necessity for it to excuse an order for its erection, without compensation, if any thing can excuse it. But we are relieved from the further investigation at present, as the whole subject is within the control of the Superior Court, on the appeal there pending; and we cannot anticipate what case may be made before that Court, nor the decision on it, but must suppose before hand that it will be legal and just on the other grounds. However the Court holds, that the decree must be reversed, with costs in this Court, and the cause remanded with directions to continue the injunction to the hearing.

PER CURIAM.   Ordered accordingly.

SAMUEL FROST vs. HUGH REYNOLDS & AL.

The interest of a vendee of land, where the contract rests in articles for a conveyance, when the purchase money shall have been paid, is not the subject of sale under execution at law, while the purchase money, or any part of it remains unpaid.

After the payment of the price, it may be sold as a trust estate, within the Act of 1812.

Where a creditor seeks to subject to the satisfaction of his debt an equitable interest of his debtor, the assignment of such interest before the filing of the bill, *bona fide* and for a valuable consideration, will bar the creditor.

Before the creditor can resort to this Court for relief against the equitable interest of his debtor, not subject to his execution at law, he must shew a judgment at law, a *fieri facias* and a return of *nulla bona*.

He cannot have relief upon the mere ground, that he had by mistake bought property at execution sale and discovered afterwards, that the estate of the debtor, did not pass by such sale. He must first establish his claim at law, under the Act of 1807. *Rev St. ch.* 45.

The cases of *Henderson* v. *Hoke*, 1 D. and B. Eq. 119, *Thorpe* v. *Ricks*, 1 D. and B. 613, *Pool* v. *Glover*, 2 Ired. 129, *Harrison* v. *Battle*, 1 Dev. Eq. 537, *McKay* v. *Williams*, 1 D. and B. Eq. 398, and *Brown* v. *Long*, 1 Ired. Eq. 190, cited and approved.

Cause transmitted by consent from the Court of Equity of Davie County, at the Spring Term, 1847.

The following case was presented by the pleadings and proofs.

On the 12th September, 1837, the defendant, Boon Frost, contracted to purchase from Archibald G. Carter a lot in the town of Mocksville, at the price of $100, payable in twelve months, with interest from the time of contract ; and he gave his sealed note to Carter therefor, and, at the same time, he took a covenant from Carter, to convey to him in fee, upon the payment of the purchase money. Boon Frost went into possession of the lot immediately and built a house, and made other improvements thereon, and made some small payments to Carter upon his note. In 1841, several judgments were taken against said Frost before Justices of the Peace; that is to say, one in favor of McRorie and Dusenbury, for $38 53; one for Bingham and Howard, for $48 91; one for R. and J. Gowan, for $49 08, besides interest and costs; and also three judgments in favor of the present plaintiff, Samuel Frost, one for the sum of $100, with interest from June 8th, 1841, and costs; one for $42 31, with interest from the same day and costs; and the other for $100, with interest as aforesaid, and costs. Executions issued on all those judgments, on which were returns, that no other property of the defendant was to be found, except the said lot, and then a levy on that lot; and thereupon the County Court ordered the sale thereof under writs of *venditioni exponas;* and in May 1842 the Sheriff offered the lot for sale, and the plaintiff became the purchaser at the price of $250. That sum was applied by the Sheriff to the satisfaction of the principal, interest and costs, on the executions of McRorie and Dusenbury, Bingham and Howard, and R. and J. Gowan; which left a balance of $94 72, applicable to the judgments of the plaintiff, and which was applied thereto as follows, viz: $66 08, in discharge of the judgment for $62 36; $10 07, in discharge of all the other costs; and $17 56 as a credit on one of the judgments for $100. The Sheriff made a deed to the plaintiff; and he on the 4th of March, 1843, paid to Carter the sum of $86, for the balance in principal and interest of the purchase money then remaining due, and requested Carter to make him a deed. The latter declined doing so, unless the plaintiff would procure and have his covenant cancelled, but professed his willingness to convey to any person, who might be entitled.

The plaintiff then filed this bill against Boon Frost, Carter, Bingham and Howard, and the other judgment creditors, and one Hugh Reynolds; and therein states, besides the foregoing facts, that he believed, when he made his purchase, and paid the residue of the purchase money to Carter, that the lot was subject to be sold under execution, and that he was entitled to a conveyance of the legal title from Carter; but that he hath since been advised by counsel, that the sale was ineffectual, and that he can not call for a conveyance. The bill further insists, that nevertheless, the plaintiff is entitled to the benefit of all the judgments which were satisfied out of the proceeds of the sale, as the substitute of those creditors, and to have the same, as well as the amount of his own three judgments, and the sum paid to Carter, paid to him by Boon Frost, or in default thereof, to have the sum raised by a sale of the lots under the directions of the Court.

The bill further states that with the view of defeating the plaintiff's rights in the premises, the defendant Frost assigned, to the other defendant Reynolds, the covenant of Carter, without any valuable consideration, and on the pretence of paying or securing some old debt from Frost to Reynolds; and, that the assignment was made on the 29th of March, 1843, with a knowledge, by both Frost and Reynolds, of the plaintiff's purchase, and of the payment by him to Carter, and that the judgments of the plaintiff were unsatisfied.

The prayer is, that the assignment to Reynolds may be declared fraudulent and void, and that Carter may be decreed to convey to the plaintiff; or that the sums, which the plaintiff paid to the other creditors, and his own judgments, and the sum paid to Carter may be declared liens in this Court on the lot; and that the same may be satisfied by a sale of the lot, if not otherwise paid by the defendants Frost and Reynolds.

Reynolds and Frost answer, that, after the knowledge of the plaintiff's purchase, the latter assigned Carter's covenant to the former: who took it for the purpose, as they state, of securing a debt, which Boon Frost owed him of about $60, on a bond, and $76 12 1-2 on account; as they were advised that the plaintiff gained nothing by his purchase, and this was the only means he had of securing this debt. Reynolds further states, that the plaintiff paid Carter the residue of the purchase money officiously, and with a knowledge of the assignment to him, Reynolds, and he insists, therefore, that he cannot claim it against the lot. These defendants however, have taken no proofs in support of their answer. Carter submits to a conveyance under the directions of the Court, and the other defendants, the execution creditors, allowed the bill to be taken as confessed against them.

No counsel for the plaintiff.
Iredell, for the defendants.

RUFFIN, C. J. The interest of a vendee of land, where the contract rests in articles for a conveyance, when the purchase money shall have been paid, is not the subject of sale under execution at law, while the purchase money, or any part, remains unpaid. After the payment of the price, it was held in *Henderson* v. *Hoke*, 1 Dev. and Bat. Eq. 119, that it may be sold as a trust estate, within the Act of 1812. But until payment there is not a pure trust for the vendee, upon the sale and conveyance of which, it was the purpose to displace the legal estate. Neither is it an equity of redemption, properly speaking. It is true that the legal estate is regarded, in equity, as being retained by the vendor as a security for the purchase money; but still it is not a security of the character of a mortgage, upon which an equity of redemption arises. There is no loan of money—no previous property in the vendor, which he, as a mortgagor, is to redeem; but the security is for the price of the land bargained for, and the right of the vendee is to a specific performance of an executory contract. There has been no instance yet, in which this interest was held to be saleable, under the Act of 1812, either as a trust, or an equity of redemption; nor any principle laid down, as far as we remember, from

which that could be adduced. And we do not feel at
liberty to carry the Act beyond its words, except in such
cases as *Thorpe* v. *Ricks*, 1 Dev. and Bat. 613. *Pool* v.
Glover, 2 Ired. 129, and *Harrison* v. *Battle*, 1 Dev. Eq.
537, in which the Court was unavoidably compelled to
go beyond the literal terms of the Act, in order to prevent
its evasion and the defeating of its plain purpose by a
debtor, who, instead of using a proper mortgage by a
conveyance on conditions, upon which an equity of redemption, technically, would arise, substitutes therefor
a species of conveyance, which has grown into common
use as a security for debt, under the name of deeds of
trusts, and is substantially a mortgage with a power of
sale. In that case the Court was obliged to hold, that the
resulting rust was in the nature of an equity of redemption, and therefore within the second section of the Act
of 1812. But that reason does not apply to the rights of
vendor and vendee under articles, which was not a case
within the contemplation of the legislature, or within the
mischief then to be redressed, as that is not a usual mode
for debtors to give a security for their debts, but only contains the terms of the contract of sale, upon the obser-
vance of which, by the parties respectively, each of them
may entitle himself to a decree for a specific performance.
It is only when the whole purchase money has been paid,
that the interest of the vendee may be taken on execution, and then it is not as an equity of redemption, but as
a pure trust under the first section of the Act. The Court,
therefore, holds, that the plaintiff gained no title under
his purchase of the lot, nor any right, which can enable
him to call for a conveyance, to his own use, from Carter
upon the payment of the purchase money to him.

The bill however seeks other relief, and of a different
character. It is that the debt to Carter, and all the judgments against Boon and Frost, as well as those that were
satisfied by the sale, as those remaining due to the plaintiff, may be declared liens on the premises, and a sale

decreed for their satisfaction, and that the plaintiff may be substituted for Carter, and the other judgment creditors, and receive all those sums to his own use.

In opposition to this claim of the plaintiff, the defendant Reynolds, in the first place, sets up the assignment to himself prior to the filing of the bill, and that would be an effectual bar to relief, in respect of the judgments, if the assignment were for valuable consideration, and *bona fide.* For, as the executions did not bind the premises, the creditor could create a lien only by filing their bill to charge this property ; and an assignee before that holds, *Harrison* v. *Battle*, 1 Dev. Eq. 537. *McKay* v. *Williams*, 1 Dev. and Bat. Eq. 398. But of course a fraudulent assignment, made to defeat the judgments, or without consideration, as was mentioned in the case last cited, forms no impediment to the relief. Of that character the Court must deem the assignment here. As far as can be seen upon the evidence, the defendant Frost owed nothing to the other defendant Reynolds. The answer states, that he owed him $60 on a bond, and also $76 1½ on an account. But the bond has not been produced, nor any proof given that it ever existed. An account for $76 1½ was exhibited with the answer ; but there is no evidence to substantiate its truth ; and besides it is actually receipted in full under the date of January 20th, 1841, more than two years before the assignment to Reynolds. There must, therefore, be a declaration, that Reynolds did not take his assignment, to secure or satisfy the debts mentioned in his answer, nor upon any valuable consideration, but that the same is fraudulent against the creditors of Boon Frost. This leaves the plaintiff's case to stand upon his rights or against the defendant Frost himself. His claims are of three kinds, and it will be proper to consider each by itself.

As a creditor by his own two judgments, one of which he alleged to be altogether due, and of the other nearly the whole, the plaintiff is entitled, upon settled princi-

93

ples, to satisfaction, or to the lot, as the equitable property of his debtor. *McKay* v. *Williams*, 1 Dev. and
Bat. Eq. 398. *Brown* v. *Long*, 1 Ired. Eq. 190. It is admitted, that the debtor has no other property out of which
satisfaction can be had, and the executions have been
returned *nulla bona*, except as to these premises; and the
Court has already said, they were not subject to executions.

But the claim upon the satisfied judgments stands upon
a different ground. The plaintiff does not come into
Court as the purchaser of these judgments, and seek to
set them up as subsisting judgments. On the contrary,
he admits they are satisfied by the return of that fact on
the executions, and the payment of the debts to the executors by the Sheriff. But he says, they were satisfied with
his money, which under a mistake he paid as the price
of this lot, which the Sheriff had not authority to sell;
and therefore, that he ought to be substituted for the execution creditors, and be allowed to set up the judgments
again in this Court, or, at all events, to claim the sum he
paid, as a debt against Boon Frost, and have a decree
for satisfaction out of the premises. But the Court is of
opinion, that in neither aspect is he entitled to relief at
present.

This Court cannot set up the satisfied judgments again
for the purpose of charging the debtor's equitable property. They are extinguished at law by payment in due
course of law, obtained by selling the debtor's property,
or a piece of land as the debtor's legal property; and we
are not aware of any principle, on which equity can put
them on foot again for the benefit of any person. Certainly it could not be done at the instance of the creditors
in those judgments; as they are satisfied, and that not
in a way, that will not amount to payment at law, because of the officious act of a stranger, but out of the
land regularly offered for sale under the executions as
the legal estate of the debtor. For the like reason, it
cannot be done at the instance of the purchaser at the

execution sale. Confining ourselves to the facts in this case, it is to be remarked, that the Sheriff did not profess to sell the precise interest of Boon Frost in this lot, as that of a vendee by articles, or as a trust, or an equity of redemption; but his sale and conveyance were of the lot itself in fee, as the legal estate of the defendant. The act of the Sheriff, then, purported to be within the scope of his authority; and consequently the contract of purchase was binding on the plaintiff, and he was obliged to pay his bid, although his title to the lot should prove defective; as every purchaser at Sheriff's sale gets only the title of the defendant in execution, and buys at the risk of getting none. *Pool* v. *Glover*, 2 Ired 120. For, as he is entitled to a conveyance from the Sheriff for the most inadequate price, so he must fulfil his part of the contract, though he may not get what he hoped for. There is no precedent for relief in equity to a purchaser at Sheriff's sale, against the defendant in execution, upon the ground of a defect of title, where there was no fraud, neither upon the proper and original rights of the purchaser, nor by substitution to those of the creditors. There cannot be, for the purchaser always gets what he thought, or ought to have thought, he would get; that is to say, the debtor's estate, whatever it might chance to be. The plaintiff's contract was for the land, or the supposed title of Frost to the land; and it was not, in form or in substance, a purchase of the judgments, but a legal payment of them, which was to extinguish them; and, consequently, the plaintiff could not claim an assignment of them, so as to make them enure to his benefit in a Court of Equity. Then, if the plaintiff claim to be relieved upon the ground, that he got no title to the land, and that, the condition failing, he paid the money to the debtor's use; the answer is, that a very just claim arises upon those facts, but that it is not one, within this jurisdiction, and in the state in which the claim is. Before the Act of 1807, Rev. St. ch. 45, there was no legal remedy for a purchaser, when the property was not in the defendant in execution ; because, as before said, he purchased at his risk. Equity did not undertake to supply that deficiency in the law ; for it was a question of pure legal policy and right, and there was no ground, on which the Court of Equity could interpose, and it was never done. It was, however, considered for the benefit of the debtor and but just to the purchaser, that the sale of the sheriff should be deemed so far the sale of the defendant himself, as to make the latter liable for the title, and upon a total defeat of property in the things sold, liable for the sum paid by the purchaser and interest thereon ; and accordingly the statute gives an action on the case for the recovery thereof. The plaintiff has, by the Act, an adequate legal remedy, and therefore cannot sue in Equity. If, indeed, there ever had been a jurisdiction of this subject in this Court, it would not be ousted by a concurrent jurisdiction, merely, being created at law. But there never was such a jurisdiction in any Court, until that conferred in 1807, and that is restricted to the action at law against the debtor and is fully adequate. It is true that here the plaintiff does not ask to change the jurisdiction, simply for the purpose of having a personal decree for the money, but he seeks satisfaction out of the equitable property of the debtor, upon the ground that he is insolvent and has no legal property that can be found. But as the demand is a legal one, namely, for the money paid for the lot, to which there was no title, it is indispensable to a bill for satisfaction here, that the plaintiff should have brought his action at law, in the first instance, to establish his demand, and issued a *fieri facias*, so as to shew, that satisfaction could then in no other manner be had. *Brown* v. *Long,* 1 Ire. Eq. 190. *Hendricks* v. *Robinson,* 2 Johns. C. C. 306.

With respect to the residue of the purchase money due to Carter, the plaintiff is clearly entitled to relief. The plaintiff was a stranger to the contract between Carter and B. Frost, and the advance of money by the plaintiff did not (as the payment of the purchase money in the other cases to the sheriff did) operate as the payment of the debt to Carter and extinguish it; but in good conscience, it entitles the plaintiff to call on Carter to do every act necessary to secure him in that sum, as by assigning to him Foot's bond, and conveying the legal title of the lot to him, if necessary to enforce the payment of the residue of the purchase money to the plaintiff. He is strictly the equitable purchaser and assignee of all Carter's rights, and the right to the money entitles him to insist that the lot should be declared a security to him for it.

It must be declared, therefore, that the plaintiff is entitled to have the sums due to him, in respect of the residue of the purchase money and interest thereon, and also in respect of his two judgments against Boon Frost for $100 each, and his costs in this suit, raised by a sale of the premises, if not paid without a sale by the defendants, Frost and Reynolds, or one of them, within a reasonable time; and it must be referred to the clerk to inquire what is due to the plaintiff upon his said demands.

Per Curiam.   Decree accordingly.

INDEX.

AGENT AND PRINCIPAL.

1. It is a well established principle in Equity, that an agent cannot make himself an adverse party to his principal, while the agency continues; he can neither make himself a purchaser, when employed to sell, nor, if employed to purchase, can he make himself the seller. In both cases, he is but a trustee for his principal. *Deep River Gold Mining Company* v. *Fox,* 61

2. But the rule applies only to agents, who are relied upon for counsel and direction, and whose employment is rather a trust than a service; and not to those, who are merely employed as instruments, in the performance of some appointed service. *Ibid.*

APPEAL.

An appeal from an order of the County Court, establishing a road or bridge, will lie for any person aggrieved thereby, either as it may affect his franchises or other property, or on the ground that he is subject to pay taxes in that county. *Smith* v. *Hawkins,* 486

BILL AND ANSWER.

1. A general allegation in a bill, specifying no facts upon which it is founded, requires no answer; or, at most, a general denial in the answer is sufficient to meet it. *Cowles* v. *Carter,* 105

1

2. A Bill should contain a statement of the title of the plaintiff and defendant, so that the pleadings may shew the titles claimed by the parties, without looking for it in the evidence alone. *Humphries* v. *Tate*, 220

3. When a defendant asks the Court to act on his answer as he does, when he moves to dissolve an injunction, it is not sufficient that he should make an answer, which merely does not admit the ground of the plaintiff's equity, but it must set forth a full and fair discovery of all the matters within his knowledge or in his power to discover, and then deny the material grounds, upon which the plaintiff's equity is founded. *Thompson* v. *Mills*, 390

4. An answer, that is evasive, that declines admitting or denying a fact positively, when it is in the party's power, if he will, to obtain information, that will enable him to admit or deny the fact; and, much more, an answer, that keeps back information that is possessed by a party upon a material fact, on the pretence, that the defendant cannot give the information with all the minuteness of which the subject is susceptible, such an answer ought not to entitle the person, who makes it, to any favor. *Ibid.*

CONTRACTS.

1. Two brothers proved the will of their father in common form. Afterwards, this probate was set aside at the instance of the widow, and an issue of *devisavit vel non* was made up. While this was pending, one of the sons, acting for the other, as he alleged, as well as for himself, entered into a written compromise with the widow, by which the property was agreed to be divided in a particular manner. Both the sons took the property assigned to them by the compromise and held it for eleven years. *Held*, that after this act and long acquiescence, they cannot now repudiate the compromise and be permitted to claim under the provisions of the will. *Washburn* v. *Washburn*, 306

2. Our Act of Assembly, Rev. Stat. ch. 50, sec. 8, which makes void all contracts for the sale of slaves not reduced to writing and signed, does not require, when the contract is by an agent, that it should be signed by the principal or by the agent in the name of the principal. *Ibid.*

3. Although equity does not

interfere with the legal operation of instruments, merely upon the want of consideration, where there is no fraud nor imposition, but leaves the parties to the law; it will, yet, not afford relief upon a voluntary executory contract, which passed nothing and created no right at law. Equity in such a case does not act for a mere volunteer, but only for a real purchaser at a fair price. *Medley* v. *Mask*, 339

4. The mere general,formal words in a deed of assignment, declaring that the assignor had been fully paid and satisfied, are not conclusive evidence that any consideration has been paid, much less an adequate consideration. *Ibid.*

5. Equity disregards penalties. *Gordon* v. *Brown*, 399

6. A penalty limits the sum which may be recovered in an action of debt for a breach of a contract. *Ibid.*

7. The party who claims for the breach of a contract is not restricted to his legal remedy by an action for the penalty, but may claim an execution of the contract, as it is understood in a Court of Equity; that is, as a stipulation, without reference to the penalty, to do

the several things stated in the condition. *Ibid.*

8. Wherever a written contract contains, by mistake, less than the parties intended, or more, and the mistake is clearly established, a Court of Equity will reform it, so as to make it conform to the precise intentions of the parties. *Braddy* v. *Parker*, 430

CORPORATION.

A corporation can only sue or be sued in its corporate name, unless the act of incorporation enables it to come into Court in the name of any other person, as its President, Cashier, &c. *Mauney* v. *Motz*, 195

COSTS.

A plaintiff in a Court of Equity is bound to give security for costs, in the same manner as a plaintiff in a suit at law. *Moore* v. *Banner*, 293

DEED.

If there be two clauses in a deed, repugnant or contradictory to each other, the first shall stand and the other be rejected. *Wheeler* v. *Wheeler*, 210

DEPOSITIONS.

1. A notice to take a number of depositions, on the 1st, 2d, 3rd, 4th, 5th, 6th, 7th, 8th, 9th and 10th, of a particular month, does not, of itself, furnish a

ground for suppressing the depositions. *Kea v. Robeson,* 427

2. Where, under this notice, the plaintiff took twenty-six depositions on the 1st and 2nd of that month, and the only one of the defendants, who complained, was present on those days, there can be no reason whatever for suppressing those depositions on the ground of the indefiniteness of the notice. *Ibid.*

DETINUE, ACTION OF.
Though, in an action of detinue for slaves, juries generally and properly, when their verdict is for the plaintiff, find the value of the property higher than it really is, in order to enforce the delivery of the slaves; yet, that is not the case, where it is known that the defendant cannot discharge himself by a delivery, as if the slaves be dead or owned by another person. *Murphy v. Moore,* 118

DEVISES.
See LEGACIES, &c.

DOWER.
See WIDOW.

ENTRY.
1. A vague entry of lands is not absolutely void, but the defect may be supplied by a survey, which renders the party's claim more specific. *Johnston v. Shelton,* 85

2. But if the entry be not so explicit, as to give reasonable notice to a second enterer of the first appropriation, and the same land is entered again, before a survey on the first entry, equity will not deprive the second enterer of his title. *Ibid.*

3. An entry of "640 acres of land, beginning on the line dividing the Counties of Haywood and Macon, at a point at or near Lowe's Bear-pen, on the Hogback Mountain, and running various courses for complement," is, in itself, too vague and indefinite *Ibid.*

EVIDENCE.
1. One, the title of whose land, as alleged by a creditor, has been sold by this creditor at execution sale, is an incompetent witness in a suit between other parties, to prove that the title was really in him. *Quinn v. Rippey,* 181

2. In a suit in Equity to recover upon a lost bond, when the answer denies that there was a bond, the same degree of proof is requisite, which a Court of law would call for, to be laid before the jury upon *non est factum* pleaded to a declaration on a lost

bond. *Morrison* v. *Meacham*, 381

8. As the declaration would have been to aver the sealing of the obliga- tion, and identify it by its date, day of payment and the sum mentioned in it, so the proof would have to come up to that descrip- tion. *Ibid.*

EXECUTIONS.

1. Where a series of execu- tions issue on the same judgment, and have been *bona fide* acted on, the last of them relates to the teste of the first and binds the property of the de- fendant from that time. *Spencer* v. *Hawkins*. 288

2. But where the original, or any intermediate writ of execution, never was delivered to the sheriff, the lien is not carried back beyond the one on which the sheriff acted *Ibid.*

3. Where an original *fi. fa.* issues to one county, and an *alias* to another, a sale by the defendant of his property situated in the latter, while the *fi. fa.* was in the hands of the sheriff of the former, is good. *Ibid.*

4. Where an execution, though made out, does not appear to have been is- sued by the clerk, it cre- ates no lien. *Ibid.*

5. The interest of a vendee of land, where the con- tract rests in articles for a

conveyance, when the pur- chase money shall have been paid, is not the sub- ject of sale under execu- tion at law, while the pur- chase money, or any part of it, remains unpaid. *Frost* v. *Reynolds*, 494

6. After the payment of the price, it may be sold as a trust estate, within the Act of 1812. *Ibid.*

EXECUTORS AND AD- MINISTRATORS.

1. An executor, like other trustees, is not to be held liable, as insurers, or for any thing but *mala fides*, or want of reasonable diligence. *Beall* v. *Dar- den*, 76

2. Where an administrator or executor delays an un- reasonable time, as, for instance, three years, to sell slaves, and they are then lost, he is answera- ble for them as assets to the creditors. *Ibid.*

3. And where an adminis- trator or executor is guil- ty of gross neglect, in suf- fering slaves to remain with an improper person, as bailee, for a long period, and the slaves are sold by such bailee, so that they are lost to the estate, the executor or administrator will be answerable for their value to the next of kin. *Ibid.*

4. Where a creditor, on the trial of a suit at law a- gainst an administrator,

relied upon his account of sales, as evidence of the assets in his hands, and afterwards discovered that the account was not correct, because the administrator, through an agent, who was returned as the purchaser of a large amount of property, had in fact bought the property himself at an under value: *Held*, that though the creditor might have called upon the administrator in equity, in the first instance, for an account of the assets, or might have filed a bill for a discovery, during the pendency of the suit at law, yet, having elected to pursue his remedy at law, he is bound by the verdict in such suit, unless he can shew that the administrator had fraudulently deceived him, by wilful misrepresentations of the state of the assets. *Wilson* v. *Leigh*, 97

5. Where the deceased had a residence in this State, a grant of administration on his estate, by the Court of any other County than that in which he resided, is absolutely void. *Johnson* v. *Corpening*, 216

6. Where an executor is in possession of a sum of money, to which his testator was entitled for the life of another, who is still living, a Court of Equity will not compel the exec-

utor to give security for the payment of the amount at the expiration of the life-interest, unless he be insolvent or in failing circumstances, or, from some other good cause, there is reason to fear the money will be lost. *Drumright* v. *Jones*, 253

7 An executor cannot take land in the payment of debts due to his testator, and his purchases are on his own account, unless at the election of those entitled to the estate. *Weir* v. *Humphries*, 264

8. Until the parties so elect to take the land, the executor is chargeable for the price given for the land, or the land itself would, in a Court of Equity, have the character of personalty. *Ibid.*

9. In the case of an executor, if the person who takes a security from him, knows that the executor is raising money on it, for purposes not connected with the affairs of the estate, and more especially when the executor uses the testator's effects to pay his own antecedent debt to that person himself, it is deemed an act of concerted fraud between the two, and the owners of the property have a right to re-claim it. *Exum* v. *Bowden*, 281

10. Where an administrator files a bill to recover back

a chose in action, which he had assigned before administration was granted to him, when it appears that there was no creditor of the intestate and that the next of kin had assented to the contract of assignment, a Court of Equity will grant him no relief. *Filhour* v. *Gibson,* 455

FRAUDS AND FRAUDULENT CONVEYANCES.

1. A. devised certain property to a trustee, in trust to apply the proceeds to the maintenance of his son, and with a proviso that no part of the property should be subject to the debts of his said son. *Held*, that this proviso was inoperative, and the creditors of the son had a right to have their claims paid out of the property. *Mebane* v. *Mebane,* 131

2. By the use of no terms or art can property be given to a man, or to another for him, so that he may continue to enjoy it, or derive any benefit from it, as the interest, or his maintenance thereout or the like, and at the same time defy his creditors and deny them satisfaction thereout. *Ibid.*

3. The only manner, in which creditors can be excluded, is to exclude the debtor also from all benefit from, or interest in the property, by such a limitation, upon the contingency of his bankruptcy or insolvency, as will determine his interest and make it go to some other person. *Ibid.*

4. When property is conveyed by a deed of trust to satisfy certain alleged debts, and the parties stand in a near relation to each other, as father and son, or brothers, and the deed is impeached for fraud, it is incumbent on the parties to offer something more than the naked bond of the one to the other, as evidence of the alleged indebtedness, especially when the bond is followed, immediately after its execution, by the deed of trust. *Hawkins* v. *Alston,* 137

5. And more especially will the Court, when a bill is filed by a creditor to set aside such conveyance, refuse to admit the validity of the bond so attempted to be secured, when the parties, being particularly interrogated, decline or refuse to set forth, fully and sufficiently, what was the consideration of the bond. *Ibid.*

6. A bond may be voluntary, and such an one, though binding between the parties, cannot stand before other debts arising out of contracts for value. *Ibid.*

7. A suppression of competition at an execution sale by the representatives of the defendant, that he was buying for the plaintiff, by means of which he purchased the land of a distressed man for a very inadequate price, will authorize a decree for the plaintiff, on a bill to redeem the land on paying the sum for which it was sold, on the ground of an undue advantage taken of his necessities, and a fraud practised in getting the title in that way, and then claiming it for his own benefit.. *Rich* v. *Marsh*, 396

8. A. purchased at execution sale a tract of land belonging to B.; afterwards the same tract of land was set up for sale under another execution against B. posterior in its lien. A. forbid the sale and then bid for the land and it was struck off to him. *Held*, that, in so doing, A. was guilty of no fraud upon B. *Markham* v. *Shannonhouse*, 411

GUARDIAN AND WARD.

1. Whether or not a guardian is bound to go to another State to sue a former guardian, who has taken off his ward's property; yet when such former guardian has given a guardian bond in this State, the subsequent guardian is bound to sue on that bond to recover the value of the property so removed; and if he neglects to do so, he is answerable to the ward for the amount of the property removed. *Horton* v. *Horton*, 54

2. Where a bond is, on its face, payable to a guardian for the benefit of his ward, this is *prima facie* notice to one, who takes an assignment of it, that it is the property of the ward and subject to his equities. *Exum* v. *Bowden*, 281

3. More especially is this the case, where the bond is taken in payment of the personal debt of the guardian, and where it is taken at an oppressive discount. *Ibid.*

4. The case of a guardian disposing of securities for money belonging to his ward, is stronger against him than that of an executor disposing of the assets of the estate; for it is not so obviously necessary that the guardian should have such a power, as that the executor should, because infants usually come to their property, as the surplus of settled estates, and can hardly be properly in arrears to their guardian. *Ibid.*

HOTCHPOT.

Devises of real estate, by a parent to a child, are not to be brought into hotchpot with land not disposed of by the will, but the land descended is to be divided, as if that were the whole real estate, of which the parent had ever been seized. *Johnston* v. *Johnston*, 9

HUSBAND AND WIFE.

1. Where a wife and her husband turn her land into money, and she does not place her part of the money with some indifferent person for her, and as her separate property, but suffers the whole to be paid to the husband, the clearest proof is requisite to rebut the presumption that it was paid to, and accepted by the husband, for himself, and not in trust for his wife. *Temple* v. *Williams*, 39

2. A. being about to be married, conveyed certain slaves to a trustee, in trust for herself and future husband during their joint lives, and, if she survived her husband, to her use only; if he survived her, then to such person or persons as she might bequeath them to by will, and, if she made no will, then to the use of the husband for life, remainder " to use of her next of kin, under the statute of distributions." *Held*, that A.

having died without executing the power, the husband was only entitled to a life estate; that he was not one of her *next of kin* under the statute of distributions, and the remainder of the slaves, after his death, belonged to her nearest relatives of her blood, who were such next of kin under the statute. *Peterson* v. *Webb*, 56

3. Even if the conveyance had been to "her legal representatives, according to the statute of distributions," the husband could not have taken, because he is her legal representative, *jure mariti*, and not according to the statute. *Ibid*.

4. A husband is in Equity entitled to slaves, held in trust for his wife, (not for her separate use,) in the same manner as he would, at law, have been entitled to such as she legally owned and he had reduced to possession. *Beall* v. *Darden*, 76

5. A husband cannot be deprived of his right to property given to his wife, except by clear and unequivocal expressions in the deed of gift or devise, leaving no reasonable doubt that the property was given to the separate use of the wife. *Ashcraft* v. *Little*, 236

6. Where a deed of gift of a negro was made to a mar-

2

ried woman and her children, (two sons,) and these words were added, "but the said gift to extend to no other person"—*Held*, DANIEL, J. *dissentiente*, that these words did not create a separate estate in the wife, especially as they extended equally to the gift to the sons, and that therefore the husband was entitled to the share of the negro so given to his wife. *Ibid.*

7. A debt, legacy or distributive share of the wife is under the control of the husband, so far as to empower him to release, assign or receive them. But if, in his lifetime, he neither releases, conveys nor receives her choses in action, but leaves them outstanding, they belong to the surviving wife. *Rogers v. Bumpass,* 385

8. Therefore, where a husband gave his bonds to the administrator of the father of the wife, of whose estate she was a distributee, for certain purchases he made at the administrator's sale, and also for money loaned to him out of the funds of the estate, there being no agreement that these were to be regard'd as payments of the distributive share of the wife; *Held*, that, after the death of the husband, the wife was entitled to recover the whole of her distributive share. *Ibid.*

See POWERS.

INJUNCTIONS.

1. Courts of Equity should be very cautious in granting injunctions to stop mining operations, because such stoppage is alike opposed to public policy, and to the private justice due to the party, who might ultimately be found to be the owner. The better course is not to prevent the working of the mine, but to appoint a receiver. *Deep River Gold Min. Co. v. Fox,* 61

2. A preliminary injunction, granted *ex parte* upon the bill alone, should be dissolved, upon an answer fully denying the facts, upon which the bill raises the plaintiff's equity. *Cowles v. Carter,* 105

3. Where a bill is for relief upon the footing, that, as a trust, the subject is one of equitable cognizance, the injunction ought not to stay the trial at law, but only the suing out of an execution, should the plaintiff at law get a judgment. *Justice v. Scott,* 108

4. Where there are two defendants in a bill of injunction, and one of them answers that he is ignorant of the facts charged, the Court will not hear a motion to dissolve the injunction, until the answer

of the other defendant is put in. *Councill* v. *Walton*, 155

5. Where there was a public sale of lands, where the vendor gave notice at the sale that there were doubts as to the title, but that he would give a warranty deed, being a man of undoubted ability to answer the warranty, and where such deed was accordingly given and the purchaser gave his bond for the purchase money, upon which the vendor afterwards obtained judgment. *Held*, that the purchaser had no right to an injunction against this judgment, that the Court of Equity would not look into the title, but would leave the purchaser to his remedy at law upon the warranty. *Merritt* v. *Hunt*, 406

6. Where a bill of injunction is filed to stay the execution of a judgment, it is improper to make the clerk, who issues the execution, and the sheriff who has received it, parties defendant. They are mere ministers of the law, and have no interest in the controversy. *Edney* v. *King*, 465

7. If the sheriff has notice of the injunction, it is a contempt in him to proceed with execution: but to that purpose a notice is sufficient, and a subpœna should not be served on him. *Ibid.*

8. An injunction to restrain the execution of a decree in equity cannot be granted. *Greenlee* v. *McDowell*, 481

9. But though an injunction cannot issue, the Court of Equity may, upon a proper case, supported by affidavits, withdraw any process it has issued, or stay an execution by granting a supersedeas. *Ibid.*

10. After an injunction has been ordered to stand to the hearing, it seems to be irregular, in effect to reverse that order, by dissolving the injunction, or motion, before the hearing. *Smith* v. *Harkins*, 486

INTEREST.

1. Interest, as between tenants in common, shall only be allowed from the time of an actual demand or from the commencement of the suit, if no previous demand has been made. *Wagstaff* v. *Smith*, 1

2. The general rule for interest on accounts in ordinary dealings, is, that it is chargeable only after an account has been rendered, so that the parties can see which is the debtor and what he has to pay, unless it be agreed otherwise, or the course of business shews it to have been otherwise understood. *Holden* v. *Peace*, 223

3. In the case of a co-partnership, without some
agreement or understand-
ing to the contrary, in-
terest is chargeable by
one partner against ano-
ther only on the balance
found due from the latter
at the time of the dissolution of the partnership,
whether that dissolution
be by death or otherwise,
and only from and after
that period. *Ibid.*

JURISDICTION.

1. Where an action is
brought at law for the recovery of negroes, con
veyed by a deed in trust,
which it is alleged was
fraudulent in its inception,
the defendant at law may
avail himself of that ob-
jection in the suit at law,
and cannot transfer the
jurisdiction to a Court of
Equity. He can only ap-
ply to the Court of Equity
for a discovery of the facts.
to be used in the suit at
law. *Justice* v. *Scott,* 108
2. But where a trustee, in
a deed made nine years
before, institutes an action
at law, against a purcha-
ser under execution a-
gainst the maker of the
deed, and the purchaser
alleges that all the debts
were paid and the whole
trust resulted to the debt-
or ; while the debtor, who
united in himself the character of creditor, by ad-
ministering upon the es-
tate of one of the credit-
tors secured in the deed,
says, that a certain debt
is not paid, and the trustee
says he does not know
whether it is or is not paid,
a Court of Equity will entertain a bill by the purchaser, as the most con-
venient and comprehen-
sive mode of determining
the rights of all the parties. *Ibid.*
3 Where a contract is
shewn to be grossly a-
gainst conscience, or grossly unreasonable, as that
the price given bore no
proportion to the real
value of the property conveyed, this may, with
other circumstances, au-
thorize the interference of
a Court of Equity. *Bar-
net* v. *Spratt,* 171
4. But where these circumstances are not proved,
and no complaint is made
by the party, now alleging
that he was circumvented,
for more than twenty
years after the contract
was entered into, the Court
will not interfere, to set
aside the contract. *Ibid.*
5. A Bill of discovery does
not ask relief, but, generally, only seeks the dis-
covery of facts, resting in
the knowledge of the de-
fendant, or of deeds or
writings in his possession
or power. in order to maintain the right or title of
the party asking it, in
some suit or proceeding

in another Court. *Pemberton* v. *Kirk*, 178

6 Where a verdict has been recovered at law, the defendant in that action cannot have relief in Equity, upon the ground that he can now produce cumulative proof as to the facts on which his defence rested at law. *Ibid.*

7. The compromise of a doubtful right, fairly entered into, with due deliberation, will be sustained in a Court of Equity. *Williams* v. *Alexander*, 207

8. Legatees, next of kin, and creditors of a deceased person, can only file a bill against a debtor to the deceased or his trustee, by charging collusion between the debtor or trustee and the personal representatives, or some other peculiar circumstances, which give right to the legatees, next of kin or creditors to bring that suit, which the personal representative might and ought to have brought. *Nance* v. *Powell*, 297

9. Collusion is the usual foundation of such a bill, and without it, or some equivalent ground, as the insolvency of the executor or the like, it will not lie. *Ibid.*

10. The facts, on which the allegation of collusion, &c. is made, ought to be stated in the bill, although the general allegation may be sufficient to prevent a demurrer, and they must be proved on the hearing. *Ibid.*

11. Legatees, next of kin, and creditors of a deceased person, cannot bring a bill against a debtor to the deceased or his trustee, for the reason, the executor could not, or that he could not prove the case, if the suit was brought by himself, but could, as a witness, prove it for the other parties. *Ibid.*

12. In a suit to set aside a deed, the plaintiff cannot, against the statements in the answer, responsive and directly contradictory to the bill, have a declaration of facts in his favor. unless upon very clear proof, that the contract, as made, was different from the representations of the answer, and that the contents of the deed, as written, were concealed from, or, at the least, unknown to the plaintiff. *Michael* v. *Michael*, 349

13. Generally, when a person makes a deed, who is able to read it, the presumption is, that he did read it ; and, if he did not, it is an instance of such consummate folly, to act upon so blind a confidence, in a bargain, where each party is supposed to take

care of himself, that it would be dangerous to relieve, upon the mere ground of a party's negligence to inform himself, as he so easily might, of what he was doing. *Ibid.*

14. Therefore, commonly, the Court ought not to act on the mere ignorance of the contents of the deed: but there should be evidence of a contrivance in the opposite party to have the instrument drawn wrong and to keep the maker in the dark. *Ibid.*

15. If a guardian, agent, or other person, standing in a confidential relation, avail himself of information which his situation puts him in possession of, or of the influence, which is the natural consequence of habitual confidence or authority, to give an undue advantage by getting obligations or conveyances, without adequate consideration, a Court of Equity will not permit them to stand. The Court regards such transactions as extremely dangerous and sets them aside, except as securities for what may have been done under them. *Ibid.*

16. But that rule does not apply, where a person claiming an equitable interest in property by an assignment from the father of certain infants, brings a suit in the name

of those infants, styling himself their next friend, he not being their guardian nor appointed an agent by any contract or agreement with them. *Ibid.*

17. A Court of Equity does not like to entertain bills to perpetuate testimony, except in cases of plain necessity. *Smith* v. *Turner,* 433

18. If the object of a bill is to perpetuate the testimony of witnesses to a deed respecting lands, the deed must be properly described, and the names of the witnesses, who are to prove it, be set forth, and also the facts, to which they are to give evidence, be specially stated. *Ibid.*

19. Such a bill must shew the interest of the plaintiff in the subject, and, in stating it, should, though succinctly, set it forth plainly and with convenient certainty as to the material facts, so that, on the bill itself, some certain interest in the plaintiff shall appear; which, indeed, is sufficient, however minute the interest may be. *Ibid.*

20. In a bill of this kind a Court of Equity only assists a Court of Law by preserving testimony, where the plaintiff's right is purely a legal one. *Ibid.*

21. But a Court of Equity will

not entertain a bill to perpetuate testimony, touching a subject of its own jurisdiction, because the party can always, though in possession, file a bill for relief, and the Court can, in its discretion, make the proper orders upon an emergency, for speeding the taking of the testimony of old, infirm, or removing witnesses. *Ibid.*

22. If not a lunatic, yet equity will grant the plaintiff relief, if his mind was so weak, that he was unable to guard himself against imposition, or to resist importunity, or the use of undue influence, if he has been imposed upon by either of these means. *Rippy* v. *Gant*, 443

23. Mere weakness will not be sufficient. *Ibid.*

24. Where there is a legal capacity, there cannot be an equitable incapacity, apart from fraud. *Ibid.*

25. Where a person receives a foreign bill of exchange, in payment of certain negroes sold, and on presentation of the bill the drawee refuses to pay, and there is no protest for non-acceptance nor notice to the drawee, nor proof that the drawee had no funds of the drawer in his possession at the time, the payee of the bill has by his negligence made the bill his own, and can have no claim in equity against

the purchaser of the negroes, either for the negroes themselves or for the price for which they were sold. *Love* v. *Raper*, 475

26. Where an appeal has been taken from a County to a Superior Court of Law, a Court of Equity has no right to decide whether the appeal was properly allowed or not. That is a question of law, which can only be decided by a Court of Law. *Smith* v. *Harkins*, 486

27. Where a creditor seeks to subject to the satisfaction of his debt an equitable interest of his debtor, the assignment of such interest before the filing of the bill, *bona fide* and for a valuable consideration. will bar the creditor. *Frost* v. *Reynolds*, 494

28. Before the creditor can resort to this Court for relief against the equitable interest of his debtor, not subject to his execution at law, he must shew a judgment at law, a *fieri facias* and a return of *nulla bona. Ibid.*

29. He cannot have relief upon the mere ground, that he had by mistake bought property at execution sale and discovered afterwards, that the estate of the debtor, did not pass by such sale. He must first establish his

claim at law, under the Act of 1807. *Rev. Stat. c.* 45. *Ibid.*

LEGACIES AND DE-VISES.

1. A bequest of Slaves to the American Colonization Society is a valid bequest under the laws of this State. *Cox* v. *Williams & al.* 15

2. A devise that land should be sold, and "the proceeds laid out in building convenient places of worship, free for the use of all Christians, who acknowledge the divinity of Christ and the necessity of a spiritual regeneration," is void for uncertainty. *White* v. *University,* 19

3. A devise to a religious congregation is valid, if the Court can see, with certainty, what congregation is intended. *Ibid.*

4. A bequest of $1000, " to be applied to foreign missions and to the poor saints: this to be disposed of and applied as my executor may think the proper objects according to the scriptures, the greater part, however, to be applied to missionary purposes, say $900. Item— It is my will, that if there be any thing over and above," (after satisfying certain legacies and devises) " that it be applied to home missions," is too indefinite and therefore

void. *Bridges* v. *Pleasants,* 26

5. To sustain a gift in trust by a testator, the trust itself must be valid; and, to make it so, it must be in favor of such persons, natural or artificial, as can legally take. *Ibid.*

6. In the case of devises to charitable purposes, the doctrine of *cy pres.* does not obtain in this State. *Ibid.*

7. A bequest for religious charity must, in this State, be to some definite purpose, and to some body or association of persons, having a legal existence and with capacity to take; or, at the least, it must be to some such body, on which the Legislature shall, within a reasonable time, confer a capacity to take. *Ibid.*

8. There is no provision in our laws for donations, to be employed in any general system of diffusing the knowledge of christianity throughout the earth. *Ibid.*

9. A testator bequeathed all his property to his brother A., except $100, which he "willed to B. to be appropriated to the use of schooling and educating the said B., in that way and at that time that shall appear to be the most advantage to the said boy. I also leave the said $100 in the hands of the said

A., to use the said money for the said purpose above written, if he should have it in his power, and, if not, to remain in common with the rest of the said property to A." The testator lived till B., the *boy*, had become a man, married, and had a family. *Held*, that this was not an absolute legacy of $100 to B., but only for his schooling and education, and that, under the circumstances existing at the death of the testator, he had no right to claim it, but it belonged to A. *Liverman* v. *Carter*, 59

10. If a bequest be to, or in trust for a legatee, to put him out apprentice, or to advance him in any business or profession, it is an absolute bequest to such legatee; except in the case, where the legacy is given over to another, in the event that the first object of the testator cannot be effected. *Ibid*.

11. A testator bequeathed to his wife a certain slave for her life, and, after her death, the slave to be sold, and the issue of the slave together with the money arising from such sale, to be equally divided among all his children "that are then living." *Held*, that the issue of such of the children, as died during the life-time of the legatee for life, took no interest

under this bequest. *Denny* v. *Closse*, 102

12. The word "children" in a will sometimes, but only under peculiar circumstances, is construed to mean "grand-children:" as where the meaning of the testator is uncertain, and the bequest must fail unless such construction be given. *Ibid*.

13. A. bequeathed as follows: "I leave my negroes (except Dan) to be sold by my executor, and divided into three shares," &c. *Held*, that this was a specific legacy of the negroes, of which the testator was possessed at the time of his death; and that one of the legatees, to whom, after the date of the will, the testator had given two negroes, was not bound to account for their value in the division of the legacy. *Guilford* v. *Guilford*, 168

14 By another clause, the testator bequeathed the negro Dan to his daughter A. M. and directed as follows: "I wish my executor to hire him out, and apply the proceeds, or so much thereof as may be necessary, to raise, clothe and educate the said child: And if the said A. M. should die before she arrives at the age of twenty-one years, then the negro boy Dan to go back and be sold by my execu-

3

tor, and the proceeds to be divided between E. L." and others. *Held*, that A. M. was entitled absolutely to all the hires of Dan, that accrued during her life-time, and was not restricted to so much only as was necessary "to raise, clothe and educate her." *Ibid*.

15. A bequest of a particular bond is a specific bequest, and the executor is not bound to collect the money due on the bond, but must deliver the bond itself to the legatees. *Howell* v. *Hooks*, 188

16. A testator devised to his wife a large real and personal estate, and then directed as follows : "It is my wish that my widow and cousin Barbara Richardson should continue to keep house together ; but should they not, I wish my executor to pay over to cousin Barbara Richardson $1,000, or that amount out of the property left my wife." The parties continued to live together until the death of the widow. *Held*, that, on the happening of that event, B. R. was entitled to receive the legacy of $1000. *Richardson* v. *Hinton*. 192

17. A testatrix bequeathed as follows, all her estate consisting of personal property : " It is my wish that all my property be equal-

ly divided among my grand-children, that are living at the time of my death ; and that their parents have the use of it as long as they live." *Held*, that the grand-children took the property *per capita*. *Hill* v. *Spruill*, 244

18. *Held*, further, that all the parents, whether the children of the testatrix or their husbands or wives, took a life estate in the shares of their respective children. *Ibid*.

19. A testator bequeathed as follows : " I give and bequeath to my five sons and daughters, to-wit, C. C., J. C., N. C., S. C., and J. H. fifteen negroes, &c. Those fifteen negroes I give to be theirs at my death. and my wife's, &c. ; these I give them with all the future increase. I hereby appoint my son C. C. guardian to my daughter N. C. The legacy I leave her is to be free and clear, and independent of her present husband, T. C., or in any wise to be subject to his debts, engagements or control, but to be wholly under the management of the guardian C. C. to act with it as he thinks best for her profit ; and after her death, all the negroes, &c. to go to his six children, &c." *Held*, that the wife was entitled to a sole and sep-

arate estate in this property; that the legal title did not pass by the words of the will to C. C. who is called guardian, but vested in the husband. But that the husband, there being no trustee, interposed, is considered in equity as the trustee for the wife, holding the property to the sole and separate use of the wife, in the same manner as another trustee would have done. *Croom* v. *Wright,* 248

20. *Held,* therefore, that one who purchased these negroes from the husband with notice of the trust, held them subject to the trusts in the will in favor of the wife and her children. *Ibid.*

21. A testator devised to his wife M. certain lands, and the will then proceeds: " I also give her the negroes I got from John Knight's estate. I also loan her $3000, and provided she has no child or children by me, that arrives to the age of twenty-one or dies under that age leaving lawful issue, I give her the said $3000. I also lend her all my household and kitchen furniture during her life or widowhood. It is also my will and desire, that the property I have given my wife and loaned her, with all the property I shall hereafter dispose of, in this my will, remain together on my plantations, under the care of my executors and trustees, which I shall hereafter appoint. and the profits arising therefrom to go to the benefit of my mother and the education of my children, should I have any, until my oldest child, should I have any, arrives to the age of twenty-one years. The balance of my property not already disposed of, both real and personal, together with the household and kitchen furniture loaned my wife, I leave in trust with my friends, A. B. and C. D., for the benefit of my child or children, should I have any to arrive to the age of twenty-one years, or the issue of such child or children at the age of twenty-one years— and for A. B., C. D., and E. F., to deliver unto them the said property." The testator left surviving him a wife and daughter. *Held,* that by this will the testator has thrown his whole property, real and personal, into a joint fund, to be held by his executors in the manner specified in this will, the profits to be divided equally between his widow and her daughter; the division of this joint fund to be contingent, upon one of two events, either

the arrival at age of her daughter or her death without issue before that period. *Held*, further, that the legacy of $3000 is still a loan; that it must be held by the exec-utors, and the widow is only entitled to the inter-est on it, until the contin-gency happens of the daughter's dying under age and without issue, in which event it will be converted into an abso-lute gift to the widow. *Held*, further, that only the original stock of ne-groes from John Knight's estate passed under the bequest, and none of the increase before the ma king of the will. *Bowers* v. *Matthews*, 258

22. A devise or legacy to a child, not *in esse* at the time the will was made, does not come within the provisions of the Act of Assembly, Rev. Stat. ch. 122, sec. 15, in relation to children, who have died in the life-time of their parents. *Lindsay* v. *Pleasants*, 320

23. That act has relation only to legacies which, but for its provisions, would have lapsed; but when the child or chil-dren were not in existence at the time the will was made, the devise or lega-cy was void *ab initio*. *Ibid.*

24. The personal property

therefore bequeathed by the will to such children goes into the undisposed of fund and must be divi-ded among the next of kin, of which the widow by the act of 1835, ch. 10, Rev. Stat. ch. 121, sec. 12, is one. *Ibid.*

25. By the will in this case the real property was di-rected to be sold and the proceeds divided among testators widow and chil-dren, naming them, and the property was sold ac-cordingly. *Held* that, three of the children be-ing dead at the time the will was made, the pro-portions of the proceeds of such sale, which would have gone to such chil-dren, if they had been living when the will was made, are still to be con-sidered as real estate and go to the testator's heirs as real estate. *Ibid.*

26. Where a testator directs his land to be turned into personalty, for particular objects, and some of those objects fail, his intention is presumed, *pro tanto*. to be defeated, and the mo-ney raised out of the lands for those objects, shall not be considered to belong to his personal estate, but is, in this Court, considered as land, and will result to the heirs at law of the tes-tator. *Ibid.*

27. It is a clear rule in Equi-ty, that where real estate

is directed to be converted into personal, for an express purpose, which fails, to consider the disappointed interest (although the land has been sold,) as realty and resulting to the heirs. *Ibid.*

28. This rule equally applies, where the proceeds of the real and personal property are blended in the devise or legacy. *Ibid.*

LIMITATIONS AND LAPSE OF TIME.

1. A tenant in common in possession is protected by the Statute of Limitations from an account to his co-tenant, of the rents and profits received more than three years before the commencement of a suit. *Wagstaff* v. *Smith*, 1

2. A Court of Equity will not interfere to enforce the performance of a contract, after the lapse of forty years from the time when it should have been executed. *Lewis* v. *Cox*, 198

LUNATICS.

1. Before the Court will direct any of the property of a lunatic to be applied to the payment of his debts, it will set apart a sufficient fund for the maintenance of the lunatic, and his wife and infant children, if he has any. Nothing that has been advanced for the prior main-tenance of the lunatic shall be chargeable on this fund. *Latham, in the matter of,* 231

2. An inquisition of lunacy, if properly taken, is, when offered in evidence, but presumptive proof against persons not parties or privies. *Rippy* v. *Gant*, 443

MARRIAGE AGREEMENTS.

1. The specific execution of marriage articles, and the reformation of settlements executed after marriage, because of their not conforming to articles entered into before marriage are among the ordinary subjects of Equity jurisdiction. *Dunn* v. *Tharp*, 7

2. Parol agreements, in consideration of marriage, entered into before our statute of 1819, Rev. St. ch. 50, sec. 8, are valid, and will be enforced in Equity. *Ibid.*

MERGER.

1. PER DANIEL, J. Merger never takes place, when it would have the effect to destroy intermediate *vested* estates in third persons. *Logan* v. *Green*, 370

2. When there is an outstanding lease for a number of years, and the reversioner makes a new lease to third persons to commence immediately, this is a vested estate;

and, although the second lessees could not take *possession* of their term, inasmuch as the possession belonged to the first lessee, they would have a *concurrent* lease and be entitled to all the rents issuing out of the term of the first lessee, and on the expiration of that term, they could legally enter and possess the land for the residue of their own term. This estate would prevent a merger when the first lessee became entitled to the reversion. *Ibid.*

3. But, if the deed, conveying this second interest, created only what is sometimes called a future lease, that is, a contract to have a lease to commence after the expiration of the first lease, then it conveyed no present *estate* in the land, either in interest or possession. It would be only an *interesse termini*, which neither makes a merger, nor prevents one, but may be accelerated in the time of its becoming an estate in the land by possession, by the merger of an antecedent vested term by the termor's purchasing in the next immediate estate in reversion. *Ibid.*

MORTGAGE.

1. In a suit for redemption, an absolute deed is not conclusive, but it can be shewn to be a mortgage by some admissions of the defendant in his answer, or by a chain of circumstances, that render it almost as certain, that it was intended as a security, as if it had been expressed in the deed : such as the disparity between the sum advanced and the value of the property— the continued possession of the former owner— written admissions, for example, in stating accounts as for mortgage money. But there is no case, in which relief has been given, upon mere proof by witnesses of declarations by the party, in opposition to the deed and the answer. *Allen v. McRae,* 325

2. In a suit brought against a mortgagor and mortgagee by one claiming to be an assignee of the mortgagor, for the purpose of setting up the assignment and redeeming, it is necessary to prove that the assignment was for a valuable consideration. *Medley v. Mask,* 339

3. If the suit had been against the mortgagor alone, it would have been sufficient to prove the assignment without proving any consideration. *Ibid.*

4. A person, who had no title to property which he mortgaged, has no right

to a decree for redemption. *Purvis* v. *Brown,* 413

5. A right to redeem property may be reserved to a stranger to the contract, but then it must be an express reservation. *Ibid.*

PARTIES.

1. A bill cannot be brought by one, who indemnifies another, upon an equity of the principal, without making the principal himself a party. *Murphy* v. *Moore,* 118

2. All the persons, however numerous, who are interested in the subject of a suit in equity, must be made parties, and, as in a declaration at common law, the circumstances constituting the case must be set forth in the Bill at large. *Hoyle* v. *Moore,* 175

3. The parties intended to be made defendants in a suit in Equity, must be specially named in the Bill, and process prayed against them. None are parties to a Bill, against whom process is not prayed. *Ibid.*

4. Therefore, where the prayer of the Bill was, "that the clerk be ordered to issue subpœnas to the proper defendants," &c. without naming them: *Held,* that the Bill should be dismissed, though certain persons came in and filed answers. *Ibid.*

PARTNERS.

Where a co-partnership owned a dwelling house, which was exclusively occupied by one of the partners and his family, *Held,* that this partner was liable for rent, though there was no special agreement to that effect, and though no charge against him for rent was made on the books of the firm during his life-time. *Holden* v. *Peace,* 223

PAYMENT.

1. If a debtor, who is indebted to the same creditor on different accounts, does not make the application of a payment at the time such payment is made, he cannot do so afterwards. *Moss* v. *Adams,* 42

2. If the debtor fails to make the application, the creditor may do so at any time afterwards before suit brought. *Ibid.*

3. Where neither debtor nor creditor makes the application of the payment, the law will apply it to that debt, for which the creditor's security was most precarious. *Ibid.*

POWERS.

1. Land was conveyed to a trustee in trust, " to receive and pay over the

rents and profits of the land unto Mrs. A. B., to her sole and separate use, free and discharged from any claim of her husband, C. D. during the natural life of said A. B.; and after her death, in trust to convey the said land unto all the children of the said A. B. that shall be living at her death, equally to be divided among them; that is to say, only in default of any such appointment by the said A. B. in nature of a will, during her life-time, as is hereinafter mentioned. But if the said A. B. shall make any appointment in writing, witnessed by two witnesses, therein appointing or giving said land to any person or persons whatsoever, then in trust to convey said land to such person or persons as the said A. B. may appoint or name, by or in any such appointment in writing as aforesaid, or in any writing executed by the said A. B. as aforesaid." *Held*, that under this power, A. B. might appoint the land to any person she chose, by deed attested by two witnesses, and that her power was not restrained to an appointment by a writing in the nature of a will. *Ex parte Britton*, 35

2. A power to the wife created by marriage articles will, though only an equitable one, bind the estate to which it refers and be supported in Equity, in the same manner as if proper legal conveyances had been made. *Newlin v. Freeman.* 312

3. Where land is conveyed to a married woman, or to a trustee, for her separate use, she has no ability to dispose of that land by will, nor otherwise, than by the ordinary mode prescribed for the conveyance of land by *femes coverts*, unless a power to that effect has been expressly given to her in the deed of conveyance. It is otherwise in respect to personal property. *Ibid.*

4. Where by marriage articles *the land, which the wife should have at the time of the marriage* and other property were agreed to be reserved to the separate use of the wife, with a power to dispose by will or otherwise of the *said land* and other property, and the wife, after the marriage, purchased, out of the proceeds of her separate estate, other land. *Held*, that she had no more right under the marriage articles to dispose of this land than if the marriage articles did not exist. the deed of conveyance not giving her any power to dispose of it. *Ibid.*

PRACTICE AND PLEAD-ING.

1. Though it is the usual course, in a suit brought by a *cestui que trust* against his trustee, for an account of the trust fund, to order a reference, yet such reference will not be ordered, when objected to by the trustee, where it appears satisfactorily on the hearing, that there is nothing due from the trustee. *Nail* v. *Martin*, 159

2. Pleadings ought to be plainly written, and the words spelt in full and without contractions, especially papers that are sworn to. If papers of a different description are sent to this Court, the Court will put the parties to the expense of making fair copies, and perhaps order the originals to be taken off the file, or dismiss the suit. *Ibid.*

3. It is not the usual course of a Court of Equity to refer partnership accounts to the master, with a set of instructions from the Court. The accounts should first be reported, and the matters in contest between the parties be brought before the Court on exceptions. *Clements* v. *Pearson*, 257

4. Where a bill is amended, and the amendment filed contains allegation directly contrary to those made in the original bill, the Court can make no decree, because they must look into all the pleadings and cannot act upon such contradictory statements. *Milton* v. *Hogue*, 415

5. The proper way in such a case is strike out so much of the original bill as is contradicted by the allegations in the amended bill. *Ibid.*

6. Every person, who claims to recover, either at law or in equity, must shew a title in the pleadings, and that ought to be done by distinct averments or plain affirmative statements. *Edney* v. *King*, 465

7. The title of a bill is no part of it. It is merely a mode of conveniently denominating a bill or cause, and it cannot be deemed a part of the statements of the bill, either as to the title or the parties. *Ibid.*

8. When a record of a bill, &c. has been lost and destroyed, the Court has full power to order a copy of the original bill to be filed. *Greenlee* v. *McDowell*, 481

9. A party to a suit is bound by the acts and agreements, made by his counsel in the management of his cause. *Ibid.*

10. A bill of review, to rehear and set aside a decree, upon the ground of newly discovered testimony, cannot be sustained,

4

if it appears, that the testimony, though unknown to the plaintiff, was to his attorney, so solicitor or agent, in time to have been used, notice to either of them being notice to the principal. *Ibid.*

PRINCIPAL
See AGENT.

REFERENCE AND REPORT.
A Clerk and Master ought not to refer back to the Court a point, which the Court has expressly referred to him, or which is necessarily involved in the enquiry, which he was directed to make. The Clerk and Master should decide every question directly, and leave it to the parties, if dissatisfied, to bring the matter up for the decision of the Court by an exception. *Rogers v. Bumpass,* 385

REGISTRATION.
The probate of a deed of settlement upon a man's family, before the Clerk of the County Court, as if it were an ordinary deed of trust, and its subsequent registration upon that probate, are void as against creditors and subsequent purchasers. *Justice v. Scott,* 108

SALES BY CLERK AND MASTER.
1 Where, on the petition of infants and *feme coverts,* for the sale of land, the land is sold, and the Court then passes this order: "Ordered, that the Clerk and Master collect the bonds as they become due, and make the purchasers title;" *Held,* that under this order, the Clerk and Master had no authority to convey the title, until the purchase money was paid. *Barnes v. Morris.* 22

2. *Held, further,* that when, in such a case, the purchaser had conveyed the land to another person, who had notice that the purchase money was unpaid, the lien on the land in favor of the original owners still continued, and the surety of the purchaser at the Master's sale, who had been compelled to pay the bond, should be substituted to the rights of the original owners. *Ibid.*

3. When an infant and another person joined in a petition, in a Court of Equity, for a sale of land, held in common, the sale was made, and the Court ordered, that, when the money was collected, the infant's share should be paid to her guardian, upon his giving bond to the Clerk and Master with sufficient

surety, that the same should be secured to the infant or her heirs, as real estate, and the Clerk and Master paid the money to the guardian without taking such bond and surety : *Held*, that he was liable to the infant by an action of law, or proceedings might be had against him in the Court of Equity, by a rule or attachment to pay the money; but that the infant had no remedy against him by an original bill in Equity. *Pool* v. *Ehringhaus*, 33

SPECIFIC PERFOR-
MANCE.

1. A Bill, praying for the specific performance of a contract for the conveyance of land, is defective, if it does not contain so particular a description that the Court may know with certainty the land, of which they are asked to decree a conveyance. *Allen* v. *Chambers*, 125

2. If a Bill be brought for the specific performance of a parol contract for the conveyance of land, although the defendant does not rely upon the plea of the statute, rendering such contracts void, yet if he denies the contract as stated in the Bill, and insists that the real contract was a different one, this Court will not permit parol evidence to be heard

in support of the plaintiff's claim. *Ibid.*

3. Part performance, such as the payment of the whole of the purchase money and the delivery of the possession to the vendee, will not, in this State, dispense with a writing, if the statute be insisted on, nor admit a parol proof of a contract, different from that stated in the answer. *Ibid.*

4. The statute of limitations does not apply in the case of a vendee bringing a bill for the specific performance of a contract. The only question, as to time, is a question of diligence. *Washburn* v. *Washburn*, 361

See LIMITATIONS.

TENANTS IN COMMON.
Without a contract between the parties, the sale of the whole tract of land and receipt of the price by one tenant in common, does not turn him into a trustee for a co-tenant, as the latter still has the legal title to his own share and can have redress on it at law. *Milton* v. *Hogue*, 415

TRUSTEES.

1. Where a clerk in a store pilfered money and goods from his employer, and laid out the proceeds in the purchase of a tract of

of land ; *Held*, that the person thus robbed could hold neither the clerk, nor his representatives after his death, as trustees of the land for his benefit so as to enable him to call for a conveyance of the legal title to himself. *Campbell* v. *Drake*, 94

2. Sales by execution must be made before the return of the writ, without respect to price, because the mandate of the writ is peremptory ; but the obligations of a trustee are not precisely like those of a Sheriff. A trustee, under a deed of trust conveying property for the purpose of a sale to pay debts, is charged with the interests of both parties, and ought not, except under very special circumstances, to sell at an enormous sacrifice. *Hawkins* v. *Alston*, 187

3. Whether a trustee had authority or not, under a deed of trust for the payment of debts, to make sale of personal property, his sale, acting in the capacity of trustee and in the presence and acquiescence of the *cestui que trust*, would give a good title, at least in equity. *Spencer* v. *Hawkins*, 288

USURY.

1. The purchase of a negotiable security for less than the real value is valid. *Ballinger* v. *Edwards*, 449

2. But that is subject to this qualification, that it must be merely a purchase of the security and at the risk of the purchaser ; and, therefore, if the person, who claims to be such purchaser, holds the person, to whom the money is advanced, responsible for the payment of the debt, it is not, in law and fact, a purchase of the security, but a loan of money upon the security, and, if the sum advanced be less than the amount of it, deducting the legal interest for the time until maturity, the loan is usurious. *Ibid.*

3. The Statute of Usury is as binding in a Court of Equity as at Law, except in cases where the borrower asks the assistance of a Court of Equity, and then the Court will compel him to do equity, by paying the principal and the legal interest. *Ibid.*

WIDOW.

1. Where an executor sells land under a power contained in the will, the purchaser claims under the will, as if the devise had been to him ; and therefore the widow of an heir of the testator has no right to dower in such

land. *Weir* v. *Humphries.*, 264

2. The wife of a mortgagee in fee, after forfeiture, may recover dower at law; but in equity she is subject to be redeemed as the husband's heir is, because equity considers the mortgagee as a trustee for the mortgagor from the first. Therefore, a Court of Equity will not decree dower in such a case, when applied to in first instance. *Ibid.*

3. Where a husband is entitled only to a remainder in fee, after the termination of a life estate, which is existing at the time of his death, the wife cannot be endowed, for the right of dower only attaches to the immediate estate of freehold as well as the inheritance. *Ibid.*

4. An estate for years, prior to the estate of inheritance limited to the husband, does not prevent the seizin of the immediate estate of inheritance by the husband, and the wife will be dowable of the land, subject to the term. *Ibid.*

5. If rent be reserved on the term, the widow, endowed of the reversion, is entitled to her share of the rent. *Ibid.*

6. But if the preceding term yields no rent, as where there is a gift by will, for example, to one for a term, remainder to another in fee, the wife of the latter, though she has a right of dower and though it may be assigned her, takes subject to the term, and can neither enter nor receive any profits, until the termination of the term. *Ibid.*

7. The same rules apply to all chattel interests in land, as well as to terms strictly speaking. *Ibid.*

8. Thus, when a testator devised a cotton factory and all its appurtenances to his three children, to be equally divided among them as also the profits, when the youngest should arrive at twenty-one years of age, and in the meantime that the factory should be carried on under the sole management and direction of the executor, until such period of division, and the profits were to be suffered to accumulate; and one of the children died before such period, leaving a widow: *Held*, that this was such a chattel interest in the executor, as though it did not prevent the assignment of dower, yet postponed the enjoyment of it until the time appointed for the division. *Ibid.*

9. A devise of land to "three children, to be kept together as *joint stock* until the youngest shall arrive

to the age of twenty-one, and then the whole property and its increase to be divided equally between them, to each one third part," creates a tenancy in common and not a joint tenancy being a gift of undivided property in joint shares. *Ibid.*

10. The act of 1784, *Rev. St. ch.* 43, *sec* 2, abolishes the right of survivorship, in the case of joint tenancy, and gives the share of the joint tenant, dying, to his heirs. But, when the heir takes *as heir*, the whole interest is neces sarily in the ancestor, and he becomes absolutely tenant of the fee, to which dower is incident, and, so also, the power of devising. *Ibid.*

11. The provision in the act of 1836, *Rev. Stat.* 121, *sec.* 1, which gives a right of dower to lands of which her husband died seized *and* possessed, is to receive the same construction as the act of 1784, which gives the dower in lands, of which the husband was "seized or possessed." The mistake is a clerical one, and none of the profession ever understood what was understood in the original law by the words "or possessed." *Ibid.*

12. In point of law, too, the owner of the inheritance is not only seized, but is said to be possessed, for the purposes of dower and curtesy, when the reversion is not after a freehold, but after a term for years only. The possession of the tenant for years is the possession of the reversioner. *Ibid.*

Ex. J. M.